lonel

MW00622601

Iceland

The
Westfjords
p195

North
Iceland
p220

West
Iceland
p168

The Highlands
p290

East
Iceland
p267

REYKJAVÍK
p42

Southwest Iceland &
the Golden Circle
p82

Southeast
Iceland
p145

**Eygló Svala Arnarsdóttir, Alexis Averbuck,
Egill Bjarnason, Meena Thiruvengadam**

CONTENTS

Plan Your Trip

The Guide

Húsavík (p249)

Strokkur geyser (p99)

BEERPIXS/GETTY IMAGES ©; TOP LEFT: ALBERTO LOYO/SHUTTERSTOCK ©; BOTTOM LEFT: ROC CANALS/GETTY IMAGES ©

Glacial ice cave (p153), Skaftafell

JAROMOND/SHUTTERSTOCK ©

Stokksnes beach and Vestrahorn mountain (p167)

ICELAND
THE JOURNEY BEGINS HERE

Iceland feels like another planet, one where spectacular waterfalls and active volcanoes come together with Viking sagas and imaginative folklore. This volcanic island is a land of fire and ice – a place where magnificent glaciers top active volcanoes, with steaming hot springs and geysers everywhere, all encircled by a rugged coastline.

This is a popular destination for hikers, climbers, birdwatchers, whale watchers, aurora chasers and fishers. While nature may be the biggest draw, there's more culture here than you might expect. Iceland gave the world Björk, Sigur Rós and Of Monsters and Men, and serves as a backdrop in many a film. Reykjavík offers a stunning concert hall alongside art museums, galleries and festivals.

Iceland may be a small country, but it's got a huge personality.

Meena Thiruvengadam

@meenathiru

My favourite experience is a late-night summer sunset, and Iceland serves up some of the best. There's nothing I find more energising than these endless stretches of daylight.

WHO GOES WHERE

Our writers and experts choose the places that, for them, define Iceland.

Seyðisfjörður (p280) is one of those places you can return to again and again, and always discover something new. This traditional fishing town of only 700 people has many quality shops and restaurants, and people are creative and welcoming towards visitors.

Eygló Svala Arnarsdóttir

Eygló has written about Iceland for various travel publications.

The highlands around **Askja** (p301) crack open my heart with their beauty. Undulating crater rows give way to iridescent volcanic pools and hidden oases. A magnificent world to be protected and revered.

Alexis Averbuck

alexisaverbuck.com

Alexis paints and writes about her adventures – like crossing the Pacific by sailboat.

On **Látrabjarg Peninsula** (p205), I take a photo of two puffins and try not to look over the edge: the cliff drops to crashing waves. Iceland's allure is a combination of beauty and perceived danger; the experience of standing alone against the forces of nature.

Egill Bjarnason

@egilssaga

Egill reports for AP and wrote How Iceland Changed the World.

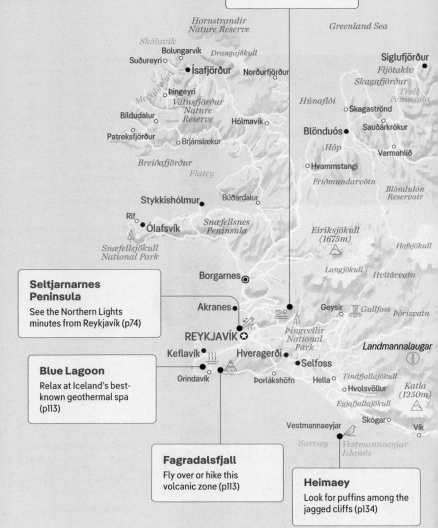

NORTH ATLANTIC OCEAN

Silfra Fissure
Swim between tectonic plates (p90)

Hornstrandir Nature Reserve

Greenland Sea

Skálavík

Bolungarvík   *Drangajökull*

Suðureyri

● **Ísafjörður**   Norðurfjörður

Siglufjörður

Fljótakiv

Skagafjörður

● Þingeyri

Vatnsfjörður Nature Reserve

Húnaflói

Troll Peninsula

○ Skagaströnd

Bildudalur

Hólmavík

○ Sauðárkrókur

Blönduós

Patreksfjörður

○ Brjánslækur

Hóp

○ Varmahlíð

Breiðafjörður

○ Hvammstangi

Friðmundarvötn

Flatey

Blöndulón Reservoir

Stykkishólmur   Búðardalur

Rif ○

● **Ólafsvík**

Snæfellsnes Peninsula

Eiríksjökull (1675m)

Hofsjökull

Snæfellsjökull National Park

Langjökull   *Hvítárvatn*

Borgarnes ◉

Seltjarnarnes Peninsula
See the Northern Lights minutes from Reykjavík (p74)

Akranes ●

Geysir ○   Gullfoss   *Þórisvatn*

Þingvellir National Park

REYKJAVÍK ✪

Keflavík ●

Hveragerði ●

Landmannalaugar

Blue Lagoon
Relax at Iceland's best-known geothermal spa (p113)

● **Selfoss**

Grindavík ○

Þorlákshöfn   Hella ○

Tindfjallajökull

○ Hvolsvöllur

Katla (1250m)

Eyjafjallajökull

Vestmannaeyjar

Skógar ○   Vík

Fagradalsfjall
Fly over or hike this volcanic zone (p113)

Surtsey   *Vestmannaeyjar Islands*

Heimaey
Look for puffins among the jagged cliffs (p134)

Húsavík
Spot blue whales off the
north coast (p249)

NORTH
ATLANTIC
OCEAN

Greenland Sea

Grímsey

Pistilfjörður

Öxarfjörður

Flatey

Í Fjörðum

Húsavík

Jökulsárgljúfur
(Vatnajökull
National Park - North)

Bakkaflói

Bakkafjörður

Dettifoss

Vopnafjörður

Akureyri

Reykjahlíð

Njarðvík

Goðafoss   *Mývatn*

Aldeyjarfoss

Egilsstaðir   **Seyðisfjörður**

Hengifossárvatn   Neskaupstaður

Móraujavatn   Eskifjörður   *Gerpir Cliffs*

Reyðarfjörður

Askja   *Hálslón*   Fáskrúðsfjörður
(1514m)   *Reservoir*

Dyngjujökull   Stöðvarfjörður

Breiðdalsvík

Bárðarbunga   *Þrándarjökull*
(2009m)   Djúpivogur

Kverkfjöll
(1860m)

Hágöngulón

Hoffellsjökull   Stafafell
Grímsvötn   *Vatnajökull*
(1719m)   *Fláajökull*   *Lónsvík*

Skaftafell
(Vatnajökull National   **Höfn**   **Stokksnes**
Park - South)

Síðujökull

Jökulsárlón
See glistening icebergs and
a diamond beach (p160)

Skaftafell

Hvannadalshnúkur
(2110m)

Kirkjubæjarklaustur

Kúðafljót

0   100 km
0   50 miles

DRIVE THE RING ROAD

This is one of the world's most iconic road trips. The 1322km Rte 1 loops around Iceland, passing through most of the country's towns and villages. In a single journey, the Ring Road can lead from the quirky northern capital of Reykjavík through the remote Arctic Coast Way, along zigzagging fjords and to coastal fishing towns. Enjoy views of jagged cliffs, towering rock formations and black-sand beaches on the way.

Visit Charming Towns

Iceland is proof the most charming things can come in small packages. There's no better way to experience the island's small towns than this road trip.

Enjoy Epic Scenery

From the dramatic Troll Peninsula, to long coastal stretches, rugged fjords and black-sand beaches, you'll find it all along this route.

Summer & Winter

Winter weather and road closures could force you to alter your itinerary. Travel in the summer for long stretches of daylight; perfect for driving remote roads.

Discover Iceland's best road trips and itineraries

❸
❷
❶
❺
❹

BEST ROAD-TRIP STOP EXPERIENCES

Get a close-up view of
❶ **Kirkjufell**, an iconic
volcanic mountain on the
Snæfellsnes Peninsula. (p186)

Take in views of picturesque
❷ **Lake Mývatn**, then
go birdwatching, soak
in geothermal lagoons
and check out the
rare Skútustaðagígar
pseudocraters. (p254)

Look for gigantic blue whales
on a whale-watching tour
off the coast of ❸ **Húsavík**.
(p250)

Hike the ❹ **Dyrhólaey
Peninsula** to take in sweeping
views of black sand beaches
and towering basalt columns,
and marvel at magnificent
rock formations near
Reynisfjara Beach. (p141)

Follow the rainbow street in
❺ **Seyðisfjörður** to the blue
church and find a cafe for
lunch. (p280)

EXPLORE VOLCANOES

Volcano tourism has exploded in popularity in recent years as the Reykjanes Peninsula has produced a steady number of mesmerising eruptions that have captured the world's attention. Visitors can hike eruption zones, fly over fresh lava fields and descend to the floor of an inactive volcano not far from Reykjavík. Explore the colourful craters that volcanic eruptions leave behind. Or walk through the long tunnels carved out by boiling lava thousands of years ago.

Hike an Eruption Zone

Hike fresh lava fields around the Fagradalsfjall volcano system on the Reykjanes Peninsula to see the effects of recent eruptions. Several companies offer guided tours.

Fly Over an Eruption

Depending on your timing, you may be able to fly over a volcanic eruption on a helicopter tour and see bubbling, flowing lava.

Explore Colourful Calderas

Experience the striking craters that volcanic eruptions leave behind by embarking on a challenging hike of the Askja caldera or an easy walk around Kerið crater.

BEST VOLCANIC EXPERIENCES

Fly over ❶ **Fagradalsfjall volcano** in a helicopter – time your tour around an active eruption and you could fly over bubbling lava. (p113)

Explore the newly formed lava fields surrounding the ❷ **Litli-Hrútur volcano** on the Reykjanes Peninsula. (p113)

Descend to the floor of ❸ **Þríhnúkagígur volcano** to make your own journey to the centre of the Earth and feel like you're in a Jules Verne novel. (p73)

Take a walk through time at the ❹ **Raufarhólshellir lava tunnel**, estimated to have formed around 5600 years ago. (p124)

Hike around ❺ **Kerið crater** for views of this colourful volcanic caldera and the bright blue-green lake at its bottom. (p122)

ENJOY THE WATER

Fire and ice may get most of the attention, but Iceland is also a country of water. Pristine lakes and rivers are teeming with fish. There are a couple of suitable areas for kayaking on the South Coast, and there's an under-the-radar beach at the southern edge of Reykjavík that's become a haven for sea swimmers. A fissure between tectonic plates allows for swimming between continents while river-rafting adventures, geothermal lagoons and epic waterfalls are plentiful.

River Rafting

If you're a beginner, go rafting down the welcoming Hvítá or West Glacial rivers. If you're looking for more of an adventure, take on the East Glacial River.

Sea Swimming

The water surrounding Iceland is cold all year, and there aren't many places to jump in. Nauthólsvík Geothermal Beach is your best bet for sea swimming.

Fishing

Fish pristine lakes and rivers for Arctic char, Atlantic salmon, and trout. Or go sea angling to fish for cod, haddock, rockfish and pollock.

❸
❶ ❹❷
❺

BEST AQUATIC EXPERIENCES

Dive into the glacial water of the ❶ **Silfra Fissure**, the only place in the world where it's possible to swim between continents. (p90)

Go rafting down the beginner-friendly ❷ **Hvítá river** in South Iceland, taking in the views as you cut through Gullfoss Canyon. (p107)

Take a more adventurous river-rafting adventure on the ❸ **East Glacial River** in North Iceland where even experienced rafters may feel challenged. (p227)

Fish for giant sea trout and salmon on the ❹ **Tungufljót river** – the best fishing conditions are from late July to August, and equipment is available to rent. (p110)

Settle into a kayak and head out from ❺ **Klettsvík Bay** in search of puffins off the coast of Vestmannaeyjar. (p134)

ANIMAL ENCOUNTERS

From petite horses and silly puffins to behemoth blue whales and playful dolphins, there's lots of wildlife in Iceland. And you don't have to worry about any of it trying to eat you. Iceland's wildlife isn't predatory, which has made it a haven for migrating birds. There are no snakes or spiders to watch out for here, and the only place you're likely to see a polar bear is on a billboard.

Go Whale Watching

Whales are frequently spotted off the coast of Iceland. Humpback and minke whales are most common, but blue whales have also been seen near Húsavík.

Look for Puffins

Look for puffins between May and August on Lundey island off the coast of Reykjavík, on the Tjörnes Peninsula on the northern coast, and on Heimaey in Vestmannaeyjar.

Ride Horses

Icelandic horses are smaller than the average horse and have five gaits instead of the typical three. They're cute and fun to ride, even for beginners.

BEST BIRDWATCHING EXPERIENCES

Take a boat tour from Reykjavík's Old Harbour to **① Akurey**, **Engey** or **Lundey**, where thousands of puffin pairs nest each summer. (p61)

See Arctic terns form a summer colony around the **② Grótta Lighthouse** and keep an eye out for the seals that occasionally come to visit. (p75)

Look for gyrfalcons hunting near **③ Lake Mývatn**, and check out the variety of ducks that call the lake home. (p256)

Head to **④ Látrabjarg Peninsula** in the Westfjords to see puffins, razorbills, white-tailed eagles and more. (p205)

Follow the coastal path to Stórhöfði, a peninsula at the southern edge of **⑤ Heimaey** that's home to a large puffin colony during the summer. (p134)

FROM LEFT: ARCTIC-IMAGES/GETTY IMAGES ©; ALEX RAMSAY/ALAMY STOCK PHOTO ©; © KASAKPHOTO/SHUTTERSTOCK ©

Find out how to see the Northern Lights

Northern Lights (p76) over Reykjavík

CHASE THE LIGHTS

Iceland is far enough north that it's almost in the Arctic Circle, and winters are marked by long, dark nights. This combination makes Iceland one of the best places in the world for viewing the Northern Lights: the magical green aurora that can take over clear skies when there's increased solar activity.

When to Go

The best time to visit for the Northern Lights is between mid-September and early April when it can be dark for up to 20 hours a night.

Where to Go

Head to dark places with minimal light pollution. Also look for clear skies or breaks in the clouds where lights can peek through.

BEST NORTHERN LIGHTS EXPERIENCES

Head to ❶ **Þingvellir National Park** to watch the Northern Lights over the birthplace of modern democracy. (p88)

Walk the trails around the ❷ **Seltjarnarnes Peninsula** to chase the Northern Lights for free. (p76)

Chase the Northern Lights around ❸ **Akureyri**, just 100km from the Arctic Circle. (p235)

Take a boat tour from ❹ **Reykjavík's Old Harbour** to see the Northern Lights not far from the capital. (p61)

See the Northern Lights over a towering waterfall at ❺ **Mígandifoss Viewpoint** on the Troll Peninsula. (p231)

GEOTHERMAL SPA DAYS

Icelandic water is some of the purest and cleanest in the world. And Icelanders have turned enjoying this natural resource into an art and a science. The Blue Lagoon is just the beginning. From sprawling lagoon complexes with multi-step bathing rituals to tiny secluded natural pools, you'll find a variety of geothermal facilities across the country.

Famous Spas

These sprawling spa complexes tap into Iceland's crystal-clear geothermal water and take things up a notch with bath rituals, massages and more.

Hidden Gems

Spending a lot of money isn't your only option. Lots of tiny geothermal pools are scattered across Iceland and cost a fraction of the price.

Local Pools

Icelanders take swimming seriously and some public pools are closer to what foreign visitors may call waterparks, but with hot tubs. Visiting is a cultural experience.

BEST GEOTHERMAL EXPERIENCES

Feel the rich silica mud between your toes as you wade into the ❶ **Blue Lagoon** to soak in its iconic blue geothermal water. (p113)

Indulge in the seven-step bath ritual at the ❷ **Sky Lagoon** and give yourself plenty of time to soak in its warm lagoon overlooking the water. (p72)

Escape the crowds and save some krónur by visiting the not-so-secret ❸ **Secret Lagoon** on the Golden Circle. (p100)

Enjoy a truly magical north coast experience at ❹ **Forest Lagoon**, where forest bathing meets Icelandic spa culture. (p239)

Relax in the ❺ **GeoSea** geothermal sea baths while enjoying endless Atlantic Ocean views. (p251)

17

EXPLORE GLACIERS

Iceland is home to an estimated 269 glaciers that cover approximately 11% of this island nation. This is a country where majestic glacial views are everywhere and memories are just waiting to be made. Vatnajökull is Iceland's largest and best-known glacier, but it's just one of many majestic ice caps offering unforgettable adventures on – or inside – ice. Go snowmobiling on Langjökull, venture into Vatnajökull's Crystal Ice Cave, sail the Jökulsárlón Lagoon or traverse the ice at Sólheimajökull.

Snowmobile Across Ice Caps

There truly is something extraordinary about snowmobiling across a magnificent glacier. Suit up for the adventure of a lifetime.

Journey into Ice Caves

Visit during winter to explore natural ice caves. A human-made ice cave within Langjökull is open year-round.

Hike a Glacier

There's nothing quite like walking on ice, and there's no better place to do it than these magical blue and white spaces.

FROM LEFT: MELBA PHOTO AGENCY/ALAMY STOCK PHOTO ©; TIM E WHITE/ALAMY STOCK PHOTO ©; PAUL BRADY/ALAMY STOCK PHOTO ©

BEST GLACIAL EXPERIENCES

Sail among magnificent icebergs on a ❶ **Jökulsárlón** glacier lagoon boat tour. (p162)

Feel like you're flying across the moon on a snowmobile ride across ❷ **Langjökull**, Iceland's second-largest ice cap. (p179)

Hike across ❸ **Falljökull** glacier on a tour from Skaftafell to walk around magical ice formations and through winding crevasses. (p150)

Head inside the ❹ **Katla Ice Cave** to tour an elaborate palace of black and blue ice that opened to visitors in 2016 and is in a constant state of evolution. (p142)

Take a guided glacial hike across remote Kverkfjöll to the ❺ **Hveradalir Geothermal Area**, a colourful oasis of steam in the highlands. (p296)

REGIONS & CITIES

Find the places that tick all your boxes.

The Westfjords

OFFBEAT ICELAND

This mountainous peninsula is sparsely populated, even by Icelandic standards. Snow and ice close the roads along the narrow fjords that define the coastline for several months each year. Travel during the summer when road conditions are best to take in the spectacular scenery in this remote region.

p195

The
Westfjords
p195

West Iceland

A MICROCOSM OF ICELANDIC ELEMENTS

West Iceland is a short drive from Reykjavík but feels like a different world. This geographically diverse area is home to volcanoes, waterfalls and Langjökull, Iceland's second-largest glacier. This is a popular destination for snowmobiling and exploring ice tunnels. It's also home to the scenic Snæfellsnes Peninsula.

p168

West
Iceland
p168

REYKJAVÍK ○
p42

Southwest Iceland &
the Golden Circle
p82

Reykjavík

A CAPITAL FULL OF SURPRISES

Iceland's national capital is also its cultural capital. This is the heart of the Icelandic art, music and nightlife scenes. Come for Michelin-star dining, vintage shopping and all-night parties under the midnight sun. Stay to hike, fish and eat your way around the world, all without leaving the city.

p42

Southwest Iceland & the Golden Circle

OTHERWORLDLY ADVENTURES, MINUTES FROM THE AIRPORT

With charming small towns, magnificent natural wonders and frequent volcanic eruptions, it's no surprise this region is Iceland's biggest draw. Soak in geothermal lagoons. Explore a rugged coastline shaped by volcanic activity and an otherworldly interior where lava fields meet bubbling hot springs, rivers and waterfalls.

p82

See the best places to visit in Iceland

North Iceland

THE LAND OF FORCE

There are few better places for viewing the Northern Lights or experiencing the midnight sun than this region at the edge of the Arctic Circle. This remote area hosts the Arctic Open golf tournament during the summer and is a popular ski destination during the winter.
p220

North Iceland p220

East Iceland

AS FAR FROM REYKJAVÍK AS POSSIBLE

This sparsely populated area is popular for skiing during the winter and a haven for artists and musicians in summer. Charming fishing towns surround picturesque natural harbours. Narrow fjords define a jagged coastline often dotted with puffin and seals, and herds of wild reindeer live in the mountains.
p267

The Highlands p290

East Iceland p267

Southeast Iceland p145

The Highlands

RUGGED, RAW, WILD ICELANDIC INTERIOR

This vast uninhabitable area – only accessible between June and September – is as off-the-beaten path as it gets. There are no towns, hotels or fancy restaurants here, just hiking huts, majestic glaciers and unbelievable landscapes. Navigating the rough gravel roads leading into the highlands requires a 4WD.
p290

Southeast Iceland

RAW GLACIAL BEAUTY, CHARMING HAMLETS

This region of Iceland puts the ice in the 'land of fire and ice'. It's best known for Vatnajökull, the country's largest glacier, and Jökulsárlón, a glacial lagoon whose majestic icebergs crash-land onto a black-sand beach, glittering like diamonds as they settle.
p145

ITINERARIES

Reykjavík & the Southwest

Allow: 5 days   **Distance:** 476km

Iceland is small enough to pack a lot into even a short trip. Base yourself in Reykjavík for easy access to Iceland's top natural wonders. Explore magnificent waterfalls, hot springs and lava fields by day, and spend the evenings meandering the streets of Iceland's liveliest city.

❶ REYKJAVÍK ⏱1½ DAYS

This walkable capital city (p42), filled with independent restaurants, one-of-a-kind boutiques and public art, will be your home base for the next few days. Dive into Icelandic history at the Settlement Exhibition or the Árbær Open Air Museum, catch a show at the Harpa concert hall and enjoy a Michelin-star meal.

Then head to the Old Harbour to spend a few hours off the coast searching for whales, puffins or the Northern Lights. It's always possible to see whales. For puffins, visit between May and August, and sail in the evenings when the birds have returned to their burrows. For the Northern Lights, visit between September and April.

❷ THE GOLDEN CIRCLE ⏱1 DAY

From Reykjavík, take yourself on a day tour of Iceland's top three sights – Þingvellir National Park (pictured), Gullfoss, and the Geysir geothermal area (p99). Rent a car for flexibility or join one of several guided Golden Circle tours. All of these stop at the three key sites, and some itineraries include excursions like snowmobiling and ice caving.

❸ KERIÐ CRATER ⏱1 DAY

Don't leave without visiting Kerið crater (p122), an overlooked natural wonder. Start the day with an easy hike around the colourful caldera – it should take under an hour, but you may find it hard to pull yourself away from these views.

Detour: Spend the afternoon exploring caves and riding horses across the red lava fields in Heiðmörk Nature Reserve. ⏱3 hours

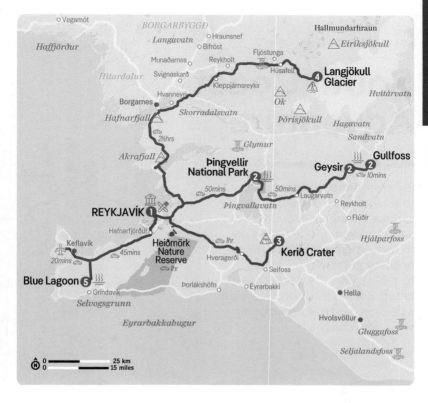

4
LANGJÖKULL GLACIER
⏱ 1 DAY

Leave Reykjavík early for a full day of adventure on Langjökull (p109), Iceland's second-largest glacier. Book a tour to ride a massive eight-wheel monster truck across this majestic chunk of ice. Strap crampons on and spend an hour wandering the world's longest human-made ice tunnel with a guide. Notice the colours – you'll see everything from cloudy white to deep blue.

5
BLUE LAGOON ⏱ ½ DAY

On your way from Reykjavík to Keflavík International Airport, give yourself at least two hours to enjoy this idyllic geothermal lagoon (p113) among the lava fields; longer if you'd like a massage, float therapy or to soak in the warm blue-tinted water rich with silica mud for just a few more minutes. If you're not driving, schedule an airport bus transfer with a Blue Lagoon stop and store your luggage at the lagoon.

ITINERARIES

South Coast Adventure

Allow: 6 days   **Distance:** 932km

Six days is enough time to get to know Iceland's South Coast without feeling rushed. Check out a glacial lagoon. Ride horses on the beach. Go paragliding, hiking or chasing waterfalls. Eat farm-to-table meals. Try hot springs bread. Soak in a lagoon. Go inside a volcano, and make memories you'll never forget.

❶ REYKJAVÍK ⏱1 DAY

Spend your first night in Reykjavík (p42). Unwind from a long flight with a luxurious dip in the Sky Lagoon. Have a traditional lamb hot dog, a Michelin-star meal, or fresh fish of the day for dinner. Visit a bar or two on Laugavegur Street, or call it an early night and have brunch at a Miðborg cafe before heading out on the Ring Road toward Seljalandsfoss.

❷ SELJALANDSFOSS ⏱1 DAY

Stop at the Hveragerði geothermal area to try fresh Icelandic rye bread baked over a hot spring. When you get to Seljalandsfoss (p131), give yourself about an hour to hike around it.

🥾 *Detour:* Hike to the top of **Skógafoss**, the misty waterfall that's become a popular filming location. ⏱3 hours

❸ VÍK ⏱1 DAY

Use Vík (p136) as your home base for exploring this stretch of the South Coast. A gateway to the Katla volcano, Vík has several hotels, restaurants, black-sand beaches, a magnificent coastline and a fairy-tale church (pictured).

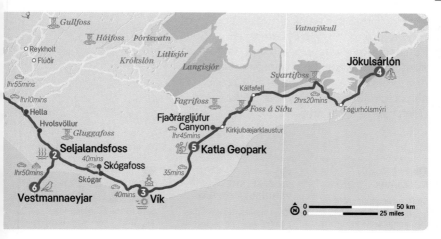

Gullfoss
Háifoss   Þórisvatn
Reykholt   Litlisjór   Vatnajökull
Flúðir   Krókslón   Langisjór
1hr55mins   Svartifoss   Jökulsárlón ④
1hr10mins   Fagrifoss   Kálfafell
Hella   Foss á Siðu   2hrs20mins   Fagurhólsmýri
Hvolsvöllur   Fjaðrárgljúfur
Gluggafoss   Canyon   Kirkjubæjarklaustur
1hr45mins
Seljalandsfoss ②   ⑤ Katla Geopark
40mins
1hr50mins   Skógafoss
Skógar   35mins
Vestmannaeyjar ⑥   40mins ③ Vík

0   50 km
0   25 miles

④ JÖKULSÁRLÓN ⏱ 1 DAY

Take a day trip from Vík to see the glittering icebergs that have washed up at Fellsfjara (Diamond Beach; pictured). Marvel at the glorious blue Jökulsárlón glacial lagoon (p160) and take a tour to get up close to the giant chunks of ice.

Detour: Stop at the **Fjaðrárgljúfur** canyon on your way back to Vík. It looks like a serpent carved into the earth and is well worth the detour. ⏱ 3 hours

⑤ KATLA GEOPARK ⏱ 1 DAY

From Vík, head out on an off-road adventure on a super-Jeep tour of Katla Geopark (p142). Take a journey deep into the Katla Ice Cave. Go ice climbing, or snowmobiling across Mýrdalsjökull glacier (pictured). You'll need a specially modified vehicle to access these areas. These aren't available for rent, so you'll need to sign up for a guided tour.

⑥ VESTMANNAEYJAR ⏱ 1 DAY

Have an early breakfast in Vík and head west on Rte 1 – drive to Landeyjahöfn and take the ferry to Vestmannaeyjar (p134) to look for puffins and visit the Eldheimar museum (pictured). Take the ferry back and stop in Selfoss at the Old Dairy food hall for dinner on your way to Keflavík International Airport.

Detour: Stop at **Leif the Lucky Bridge** and cross the rift between the North American and Eurasian tectonic plates. ⏱ 1 hour

ITINERARIES

Full Circle

Allow: 7 days   **Distance:** 1538km

This itinerary will take you around the entire country in a week. From artsy Reykjavík and the wild Snæfellsnes Peninsula, to a whale haven and endless stretches of black-sand beaches, you can experience every scene and season as you circle the country, even if you don't have a lot of time.

① REYKJAVÍK ⏱ 1 DAY

Spend your first night in Reykjavík (p42) preparing for an unforgettable trip on Rte 1, the scenic Ring Road that loops around Iceland. Unwind in the Sky Lagoon after a long flight. Have a Michelin-star meal, a Bill Clinton–approved hot dog or langoustine soup for dinner, and set out on the road trip of a lifetime after breakfast.

② SNÆFELLSNES PENINSULA ⏱ 1 DAY

Head out early to drive the Snæfellsnes Peninsula (p168). This is one of Iceland's most scenic drives. See the volcano that inspired Jules Verne and Kirkjufell, the cone-shaped mountain that's the most photographed in Iceland.

③ AKUREYRI ⏱ ½ DAY

Stop in Akureyri (p235) to wander the charming streets of Old Town where many buildings are finished with corrugated iron to protect them from harsh weather. See mid-century stained-glass windows at the striking Akureyri Church, or step back in time at Gásir, which hosts a medieval festival each July.

④ HÚSAVÍK ⏱ 1 DAY

Spend your morning on a whale-watching boat tour from Húsavík (p249). Prepare to be charmed by humpback whales, minke whales, porpoises and dolphin pods. Keep an eye out for the rare giant blue whale. If you see this species in Iceland, it'll be here. After lunch in town, get back on the Ring Road to Seyðisfjörður.

TRAVELPIX/ALAMY STOCK PHOTO ©

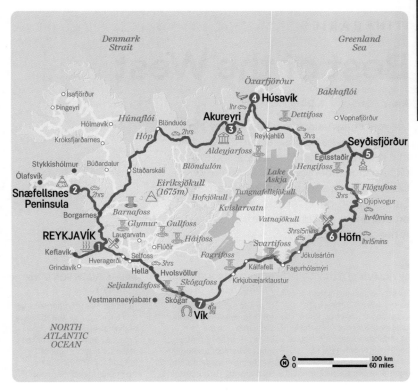

Denmark
Strait

Greenland
Sea

Öxarfjörður

Bakkaflói

🦅 **4 Húsavík**

○ Ísafjörður
○ Þingeyri

1hr

○ Vopnafjörður

Hólmavík ○

Húnaflói Blönduós

Akureyri 🏛 Dettifoss

3hrs

Króksfjarðarnes ○

Hóp 2hrs

3 Reykjahlíð

Seyðisfjörður

Stykkishólmur Búðardalur

Staðarskáli

Aldeyjarfoss 🏛

Egilsstaðir

5

Ólafsvík

🏛

Blöndulón

*Lake
Askja*

Hengifoss 🏛

🏛 *Flögufoss*

**Snæfellsnes
Peninsula** **2**

*Eiríksjökull
(1675m)* △

Hofsjökull

Tungnafellsjökull

3hrs

○ Djúpivogur

2hrs

Borgarnes

Barnafoss 🏛

Kvíslarvatn

1hr40mins

REYKJAVÍK

Glymur 🏛

Gullfoss

Vatnajökull

Laugarvatn

🏛 *Háifoss*

3hrs15mins 🍴

Keflavík ●

○ Flúðir

Svartifoss

6 Höfn

1hr15mins

Grindavík ○

Hveragerði

Fagrifoss

Jökulsárlón

Selfoss

3hrs

Kálfafell

Fagurhólsmýri

Hella

Hvolsvöllur

Kirkjubæjarklaustur

Seljalandsfoss 🏛

Skógafoss 🏛

Vestmannaeyjabær ●

Skógar

7

🐎 **Vík** ⛪

*NORTH
ATLANTIC
OCEAN*

Ⓝ 0 ———————— 100 km
0 ———————— 60 miles

5 SEYÐISFJÖRÐUR ⏱1 DAY

Follow the rainbow path (pictured) to the light-blue church in the charming village of Seyðisfjörður (p280). Don't miss the Tvísöngur sound sculpture or the chance to experience a thriving local arts scene.

🔁 *Detour: Stop in **Djúpivogur** to check out 34 granite eggs lined up along the shore. Each represents a species of bird that nests here.*
⏱ *1 hour*

6 HÖFN ⏱1 DAY

Let Höfn (p166), Iceland's langoustine (pictured) fishing capital, welcome you with a fresh seafood dinner. Peak langoustine season is from mid-May to August. Each July, the town hosts a festival celebrating this type of lobster.

7 VÍK ⏱1½ DAYS

Finish with a day in Vík (p136). Have breakfast overlooking the rugged coastline and check out the views from its charming small-town church. Go horse riding on the beach, take a scenic hike or go paragliding over magnificent rock formations before flying out of Keflavík International Airport.

Best of the West

Allow: 5 days   **Distance:** 517km

Let your imagination run wild on a day trip to the Snæfellsnes Peninsula. See the volcano that inspired a Jules Verne novel and the picturesque mountain that's become a *Game of Thrones* regular. Take a scenic hike. Sample fresh-baked *hverabrauð* (hot spring bread), and walk from Europe to North America.

❶ REYKJAVÍK ⏱ 1 DAY

Spend your first two nights in Reykjavík (p42). Have fresh Icelandic fish and chips, visit a local museum, check out street art and shop adorable boutiques. Depending on when you're travelling, chase the Northern Lights or revel in the midnight sun.

❷ ÞINGVELLIR NATIONAL PARK ⏱ 1 DAY

Dive into the Silfra Fissure (p90) for an unforgettable swim between tectonic plates. See the birthplace of modern democracy and the first home of Iceland's Alþingi (Parliament). Go horse riding, traverse lava fields or simply enjoy the views.

❸ LAUGARVATN FONTANA ⏱ ½ DAY

At this relaxed geothermal spa and bakery (p100), the specialty of the house is Icelandic lava bread: a rye that's been baked in the sand by the heat of hot springs. Try some of this traditional *hverabrauð* with fresh Icelandic butter after a long soak in a warm pool and a quick dip in the cold lake. This complex is less crowded than the Sky Lagoon and Blue Lagoon, and admission is a fraction of the price.

❹ HVERAGERÐI ⏱ ½ DAY

Hike the Reykjadalur Valley in Hveragerði (p127) and reward yourself with a soak in a warm geothermal river. Check out steaming vents and bubbling mud pools along a meandering 3km path that passes canyons and waterfalls as it cuts through this colourful valley. There are public bathrooms at the trailhead. Spend the night in town, and stop for locally made ice cream at Bongó ísbúð or Ísbúðin okkar.

Geothermal river, Hveragerði (p127)

⑤ GRINDAVÍK ⏱1 DAY

Check out the small fishing town of Grindavík (p111). From here, hike the Fagradalsfjall lava fields (pictured) where eruptions have become increasingly frequent in recent years. Or learn about saltfish at the Kvikan museum, and dine on fresh cod at Hjá Höllu or Salthúsið.

⑥ BLUE LAGOON ⏱ ½ DAY

Step into the light-blue water of the Blue Lagoon (p113). Bask in its warmth while slathering your skin with mineral-rich silica mud, and treat yourself to an in-water massage or Michelin-star meal.

⑦ LEIF THE LUCKY BRIDGE ⏱ ½ DAY

There's no other place in the world where you can walk from Europe to North America. This spot along the Mid-Atlantic Ridge on the Reykjanes Peninsula is a place where the North American and Eurasian tectonic plates meet. Use the Leif the Lucky Bridge (p117) to walk across the continental rift, or explore the sandy fissure between the plates.

WHEN **TO GO**

For the Northern Lights, travel between September and March. For the midnight sun, travel in June or July.

It's always a good time to visit Iceland, but you can expect a very different experience depending on when you go.

Long nights offer ample opportunity for taking in dazzling Northern Lights displays during the winter. Long summer days are perfect for lengthy hikes, revelling in the streets and taking in midnight sunsets.

Iceland has four distinct seasons. If a full Ring Road trip or multiday hikes in the highlands are on your agenda, travel between July and September when mountain roads are usually open, days are long and the winter thaw has passed. For puffins, travel between mid-May and early August. Ski areas are generally open from December to April. You'll find the best conditions in February and March.

You can go whale watching, snowmobiling, glacier hiking and horse riding year-round. November to March is best for ice caving. Travel between May and October if you want to take a Jökulsárlón boat tour.

Bláhver (p297)

> ⊛ **I LIVE HERE**
>
> ### SUMMER IN ICELAND
>
> **Jewells Chambers is the founder and host of the All Things Iceland podcast and YouTube channel.**
> **@allthingsiceland**
>
> This is the season when Iceland's enchanting landscapes, from cascading waterfalls to verdant moss-covered valleys, truly shine. The midnight sun, adorable puffins, hiking in gorgeous mountain ranges and rejuvenating soaks in hot springs late into the bright evenings all make visiting at this time of year a unique and amazing experience.

PREPARE FOR EVERYTHING

There's only one predictable thing about the Icelandic weather: it's unpredictable. Be prepared to experience four seasons in a single day and for dramatic changes in wind, rain and winter weather, especially in the countryside and mountains.

Weather Through the Year (Reykjavík)

	JANUARY	FEBRUARY	MARCH	APRIL	MAY	JUNE
	❄	☁	☔	⛅	☀	☀
Average daytime max:	3.1°C	3.3°C	4°C	6.8°C	9.8°C	12.7°C
Days of rainfall:	15	14	14	11	10	9

MILD WINTERS & CHILLY SUMMERS

This country's name may be Iceland, but don't let that fool you. Because of the Gulf Stream, winters here are milder than you might imagine with average temperatures around freezing. Icelandic summers are pleasant, but you'll want to bring a light jacket.

Summer Festivals Galore

Summer is festival season in Iceland. Visit on 17 June to experience **Iceland Day**, a nationwide celebration of Icelandic independence, with family-friendly parades, local fairs and Icelandic-flag-themed treats. **June**

Head to Seyðisfjörður for the **LungA Art Festival**; a celebration of art and creativity swells the population of the tiny town on Iceland's eastern edge. The festival includes concerts, dance parties, exhibitions, panel discussions, and swim and sauna sessions. **July**

Or travel in August to experience **Reykjavík Pride** or the **National Festival** in Vestmannaeyjar. The National Festival draws thousands of visitors each August for a long-weekend campout. It includes a Friday night bonfire, a Sunday folk music singalong with a well-known local musician, and a light show meant to represent Iceland's volcanic flames. **August**

See a full calendar of events and more

Eclectic Music Festivals

Iceland Airwaves is the biggest music event on the Icelandic calendar. The four-day multi-genre festival features hundreds of bands from around the world. Held at venues across Reykjavík. It includes a conference with talks on the music business, Icelandic films and more. **November**

Check out the **Reykjavík Jazz** festival, which celebrates everything from contemporary jazz and gospel music to Latin jazz and big bands. **August**

Eistnaflug Metal Festival brings dozens of metal bands to the tiny town of Neskaupstaður, doubling its population. **Second weekend of July**

There are only 800 tickets sold for the **Bræðslan** music festival in Borgarfjörður Eystri, but don't let this party's size fool you. This exclusive festival hosts intimate performances from some of the biggest names in music. **Late July**

I LIVE HERE

COSY WINTERS

Anna Lisa Terrazas is a native Icelander living and working in Reykjavík.

I love the winter months. They are cosy with lots of candlelit nights. People go downhill skiing, cross-country skiing and snowmobiling. There are geothermal pools where you can be outside and still stay warm. And of course, there's the chance to see the Northern Lights. I spend winter wearing cosy sweaters and around March, I like being able to feel and see the days growing longer.

RARE THUNDERSTORMS

Thunderstorms are rare in Iceland, which sees maybe a handful of them each year. Those that do occur typically happen during the summer and are usually caused by warm-air masses coming up from Europe.

JULY	AUGUST	SEPTEMBER	OCTOBER	NOVEMBER	DECEMBER
Average daytime max: 14.6°C	Average daytime max: 13.9°C	Average daytime max: 11.1°C	Average daytime max: 7.5°C	Average daytime max: 4.5°C	Average daytime max: 3.3°C
Days of rainfall: 10	Days of rainfall: 11	Days of rainfall: 15	Days of rainfall: 13	Days of rainfall: 13	Days of rainfall: 14

More essential tips for visiting Iceland

Top: Jökulsárlón (p162). Right: *Game of Thrones*.

GET PREPARED FOR ICELAND

Useful things to load in your bag, your ears and your brain.

Clothes

Layers Iceland weather is unpredictable, and layering is your best strategy regardless of when you're travelling. Pack a lightweight puffer jacket and sturdy waterproof hiking boots for summer travel. Choose waterproof trousers over jeans for hiking, and leave the vest tops, sandals and shorts at home – you won't need them, even in July.

Winter gear Winters are milder than you might expect, with temperatures rarely dipping below 0 °C. Pack snow pants, snow boots and a warm coat. Don't forget gloves, a hat and thermal base layers. Excursion operators provide heavy winter gear for activities like snowmobiling and glacial hiking, but bundle up for aurora expeditions.

Manners

Always shower before getting into a pool or sauna. Don't wear your shoes or socks into the locker room.

Tipping is not required but may be appreciated where businesses put out tip jars.

Take shoes off when entering someone's home.

Only use designated areas for **camping**.

Casual vs formal Icelanders dress casually, so you can leave the heels, sport coats and formalwear behind.

Jackets A rain jacket is always a good idea.

📖 READ

Journey to the Center of the Earth (Jules Verne; 1864) This science fiction classic takes place on Iceland's Snæfellsnes Peninsula.

The Little Book of Tourists in Iceland (Alda Sigmundsdóttir; 2022) An easy read on being a responsible traveller in Iceland.

The Little Book of the Icelanders (Alda Sigmundsdóttir; 2014) Insights into the quirks of Icelandic culture through 50 miniature essays.

Secrets of the Sprakkar (Eliza Reid; 2022) A glimpse of a more gender-equal world from Iceland's First Lady.

Words

Most Icelanders speak English, so don't worry about getting around without any Icelandic. Icelanders understand that their language, which hasn't changed much since the 9th century, can be difficult for visitors to learn.

Icelandic is mainly spoken in Iceland and is most closely related to Faroese, which is spoken in the neighbouring Faroe Islands. Icelandic has 32 letters in its alphabet – six more than English. It's missing a handful of familiar consonants and has two additional vowels.

A few helpful words and phrases:
Halló (hah-lo) 'Hello'.
Góðan daginn (go-thah-n die-in) 'Good day'.
Vinsamlegast (vin-saam-leh-gast) 'Please'.

Takk (thak) 'Thank you'.
Já (y-ow) 'Yes'.
Nei (neigh) 'No'.
Bless (bles) 'Goodbye'.
Hvar er...? (kva-r-eh-r) 'Where is...?'
Klósett (k-low-seht) 'Toilet'.
Hvað kostar þetta? (hvahth kost-ar thet-ta) 'How much does this cost?'
Ég tala ekki Íslensku (yeh tah-la ekkee ees-len-skew) 'I don't speak Icelandic'.
Skál (sk-owl) 'Cheers'.

A few tips:
The Icelandic 'j' sounds like the English 'y'.
The character 'Þ' is pronounced 'th' like 'then'.
The character 'Ð' is pronounced 'th' like 'the'.
'Reykjavik' is pronounced 'Rayk-yah-veek'.
'Rs' get rolled.

▶ WATCH

Die Another Day (Lee Tamahori; 2002) The car-chase scene was shot at Jökulsárlón lagoon.

Game of Thrones (2012) Look for Þingvellir, Fjaðrárgljúfur canyon, Þórsmörk and Reynisfjara.

The Secret Life of Walter Mitty (Ben Stiller; 2013) Features Skógafoss and Vatnajökull.

Children of Nature (Friðrik Þór Friðriksson; 1991) The only Icelandic film ever nominated for the best foreign language Oscar.

Katla (Baltasar Kormákur Baltasarsson; 2021) The South Coast stars in this Netflix series on a catastrophic volcanic eruption.

🎧 LISTEN

Greatest Hits (Björk; 2002) A collection of fan favourites from Iceland's most famous singer, songwriter, record producer and actress.

My Head Is an Animal (Of Monsters and Men; 2011) The album that vaulted this Icelandic folk rock band to global fame.

I Made an Album (Daði Freyr; 2023) The debut English-language album from a beloved Reykjavik-born Eurovision finalist.

Kveðja (Bríet; 2020) The award-winning breakout album from a young Icelandic musician who began playing Iceland Airwaves as a teenager.

Explore more of Iceland's food and drink

Harðfiskur

THE FOOD SCENE

Don't be fooled. There's far more to the Icelandic food scene than fish, meat and potatoes.

The Icelandic food scene has come a long way. While the traditional fermented and dried foods of the past can still be found, freshly caught fish, delicious gamey lamb, and creamy *skyr* (yoghurt-like dessert) are staples of the modern diet.

Icelandic food is some of the freshest and purest in the world. The North Atlantic provides an abundance of fish, mussels and scallops. Geothermal energy allows farmers to grow a variety of fruits and vegetables year-round.

Traditional Foods

For many years, people here had to make the most of what they had and make it last through long, harsh winters. Salt and fermentation extended the shelf life of the available food, and eating every part of every creature became the norm. Dishes like *harðfiskur* (a dried fish snack), *svið* (a boiled sheep's head cut in half) and *hákarl* (fermented shark) were common. Horse was – and occasionally remains – on the menu. Icelandic rye bread, sometimes cooked over a hot spring, accompanied meals. This *hverabrauð* is still available today.

Modern Icelandic Cuisine

Iceland's culinary star has been on the rise. Michelin-star chefs whip up creative tasting menus featuring farm-fresh ingredients and unforgettable fine-dining experiences. Casual cafes and coffee shops dot Reykjavík and are spreading across the countryside.

Modern Icelandic cuisine is farm-to-table dining at its best. Most restaurants serve freshly caught fish of the day and locally grown fruit, vegetables and berries. High-end dining is just part of what Iceland has to offer. Its casual foods are some of its most memorable. Have farm-fresh ice cream at a dairy. Try cake made with fresh *skyr*. Or stop for a famous Bæjarins Beztu Pylsur (p55) lamb hot dog, a local staple that's won over visitors from around the world.

Beer & Liquor

Beer was illegal in Iceland until 1989, but you can now find quality craft breweries across the country. Beer is also sold at government liquor stores. Icelandic beer is made with Icelandic water, giving these lagers, pilsners, pale ales and stouts an exceptional taste.

Iceland is also the home of a growing distillery business. It's best known for Reykja, a small-batch producer that finishes its vodka in the coastal village of Borgarnes. Several distilleries are located in the southwest and produce spirits including gin, rum, whisky and Brennivín.

Local Specialities

Fresh from the Sea

Atlantic cod Lean flaky fish that's a staple of the Icelandic diet.

Arctic char Restaurant menu staple fished from rivers and lakes across Iceland.

Wolffish Meaty white fish with a sweet taste and crab-like texture.

Langoustine Small lobster that's fished off the southern coast. Often served in soup.

Haddock Versatile white fish with a fine texture and delicate flakiness.

Fresh from the Farm

Lamb Free-roaming sheep graze on wild herbs and grasses, making Icelandic lamb especially tender and flavourful.

Beef High-quality, grass-fed local meat, free of hormones and antibiotics.

Tomatoes Greenhouse-grown with glacier water, Icelandic tomatoes are flavourful and pesticide-free.

Snacks & Sweets

Harðfiskur A traditional dried fish snack often eaten with butter.

Pönnukökur Similar to a sweet crepe, often with jam and whipped cream.

Laufabraud A leaf-shaped flatbread eaten during the holiday season.

Kleinur Fried twisted doughnuts flavoured with vanilla or cardamom.

Dare to Try

Hákarl Fermented shark often with a shot of Brennivín.

Svið A boiled half of a sheep's head with potatoes or turnips.

Hrútspungar Sour ram testicles in gelatin or whey eaten as a pâté.

Reindeer Lean gamey meat served in Reykjavík and eastern Iceland.

Hestur Horse meat, often served in stews.

Laufabraud

FOOD FESTIVALS

Food and Fun Festival (p46) Held in Reykjavik each spring, this is Iceland's premier food festival. The Food and Fun Festival brings chefs from around the world to Iceland, challenging them to create affordably priced gourmet menus using only Icelandic ingredients over the course of a weeklong competition.

Þorrablót (p224) This February food festival is a celebration of Iceland's pagan history. Traditional feasts include dried fish, boiled sheep's head, dung-smoked lamb, and pickled ram's testicles.

Great Fish Day (p247) The village of Dalvík in North Iceland celebrates the country's rich fishing heritage with a free all-day seafood buffet every August.

Humarhátíð (p166) Höfn is the lobster capital of Iceland, and it celebrates its bounty with a festival each June. Try delicious Icelandic lobster while experiencing an authentic small-town festival.

SURYA MJÖLL/WIKIMEDIA COMMONS © CC BY-SA 4.0

THE YEAR IN FOOD

SPRING

Have an Easter feast of lamb, fish, potatoes and vegetables and a *skyr* cake topped with chocolate eggs. Brown-trout and sea-trout fishing begin in April, with prime season between July and October.

SUMMER

June brings candy floss and Icelandic-flag-themed sweets for Iceland Day, and the start of salmon season. Berry season can begin any time from late July to the end of August.

AUTUMN

Icelandic lobster (langoustine) fishing begins in April and tapers off in September. You'll also find the freshest lamb as flocks will have spent their summers eating wild herbs and grasses.

WINTER

Enjoy Christmas meals of savoury smoked lamb and vegetables and warm bowls of soup and stew. Or feast on traditional Viking fare during the Þorrablót festival in February.

DAVID VARGA/SHUTTERSTOCK ©

Laugavegur trail (p135)

THE **OUTDOORS**

With spectacular scenery, excellent infrastructure and an endless list of things to do, you may never want to go inside.

The best things in Iceland are outdoors. Prepare for stunning mountains, gargantuan glaciers, expansive lava fields and beautiful black-sand beaches along a rugged coast. Iceland is known for its spectacular natural beauty, and there's no shortage of ways to experience it. Hike a glacier or explore an ice cave. Go snowmobiling, skiing, snowboarding or mountain biking. Spend your days hiking and fishing and your evenings enjoying candlelit campsite dinners. Whatever you choose, you'll find endless waterfalls and stunning views.

Walking & Hiking

From the smooth path along the Reykjavík waterfront to the emerald kingdom that is the Þórsmörk Valley, you'll find countless adventures on foot here. Iceland's towering mountains, calm valleys, rugged coastlines and endless waterfalls are made for hiking. You'll find easy trails across the country as well as difficult mountain treks to challenge even the most experienced hikers.

The Fagradalsfjall volcano has taken off as a hiking destination thanks to several recent eruptions. You'll also find well-marked and well-maintained trails in national parks, along rugged coastlines and through idyllic valleys. The Laugavegur and Fimmvörðuháls trails are two of Iceland's most popular. Laugavegur offers experienced hikers an unforgettable journey through caramel-coloured dunes and the

Adrenaline Adventures

PARAGLIDING
Soar over Vík's black-sand beaches and the magnificent Reynisdrangar (p138) rock formations off Iceland's southern coast.

SKIING & SNOWBOARDING
Ski or snowboard down jagged mountain peaks towards the sea at Siglufjörður (p245) on the Troll Peninsula.

SCUBA DIVING & SNORKELLING
Dive into the Silfra Fissure (p90), the only place in the world where you can swim between tectonic plates.

FAMILY ADVENTURES

Bundle up and bring your warmest hats because you'll find Iceland's best family adventures outdoors. Ride precious Icelandic horses across Þingvellir National Park or on a beach near Vík. Head out for an unforgettable whale-watching tour from Reykjavík's Old Harbour, or take children 14 and older on a kayak tour in search of puffins off the coast of Vestmannaeyjar. Chase waterfalls across the South Coast and beyond. Traverse wild topography on a snowmobile, ATV or mountain bike. Take memorable family hikes, soak in idyllic lagoons and have candlelit dinners in caves. Go fishing, enjoy local pools that feel like waterparks or set out to see the Northern Lights. No one's getting bored here.

Icelandic desert. Fimmvörðuháls follows a trail of waterfalls leading from Skógafoss to Þórsmörk.

Cycling

The Ring Road is a popular route for visitors looking for an Icelandic cycling adventure. It's paved throughout and passes through most major towns, but there are no designated bike lanes. Outside of Reykjavík, the two-lane Rte 1 sometimes narrows to one lane. You'll need to be comfortable sharing roads with vehicles as well as the occasional sheep or horse.

This ride is best tackled during the summer when campsites are open, road conditions are at their best and there's ample daylight for long rides. Be prepared for rain, especially in June and July, and the occasional summer snow. Cyclists are not allowed to pass through the Hvalfjörður Tunnel, but cycling the fjord is a far more scenic experience. Cyclists will also need to switch to local paths in Reykjavík.

Mountain biking is growing in popularity but trails are limited because of the delicate ecosystems they'd have to pass through. You'll find some pristine sections of singletrack in places like Þórsmörk, and welcoming trails such as Laugavegur and those in the Reykjadalur Valley. It's often acceptable for mountain bikers to use existing sheep trails. Tour operators in Reykjavík (Icebike Adventures) and Húsavík (Mountain Bike Húsavík) offer scenic rides and heli-biking.

Resources

Safe.is is the official source for driving tips and safety alerts and road.is has the latest information on road conditions and the weather. Fi.is provides information on cabins and mountain huts for hikers, and has a list of hiking trails with estimated difficulty levels.

Hut on Laugavegur trail (p135)

See Iceland's beautiful beaches

RIVER RAFTING	SNOWMOBILING	GLACIER HIKING	ICE CAVING
White-water raft the Hvítá river (p296), which carves its way through Gullfoss Canyon and is suitable for beginners.	Zoom across magnificent Langjökull glacier (p109) on a snowmobile. Crisscross this snowy expanse while enjoying pristine mountain views.	Hike across the marble-like blue and black ice of Sólheimajökull glacier (p143). Walk across a volcanic ash field along the way.	Venture inside the wild blue and black ice caves at the Katla volcano (p142).

ACTION AREAS

Where to find Iceland's
best outdoor activities.

NORTH ATLANTIC OCEAN

Hornstrandir Nature Reserve

Greenland Sea

Skálavík

Bolungarvík
Suðureyri ○
Drangajökull
● **Ísafjörður**
Norðurfjörður
Siglufjörður

þingeyri ○
Skagafjörður
Troll Peninsula

Bíldudalur ○
Vatnsfjörður Nature Reserve
Húnaflói Skagaströnd ○
Sauðárkrókur ○

Patreksfjörður ○
Hólmavík ○
Blönduós ●

○ Brjánslækur
Hóp
Varmahlíð ○

Breiðafjörður
○ Hvammstangi

Flatey
Friðmundarvötn
Blöndulón Reservoir

Stykkishólmur ●
Búðardalur ○

Rif ○
Ólafsvík
Snæfellsnes Peninsula
Eiríksjökull
Hofsjökull

Hvítárvatn

Borgarnes ◉

Akranes ●
Geysir ○ *Gullfoss*
Þórisvatn

REYKJAVÍK ✪
Hveragerði ○

Keflavík ●
● **Selfoss**

Grindavík ○
○ þorlákshöfn
Hella ○ *Tindfjallajökull*

Hvolsvöllur ○
Katla

Vestmannaeyjar
Skógar ○

Surtsey
Vestmannaeyjar Islands
Vík ○

Walking/Hiking

❶ Mt Esja (p177)
❷ Laugavegur Trail (p135)
❸ Fimmvörðuháls (p135)
❹ Þórsmörk (p135)
❺ Dettifoss to Ásbyrgi canyon (p262)
❻ Kerlingarfjöll Loop (p296)
❼ Askja Trail (p301)

Discover more of Iceland's best hikes

Cycling

1. Svalvogar Circuit (p202)
2. Westfjords Way (p206)
3. Iceland Bike Farm (p156)
4. Kjölur Route (p294)
5. Akureyri (p241)

Greenland Sea

Skiing/Snowboarding

1. Siglufjörður (p240)
2. Ísafjörður (p211)
3. Hlíðarfjall (p240)
4. Dalvík (p240)
5. Ólafsfjörður (p246)

Grímsey

Þistilfjörður

Öxarfjörður

Flatey

Í Fjörðum

Bakkaflói

Húsavík

Bakkafjörður

Dettifoss

Vopnafjörður

Akureyri

Reykjahlíð

Njarðvík

Goðafoss

Mývatn

Aldeyjarfoss

Egilsstaðir

Seyðisfjörður

Hengifossárvatn

Neskaupstaður

Mórauðavatn

Eskifjörður

Gerpir Cliffs

Askja

Hálslón Reservoir

Reyðarfjörður

Fáskrúðsfjörður

Dyngjujökull

Stöðvarfjörður

Breiðdalsvík

Bárðarbunga

Kverkfjöll

Þrándarjökull

Djúpivogur

Hágöngulón

Vatnajökull

Hoffellsjökull

Stafafell

Fláajökull

Lónsvík

Grímsvötn

Höfn

Stokksnes

Siðujökull

Hvannadalshnúkur

Skaftafell

Glaciers/Ice Caves

1. Katla Ice Cave (p132)
2. Langjökull (p179)
3. Sólheimajökull (p143)
4. Mýrdalsjökull (p142)
5. Vatnajökull (p150)
6. Snæfellsjökull (p187)
7. Kverkfjöll ice caves (p306)

Kirkjubæjarklaustur

Kúðafljót

National Parks

1. Þingvellir National Park (p88)
2. Vatnajökull National Park (p301)
3. Snæfellsjökull National Park (p187)

0 — 100 km
0 — 50 miles

THE GUIDE

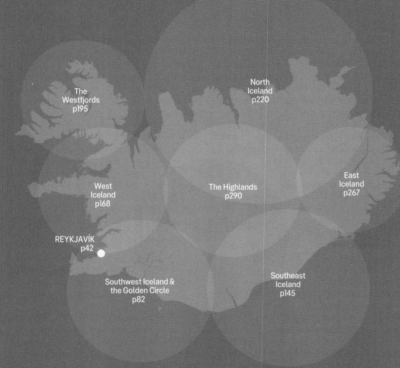

The Westfjords
p195

North
Iceland
p220

West
Iceland
p168

The Highlands
p290

East
Iceland
p267

REYKJAVÍK
p42

Southwest Iceland &
the Golden Circle
p82

Southeast
Iceland
p145

Chapters in this section are organised by hubs and their surrounding areas. We see the hub as your base in the destination, where you'll find unique experiences, local insights, insider tips and expert recommendations. It's also your gateway to the surrounding area, where you'll see what and how much you can do from there.

View of Lómagnúpur cliffs (p156)

REYKJAVÍK
A CAPITAL FULL OF SURPRISES

Eat your way around the world, soak in geothermal lagoons, seek out puffins, chase the Northern Lights or dance all night under the midnight sun.

Reykjavík is the capital and largest city in Iceland, a country of fewer than 400,000 people spread across an island about the size of Switzerland. More than 60% of Icelanders live in the greater Reykjavík area, which is the commercial, industrial and cultural centre of the country.

This is a city that feels like a small town but has a huge, quirky personality. Vintage stores, independent cafes and souvenir shops line its streets, punctuated by pleasant surprises, such as a sprawling bar dedicated to the movie *The Big Lebowski* and *The Black Cone*, a giant slab of cracked rock that celebrates the power of civil disobedience.

Most international travellers arrive at Keflavík International Airport, making Reykjavík a natural starting point for any Iceland trip.

Unwind from a long flight with a soak at the Blue Lagoon or Sky Lagoon. Take a stroll along the waterfront, stopping at Harpa, the glistening concert hall that hosts the Iceland Symphony Orchestra, Icelandic Opera and more. Spend a moment at the iconic *Sun Voyager,* an excellent vantage point for enjoying late summer sunsets.

Visit the Settlement Exhibition to learn how this area went from farmland to European capital. Wander through historic turf houses at the Árbær Open Air Museum where guides in period costumes will transport you to another era. Learn about how Iceland came to be – and check out the first full Bible printed in Icelandic – at the National Museum of Iceland.

For a bird's-eye view of the city, head to Hallgrímskirkja, whose soaring church tower is among the tallest structures in the country. The church anchors a charming city centre that's home to iconic stretches including Rainbow Street and the pedestrian-only Laugavegur Street. Take the time to wander these cobblestone streets, check out colourful street art and find a new favourite bar or cafe.

This is a city where chain restaurants are rare and where fresh, local seafood often leads menus. Reykjavík has become more vegetarian-friendly and offers a surprising variety of global cuisines for a city of its size.

Just don't go looking for McDonald's. There isn't one in Iceland.

OLEG SENKOV/SHUTTERSTOCK ©

THE MAIN AREAS

MIÐBORG	**VESTURBÆR**	**LAUGARDALUR & HLÍÐAR**	**ARBÆR**
Lively city centre.	Historic Old Harbour.	A scenic shoreline.	Open-air turf house museum.
p48	**p56**	**p62**	**p67**

Above: Panoramic view of Reykjavík. Left: Rainbow Street

KÓPAVOGUR
Nature, industry and a lagoon.
p70

SELTJARNARNES
A scenic peninsula.
p74

**HAFNARFJÖRÐUR &
GARÐABÆR**
Vikings and distilleries.
p77

SCOOTER

You'll quickly notice people zipping around central Reykjavik on the kinds of electric scooters that have been popping up in cities around the world. You can join them by renting an electric scooter from Zolo, Hopp or Wind.

FROM THE AIRPORT

Two private bus companies connect Keflavík International Airport with Reykjavik in under an hour for around 4000kr. Or take the 55 bus for 2300kr – the journey takes an hour and twenty minutes. Expect to pay at least 12,000kr for a private transfer or taxi.

Viðey Island

Sundahöfn Harbour

Kattðagerði

Laugardalslaug

Reykjavik Art Museum – Ásmundarsafn

Elliðaárdalur

Árbær Open Air Museum

Árbær
p67

Vesturlandsvegur

Réttarholtsvegur

Bústaðavegur

Háaleiti

Nýbýlavegur

Sæbraut

Borgartún

Laugavegur

Höfði House

Hlíðar

Reykjavik Art Museum – Kjarvalsstaðir

Laugardalur & Hlíðar
p62

Langholt

Háaleitisbraut Kringlumýrarbraut

Almgerði

Enniland

Atholsvegur

Miklabraut

Öskjuhlíð

Bústaðavegur

Nauthólsvegur

Fossvogur

Nauthólsvík Geothermal Beach

Sky Lagoon

Kópavogur

Bessastaðatjörn

Hólmar

Enney

Sun Voyager

Harpa

Hverfisgata

Hallgrímskirkja

Miðborg
p48

Lake Tjörnin

Settlement Exhibition

Reykjavik Domestic Airport

Einarsnes

Suðurgata

National Museum of Iceland

Reykjavik Art Museum – Hafnarhús

Old Harbour

Vesturbær
p56

Fiskislóð

Hólmurinn

Norðurströnd

Valhúsahæð

Suðurströnd

Seltjarnarnes
p74

North Atlantic Ocean

Grótta Lighthouse

Bakkatjörn

Seltjarnarnes Golf Club

44

Explore
Reykjavik's
neighbourhoods

Reykjanesbraut

Kópavogur
p70

Hafnarfjörður
& Garðabær
p77

ALFTANES

Lake
Vifilsstaðavatn

Museum of Design
and Applied Art

Urriðaholt

Höfðaskógur
Forest

Hafnarfjörður

Hellisgerði
Park

Suðurgarður Park

Ástjörn

Reykjanesbraut

Hraunholtsbraut

Hafnarfjarðarvegur

Strandgata

Elliðavatn

Garðavegur

Herjólfsgata

Hvaleyrabraut

Miðvangur

Hraun

Reykjanesbraut

Hvergata

Find Your Way

Reykjavik is a small, walkable city. It's easy to get around without a car, but you may want to take the bus if you're heading across town or to a further-flung neighbourhood. Uber and Lyft are not available here, and there are no trains in Iceland.

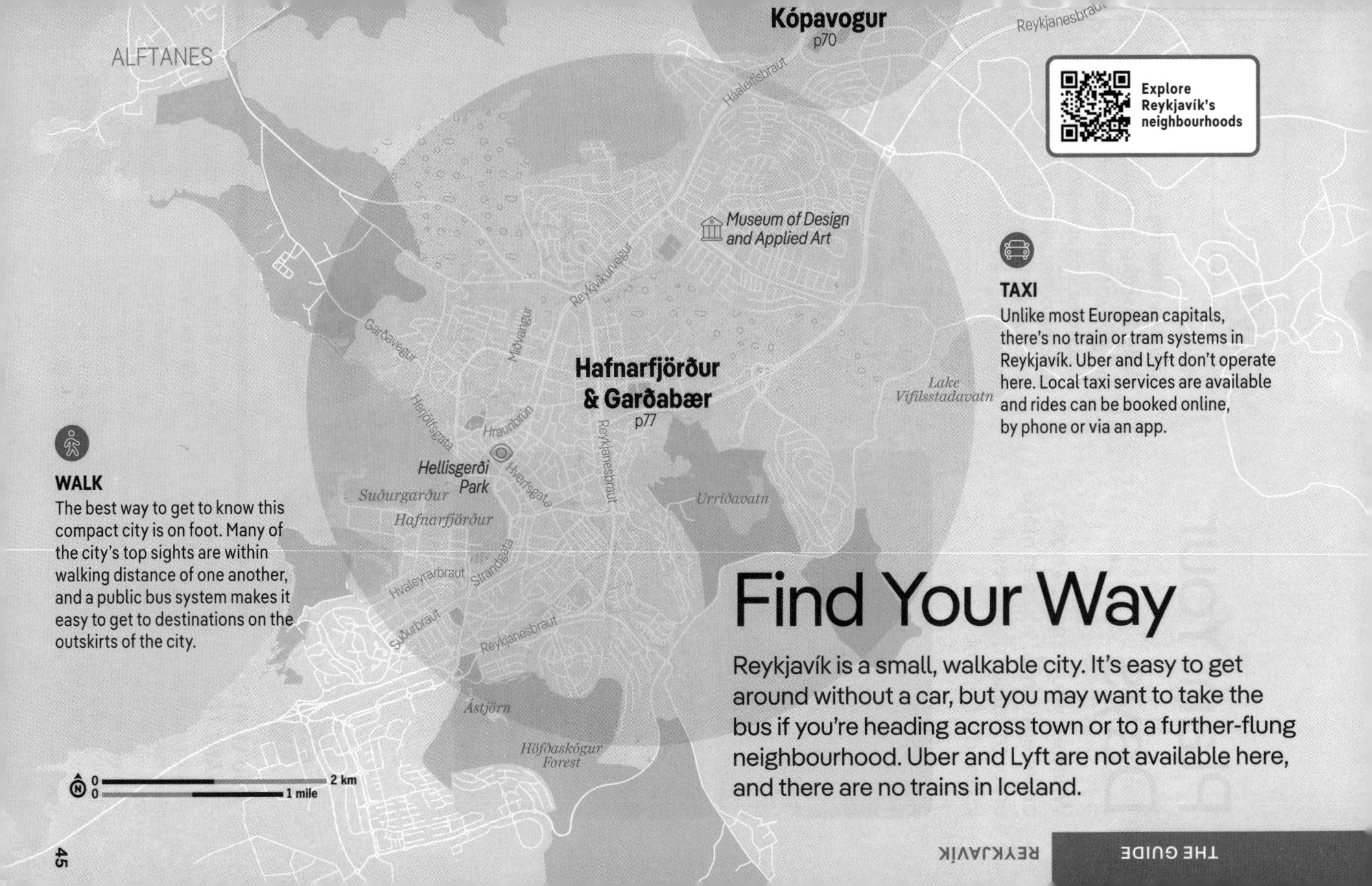

WALK

The best way to get to know this compact city is on foot. Many of the city's top sights are within walking distance of one another, and a public bus system makes it easy to get to destinations on the outskirts of the city.

TAXI

Unlike most European capitals, there's no train or tram systems in Reykjavik. Uber and Lyft don't operate here. Local taxi services are available and rides can be booked online, by phone or via an app.

0   1 mile
0   1   2 km

45

Plan Your Days

Whether you've got 24 hours or several days, you can make unforgettable memories in Iceland's capital.

KERRY TAYLOR/ALAMY STOCK PHOTO ©

Lebowski Bar (p55)

Day 1

Morning
Spend your morning at **Hallgrímskirkja** (p49) and take in the views from the top of the tower, then stop at **Mokka Kaffi** (p52) for coffee and a waffle, and take yourself on a street art tour through the city centre.

Afternoon
Have lunch at **Cafe Laundromat** (p52) and browse its expansive book collection. Shop the independent boutiques and vintage stores on **Laugavegur Street** (p55), and check out **Harpa** (p52), Reykjavík's gorgeous concert hall on the water's edge. Enjoy a waterfront stroll to the **Sun Voyager** (p54) sculpture, and check out **Höfði House** (p63) and the 3.8-tonne chunk of the Berlin Wall that's not far from it.

Evening
Finish your day with dinner at **Reykjavík Kitchen** (p66).

YOU'LL ALSO WANT TO...
You could spend weeks roaming around Reykjavík and still not discover everything this tiny European capital has to offer.

SHOP ARTSY BOUTIQUES
Foreign chains are few and far between. Independent boutiques and galleries offer things you won't find anywhere else.

ENJOY A GOURMET FOOD FESTIVAL
Sample locally sourced menus prepared by international chefs at the annual winter Food and Fun Festival.

TAKE A DIP
Icelanders are avid swimmers and local pools are as much social scenes as they are places to swim. You'll find pools across the country.

Day 2

Morning

Stop at the historic **Sandholt Bakery** (p54) for a hearty breakfast before heading out on a **whale-watching tour** (p60). Spend a few hours looking for these majestic creatures from a boat before returning to shore.

Afternoon

Have lunch at **Grandi Mathöll** (p59), then visit the **Settlement Exhibition** (p51) to learn about Iceland's roots and early Reykjavík. Take a leisurely stroll around **Lake Tjörnin** (p54), admiring its quirky sculptures and vibrant community of ducks.

Evening

Take a relaxing soak in the **Sky Lagoon** (p72). Give its multi-step bathing ritual a try before heading to **Brasserie Kársnes** (p72) for dinner.

Day 3

Morning

Start your day with breakfast at **Cafe Loki** (p52), then take a walk through Icelandic history at the **Árbær Open Air Museum** (p68).

Afternoon

Stop at **The Gastro Truck** (p69) for lunch, then head out to explore the lava fields, craters and caves at the **Heiðmörk Nature Reserve** (p71).

Evening

Have a Viking-inspired dinner at **Fjörugarðurinn** (p81), then start a night of bar-hopping at **Lebowski Bar** (p55). If you're travelling during the winter and the forecast is good, bundle up and head to the **Seltjarnarnes Peninsula** (p76) in search of the Northern Lights.

 Explore Reykjavík's best experiences

SEE A SHOW AT HARPA

Harpa (p52) regularly hosts musical performances and comedy. Catch a show here if you can.

RIDE HORSES

Icelandic horses are unlike any other horses in the world. They are more petite, and have five gaits, essentially paces, instead of the usual three.

GO SKIING

You'll find ski slopes just a half-hour's drive from the city. Ski season typically runs from January to mid-April, depending on snow conditions.

WALK ON A BEACH

Walk along a sandy beach and enjoy a soak in a scenic beachside geothermal pool. Up for cold water? Consider a dip in the Atlantic Ocean.

MIÐBORG

A VIBRANT, QUIRKY CITY CENTRE

This central neighbourhood is the cultural heart of Reykjavík. If you're looking to spend a day museum-hopping, shopping at independent boutiques and snacking on street food, this is the place to do it.

Miðborg contains the city's main bus terminal, where airport buses stop and several tours depart. This area is home to the Reykjavík architectural icons including Hallgrímskirkja and Harpa, the glistening concert hall along the city's waterfront. It's also where you'll find the country's leading museums, top hotels and government offices.

This neighbourhood is filled with vibrant street art, international restaurants, colourful houses and so many surprises, like a small monument dedicated to civil disobedience and another that recognises the unknown bureaucrats of the world. Several bars and dance clubs dot this neighbourhood, making it the best place for a bar crawl under the midnight sun.

TOP TIP

No one wants to spend their holidays doing laundry, but sometimes you just need clean clothes. One of the best cafes in Reykjavík doubles as a launderette, making it easy to wash and dry your clothes while you enjoy a delicious meal in a vibrant diner that could also double as a library.

ANTON_IVANOV/SHUTTERSTOCK ©

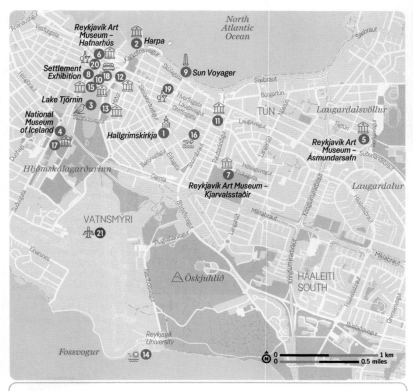

HIGHLIGHTS

1 Hallgrímskirkja
2 Harpa
3 Lake Tjörnin
4 National Museum of Iceland
5 Reykjavík Art Museum – Ásmundarsafn
6 Reykjavík Art Museum – Hafnarhús
7 Reykjavík Art Museum – Kjarvalsstaðir
8 Settlement Exhibition
9 Sun Voyager

SIGHTS

10 Alþingi
11 Icelandic Phallological Museum
12 Icelandic Punk Museum
13 National Gallery of Iceland
14 Nauthólsvík Geothermal Beach
15 Reykjavík City Hall
16 Sundhöllin
17 University of Iceland

SLEEPING

18 Hótel Borg

DRINKING & NIGHTLIFE

19 Dillon
20 Ingólfur Square

TRANSPORT

21 Reykjavík Domestic Airport

Hallgrímskirkja

A TOWERING PRESENCE

This iconic church has defined Reykjavík's skyline since 1986. It is known for its soaring tower (74m) and unique side wing, constructed to resemble the basalt lava flows that are common across the country. Its best-kept secret may be its organ recitals and 50-person choir that regularly performs concerts here.

Hallgrímskirkja is one of the best places in Reykjavík to get a bird's-eye view of the city. Head to the top of the tower to look out on the colourful houses, the Atlantic Ocean and Mt Esja. On a clear day, it's possible to see as far as Snæfellsjökull.

VISITING THE CHURCH

It's free to visit this church, but admission to the tower is 1000kr. A lift carries visitors part of the way up the tower, but you will have to climb a few flights of stairs to reach the top.

Hótel Borg

A HOTEL WITH STORIES TO TELL

This Art Deco luxury hotel on Reykjavík's main square ran Iceland's only legal pub in the 1940s. Its founder made a fortune as an American circus performer and dreamed of investing in a magnificent luxury hotel back home. Since opening in 1930, Hótel Borg has become a magnet for heads of state and visiting celebrities. The property has 99 rooms, a glamorous restaurant and a drool-worthy spa. It's steps from the Settlement Exhibition and the stylish Apotek Kitchen & Bar, which is located inside a historic pharmacy.

Hótel Borg

Icelandic Punk Museum

A PUNK DREAM COME TRUE

If you're into punk music or Björk, Iceland's best-known musician, you can't miss the small Icelandic Punk Museum in the heart of Reykjavík. This may be the only museum in the world that occupies a city's former public toilets. Follow the music and head downstairs to enter this ode to punk culture. Walk through exhibits that wind through converted toilet stalls lined with news clippings, quotes and the stories of punk legends. There's also a listening station featuring music from artists including the multifaceted Björk, who was in an all-girl punk band as a teenager.

Icelandic Punk Museum

Icelandic Phallological Museum

A DIFFERENT MUSEUM

If you're looking for a truly phallic experience, Reykjavík has the museum for you. The Icelandic Phallological Museum is believed to be the only museum in the world dedicated to displaying a broad collection of phalluses. The family-owned museum traces its history to 1974 when its founder was given a bull's penis as a gift while working as the headmaster of a school in the town of Akranes. The collection has grown to include donations from around the world. The museum houses a variety of specimens, including examples from several types of whales.

Alþingi

WHERE DEMOCRACY CONTINUES

The large grey Alþingi (Parliament House) is the centre of modern Icelandic government. It's also home to the oldest public garden in Iceland. The building was built in the late 1800s to replace the Althingi's original meeting place in what's now known as Þingvellir National Park. Almost all government meetings have been held here since it opened its doors in 1881. The building itself is made of Icelandic stone. It was designed by Danish architect Ferdinand Meldahl when Iceland was under Danish rule.

Alþingi

National Museum of Iceland

National Museum of Iceland

THE STORY OF ICELAND

Head to Þingvellir National Park to see how Iceland formed geologically, but go to the National Museum of Iceland to see how this wild volcanic island 805km from its closest neighbour became a country. Start your visit with a look at the kind of ship medieval explorers would have used on their journey to Iceland. Don't miss the 13th-century Valþjófsstaðir church door, which tells the story of a knight and his lion's battle with a pack of dragons. There's also a giant bronze Thor and Guðbrandur's Bible. The Bible was the first book printed and widely distributed in Iceland. About 500 copies of this Bible were printed, and this one still has its original binding intact.

Settlement Exhibition

FROM FARM TO CAPITAL

This is one of those museums kids visit on school field trips and for good reason. The Settlement Exhibition is built around the ruins of a 10th-century Viking long house. Through a series of interactive exhibits, the museum tells the story of how Reykjavík came to be. Learn how this remote farmland became a national capital and a global powerhouse. Check out one of the oldest houses in Reykjavík and wander through a replica old general store. This is the kind of museum that makes adults want to dig in and keeps kids engaged through a series of interactive exhibits.

Go Inside Harpa

A CONCERT HALL WORTH VISITING

Don't make the mistake of marvelling at Harpa's beauty from the outside but not making the time to go inside. This is a one-of-a-kind building that has an interior just as gorgeous as its exterior.

Harpa is the home of the Iceland Symphony Orchestra, Icelandic Opera, Reykjavik Big Band, a classical music series, and a local jazz club. It hosts the annual children's music awards, comedians and several special events, but even a wander inside when nothing is happening is an experience.

The award-winning glass facade was designed by Icelandic-Danish artist Olafur Eliasson. It's made of glass and steel assembled to look like stacked glass bricks. His mission was to mirror the city, its light and Iceland's changing weather in kaleidoscopic reflections inside the building. From the outside, these glass bricks look almost like the crystallised basalt columns found all over Iceland.

The concert hall's acoustics were designed by the same company that worked on the Lincoln Center Jazz Concert Hall in New York. Harpa hosted its first concert in 2011, more than 100 years after the Icelandic press first floated the idea of a local concert hall.

Party under the Midnight Sun

PREPARE FOR A LATE NIGHT

There's nothing quite like not seeing darkness for days on end. The only thing more interesting may be partying all night under the midnight sun. If you're up for a late summer night out unlike anything you've experienced, head to the historic city centre to experience a taste of Iceland's unique nightlife.

Start your night near **Ingólfur Square** where you'll find several Irish pubs, a craft beer bar, live music venues and nightclubs. Don't be surprised when you wander out of a venue and into the bright light of a long summer day and revel in the streets enjoying the sunshine.

Stop for a late-night hot dog that might feel more like lunch and begin working your way east where you'll find several quirky bars, including Dillon, which has an expansive whisky selection to finish the night. Remember, Iceland's nightlife scene doesn't get going until late, so don't be deterred if you can't find a lively spot before midnight.

BEST CAFES IN MIÐBORG

Cafe Laundromat
There's something for everyone at this spacious restaurant that serves brunch until 4pm every day. €€

Cafe Babalu
This adorable cafe is best known for its crepes and coffee, but also gets good reviews for its tomato soup and hot chocolate. €

Cafe Loki
The place to go for classic home-style Icelandic dishes and delicious *skyr* (Icelandic cheese that's more like a yoghurt) desserts. €€

Mokka Kaffi
Come for the coffee and waffles at this cosy coffee shop, but stay for the vintage charm and local art. €

 WHERE TO STAY IN MIÐBORG

Radisson Blu 1919
A stylish centrally located hotel that's a favourite among business travellers and home to Iceland's first lift shaft. €€€

The Reykjavik EDITION
Steps from Harpa, the city's first 5-star hotel is an oasis of luxury with rooms that feature panoramic harbour views. €€€

Loft HI Hostel & Bar
A clean casual hostel with dorms, private en suite rooms, a kitchen and a cafe. €

Take a Helicopter Tour
SOAR ABOVE WILD TOPOGRAPHY

A helicopter tour may be the most expensive way to see Iceland, but seeing this topography from above can be worth the price. Several companies offer a variety of tours from Reykjavík Domestic Airport. Fly over volcanic eruptions and geothermal areas. See hot springs and colourful landscapes from above. Land on a glacier, a volcano, or both.

Helicopter tours from Reykjavík will set you back 40,000kr to 75,000kr, but they provide a view that no bus, snowmobile, ATV or walking tour can match. There's nothing quite like flying over stretches of the Earth that look like the moon, touching down on remote glaciers, and seeing volcanic lava flowing while circling above.

If you're going to treat yourself to a helicopter flight somewhere, Iceland is a great place to do it. And because tours depart from and return to Reykjavík Domestic Airport, you'll also get aerial views of the Blue Lagoon and the city centre.

Helicopter tours can range from half an hour to two hours, and tours that include one or more landings typically take longer. It's often possible to arrange hotel pick-up.

Check Out Icelandic Art
PAINTINGS, SCULPTURE AND POP ART

The Reykjavík Art Museum is Iceland's largest institution dedicated to the visual arts. The museum is split across three locations in Reykjavík. One is in an old warehouse near the Old Harbour, another is in Klambratún Park and the third is in Laugardalur.

Reykjavík Art Museum – Hafnarhús in the Old Harbour hosts events ranging from rock concerts to poetry readings. It exhibits the work of Icelandic artist Erró who is best known for his pop-art collages of images from comic books and advertisements.

Reykjavík Art Museum – Kjarvalsstaðir is located in Klambratún, an urban green space not far from the city's core. The building features 20th-century art and exhibits the work of one of Iceland's top painters, the late Jóhannes S Kjarval.

The third site, **Reykjavík Art Museum – Ásmundarsafn**, is in Laugardalur and exhibits the sculptures and drawings of Icelandic artist Ásmundur Sveinsson. The museum is his former home and studio.

Each building has its own architectural style, and they're all just as interesting from the outside as they are from the inside.

BEST PUBS IN MIÐBORG

Bastard Brew & Food
This pub has a creative menu, delicious sweets and offers a bottomless weekend brunch with a selection of 25 small courses. There's an optional bottomless drinks pairing.

Prikið
A coffee shop and diner by day, this spot opened its doors in 1951 and turns into a pub and live music venue at night.

The Drunk Rabbit
An authentic Irish pub in the heart of Reykjavík. There's live music every night, sports on TV and happy hour from noon to 7pm.

Skuli Craft Bar
This bar stocks 130 craft brews and has 14 rotating taps. Beer flights are available.

 WHERE TO STAY IN MIÐBORG

Center Hotels Plaza
Clean, comfortable, and within walking distance of several of the city's top sights. €€

Apotek Hotel
This boutique hotel is the perfect blend of comfort and style in an unbeatable location. €€

Reykjavik Konsulat Hotel
A boutique hotel offering plush rooms and a trendy wine bar in a historic building. €€€

Lake Tjörnin

COFFEE SHOPS & BAKERIES IN MIÐBORG

Emilie and the Cool Kids
There's no better place for a freshly baked cookie than this Icelandic outpost of a small bakery chain from the south of France that serves cookie chunks with its coffees. €

Te & Kaffi
This local chain has several locations and is a solid bet for coffee or a quick lunch. Menu items include sandwiches, bagels and pastries. €

Sandholt Bakery
This family bakery with an experimental approach to traditional baking methods has served Reykjavik since 1920. The bakery also offers a selection of heartier breakfast fare and lunch items. €

Beyond these museums, you'll find unique sculpture like the *Sun Voyager,* a gleaming waterfront steel sculpture by Jón Gunnar Arnason, and others all around town.

Head to the Beach
FEEL THE SAND BETWEEN YOUR TOES

Believe it or not, Reykjavík is a beach town. **Nauthólsvík Geothermal Beach** is a small sandy beach at the southern edge of central Reykjavík near the city's domestic airport. Warm geothermal baths overlooking the beach are free to use though you will have to pay for the on-site changing rooms. This beach is a great option for anyone looking to experience Icelandic sea swimming. Prepare yourself for the cold water of the North Atlantic and be grateful for the warm pools just across the sand. Depending on the tide, there's a natural geothermal lagoon on the beach that you can soak in as well. The water here is sulphuric, and you may notice the scent when you arrive. You'll find more locals than tourists here, and a visit to the beach is an excellent alternative to happy hour.

Stroll Lake Tjörnin
SCENERY AND SURPRISES

Take a stroll around idyllic Lake Tjörnin and you'll find lots of surprises, like the duck population that lives in the geothermally heated portion of the lake year-round. It's not un-

 WHERE TO EAT VEGETARIAN & VEGAN FOOD IN MIÐBORG

Mama Reykjavik
Features a variety of hearty globally-inspired vegan stews as well as juices, salads and sandwiches. €€

Sónó Matseljur
Aims to give foraged plants a more prominent place in the restaurant world. Endlessly creative. €€

Cafe Gardurinn
Perfect for a quick and affordable vegetarian, vegan or gluten-free bite; the menu changes daily. €€

usual to spot swans, geese, Arctic tern and other birds here during the summer, though you will need to head out onto the water if you're looking for puffins.

The lake is adjacent to **Reykjavík City Hall**, which houses a topographical map of Iceland – a good way to get acquainted with this unique terrain. The National Gallery of Iceland, the National Museum of Iceland (p51), the University of Iceland and the office of the president are also nearby. The lake is surrounded by a park on the south side, and you'll find a collection of interesting sculptures surrounding and to the north of the lake. Take a minute to check out *The Unknown Bureaucrat*, a sculpture of a man being crushed by a rock, and *The Black Cone*, a cracked rock-based sculpture designed as an ode to peaceful civil disobedience.

Shop for Vintage Goods & Sweaters
A SECONDHAND SHOPPER'S PARADISE

Everything is more expensive in Reykjavík, and that's made vintage shopping an art here. You'll find several well-curated vintage shops in the city centre. Independent boutiques, restaurants and souvenir shops dominate **Laugavegur Street**, making it easy to spend hours browsing handmade jewellery, local crafts, and vintage bags and clothes.

Something you won't see: major Western chains like Starbucks, McDonald's or Urban Outfitters.

If you're looking for a wool sweater that won't break your budget, browse the Kolaportið flea market. This is Iceland's only indoor flea market, and it may be one of the most affordable places in town to pick up a handmade Icelandic sweater.

This is one of the few places in Iceland where credit cards aren't widely accepted. Bring some cash in case that must-have item's seller doesn't take cards or digital payments.

Soak in a Rooftop Hot Tub
SUNDHÖLLIN PUBLIC BATHS

Iceland's public pools are some of the best in the world, and Sundhöllin is particularly special. This city pool complex near Hallgrímskirkja has a sauna, steam rooms, cold plunge pools and several heated pools. It has a relaxing rooftop hot tub and at 1210kr, admission costs a fraction of what you'd pay for the Blue Lagoon or the Sky Lagoon. It's also a very local experience. This place in the centre of Reykjavík is about enjoying the water. There are no cocktails to sip or selfie spots to visit, just warm Icelandic water and a truly authentic local experience.

BEST FAST FOOD IN MIÐBORG

Bæjarins Beztu Pylsur
The simple hot dog stand that won over Bill Clinton, Anthony Bourdain and Kim Kardashian. Its hot dogs are made of lamb, pork and beef, and served with your choice of ketchup, sweet mustard, remoulade, and crispy fried onion or raw onion. €

Hamborgarabúlla Tómasar
This fast casual spot has been serving up burgers and fries in Reykjavík since 1981. Come here for a relaxed vibe, fresh beef and vegetables, and freshly baked buns. €

101 Reykjavik Street Food
It's not quite street food, but this casual spot in the centre of town is perfect for a quick bowl of soup or a feast of fish and chips. €

WHERE TO DRINK IN MIÐBORG

Lebowski Bar
With *The Big Lebowski* playing on multiple screens, this is the fan bar you didn't know you needed. €€

Kiki Queer Bar
Reykjavík's leading gay bar, Kiki is a small venue with a friendly vibe and regular drag shows. €€

Slippbarinn
An excellent place to sip an old favourite or try something new while looking out onto the Old Harbour. €€

VESTURBÆR

A CHARMING OLD HARBOUR

This square mile of Reykjavík includes several distinct neighbourhoods as well as the city's historic harbour. This natural harbour was a key force in helping Reykjavík transform from remote farmland into a national capital and fishing powerhouse.

This is where you'll find the University of Iceland and some of the most expensive homes in the city. It's just as charming as Miðborg, but without the museums, volume of historic sites and tourist traffic.

If you're looking for a relaxing walk through charming streets, you'll find it here. Or head to Grandi, the redeveloping area that's home to Reykjavík's most popular ice-cream shop. Puffin, whale watching and Northern Lights tours depart from the port here. Or see whales and Northern Lights without leaving land at museums dedicated to each.

And unlike a whale-watching cruise, at Whales of Iceland, visitors can get up close to models of these giant creatures.

TOP TIP

Icelanders love ice cream and even cold weather won't keep them from indulging in simple ice-cream cones and elaborate sundaes. You'll find Valdis, one of the best and most creative ice-cream shops in the country, here in the Old Harbour area. The menu includes unique flavours like rhubarb, licorice and Turkish pepper.

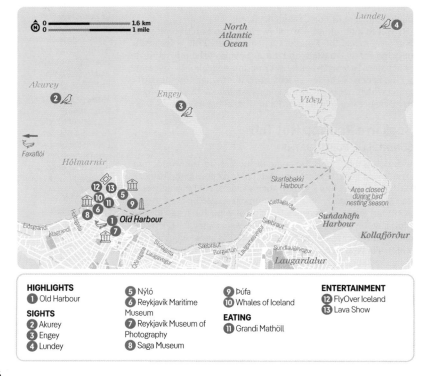

HIGHLIGHTS
1 Old Harbour

SIGHTS
2 Akurey
3 Engey
4 Lundey

5 Nýló
6 Reykjavík Maritime Museum
7 Reykjavík Museum of Photography
8 Saga Museum

9 Þúfa
10 Whales of Iceland

EATING
11 Grandi Mathöll

ENTERTAINMENT
12 FlyOver Iceland
13 Lava Show

Reykjavík Maritime Museum

THE CITY AND THE SEA

To understand Iceland, you have to understand how the country has been defined by its relationship with the sea. There's no better place to do that than the Reykjavík Maritime Museum. This museum chronicles 150 years of fishing. Learn how traditional and modern fishing methods differ and what it took to survive the rough seas without the technology of today. The museum is housed in a building that used to be a fish-freezing plant and there's an 816-tonne Icelandic coastguard ship on-site.

Reykjavík Maritime Museum

The Living Art Museum

SUPPORT LOCAL ART

This artist-run exhibition space features a rotating roster of local artists. Nýló (The Living Art Museum) was founded by a group of local artists in 1978 and houses a collection of more than 2000 items dating as far back as the 1960s. The space was designed to serve as a canvas for artistic experimentation, a place for up-and-coming artists to display even their most avant-garde projects. It's also a great way to catch up on the evolution of the Icelandic contemporary art scene since the 1960s. The museum closes between exhibitions, so check its schedule before you go.

The Living Art Museum

Reykjavík Museum of Photography

NATURE, FAMILY PORTRAITS AND NEWS PHOTOS

Dive deep into Icelandic photography at the unassuming Reykjavík Museum of Photography, which shares a building with the city library and the city archives. The museum's collection includes more than six million photographs dating as far back as 1860, with work from professional photographers as well as amateurs. This collection is broader than what you might find at the average museum. It includes industrial and commercial photography in addition to press photographs and portraits. There are also some personal photo collections here.

And if seeing these collections inspires you to think about your own photo archive, you're in luck. The museum has a photo studio and hosts events aimed at helping visitors preserve their photos.

AMADA EKELI/SHUTTERSTOCK © BOTTOM: LAVA SHOW ©

Whales of Iceland

Whales of Iceland

SEE FULL-SIZED MODEL WHALES

You don't have to go out on a boat to get up close to whales in Iceland. Head inside Whales of Iceland to see a collection of nearly two dozen life-sized whale replicas. Each of these creatures can be found in the water surrounding Iceland. See a huge blue whale like those that surface off the coast of Húsavík. Check out a sperm whale and snuggle up to an adorable beluga whale. These models are soft, squishy and made to be touched. The museum worked with marine biologists to create a collection of audio guides in more than a dozen languages. One of its missions is to promote marine preservation through education.

Lava Show

WATCH SIZZLING LAVA FLOW

It isn't always possible to time your Icelandic holiday with a volcanic eruption. Even if you can, you might not want to. That doesn't mean you can't see real flowing lava. Started by an Icelandic couple who visited the site of the Fimmvörðuháls volcanic eruption in 2010 and haven't been able to stop thinking about it, Lava Show recreates a volcanic eruption by superheating real molten lava and letting it flow. Hear lava sizzle and feel the heat no matter when you're visiting. Lava Show has a second location in Vík.

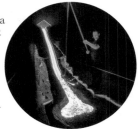

Lava Show

FlyOver Iceland

ICELAND IN UNDER AN HOUR

As close as Iceland gets to an IMAX theatre, FlyOver Iceland is an excellent indoor activity for a cold rainy day. It does one thing that's impossible to do on a single trip in real life: experience Iceland in every season. It's also a way to catch a glimpse of remote destinations like Landmannalaugar that are only accessible for a few months each year.

Grandi Mathöll

A STREET-FOOD FEST

Food halls have taken off in a big way across Iceland, and Grandi Mathöll in the trendy Grandi area is well worth a visit, especially if you're spending the day museum-hopping or cruising for wildlife. This food hall specialises in street food and offers more than half-a-dozen options including one spot that dishes up fish and chips, another that highlights Korean street food, and one that serves Icelandic meats prepared in a variety of ways. Vegetarian options are available on several menus.

Grandi Mathöll

Saga Museum

Þúfa

WORTH THE CLIMB

This piece of public art in Grandi comes from Ólöf Nordal, the same artist who created the Kvika Footbath on the Seltjarnarnes Peninsula. This 8m perfectly round grassy mound is made from about 4080 tonnes of gravel. Þúfa is one of the largest pieces of public art in Iceland, and it's a reminder of the country's rich fishing history. The hill is topped with a type of hut that would have historically been used to dry fish. Climb the hill for sweeping views of Reykjavík's harbour and Faxa Bay.

Saga Museum

JOURNEY INTO ICELAND'S VIKING PAST

Come here to see Iceland's Viking past come to life. Saga Museum aims to recreate Icelandic history through a series of detailed exhibits realistic enough that you may feel you've walked into another era. Some of these wax figures look so real you might become convinced they are. This is one museum where the audio guide is well worth picking up and filled with detailed information about days gone by. At the end of the exhibits, there's a station where visitors can try on Viking gear for photos.

RPBA/AO/SHUTTERSTOCK ©, TOP: CAROLYNE PARENT/SHUTTERSTOCK ©

LOUISE KURIR NEUMANN/SHUTTERSTOCK ©

Puffins, Lundey

BEST PLACES TO STAY IN VESTURBÆR

Grandi by Center Hotels
Simple, spacious rooms located steps from the harbour and the centre of Reykjavík. Some rooms have balconies and expansive city views. €€

Reykjavik Marina (Berjaya Iceland Hotels)
This hotel is comfortable with a hint of rustic charm. It has a variety of room types, including single rooms and family rooms. €€

Exeter Hotel
Don't let its simple exterior fool you. Exeter Hotel is a stylish, industrial, chic property with a bakery, restaurant and sauna on-site. An oasis of relaxation in the heart of a busy harbour. €€€

Go Whale Watching
AN ALMOST-GUARANTEED SIGHTING

Iceland is one of the best places in the world for whale watching, and you don't have to travel far from Reykjavík to spot these magnificent creatures. Several whale-watching cruises depart from Reykjavík's Old Harbour, and it's not uncommon to spot whales within 16km of the coastline.

It's possible to see whales off the coast of Reykjavík all year long, but you might want to plan your travel between April and September if whale watching is high on your list – reasonable temperatures and ample daylight hours make these the best months.

The most commonly spotted whales near Reykjavík are humpbacks and minke whales, though porpoises and dolphins are also known to make appearances. Iceland is home to more than 20 species of whale, and if you're lucky you might just catch a glimpse of a majestic black and white orca.

Whale-watching tours typically last about three hours and take guests to **Faxaflói** bay. You'll want to dress warmly, especially if you're travelling during winter though whale-watching boats typically offer indoor and outdoor viewing areas.

 WHERE TO EAT IN VESTURBÆR

Matur og Drykkur
This Michelin-star restaurant serves a seasonal six-course tasting menu inspired by old Icelandic recipes. €€€

Reykjavik Fish Restaurant
This relaxed restaurant is an excellent place for fish and chips and traditional fish stew. €€

Kaffivagninn
This historic harbourside restaurant serves breakfast, lunch and dinner with a view. €€

An Evening with Puffins
LOOK FOR THEIR ORANGE BEAKS

Puffins may just be the cutest birds of them all. They're best known for their bright orange beaks and huge personalities. Puffins spend most of the year at sea but seek out land each spring to breed and birth pufflings, their even more adorable baby puffins.

Three uninhabited islands off the coast of Reykjavík, **Akurey**, **Engey** and **Lundey**, are known hot spots for Atlantic puffins during breeding season. They're often referred to colloquially as the Puffin Islands. Some tour operators are so confident visitors will see puffins here that they offer sighting guarantees.

Peak puffin season is from May to July, though you may see early birds in April and laggards leaving in August.

The Atlantic puffins in Iceland are the smallest of three types of puffins found around the world and weigh about as much as a loaf of bread. They're fast flyers and excellent swimmers, so don't expect to get a chance to make that weight comparison yourself.

Puffins tend to spend their days fishing at sea, so try to plan your puffin-spotting excursions in the evenings after they've returned to their burrows on land.

Set Sail for the Northern Lights
UNSPOILED AURORA BOREALIS VIEWS

Witnessing the aurora borealis anywhere can be magical, but there's nothing quite like watching the Northern Lights dance above you at sea. And you don't have to commit to a cruise to experience a magical night under the aurora.

Northern Lights cruises depart from Reykjavík's Old Harbour during the evenings from September to April. Choose between a boat or yacht cruise and set out in search of the lights.

The aurora borealis can be fickle, requiring solar activity and clear dark skies. Being at sea virtually guarantees light pollution won't be a problem, and unlike a bubble hotel – a clear dome accommodation designed for comfortable aurora viewing – a ship captain can change locations for better viewing conditions.

Northern Lights cruises are typically between two and three hours long. Like many aurora tours, they offer the option of another free cruise should your search not pan out the first time. And you might just find a boat to be more comfortable than a bus tour, setting out on foot, or having to drive yourself.

BEST PLACES TO EAT ICE CREAM IN VESTURBÆR

Valdis
This may be one of the most creative ice-cream shops in the world. Valdis has tested hundreds of ice-cream flavours over the years, including bacon, curry, rye bread and lavender. Two of its most popular flavours are Turkish pepper, and salted peanut and caramel. €

Omnom Chocolate Ice Cream Shop
This small-batch ice creamery got its start inside a converted petrol station where its owners perfected their chocolate recipe before venturing into the ice-cream business. Its colourful creations are adventurous works of art with homemade toppings and sauces. €

WHERE TO DRINK IN VESTURBÆR

Hygge Coffee & Micro Bakery
Excellent coffee, fresh bread and creative pastries like pear croissants with almond cream, and blue birch rolls. €

Lady Brewery
This woman-owned brewery has an impressive lineup with a signature lager that's available year-round. €

Bryggjan Brugghús
Come for the fresh meat, fish and seasonal produce. Stay for the wide selection of local beer. €€€

LAUGARDALUR & HLÍÐAR

MORE THAN A HISTORIC WATERFRONT

These neighbourhoods on the edge of town are excellent for getting outside without leaving the city. Stroll to Laugardalur from Harpa and you'll pass the iconic *Sun Voyager* and lesser-known *Partnership* sculptures as well as the bright yellow Höfði Lighthouse. Keep walking and you'll find a collection of waterfront museums and even a small beach. Head inland in Laugardalur for a huge park and pool complex, Iceland's national football stadium and a charming botanic garden. Public pools are a huge part of Icelandic culture, and this is one not to miss. Southwest of Laugardalur, Hlíðar has more green spaces as well as Perlan, a natural history museum with epic city views from its observation deck. This building is unlike any other you'll see in Iceland. Keep an eye out for the giant dome on the hill.

TOP TIP

Nights out are expensive in Reykjavík, but they don't have to be. Head to Kaffi Laugalækur, the restaurant and bar on the first floor of the Lækur Hostel, for a double happy-hour deal – drink at a discount between 4pm and 7pm and between 10pm and 11pm each night.

EWY MEDIA/SHUTTERSTOCK ©, RIGHT: ICEROCK/GETTY IMAGES ©

Höfði Lighthouse

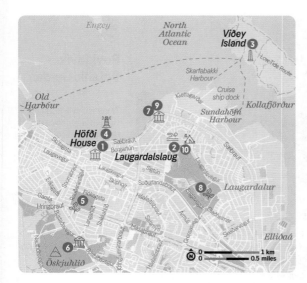

Höfði House

A COLD WAR ICON

Höfði House

Gleaming white-washed wooden Höfði House overlooking the water is where the Cold War began winding down. US president Ronald Reagan and Soviet president Mikhail Gorbachev met here in 1986. Reagan had come to discuss human rights and the Soviet occupation of Afghanistan while Gorbachev was squarely focused on limiting arms control. No agreements were announced here, but the meeting is seen as a major breakthrough. The discussions marked the first time human rights entered the conversation between the US and the Soviet Union.

The building's pieces were imported from Norway, and the structure was constructed in Iceland for the French consulate in the early 1900s. Höfði House isn't open to the public though it's occasionally used for official events. Visitors can still walk around the house. There are a few sculptures on the grounds and another remnant of the Cold War, a chunk of the Berlin Wall, a short walk away. The 3.8-tonne chunk of wall was a gift commemorating the 25th anniversary of German reunification.

Höfði Lighthouse

ENDLESS OCEAN VIEWS

Completed in 2019, this cheery bright yellow lighthouse is a relatively new addition to the Reykjavík waterfront. Designed to resemble the lighthouses that stood along Reykjavík's Old Harbour in the early 1900s, it was built as a replacement for another that had to be decommissioned. Höfði Lighthouse cost more than 150 million króna to build. Its completion required crews to extend the shoreline into the sea with landfill. On a clear day, it offers excellent views of Faxaflói bay and majestic Mt Esja.

Reykjavík Botanic Garden

Reykjavík Botanic Garden

A LOT CAN GROW HERE

The Reykjavík Botanic Garden is a lush oasis not far from the local pool. This botanic garden is home to more than 3000 plant species arranged over eight sections. The garden aims to help visitors understand the variety of flora that can flourish even in northern climates where harsh conditions are common. Iceland is home to nearly 500 flowering plants and ferns, 300 of which can be viewed at the city's botanic garden. An alpine garden shows off perennials and bushes from the world's mountain ranges. Don't miss the rose garden or Flóran, the Botanic Garden's cafe. The menu is small, but this greenhouse-style cafe may be one of the most peaceful places for lunch or coffee in the city.

Laugardalslaug

AN AUTHENTIC LOCAL POOL EXPERIENCE

This pool complex is a local favourite. It's not as fancy as the Blue Lagoon or Sky Lagoon, but Laugardalslaug is a place where you're likely to hear far more Icelandic than foreign accents. The property includes a 50m pool primarily used for training as well as a separate indoor pool, a children's pool, several hot tubs and water slides. There's an accessible pool and a wading pool at the facility, plus a fitness trail, running routes, mini golf, a steam bath, a saltwater tub and beach volleyball. A visit here really is a uniquely Icelandic experience.

Laugardalslaug

Sigurjón Ólafsson Museum

A SCULPTOR'S PARADISE

This museum is dedicated to Icelandic sculptor Sigurjón Ólafsson. Started by his widow in 1984 at the waterfront home the couple shared before his death in 1982, this is now an offshoot of the National Gallery of Iceland. Several sculptures surround the Sigurjón Ólafsson Museum, making it easy to get acquainted with the artist's work even after the museum has closed. Inside the museum, you'll find work by Ólafsson and other Icelandic artists. Ólafsson had a studio at his home, and much of his research remains on-site.

Reykjavík Campsite

CAMP IN THE CAPITAL

Hotels are expensive in Reykjavík. But there is another option for travellers looking for accommodation near the city centre. Reykjavík Campsite offers access to washrooms, showers, kitchens, luggage storage and laundry at a fraction of the cost of a hotel. It's within walking distance of the city centre and on a major bus line, Strætó Route 14. The site has room for about 300 tents and 50 sites for RVs in need of outlets. There are another 50 spots for camper vans that don't need to plug in.

Reykjavík Campsite

Perlan

Klambratún

GREEN SPACE FOR EVERYONE

One of the largest public parks in Iceland, there's something for everyone in this expanse of urban green space. Visit an outpost of the Reykjavík Art Museum on the northern edge of Klambratún, or find out why Icelandic people are such avid frisbee players. There's also a basketball field, beach volleyball court, football field and playground. There's a vehicle charging station at the north end of the park, and lots of benches for sitting around and soaking in the greenery.

Perlan

PEARL OF ICELAND

This unique natural history museum sits on top of Reykjavík's highest hill. Inside the dome, visitors can get a taste of volcanoes, ice caves and the natural forces that shape Iceland. There's a planetarium where it's always possible to see the Northern Lights in high definition, a volcanic lava show, and a human-made ice cave to explore.

Some exhibits, like a virtual fish tank, incorporate augmented reality, and there's an entire section dedicated to climate change.

Perlan has a restaurant, bar and ice-cream shop. There's also an observation deck for taking in 360-degree city views. It's possible to visit just the observation deck, but you'll need to buy that ticket on-site. Museum tickets can be booked online.

BEST PLACES TO STAY IN LAUGARDALUR & HLÍÐAR

Hilton Reykjavik Nordica
This clean comfortable hotel offers spacious rooms and Michelin-star dining a short walk from the city's bars, restaurants and boutiques. €€

Fosshotel Reykjavík
This 16-storey hotel offers clean spacious rooms just far enough away from the city centre that weekend noise won't be a bother. €€

Lækur Hostel
You'll find clean dorm rooms with shared bathrooms and kitchen facilities at this airy hostel where sheets and pillowcases are provided. €

Dalur HI Hostel
The bus stops just outside this clean hostel with family rooms and electric car charger. €

J. HELGASON/SHUTTERSTOCK ©

Viðey Island

MORE IN LAUGARDALUR & HLÍÐAR

Explore Viðey Island
NATURE'S ART PARK

This island off the coast of Reykjavík makes for a great day trip. It's a short ferry ride from Reykjavík, but it feels like an entirely different world, and in a different way than other parts of Iceland. Viðey island is best known as the home of Imagine Peace Tower, a piece of art by Yoko Ono that's dedicated to John Lennon and meant to serve as a wish for World Peace. The tower is made of a collection of lights that come together to form what appears to be a single beam – its intensity and brilliance changes with the weather and atmospheric conditions. The island is also home to a collection of pillars by American sculptor Richard Serra, one of the most influential sculptors of the postwar era. If you're looking for a charming off-the-beaten-path picnic spot, this is it.

Recycled House
A HOME LIKE NO OTHER

A Viking warrior greets visitors to Hrafn Gunnlaugsson's unusual property along the coast. Here you'll find small temples paying homage to Norse gods, Christian deities and Buddhist icons. This is a place where many things coexist in peace. Tribal masks and religious talismans cover the exterior of Gunnlaugsson's small house.

Visitors often come to check out what's come to be known as the 'Recycled House' but has nothing at all to do with recycling. Gunnlaugsson purchased the run-down house with a quiet stretch of shoreline so he'd have a place to build scenery for his films. It may not be the backdrop of global blockbusters, but it is a one-of-a-kind cultural icon.

 WHERE TO EAT IN LAUGARDALUR & HLÍÐAR

Borg29 Mathöll
A small food hall with affordable prices, international cuisine and more than a dozen restaurants. €

Perlan Restaurant & Cafe
Dine on salads, pizza and fish under a glass dome with 360-degree views of Reykjavík. €€

Reykjavík Kitchen
A family-owned restaurant specialising in fresh fish, beef and lamb. It only serves Icelandic beer. €€

ARBÆR

A STEP BACK IN TIME

The residential area of Arbær is a collection of smaller neighbourhoods that house about 13,000 people. Much of the architecture is relatively modern, tracing its history to the 1960s and later.

The biggest draw for visitors is the Árbær Open Air Museum where you can wander through old Iceland, checking out turf houses and learning how Iceland has developed over the past century. The name of this district means 'the farm by the river'. One look around this museum is all it takes to understand how Arbær got its name.

This is where you'll find Iceland's oldest brewery as well as the Icelandic Riding Center, which specialises in unforgettable rides through rocky red landscapes that look like film sets. ATV tour companies operate just outside the district, making it an excellent jumping-off point for off-road adventures.

TOP TIP

The best time to visit the Árbær Open Air Museum is during the summer when costumed staff bring this open-air folk village to life. See how wool was spun and how daily life was lived in and around early Reykjavík. The museum hosts free guided tours every afternoon at 1pm.

WALK THROUGH HISTORY

Visiting this outdoor museum is like taking a stroll through Icelandic history. Walk through a general store, homes made partly of stone, and a farmhouse that still stands on its original spot. The exhibits inside these buildings are as interesting as the structures themselves. Check out the toys Icelandic kids played with in the last century. See the American classic cars that still have a fan base here, and learn how Reykjavík – once sparsely populated farm land – became the thriving European capital it is today. It's easy to spend hours getting lost in the history here, so plan your day accordingly.

Árbær Open Air Museum

JOURNEY TO OLD ICELAND

Don't be surprised to see history walking past you in the form of costumed staff at this local history museum at the edge of Reykjavík. Árbær Open Air Museum is built on old farmland and is made up of several historic buildings mostly transported here from other parts of Iceland. The property includes an old shop from Reykjavík's most famous shopping street, a 19th-century labourer's cottage, the first Boy Scout cabin built in Iceland, and homes of local blacksmith and fishing families. Walk through an old city-centre stable, and learn about historic building techniques and how turf houses were able to withstand harsh Icelandic winters and unpredictable rainy summers.

The 20 historic buildings at this open-air folk museum are arranged to form an old town square, a village and a farm. During summer, expect to see staff dressed in period costumes spinning wool, milking cows and smoking meat here.

The museum is open from 10am to 5pm between June and August, and from 1pm and 5pm between September and May. It's closed over the Christmas, New Year and Easter holidays.

GAGLIARDIPHOTOGRAPHY/SHUTTERSTOCK ©

ATV riders

MORE IN ARBÆR

Hop on an ATV

OFF-ROAD ADVENTURES AWAIT

You don't need to have a monster truck to get off-road in Iceland, or go far from Reykjavík to have an off-road adventure.

All-terrain quad bikes are an excellent way to explore the rugged landscape surrounding Reykjavík. Much of this area can't be accessed by car, making these ATVs the only way to really experience the area. And there may be no more fun way to explore this terrain.

Ride solo or partner up with a friend on a dual-passenger bike. Safety equipment and thermal suits are provided by tour operators. You can also expect a short orientation and a little bit of time to practise before you set off on your adventure. Expect to visit a mountain peak or two depending on which ATV experience you choose to book.

Drive to the top of Reykjavík Peak for sweeping city views and spectacular photos. Head up Wolf Peak Mountain for views of Mt Esja, the Blue Mountains and the Icelandic countryside.

Feel the adrenaline rush of climbing steep hills, manoeuvering through mud, and powering across rocky terrain in a vehicle built for the adventure. Traverse snow and ice, literally getting off the beaten path.

If you're short on time, opt for a one-hour ride across the lowland trails and rocky lava fields at the edge of the city. Regardless of what you choose, you can expect a truly off-the-beaten-path adventure you'll never forget.

ATV SAFETY & RULES

Much of the land in Iceland is inaccessible to traditional vehicles. Off-road vehicles such as ATVs and snowmobiles are key for exploring certain areas and can make for an exhilarating ride.

Tour operators will provide safety instructions, helmets, overalls and gloves, but you'll need to dress in warm layers and plan for unpredictable weather when you're off-roading. Always keep your helmet and goggles on when riding or driving, and never exceed the speed limits set by your guide.

Children as young as six can join ATV tours as passengers. To drive an ATV in Iceland, you must hold a driving licence in your home country and be at least 17.

  WHERE TO GET A SNACK IN ARBÆR

Mathöll Höfða
Eat your way around the world at this casual food hall. €

The Gastro Truck
Visit this food truck inside Mathöll Höfða for excellent chicken sandwiches, burgers and wraps. €€

Kaffitár Stórhöfða
A casual coffee shop and cafe with a wide variety of pastries, jams and teas. €

KÓPAVOGUR

A SUBURB OF SURPRISES

There's more to this suburb than the warehouses and residential buildings that greet visitors at the southern edge of Reykjavík. This area is home to Iceland's tallest building, a 20-storey office and retail tower, as well as a handful of museums.

Kópavogur makes it easy to escape into nature just a few kilometres away from the capital. The Heiðmörk Nature Reserve sits at the eastern edge of Kópavogur, spilling into Reykjavík and Garðabær. Wander through natural lava caves, jog some of the most scenic running trails in the world, hike towering red rocks, or have a picnic you'll never forget.

Sky Lagoon, one of the most idyllic spots in Kópavogur, is located at the eastern edge of town. Relax in its geothermal water, try the multi-step bathing ritual, and enjoy the peaceful views in a place that feels like it's the edge of the Earth.

TOP TIP

The Sky Lagoon may get all the attention, but don't leave this area without venturing into the magnificent Rauðhólar pseudocraters at the Heiðmörk Nature Reserve. These pseudocraters are bright red because of iron in the lava and there may be no place that feels more like Mars than this.

HIGHLIGHTS
1 Sky Lagoon

SIGHTS
2 Gerðarsafn Kópavogur Art Museum
3 Natural History Museum of Kópavogur
4 Þríhnúkagígur Volcano

ACTIVITIES, COURSES & TOURS
5 Heiðmörk Nature Reserve
6 Rauðarvatn
7 Rauðhólar

Heiðmörk Nature Reserve

TOWERING TREES, CRATERS AND CAVES

You don't have to go far to get a world away from Reykjavík. Heiðmörk Nature Reserve is about a half-hour's drive from Reykjavík, but it feels like an entirely different planet. Walk among towering Sitka spruce trees. Wander across Rauðhólar, a collection of vibrant red craters that are part of a larger lava field. Explore natural caves. Go for a hike, check out the wildflowers or simply take in the silence and solitude at this nearly 32-sq-km urban oasis.

Heiðmörk Nature Reserve

Natural History Museum of Kópavogur

GEOLOGY AND ZOOLOGY

The small Natural History Museum of Kópavogur shares a building with the town's public library, but it packs a lot into a small space. The museum is divided into two parts: one that focuses on geology and another that highlights Icelandic birds, mammals, fish and invertebrates. A small collection of live fish, including Atlantic cod, Atlantic footballfish and deep-sea anglerfish live in on-site marine and freshwater aquariums. There are also several stuffed examples of Icelandic wildlife, and don't miss the rock and mineral sections. This is an excellent indoor option for diving into the geological development of Iceland.

Atlantic cod

Gerðarsafn Kópavogur Art Museum

SCULPTURE AND STAINED GLASS

The modern and contemporary Gerðarsafn Kópavogur Art Museum is the only museum in Iceland that was built to honour a female Icelandic artist, the sculptor and stained-glass artist Gerður Helgadóttir. Several of her pieces are on display in this intimate museum alongside exhibits by Icelandic and international artists. Helgadóttir was trained in Denmark, Italy and France, and her work is scattered across Iceland. She created stained glass for the Skálholt cathedral as well as the local church in Kópavogur.

71

Best swimming spots in Reykjavík

LAGOON & POOL ETIQUETTE

One thing you won't notice at Iceland's geothermal lagoons and swimming pools is the scent of chlorine. Icelanders follow strict hygiene rules to keep bathing water clean while keeping chemicals out.

When visiting a geothermal spa like the Sky Lagoon or a public swimming pool, always remember to take off your shoes before entering changing rooms. You'll often find a rack outside for just this purpose.

Before getting in the water, shower completely naked. Some facilities have open locker-room showers with attendants to help ensure everyone follows the rules. The Sky Lagoon offers an upgraded entry package with access to private showers and changing spaces.

FRANKONLINE/GETTY IMAGES ©

Inside Þríhnúkagígur volcano

MORE IN KÓPAVOGUR

Sky Lagoon
A SOAK WITHOUT SILICA

You'll find this idyllic oasis just beyond the warehouses and industrial buildings that dominate the area. This really is a place where the sea meets the sky, and there's nothing like soaking in the warm water while taking in an ocean view.

Sky Lagoon is a human-made geothermal lagoon that's similar to the Blue Lagoon, but with two key differences. There's no silica in the water here – that means there's no blue tint to the water and no need to condition or cover your hair. And instead of lava fields, you'll look out onto the sea as you soak.

Sky Lagoon offers three options: a simple dip into the lagoon for 8500kr; a dip in the lagoon plus access to a sauna and salt scrub as part of a seven-step bathing ritual for 11500kr; and a premium package with a private changing room instead of the standard shared changing rooms for 14500kr.

There's a swim-up bar and cascading waterfall inside the lagoon as well as a cascading on-site cafe. The seven-step bath ritual includes a cold plunge, a sauna with a view, and homemade salt scrub. Expect to queue if you're visiting during peak summer.

 WHERE TO EAT IN KÓPAVOGUR

Brasserie Kársnes
This local favourite offers a creative à la carte menu and a four-course chef's tasting menu. €€€

Mossley
A comfortable neighbourhood restaurant serving up burgers, tacos, sandwiches and more. €€

Craft Burger Kitchen
All kinds of burgers plus fries, chicken wings, salads and family meal options. €€

Go Inside a Volcano

DESCEND INTO THE CRATER

If you loved Jules Verne's *Journey to the Center of the Earth*, this is an experience you can't miss. Head inside the dormant **Þríhnúkagígur volcano**, making the 122m descent to the bottom of the crater in an open cable lift.

The volcano last erupted around 4000 years ago, and the descent to the floor takes just six minutes. The system used to carry people to and from the floor of the volcano is the same system window cleaners use on high-rise buildings. It's essentially an open lift connected to a crane that's moved up and down with massive cable wires.

It's a memorable way to take in a space that really does feel like the centre of the Earth, especially when you touch down on the ground of the magma chamber.

Visitors can either hike to the volcano or opt for a helicopter ride above the lava fields. The tour operator rates the difficulty of this hike as two out of five. The surface can be uneven and the last 10 minutes are described as especially challenging.

This experience operates from early May to late October, and children eight and above are welcome to join as long as they're comfortable hiking 7km.

Ride Horses Across Lava Fields

AN UNFORGETTABLE RIDE FOR ALL LEVELS

There are lots of places in Iceland to go horse riding, but there's no place like the wild **Rauðhólar** (Red Hills) that are part of the 32-sq-km Heiðmörk Nature Reserve at the eastern edge of Kópavogur.

Many tour operators offer beginner-friendly rides across this unusual landscape of red craters and rocks that are part of a larger lava field.

New riders may appreciate traversing this area on Icelandic horses, which are slightly smaller than their foreign counterparts. Icelandic horses have five gaits, essentially speeds, as opposed to the three used by most horses. One of these additional gaits is a slow, relaxed walk perfect for sitting back, relaxing and enjoying the spectacular scenery at this hidden gem just a 20-minute drive from Reykjavík.

A route for more advanced riders leads around the **Rauðarvatn**, a lake within the reserve. Both routes feature natural riding trails. The trail surrounding the lake is 4km long.

VOLCANO TOURISM

Volcanic eruptions have become a big draw for tourists around the world, but viewing them takes a special type of preparation.

You'll need to be flexible with your travel arrangements. New eruptions can happen at any time and viewing points may close if they're deemed unsafe.

You'll want to pack your sturdiest hiking boots and prepare for a six- to eight-hour hike across several kilometres of rough, rocky ground. Visibility can be low, and there may be gas in the air.

You won't able to get too close because new fissures and craters can emerge at any time, but helicopter tours can give a bird's-eye view, and hiking tours lead to viewing points.

 WHERE TO EAT IN KÓPAVOGUR

Mandi Kópavogur
Come here for cheap kebabs, shawarma and spicy late-night falafel. €

Krua Thai
Authentic Thai food with rich flavours, generous portions and reasonable prices. €

Brikk
A bright bakery with lots of pastries and light lunch items like soups and sandwiches. €

SELTJARNARNES

A WILD PENINSULA A WALK AWAY

You won't find many museums, shops, bars or clubs here, but you won't miss them. Seltjarnarnes is Iceland's smallest township. Surrounded by the ocean, this peninsula at the western edge of Reykjavík is a place to escape into nature.

Play a game of golf as wild Atlantic waves crash into the coastline. Take a long bike ride or an invigorating hike around the peninsula, enjoying sweeping mountain and sea views as you go.

If you're a birdwatcher, spend your time near the Grotta lighthouse, a favourite spot for about 110 visiting bird species. Soak your tired feet in a tiny geothermal pool after crossing new birds off your list. If it's a cold, dark winter night, keep an eye out for the Northern Lights that are known to frolic here. This is one of the best places to see the Northern Lights within walking distance of central Reykjavík.

TOP TIP

You don't have to rent a car or book an expensive tour to see the Northern Lights. When the conditions are right, the aurora borealis can be spotted at the edge of the Seltjarnarnes Peninsula about a half-hour walk from central Reykjavik. It is harder to chase the lights without wheels, but it won't matter when they come to you.

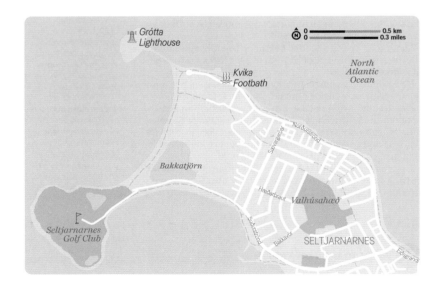

Kvika Footbath
ART MEETS NATURE

This tiny geothermal pool is an idyllic piece of art by Icelandic visual artist Ólöf Nordal. Nordal carved the Kvika Footbath out of a rock near the edge of the coast. It's just 90cm in diameter and about 30cm deep. It's fed by a nearby spring, and there's just enough room for one or two people to sit around the edge soaking their tired feet in piping-hot water while taking in mountain and water views. As you might imagine, this footbath makes for a popular local date spot.

Kvika Footbath

Grótta Lighthouse
BIRDS, AURORA AND CRASHING WAVES

This postcard-perfect lighthouse anchors a nature reserve on the tip of the Seltjarnarnes Peninsula. Grótta Lighthouse is surrounded by black sand and a rugged coastline. The Atlantic Ocean churns just beyond the coastline, and on a clear day you can see as far as the Snæfellsnes Peninsula. This is one of the best birdwatching sites near Reykjavík – several species nest here during the summer. Arctic terns form a colony on the rocks while tufted ducks hang out in an adjacent pond. Keep an eye out for the occasional seal, and stick to marked walking paths in June when Arctic terns are nesting here. Low levels of light pollution make this a popular spot for Northern Lights viewing in the winter.

Grótta Lighthouse

An Urban Hike
WALK THE PENINSULA

For a scenic hike without crowds or having to leave the capital area, follow the 5.5km loop that encircles the tiny Seltjarnarnes Peninsula. The route is popular with runners, hikers and road bikers, and is considered an easy trail. The trail has an elevation gain of 74m and can be completed in under an hour and a half. Expect sweeping sea views, an idyllic lake and seasonal bird sightings on this oceanfront trail.

THOMAS H. MITCHELL/GETTY IMAGES ©

Northern Lights, Seltjarnarnes Peninsula

WHY I LOVE REYKJAVÍK

Meena Thiruvengadam, writer

I love to *flâneur*, a French word that essentially translates to wandering around soaking in one's surroundings. Reykjavík is perfect for that.

Reykjavík is a compact city with a vibrant, lively centre full of surprises. Each time I visit, I find something new or a reason to venture to a further-flung part of town on foot.

Having lived in big cities for most of my life, I appreciate Reykjavík's small-town charm, friendliness and surprises. For me, this city is a reminder to take a closer look at places I know well and to discover new reasons to love them.

MORE IN SELTJARNARNES

Chase the Northern Lights on Foot
WATCH AURORA DANCE OVERHEAD

Here's a hack for seeing the Northern Lights for free if you're staying in Reykjavík: walk.

Northern Lights tours can be expensive, and renting a car to chase them yourself isn't cheap either. Luckily for travellers on a budget or without a driving licence, several excellent viewpoints on the Seltjarnarnes Peninsula are within walking distance of central Reykjavík.

Follow coastal walking paths as you search for green and red flickers of light to emerge from the sky above. Head towards the Grótta Lighthouse or the Kvika Footbath. Or go further out towards the golf course. There's little light pollution here at the edge of Iceland, making for ideal Northern Lights viewing conditions. As long as the solar conditions are right and the skies are clear, you might just be able to experience this magical natural phenomenon without having to pay for a tour or car hire. And if the skies are cloudy, a short walk could be all it takes to find a patch of clear sky among the clouds.

It's likely to be cold, so bundle up in your warmest winter gear and bring a thermos of your favourite warm beverage. Hand and foot warmers are also well worth the investment for this type of excursion.

If you're not up for a long walk, you can take the Strætó Route 11 bus. If you've rented a car, it's about a 10-minute drive from central Miðborg to the Grótta Lighthouse.

 WHERE TO EAT IN SELTJARNARNES

Ness
Come here for seasonally rotating menus featuring fresh fish, local produce and expansive views. €€

Raðagerði Veitingahús
A cosy Italian restaurant that masterfully works Icelandic birch smoked salmon into its menu. €€

Ísbúð Huppu
This is the place to go for soft-serve ice cream and milkshakes. €

HAFNARFJÖRÐUR & GARÐABÆR

VIKINGS AND PRESIDENTS

These growing towns at the edge of Reykjavík are considered part of the capital region. Hafnarfjörður is best known for its annual Viking festival. People flock here each June to don Viking garb and engage in traditional Viking activities like longbow shooting. For anyone not visiting in June, Hotel Viking will give you a taste of the experience. Hafnarfjörður is built on top of Holocene lava fields from a volcanic eruption and has been a trading hub for English and German merchants – Iceland's first fishing trawler set off from here in the early 1900s, laying the groundwork for it to become the fishing and import/export hub it is today. People have lived in neighbouring Garðabær since at least the 9th century. The home of Iceland's president is also here.

TOP TIP

Visiting the home of Iceland's president is very different from visiting other high-profile presidential palaces where fences and security make it hard to get a close-up view. Here, visitors are welcome to walk around the home and check out the grounds, which include an idyllic church and expansive ocean views.

SIGHTS
1 Bessastaðir
2 Hellisgerði
3 Museum of Design and Applied Art

ACTIVITIES, COURSES & TOURS
4 Keilir Golf Course

DRINKING & NIGHTLIFE
5 Eimverk Distillery
6 Hovdenak Distillery
7 Thoran Distillery

ENTERTAINMENT
8 Bæjarbíó

PHOTOGRAPHY BY SC/SHUTTERSTOCK ©. BOTTOM: CAVAN IMAGES/GETTY IMAGES ©

Hellisgerði
A HIDDEN WORLD

If this magical garden feels like a fairy wonderland, there might be a very good reason for that. According to folklore, Hafnarfjörður is home to one of Iceland's largest colonies of hidden people. Icelandic elves, dwarfs and fairies are said to live in this enchanted oasis where moss blankets lava formations. The centre of the Hellisgerði is made up of several small caves that look like they could be entryways to secret worlds. If there's any place in the world elves, dwarfs and fairies would live, it's here. There's a small souvenir shop during the summer.

Hellisgerði

Leiðarendi Lava Cave
JOURNEY INTO THE EARTH

Head under the surface of the Reykjanes Peninsula and into the rugged Leiðarendi Lava Cave where you'll be met with colourful rock formations, ancient stalagmites and a hike unlike anything you've experienced.

This is a place where cooling lava has become a collection of intriguing rock formations that tell thousands of years of history. The tunnel is the result of lava that flowed here 2000 years ago, hardening after having carved out this path. The untouched lava tunnel doesn't have the tourist infrastructure of Iceland's better-known lava caves. You'll have to crawl to access certain areas of this nearly 915m tunnel. If you're an inexperienced hiker or claustrophobic, you should consider another lava tunnel first.

Leiðarendi Lava Cave

Bæjarbíó
A GLIMPSE OF ICELAND IN 1945

This venue opened in 1945 and is the only 20th-century Icelandic cinema that's been preserved in its original form.

Nowadays Bæjarbíó mostly hosts concerts and theatre, and there's no better place to get a glimpse of what Icelandic life was like as Europe emerged from WWII than this well-preserved mid-century cinema.

Bessastaðir

HOME OF ICELAND'S PRESIDENT

The official residence of Iceland's president, Bessastaðir is a site that's played a key role in Icelandic history. This spot was settled around 1000 CE and claimed by the king of Norway after the murder of beloved Icelandic poet and historian Snorri Sturluson who had operated it as a farm. The understated white building here has been a school and a residence. It was donated to the state in 1941 and eventually turned into the presidential residence. Visitors are welcome, and events are frequently hosted here.

Bessastaðir

Hafnarfjörður Viking Festival

Hafnarfjörður Viking Festival

TRAVEL BACK IN TIME

Once a year, the tiny town of Hafnarfjörður on the Icelandic coast turns into a vibrant village of Vikings. Arrive here in mid-June, and you may feel you've travelled back in time 1000 years to an era when Vikings roamed this area. Sample freshly roasted lamb, swap stories with new friends and experience a festival unlike any other.

This is a chance to live like a Viking and write your own Icelandic saga, at least for a few days. And don't be too surprised if you walk into a sword fight. Dozens of members of a local Viking club reenact Viking battles during the four-day festival.

Entrance to the annual Viking Festival is free.

Museum of Design and Applied Art

ODE TO ICELANDIC DESIGN

The quirky Museum of Design and Applied Art is an ode to Icelandic design. The museum's collection includes about 5000 items dating as far back as 1900. A permanent exhibition of about 200 items is set up as a sort of blueprint of an Icelandic home. Different objects from different eras are placed side by side as if they had occupied the same slice of history. This museum isn't huge, but it's creative and thought-provoking. If you're looking for design inspiration, this is a good place to start.

ARCTIC-IMAGES/GETTY IMAGES ©, TOP: UP IN THE NORTH/SHUTTERSTOCK ©

Hotel Viking

WHERE TO STAY IN HAFNARFJÖRÐUR & GARÐABÆR

Hotel Vellir
Rates at this straight-forward boutique hotel in Hafnarfjörður include parking and breakfast. Expect clean rooms and a short drive to Reykjanes' eruption sites. €€

Hotel Viking
Can't make the Viking Festival? Stay at this unique Hafnarfjörður hotel for family-friendly rooms and decor that's sure to make you feel like a Viking. €€

Hlid Fisherman Village
This charming collection of cabins not far from the president's home in Álftanes offers privacy, family-friendly rooms and an on-site restaurant with a seasonal menu. €

MORE IN HAFNARFJÖRÐUR & GARÐABÆR

Golf in the Midnight Sun
A TRUE TEST OF SKILL

The top-ranked golf course in Iceland, **Keilir Golf Course** is just a 15-minute drive from downtown Reykjavík, and it's unlike anything you've ever experienced. This 18-hole golf course offers spectacular views and is a test of skill and accuracy.

The front nine holes are surrounded by lava, creating a unique challenge for even experienced golfers. This is a course where power and distance take a backseat to the kind of prow-

 ## WHERE TO EAT IN HAFNARFJÖRÐUR & GARÐABÆR

Von Mathus & Bar
Come here for creative small plates, hearty main courses and an affordable three-course set menu. €€

Mathús Garðabæjar
A pub-style restaurant with a daily fish, meat and soup of the day. €€

Noodle Station
A comfortable spot for a steaming bowl of Asian noodle soup on a cold night. €

ess it takes to navigate such unique terrain. Can you keep the ball on the fairway and off the lava rocks surrounding it?

The back nine sits on a small peninsula at the entrance to the Hafnarfjörður harbour, providing views as far as the Álftanes Peninsula and Snæfellsjökull glacier. Playing here feels like playing two separate nine-hole courses. There really is no other golf course quite like it.

You can book tee times online. Expect to pay around 20,000kr including golf-club rentals, and don't miss the clubhouse restaurant. It's so good some people skip the golf and come just for lunch. And don't worry if you're travelling alone – this club is great at matching solo golfers with groups near their level.

Keilir Golf Course is typically open until 10pm every night, but golfers can request midnight tee times in June and July when the sun shines practically around the clock. If you've ever wanted to play a game of golf in the midnight sun, this is your chance.

Visit Local Distilleries
CHEERS TO LOCAL LIQUORS

This area of the capital region is a hub of the Icelandic distillery business and home to three separate distilleries that make a variety of Icelandic liquors. That's almost half of the legal distillers in Iceland.

Visit the **Thoran Distillery** to learn about how Icelandic gin is made and sample its Marberg gin. This award-winning small-batch gin is made of 22 botanicals including Iceland dulse seaweed, angelica root, cardamom and Icelandic birch leaves. Or visit the **Hovdenak Distillery**, which opened in 2018 and makes gin, vodka, rum and aquavit. Hovdenak's distillery tours begin with a gin and tonic and offer the opportunity to sample all of the company's spirits. If you're looking for something a little different, try the Rökkvi Espresso Martini liqueur, which is made with cold-brew coffee.

Head to **Eimverk Distillery**, a family-run distillery that opened in 2009, to learn how it makes Iceland's only single-malt whisky using local ingredients. This distillery makes Floki, the single malt, as well as Vor, a pot-distilled gin, and Viti, a signature Icelandic Brennivín. Floki is the first single-malt whisky ever distilled in Iceland – it's made of Icelandic barley, which brings a sweet maltiness to the blend. A version of the whisky is smoked in sheep dung; a whisky truly like none other in the world.

BEST PLACES TO EAT IN HAFNARFJÖRÐUR & GARÐABÆR

Fjörugarðurinn
Feast on a three-course Viking dinner. Try sipping Brennivín from a lamb horn. Enjoy live entertainment from singing Valkyries and Vikings, and try your hand at being crowned an honorary Viking. €€

Krydd Restaurant
This restaurant has a creative menu of locally sourced dishes, colourful Icelandic artwork on the walls, and a bar made of reclaimed wood from the harbour. €€

Norðurbakkinn
This cosy cafe with a gigantic book selection is perfect for light meals, coffee or dessert. €

Pylsubarinn
A casual stop for affordable hot dogs, burgers and dishes like fish and chips. €

Pallett
A cute coffee shop and casual cafe that feels more like an independent bookshop. €

A. Hansen Restaurant & Bar
A steakhouse serving local meats, a few vegan options and karaoke on the weekends. €€

SOUTHWEST ICELAND & THE GOLDEN CIRCLE

OTHERWORLDLY ADVENTURES, MINUTES FROM THE AIRPORT

Seemingly endless lava fields, charming coastal towns and outdoor adventures galore: come here to sample the best of Iceland.

Southwest Iceland brings to life the natural landscapes from even the wildest imaginations. This is where you'll find the rugged Reykjanes Peninsula, an area of sprawling lava fields, little vegetation and renewed volcanic activity. Southwest Iceland encompasses the Golden Circle – a scenic drive that connects thundering waterfalls, magnificent geysers and Iceland's first national park, the only place in the world where visitors can swim between the North American and Eurasian tectonic plates.

This area is home to Keflavík International Airport, where most international visitors arrive, and the national capital Reykjavík, where two-thirds of the Icelandic population lives. Use Reykjavík as a base for hiking in ice caves, snowmobiling on glaciers, horseback riding and discovering the shipwrecks time has forgotten. Or follow Iceland's famed Ring Road along the southern coast, staying in charming villages or well-equipped campsites or cabins while stopping to marvel at cascading waterfalls, towering volcanoes and beautiful barren landscapes along the way.

With its extensive wetlands, highlands, rivers and coastline, this region of Iceland is a dream for birdwatchers. It's home to the world's largest colonies of puffins, pink-footed geese and great skua. It's heaven for whale watchers in search of rare blue whales, humpbacks and orcas, and home to a growing sanctuary for beluga whales.

Go fishing. Play golf. Hike landscapes that look like paintings. It's all here.

HENNER DAMKE/SHUTTERSTOCK ©

THE MAIN AREAS

ÞINGVELLIR NATIONAL PARK	**HAUKADALUR VALLEY**	**GULLFOSS**	**GRINDAVÍK**
Where Iceland began.	Geysers galore.	A powerful glacial waterfall.	A fishing village with blue lagoons.
p88	p98	p105	p111

Above: Brúarfoss (p102). Left: Great skua

SELFOSS	**SKÓGAFOSS**	**VÍK**
The largest town in South Iceland.	Impressive 61m cascading water.	Black-sand beaches, glaciers and volcanoes.
p121	p129	p136

0 — 40 km
0 — 20 miles

Þingvellir National Park, p88
Iceland's first national park and the site of Iceland's first parliament. The only place in the world you can snorkel between continents.

Glymur

Akranes

Kálfstind (824m)

Skálafell (774m)

Hrafnabjörg (763m)

Skálabrekka

Laugarvatn

Faxaflói

Mosfellsbær

Seltjarnarnes

Þingvallavatn

Apavo

★REYKJAVÍK

Nesjavellir

Garðskagi

Garður

Hengill (805m)

Sandgerði

Keflavík

Hveragerði

Keflavik International Airport

Vogar

Núpar

Hvíta

Ölfusa

Selfoss

Hafnaberg Cliffs

Hafnir

Keilir (379m)

Flói Nature Reserve

Vatnshc

Sandvík

Hlíðarvatn

Þorlákshöfn

Eyrarbakki

Reykjanesviti

Grindavík

Krýsuvíkurberg Cliffs

Gaulverjask

Selvogsgrunn

Grindavík, p111
A charming fishing village and home to Iceland's famous Blue Lagoon hot springs.

Selfoss, p121
Gateway to historic caves and epic craters.

NORTH ATLANTIC OCEAN

Find Your Way

Road trips are huge in Iceland. The Golden Circle takes you to three of the Southeast's main attractions: Þingvellir National Park, Gullfoss waterfall and Geysit geothermal area.

Haukadalur Valley, p98

Iceland's most famous collection of geysers, mud pools and hot springs.

Gullfoss, p105

A dramatic glacial waterfall that's a key stop on the Golden Circle.

CAR

There are several car rental companies in Iceland, including locally owned Blue Car Rental, and international chains Enterprise and Hertz. Rent a car at Keflavík International Airport to start your South Iceland road trip or take the bus into Reykjavík and pick up a car.

BUS

Iceland's public bus system, Strætó (straeto.is), operates across the country, not just in Reykjavík. If you don't drive or rent a car, you can travel the South Coast using Strætó. It's possible to reach Gullfoss and Geysir by public bus but not Þingvellir National Park.

HITCHHIKE

Hitchhiking is still a fairly common way for budget travellers to get across Iceland because public transit is extremely limited in this area. Prepare for inclement weather and potentially long waits between rides. Be sure to pack lots of snacks and drinks as well.

Skógafoss, p129

A heavenly campsite, 61m of cascading water and scenic hiking trails.

Vík, p136

Black basalt beaches in the shadows of glaciers and volcanoes.

Plan Your Time

Get a taste of South Iceland on a long layover or spend several days exploring the nooks and crannies of this wild volcanic landscape.

KASAKPHOTO/SHUTTERSTOCK ©

Katla Ice Cave (p142)

A Layover That's Worth Leaving the Airport

● If you have just 24 hours in Iceland, make the most of it with a Golden Circle tour. Visit **Þingvellir National Park** (p88), **Gullfoss** (p105) and the **Geysir geothermal area** (p99) in about seven hours on a group tour or rent a car and travel at your own pace. Add a stop at colourful **Kerið crater** (p122), a small-town farm-to-table restaurant like the **Flúðasveppir Farmer's Bistro** (p100) where mushrooms are a speciality, and a local ice-cream shop. Stop at the **Blue Lagoon** (p113) for a blissful spa break and a Michelin-starred meal on the way to the airport.

SEASONAL HIGHLIGHTS

Winter brings long stretches of darkness, ideal for aurora viewing. In summer, there are days when the sun barely sets and Iceland enters the season of the 'midnight sun'.

APRIL–AUGUST

Peak puffin season. Puffins arrive into Iceland in late April or early May and stick around until August.

MAY

Fishing season gets underway. Catch brown trout and Atlantic salmon, but wait until June to fish for Arctic char.

JUNE

Celebrate Icelandic National Day (17 June). There's a parade and community festival in Reykjavík. Most small towns mark the occasion.

HARRY COLLINS PHOTOGRAPHY/SHUTTERSTOCK ©, VICPHOTORIA/SHUTTERSTOCK ©, ARCTIC-IMAGES/GETTY IMAGES ©

Three Perfect Days Filled With Nature

● If you're in the region for three nights, spend the first two near **Þingvellir National Park** (p88). Visit **Gullfoss** (p105), the geysers in the **Haukadalur Valley** (p99), and the geothermal bakery at **Laugarvatn Fontana** (p100). Go snowmobiling on a glacier, chase waterfalls, explore caves, and dine inside a greenhouse where tomatoes grow year-round. Spend your last evening on the Reykjanes Peninsula, stopping at **Kerið crater** (p122), dramatic waterfalls and charming fishing villages along the way. Spend some time soaking in the geothermal water of the **Blue Lagoon** (p113) while looking out onto the seemingly endless lava fields before you go.

Take Your Time

● If you have four or more nights, split your time between the Golden Circle and the South Coast. Visit **Þingvellir National Park** (p88), **Gullfoss** (p105) and the famous geysers in **Haukadalur Valley** (p99). Take your time checking out hot springs, geothermal bakeries and massive volcanic craters. Get adventurous on the South Coast – snowmobiling on a glacier, walking through an ice cave at the **Katla volcano** (p142) and riding horses on a beach. Take scenic hikes, chase majestic waterfalls and have picnics. Make a stop at the **Blue Lagoon** (p113) on your way into Iceland or before you leave the South Coast.

JULY
Check out the Icelandic Horse Competition in Hella or run an ultramarathon in the highlands.

AUGUST
Enjoy concerts, bonfires and fireworks displays at the Vestmannaeyjar National Festival. Don't skip the Sunday singalong.

SEPTEMBER
The autumn equinox creates prime Northern Lights viewing. Look for a viewing spot with clear skies and minimal light pollution.

DECEMBER
This is one of Iceland's coldest and darkest months. Expect excellent aurora viewing conditions and unique Christmas traditions.

ÞINGVELLIR NATIONAL PARK

This national park is the result of massive volcanic eruptions, powerful lava flows and slowly melting glaciers. It's a place that brings geology to life through sprawling lava fields, rocky canyons and crystal-clear glacial water, and there's no better place to see how Iceland came to be.

This is the birthplace of Icelandic government and a key location in the development of Icelandic culture. Not only is it where Norwegian settlers chose to build Iceland's earliest recorded community, it's where Iceland was governed for centuries, and a place where countless Icelanders came together to the lay the roots of what would become modern Icelandic culture.

Today, Þingvellir National Park is one of three national parks in Iceland and a top attraction. It's home to the only place in the world where it's possible to swim between continental plates, as well as well-worn riding trails and endless fields of lava.

REYKJAVÍK ⭐ Þingvellir
National Park

TOP TIP

The dark skies found here make for ideal aurora-borealis viewing conditions. And the only thing more unreal than seeing the bright greens, reds and pinks dance through the sky may be seeing it happen against a backdrop of lava fields and tectonic rifts.

YURIY CHERTOK/SHUTTERSTOCK ©

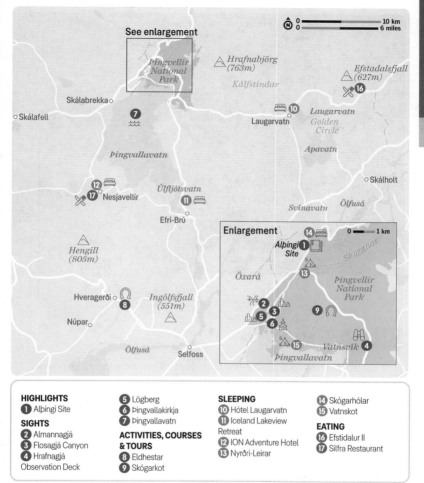

HIGHLIGHTS
1 Alþingi Site

SIGHTS
2 Almannagjá
3 Flosagjá Canyon
4 Hrafnagjá Observation Deck

5 Lögberg
6 Þingvallakirkja
7 Þingvallavatn

ACTIVITIES, COURSES & TOURS
8 Eldhestar
9 Skógarkot

SLEEPING
10 Hótel Laugarvatn
11 Iceland Lakeview Retreat
12 ION Adventure Hotel
13 Nyrðri-Leirar

14 Skógarhólar
15 Vatnskot

EATING
16 Efstidalur II
17 Silfra Restaurant

Explore Þingvellir National Park on Foot

TRAILS FOR EVERYONE

This is the kind of national park that will make even the hardcore urbanite put their phone away and look for a pair of hiking boots. Several trails cut across Þingvellir National Park leading to such places as the 6.4km rift that marks

 WHERE TO EAT IN & AROUND ÞINGVELLIR NATIONAL PARK

Þingvellir National Park Service Center
This cafeteria near the Leirar campsite is the only place to eat inside the park. €

Silfra Restaurant
Beautifully presented, well-proportioned meals featuring locally sourced, seasonal ingredients. €€€

Efstidalur II
This farm-to-table restaurant is actually at a farm and produces its own dairy products. €€

VICPHOTORIA/SHUTTERSTOCK ©

Scan this
QR code to book
snorkelling and diving tours

TOP SIGHT

Silfra Fissure

This water-filled crack between the North American and Eurasian
tectonic plates is the only place in the world where you can swim
between continents. The crystal-clear water here flows from the
Langjökull glacier, winding through porous lava rock for decades
before emerging here. The name 'Silfra' means silvery.

DON'T MISS

Silfra Big Crack –
deep, expansive
canyons

Silfra Hall –
towering rock
formations

Silfra Cathedral –
otherworldly deep
blue water

Silfra Lagoon –
lagoon with a view

Dive Between Continents

Silfra is a diving destination that tops many travellers' buck-
et lists. The water is cold. There aren't many fish. But where
else in the world are you going to dive between continental
plates? Besides, the water here is crystal clear, giving divers
unforgettable views for hundreds of feet.

Dive into the Silfra Big Crack. Swim between the towering rock formations on either side of Silfra Hall, a space that
looks like a cathedral. Or head deeper into the fissure into
Silfra Cathedral where you'll find several mesmerising shades
of blue. This is an area filled with intricate rock formations
and crevices and a favourite of experienced divers. Dives end
at a lagoon that's a blend of freshwater and glacial meltwater.

Dives generally last between 30 and 45 minutes, giving divers ample time to explore magnificent rock formations underwater. Dives may be as deep as 18m, though they're more

commonly around 10m. Silfra is one of two places where scuba diving is allowed in Þingvellir National Park. Advanced permits are required and all divers must hold drysuit certifications. Dive tour companies typically require PADI Open Water Diver certification or an equivalent, and either drysuit dive certification or a record of 10 drysuit dives within the two prior years. If you go this route, you'll need to provide written proof from dive instructors.

Snorkel Between Continents

You don't have to be a diver to get under the surface of Silfra. Several companies offer snorkelling tours, sometimes combining snorkelling with activities like whale watching, Northern Lights chasing and horseback riding. These tours typically last between 30 and 45 minutes.

Snorkellers are allowed to bring their equipment but must use open-heeled fins that fit over drysuit boots. Full-face snorkelling masks are not allowed because they don't work with the drysuits necessary for snorkelling in this cold water that's just a few degrees above freezing. If you don't have your own gear, don't worry. Snorkelling tour companies will have everything you need. However, you will need to be a competent swimmer to join snorkelling tours. The drysuits used for snorkeling here are buoyant and can help keep you afloat, but it's still key for snorkellers to have basic swimming skills and be comfortable in the water.

The Ultimate Photo Spot

This entire area is photo-worthy, and most tour operators take photos to capture the experience for divers and snorkellers on their tours. So go ahead and enjoy yourself and leave the documenting to someone else. If you're looking for a specific shot, talk to your guide before you dive in.

Without Getting Wet

You don't have to get in the water to get a peek at this crystal-clear glacial meltwater. If you're not a swimmer, park in lot number 5 for a peek at the divers and snorkellers heading to and from the site's entry point. This lot is near walking trails that will guide you across this beautiful landscape where you'll be able to catch glimpses of the fissure and marvel at the rocks you see through the pure glacial water.

DIVE ALL YEAR
Scuba diving and snorkelling are year-round activities at the Silfra Fissure where water flows underground from the Langjökull glacier 60km away. This glacial water maintains a consistent temperature of 2°C to 3°C because it flows underground, and it doesn't freeze over at the Silfra Big Crack.

TOP TIPS
- Diving and snorkelling are only allowed on guided tours.
- There is no fish or coral here. Þingvellir Lake is home to a number of fish species, but they rarely venture far into the Silfra Fissure.
- Marine life is limited to bright green algae, colloquially called 'troll hair', and other types of algae.
- Narrow passageways, strong currents and and a tunnel known as 'the toilet' make this a particularly dangerous dive site.
- Some tour operators offer guests the option to get drysuit certified the day before a Silfra Fissure dive.

the eastern edge of the North American tectonic plate. Trails are 1.5km to 10.5km long, making it easy to find a hike that fits your schedule and fitness level. The easiest trail is 1.6km each way and connects the site of Iceland's first parliamentary assembly with a seemingly idyllic pool of crystal-clear water that was used to carry out executions in the 1600s. The elevation gain on this hike, which can be done in under an hour, is less than 120m. The longest trail has an elevation gain of just over 335m, and while it's considered moderately challenging, it may not wow avid hikers, except for the scenery. Start at the park's visitor centre to map out your trek, and be sure to stop at **Lögberg**, the original meeting site of Iceland's Alþingi. If you're not diving Silfra, go to **Peningagjá** to peek at clear glacial water flowing through a rocky crevice. There was a time when people used to throw coins in this water hoping for good fortune. **Flosagjá** is a beautiful canyon with glittering water and majestic views that's also a must-see.

Enjoy Iceland's Largest Lake
GO FISHING

Fish for brown trout and Arctic char on **Þingvallavatn**, Iceland's largest lake, from late April to mid-September. The northernmost part of Þingvallavatn is inside Þingvellir National Park and it's a haven for fly-fishing early in the season. Only fly-fishing is allowed between the beginning of the season and 1 June. Brown trout caught during these months must be released back into the lake. Fly, spoon and worm fishing is allowed for the rest of the season. Whatever you prefer, you'll find this is a peaceful place to cast your rod and enjoy rare moments of silence.

Go Horseback Riding
ICELAND IS HORSE COUNTRY

Icelanders have been crisscrossing this area on horseback for generations, and you can too. A few designated horse trails now run through Þingvellir National Park. They converge at **Skógarkot**, an abandoned farm where a few ruins of the past remain. Visit **Skógarhólar**, a camp where horses have long grazed while their riders snoozed in sleeping bags. Stay overnight in the rustic five-bedroom house with a barbecue grill and a full kitchen. Enjoy sweeping park views and the serenity of your horse's rhythmic gait in between stops. The park doesn't offer horse rentals or tours itself, but several private companies do. **Eldhestar** is one operator that takes guests

EARLY ICELAND

Þingvellir is where Iceland began. Iceland's Alþingi (general assembly; the parliament that set its earliest laws and managed disputes), met here for more than 800 years from 930 until 1798.

In the early 19th century, this vast spread of lava fields, canyons and moon-like landscapes became a symbol of Icelandic independence, after centuries of being ruled by Norway and Denmark. Iceland gained its independence in 1918 and broke away from Denmark in 1944.

Þingvellir became a national park in 1930 and a UNESCO World Heritage Site in 2004.

BEST HOTELS NEAR ÞINGVELLIR NATIONAL PARK

ION Adventure Hotel
This modern hotel is a perfect home base for fishing, riding and other outdoor activities. €€€

Iceland Lakeview Retreat
With a glass wall that's perfect for Northern Lights viewing, this is one of Iceland's dreamiest cabins. €€€

Hótel Laugarvatn
Small hotel with single, double and family rooms. Offers breakfast buffet and Nordic tasting menu. €€

on a 125km ride through Maradalur, a valley of unusual volcanic formations known as the Valley of the Horses, before cutting across the park's lava fields and forests. Horses aren't allowed on automobile roads that cut through the park, at the old assembly site, or at the Almannagjá fault.

Search for Unreal Scenery
WILD VOLCANIC LANDSCAPES ABOUND

There's no shortage of scenic spots to discover in this unique national park. Get the lie of the land with a stop at the **Hrafnagjá Observation Deck**. Check out the **Flosagjá Canyon**, a rift valley on the Mid-Atlantic Ridge. This is where the North American and Eurasian tectonic plates meet and is a great alternative for anyone looking for tectonic experience without having to dive into cold water. Marvel in the fresh spring water flowing through this rocky crevice.

See **Almannagjá**, a 6.4km rift that marks the eastern boundary of the North American tectonic plate. There's a beautiful waterfall here and unreal landscape views in every direction. Stop at Stekkjargjá, a rocky spot where people used to milk sheep. See **Lögberg**, the rocky spot where Iceland's first parliament met. Wander through wild volcanic landscapes. Get lost among giant rocks. Listen to the sound of flowing glacial water, and feel the pull of everything around you.

Visit Iconic Þingvellir Church
COSY AS A CABIN

If you've seen photos of Iceland, you've probably seen **Þingvallakirkja**, one of Iceland's best-known churches. This simple church looks like something from an old postcard. Built in 1859, it sits on the place where Iceland's first parliament met for more than 800 years. These general assemblies moved in 1798, making way for the church's construction. The wood for the church came from Norway as did the church bells, a gift from King Olaf.

Þingvellir Church's clean lines, green shutters and simple architecture blend well with the landscape here. The church's interior feels more like a cosy cabin than a formal religious space. Still, it carries on a tradition. An earlier church is believed to have been built near this location around the time Iceland adopted Christianity in the year 1000. There's a small cemetery outside the church.

Þingvallakirkja

WHERE TO CAMP

There are no hotels inside Þingvellir National Park, but there are several campsites. Permits are required and available at the park's service centre, which is near the sites.

Two campsites, at **Leirar** and **Vatnskot**, are open for summer camping from 1 June through 1 September. A campsite at **Nyrðri-Leirar**, adjacent to the park's service centre, is open year-round.

For all sites, restrooms and laundry are available year-round, but the showers here close from December through March. Camping for adults is 1300kr per night. Electricity access is an additional 900kr per night. Children aged 17 and under camp free.

GETTING AROUND

For the most flexibility, you'll want to rent a car. If you don't want to drive, consider joining a group tour. Public buses don't run directly to Þingvellir National Park. You would need to take an expensive taxi from the last stop to the park. There are several car parks and paved roads inside the park, as well as hiking and horseback-riding trails.

Beyond Þingvellir National Park

Þingvellir National Park

Gjábakkahellir

Take a scenic drive along a fjord and head into a lava tube.

Þingvellir National Park is a key stop on the Golden Circle. Three other stops along an extended version of the sightseeing route are nearby: Gullfoss, the Geysir geothermal area and Kerið crater. It's possible to visit all four sites in one day, though you may prefer to slow down and enjoy the idyllic lagoons, secluded hot springs and farm-to-table dining along the way. Hike across a lava field and venture into a lava tunnel that is accessible to the public. Or drive one of the most scenic routes in Iceland. There aren't a lot of hotels in this area, but you will find well-equipped campsites, cute cottages and vacation rentals.

TOP TIP

To cut your drive time, use the Hvalfjörður Tunnel – one of Iceland's long tunnels – to reach the scenic route along the fjord.

MARTI BUG CATCHER/SHUTTERSTOCK ©

Hvalfjörður scenic drive (p97)

Gjábakkahellir

Journey into a Lava Tube

WALK AMONG LAVA FALLS

With its abundant lava formations and ice sculptures, **Gjábak-kahellir**, a 20-minute drive from Þingvellir National Park, is a textbook example of an Icelandic lava tube. Gjábakkahellir is also the one lava tube in Iceland that visitors can walk all the way through. Lava falls and shark-tooth stalactites welcome you as you enter a 335m-long passage, discovered by construction workers in 1907. Over the centuries, cooling rock and the shifting ground have created a tunnel here that's lined with layers of mineral-rich rock. The cave floor is also covered in rocks that fell from the ceiling as the lava fields here were cooling. Because of this, the pathway through the tunnel is bumpy and requires some scrambling over the rocks. Gjábakkahellir is one of several lava tunnels in Iceland, but this one is well-suited for first-time cavers who may appreciate the tunnel's spacious chamber during their first journey into an underground cavern. It's possible to visit the cave independently or on a guided caving tour.

CAMPING IN ICELAND

Resist the urge to pitch a tent or pull over your camper van just anywhere in Iceland. Wild camping isn't allowed anywhere in the country, and camper vans and motorhomes are only allowed to be set up in specific areas.

Iceland is dotted with campsites, some of which are in spectacular locations. Most Icelandic campgrounds offer toilets, electricity and common houses with kitchen or outdoor barbecue grills. Some even offer playgrounds or candlelit caves. Camping generally costs between 1500kr and 2500kr a night. Electricity, laundry and shower access may incur additional fees.

It's easy to rent camping equipment in Reykjavík, including tents, sleeping bags, cooking sets, crampons and wi-fi hot spots.

THINGS TO SEE IN AKRANES

Akranes Folk Museum
A folk museum with an open-air section where you can see 19th-century boats and buildings.

Old Akranes Lighthouse
A popular spot for Northern Lights photography. The larger lighthouse is open to the public.

Höfrungur AK 91
Admire remains of an old herring fishing boat that was built here in the 1950s.

SKÁLHOLT CATHEDRAL

The current Skálholt Cathedral site was the backdrop to about 700 years of Icelandic history; it's where the country's early political, spiritual and cultural identity was formed. A cathedral was first built on this site in 1056, a time when religious disputes were common, as Christianity was trying to take hold of an island where pagan belief systems were the norm. This is also where the last Catholic bishop of Iceland, Jón Arason, was killed in 1550. The idyllic white building with impressive altarpiece and stained-glass windows dates from 1963 and is the 10th cathedral to stand at this site. There's a museum here as well as a mysterious underground tunnel in the church cellar.

Meet the Cave People

TRAVEL BACK IN TIME

Less than 100 years ago, it wasn't uncommon for Icelanders to live in caves. The **Cave People Museum** invites visitors to get to know some of these people through half-hour guided tours of two human-made caves just 20 minutes' drive from Þingvellir National Park. Look for the windows and door peeking out from the earth. When you see them, you'll feel like you've arrived at another time in history. In an experience that's part live performance and part museum, characters in period costumes will reveal what rural Icelandic life was like within these cave walls just a century ago. The storytelling alone is worth the drive, but even the exterior of the cave is something to see. It looks like a chunk of earth laid on top of a home, almost as if it were a blanket. The interior has been meticulously restored with dishware, linens and other items that were key to rural Icelandic life at the time. Shelves and storage are carved into the walls of the cave. The tables have been set. All that's left is for you to enter and let your imagination lead the way. You can book tours of The Cave People online or contact the site's operator to book private tours or tours at other times.

BRANISLAV KUCINSKY/SHUTTERSTOCK ©

Glymur waterfall

HIKING & SWIMMING SPOTS

Akrafjall Hiking Area
A steep, challenging trail with panoramic views that even the rain will struggle to diminish.

Guðlaug Baths
Heated geothermal pools, steps from the beach. Don't miss the views from the infinity pool.

Langisandur
Take a walk along a calm, sandy beach before or after you visit Guðlaug Baths.

Drive Hvalfjörður Fjord

ONE OF ICELAND'S MOST SCENIC DRIVES

This scenic route an hour's drive from Þingvellir National Park will leave you feeling blissful. Enjoy unblemished natural landscapes and watch fields of green melt into the Atlantic Ocean.

If you come here looking for whales, you'll be out of luck. This fjord didn't get its name by having an abundance of whales, though it is home to Iceland's only whaling station. The name is a nod to an Icelandic folk story about an elf woman who turns her human lover into a redheaded whale who angrily attacked area ships before being killed by a local priest.

Many travellers choose to start this journey with a drive through the roughly 6.4km tunnel that runs underneath the fjord. A longer, more scenic route passes by what was once Iceland's tallest waterfall.

Hike to Iceland's Second-Highest Waterfall

AN ASCENT WORTH THE EFFORT

The **Glymur** waterfall sits between Þingvellir National Park and the Hvalfjörður fjord, and is about 35 minutes' drive from the park. Since the discovery of an even taller waterfall in 2011, it has become Iceland's second-tallest waterfall. You can only reach this off-the-beaten-path waterfall on foot. Round trip, the hike comes in at just over 6.4km and involves a 426m climb. Sturdy hiking boots and hiking poles are recommended. The hike is considered moderate and estimated to take between three and four hours to complete. If you plan to attempt this hike, you'll need to visit between June and September when the ground here is clear of snow and a log has been put in place to facilitate a river crossing. The hike offers two potential routes, passes through two river crossings, and includes a short walk through a cave. You can also expect countless views of the magnificent 198m waterfall.

WHERE TO EAT & DRINK

Lindin
This cosy restaurant in Laugarvatn has a menu of local produce and meats, such as Arctic char, lamb and reindeer. €€

Gamla Kaupfélagið
A casual spot in Akranes with elevated lobster, fish and vegetarian dishes. Pick up some seasoned salmon for self-catering. €€

Kallabakarí
Ideal for road-trip pastries, an indulgent breakfast or laid-back lunch. In Akranes. €

Laxárbakki
Cosy restaurant in Akranes serving staples like lamb soup and pan-fried cod in a family-run hotel. €€

Vínstofa Friðheima
A wine bar with an extensive selection, located inside a greenhouse that opened in Selfoss in the summer of 2023. €€

 GETTING AROUND

While there is bus service between Reykjavík and Akranes, public transit is limited in this area. You'll need to rent a car, or hire a car and driver service, to drive this scenic fjord and explore sights beyond Þingvellir National Park.

HAUKADALUR VALLEY

REYKJAVÍK

● Haukadalur Valley

Haukadalur is a colourful geothermal valley about a 90-minute drive from Reykjavík. You'll notice the smoke rising on the horizon as you approach and vibrant shades of yellow, green and red colouring the ground. The yellow colour comes from sulphur. Copper gives it greens, while iron gives it hints of red.The geysers here have been drawing visitors for more than 100 years. The best-known of them is Geysir, which at one point was spouting water nearly 150m at regular intervals. Nowadays, nearby Strokkur is the valley's most active geyser. Strokkur may not shoot water as high as Geysir, but it's far more reliable and goes off about every 10 minutes. Geysir and Strokkur may be symbols of Iceland, but they aren't the only attractions in this area, where you'll also find dozens of mud pools, hot springs and fumaroles – vents in the earth that emit volcanic gasses.

TOP TIP

Geysir and Strokkur might be the stars of the geyser show here, but don't overlook the idyllic turquoise pools – such as Blesi – and this colourful valley itself, which is almost like a painting. Blesi doesn't bubble anymore, but even watching steam rise above this dormant geyser can be mesmerising.

IZZET KERIBAR/GETTY IMAGES ©

Geysir

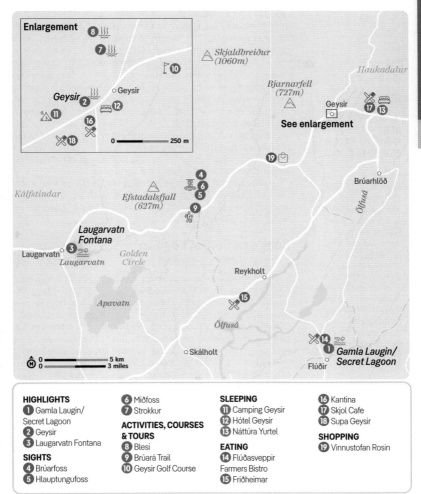

Enlargement

Skjaldbreiður
(1060m)

Haukadalur

Bjarnarfell
(727m)

Geysir

See enlargement

Geysir

Geysir

Kálfstindar

Brúarhlöð

Efstadalsfjall
(627m)

Ölfusá

**Laugarvatn
Fontana**

Laugarvatn

Laugarvatn

Golden
Circle

Reykholt

Apavatn

Ölfusá

Gamla Laugin/
Secret Lagoon

Skálholt

Flúðir

0   5 km
0   3 miles

| HIGHLIGHTS | | ACTIVITIES, COURSES & TOURS | SLEEPING | SHOPPING |

HIGHLIGHTS
1 Gamla Laugin/
Secret Lagoon
2 Geysir
3 Laugarvatn Fontana

SIGHTS
4 Brúarfoss
5 Hlauptungufoss

6 Miðfoss
7 Strokkur

ACTIVITIES, COURSES & TOURS
8 Blesi
9 Brúará Trail
10 Geysir Golf Course

SLEEPING
11 Camping Geysir
12 Hótel Geysir
13 Náttúra Yurtel

EATING
14 Flúðasveppir
Farmers Bistro
15 Friðheimar

16 Kantina
17 Skjol Cafe
18 Supa Geysir

SHOPPING
19 Vinnustofan Rosin

Walk among Geysers & Hot Springs

ALMOST GUARANTEED GEYSER ERUPTIONS

This area is a hotbed of activity, and there's far more here than the soaring sprays and reliable eruptions that have made it famous. Look for colourful pools on the ground as you watch smoke rising from the earth. The heat here is enough to bake bread and fry eggs. Sample these local delicacies and hang out for a little while. You're bound to see a geyser eruption, but it'll more likely come from **Strokkur** than **Geysir**, the geyser that made this site famous with the regularity of its eruptions. Strokkur can spout water as high as 30m and still erupts regularly.

Geysir and Strokkur may get most of the attention, but they aren't the only sites worth checking out in this area. In its calmest moments, the **Blesi** hot springs are beautiful pools of blue and turquoise with hints of green. Steam rises off the boiling water, immensely calming to watch. This geyser doesn't erupt regularly, but it doesn't have to. This is an idyllic hot spring even in stillness. And who knows? Blesi geyser may surprise you with a well-timed eruption. A 2.2km hiking route connects Geysir, Strokkur and Blesi. Most people would describe this path as more of a walking trail than a vigorous hike. The elevation gain is 110m and the loop can be completed in under an hour, making it a great option for photographing wildflowers, as well as getting up close to Strokkur and seeing Blesi's blues on a tight schedule.

Or play a game of golf at the **Geysir Golf Course** across the way from the hot spring. The course's nine holes meander around rivers and summer cottages, and the course was designed for minimal disturbance to the terrain.

Soak in a Secret Lagoon

A SPA WITHOUT THE CROWDS

Unwind with a relaxing dip in Iceland's oldest swimming pool, a remote oasis that traces its history to 1891. Many Icelanders learned to swim here in the early 1900s, but the pool eventually closed when a newer alternative opened nearby. **Gamla Laugin**, the old pool, reopened as the **Secret Lagoon** under private ownership in 2014. The Secret Lagoon isn't as picturesque as the Sky Lagoon (p72) or Blue Lagoon (p113), but it's a peaceful place for a relaxing soak in nature at a fraction of the price. There's only one human-made pool here, but warm water from local hot springs refills it every 24 hours, ensuring a steady supply of fresh, clean water. The water is consistently around 38°C. There are no eucalyptus steam rooms, multi-step bathing rituals, saunas or swim-up bars, but the Secret Lagoon does have the basics covered. You'll find changing rooms, restrooms, showers, lockers and a cafe on-site. Swimsuits and towels are available for rent. Adult entry to the Secret Lagoon is 3300kr. Children of all ages are welcome, and those under 14 enter for free.

Geothermal Bread & a Spa Day

A BAKERY LIKE NO OTHER

Recharge on a road trip with a visit to **Laugarvatn Fontana**, a spa complex that brings together natural geothermal pools, bubbling hot springs and cool refreshing lake water. Locals

BEST FARM-TO-TABLE EXPERIENCES

Friðheimar
Farm-to-table dining in a greenhouse where the restaurant's tomatoes are grown year-round. The menu includes rarities like tomato beer and tomato ice cream. The farm grows four varieties of tomatoes and was the first to cultivate plum tomatoes and Flavorino cocktail tomatoes year-round. €€

Flúðasveppir Farmers Bistro
It doesn't get more farm-to-table than this restaurant run by the operators of Iceland's only mushroom farm. The restaurant is located on the farm, which grows three types of mushrooms (white, chestnut and portobello), and the menu includes the likes of mushroom soup and mushroom ice cream. €€

 QUICK BITES NEAR GEYSIR

Supa Geysir
This laid-back spot always offers a vegan option and serves soups with fresh bread. €

Kantina
Fast food in a large casual dining room. Don't skip the soups and stews. €

Skjol Cafe
Come to this laid-back backpacker hangout for pizzas, salads, and fish and chips. €

Secret Lagoon

NATURE'S OVEN

Icelanders have used the hot springs here to bake rye bread for generations. *Hverabrauð* (hot-spring bread) is steam-cooked underground for 24 hours in the heat of the geothermal springs. Bakers bury stainless steel pots of flour, sugar, baking powder, salt and milk, digging up the pots of the bread the next day. The Icelandic rye that emerges is cakey with just a hint of sweetness, and goes perfectly with smooth, creamy Icelandic butter. Until Laugarvatn Fontana opened in 2011, this is just how local bread was made. Now there are up to three bread-making tours every day at Laugarvatn Fontana, giving visitors a chance to sample it for themselves.

have been enjoying natural steam baths here since 1929. Steam simmers up from the ground through grids in the wooden floors of three traditional steam rooms. Temperatures range from around 40°C to 50°C with high humidity. These steam rooms are located directly on top of the hot springs, allowing the sounds and scents of the hot springs to seep in and making it hard to do anything but relax. The complex also includes a collection of outdoor mineral baths with varying temperatures and depths. Don't miss the playful stone artwork surrounding the pool or the panoramic view from the hot tub. If you'd prefer a traditional Finnish sauna, there's one of those here as well. And when it's time to cool off, take a walk along a black-sand beach and into the lake.

Time your visit around daily geothermal bakery tours to watch fresh pots of bread emerge from hot black sand. Sample this one-of-a-kind fresh bread with local smoked trout and Icelandic butter. Depending on the hot-spring activity, you can buy rye for the road. Tours are available twice a day year-round at 11.45am and 2.30pm. During the summer, there's a third tour at 10.15am.

Admission to Laugarvatn Fontana is about 5000kr, around half of what it costs to go to the Blue Lagoon.

 WHERE TO STAY NEAR GEYSIR

Hótel Geysir
This stylish hotel is a cosy escape: 77 rooms, 5-minute walk from its namesake geyser.
€€

Náttúra Yurtel
Mongolian yurts with electricity, private toilets, underfloor heating. Leave your yurt for a private shower. €€

Camping Geysir
This campground, a short walk from the geysers, has mountain views, laundry and playground. €

MORITZ WOLF/GETTY IMAGES ©

Hlauptungufoss waterfall

BUY YOUR WOOL SWEATER HERE

If you're looking to take home an authentic Icelandic sweater, make a detour to **Vinnustofan Rosin**, about 10 minutes' drive from Strokkur and Geysir.

This small shop sells handmade wool sweaters, socks and mittens that are good value. The family who runs the shop also has a sheep farm, so you could call these farm-to-hanger sweaters. Don't be surprised to see sheep running around the property when you visit.

If you don't see something you like, the shop can create your dream Icelandic sweater for you in about a week. Just be sure to bring cash. This is one of the few places in Iceland that doesn't accept credit cards or digital payments.

See Bright Blue Waterfalls

BRÚARFOSS' BLUE LAGOON IMPERSONATION

If the Blue Lagoon (p113) fed into a waterfall it would probably look like **Brúarfoss**. But unlike those geothermal pools, this waterfall originates at the Langjökull glacier. It's that glacial meltwater flowing through the Bruar and Hvítá rivers that gives this waterfall its bright blue colour. The Blue Lagoon, on the other hand, gets its bright blue hue from silica in the water that reflects light.

A new car park opened in early 2023, making Brúarfoss significantly easier to access. You'll have to pay to park, but the waterfall is just a few minutes' walk away. Or, take the scenic route by parking for free in the **Brúará Trail** car park and make the 7km round-trip hike to the waterfall. Give yourself about an hour each way, longer if you stop frequently and take lots of photos. And there's plenty to stop for on this hike, including unbelievable river views and two more bright blue waterfalls. **Hlauptungufoss** isn't the biggest waterfall you'll see in Iceland, but it bottlenecks to create a forceful stream of blue water cascading over the edge, which stands out in this landscape. **Miðfoss** sits between Brúarfoss and Hlauptungufoss. It's smaller – with a drop under 2m – but still has that gorgeous hue. At Brúarfoss, the bright blue water plunges 3m into a bright blue pool of water punctuated by white rapids. The trail here isn't particularly steep, making this hike accessible to beginners with sturdy footwear.

GETTING AROUND

A car will give you the most flexibility when exploring this area. You can also take public buses to Geysir from Reykjavík, Selfoss and Reykholt. All Golden Circle tours visit the geysers Strokkur and Geysir.

Beyond Haukadalur Valley

You'll quickly notice you're surrounded by greenhouses. Discover colourful canyons, thundering waterfalls and a sustainable paradise for produce production.

Haukadalur Valley

Keldur

Haukadalur Valley is near Gullfoss and Þingvellir National Park, making it easy to visit all three in a single day if you're tight on time. You'll find idyllic hot springs, lovely lagoons, and the country's only mushroom farm a short drive away, but you'll want to rent a car – or hire a car and driver – for the most flexibility with your itinerary. Haukadalur Valley sits at the edge of an area dotted with greenhouses, where tomatoes, bananas and more are grown all year long. Most restaurants here are farm-to-table. You'll eat well while respecting the environment. These are some of the most sustainable produce farms in the world and are run by geothermal power.

TOP TIP

Thanks to greenhouses, Iceland is able to grow tomatoes year-round without using pesticides. Don't leave without trying a local tomato.

RALF BROSKVAR/SHUTTERSTOCK ©

CHERYLRAMALHO/SHUTTERSTOCK ©

Commonwealth Farm

STAY IN A MODERN TURF HOUSE

Instead of just checking out turf houses, stay in one at Torfhus Retreat. While they may look like it from the outside, these are no ordinary turf houses. On the inside, they're luxury cabins made of reclaimed oak, furnished with rustic handcrafted items, and complete with every creature comfort you could imagine. One-bedroom retreats come with private bathrooms and verandas, in-room coffee makers and a minibar that's restocked every day. Each retreat comes with access to a shared geothermically heated basalt stone hot pool. This is an experience that comes at a high price, with a two-night minimum stay.

A 900-Year Journey Minutes from the Road

A RECONSTRUCTED FARMHOUSE

Journey back in time to a reconstructed farm that was buried under a volcanic eruption during the Middle Ages. The **Commonwealth Farm** (open from 1 June to 31 August), in the Þjórsárdalur Valley, about an hour's drive from the Haukadalur Valley, is a replica of the manor farm that once stood here. The farm opened to visitors in 1977, and this area is believed to have been home to about 20 towns and farms. An estimated 400 to 600 people lived here until the volcano Hekla erupted. The ruins of one of those farms, Stong, were discovered centuries later. Take a seat around the small fire and let your imagination take you on a journey through Icelandic history.

Visit Iceland's Oldest Turf House

EXPERIENCE VIKING ICELAND

Before 1947, **Keldur** was a thriving village of about 20 buildings. This village is home to what's believed to be the oldest turf house in Iceland. The farmhouse traces its history to the 12th century. It's not a staple of local group tours, so you'll need a car to visit (one hour and 20 minutes from Haukadalur Valley). This is a detour worth the drive. There's a tunnel from a main cabin that is believed to have been used as an escape route during a violent period of Viking history in the 13th century. The well-kept property even plays a role in local folklore as the setting for a 13th-century Icelandic saga. It's only open to visitors during the summer, but you'll be able to check out the outside of these structures at other times of the year.

 WHERE TO STAY IN FLÚÐIR

Hotel Flúðir
A collection of modern cabins around a garden of hot tubs, with on-site vehicle chargers. €

Flúðir Camping Ground
With ample space, this campsite is ideal for travellers in camper vans and motor homes. €

Guesthouse Flúðir
This cute guesthouse has a pool, free breakfast and a restaurant that's popular among locals. €

GULLFOSS

SOUTHWEST ICELAND & THE GOLDEN CIRCLE GULLFOSS

This powerful waterfall isn't the highest or widest in the world, but it is Iceland's best-known waterfall. A key stop on Golden Circle tours, it certainly makes a statement. From the car park, it looks almost as if the river leading to this waterfall plunges straight into the earth, but walk toward the viewpoints and you'll see the famous falls plunging 30m into a rugged crevice. Gullfoss is a thundering two-tier waterfall with a 11m drop and another more dramatic 21m drop. During the winter, icicles dangle all around and chunks of ice plunge into a snow-covered ravine. In the summer, Gullfoss is at its fullest and mist rises over carpets of bright green moss. Gullfoss is surrounded by 3.2km of walking paths and has two observation decks. It's free to visit, open around the clock and accessible year-round.

TOP TIP

Don't let winter weather deter you from visiting Gullfoss. This waterfall is particularly spectacular during the winter when it freezes in places. You won't see the same thundering flow as you would in the summer, but you might get to see a majestic waterfall literally frozen in time.

HIGHLIGHTS
1 Gullfoss

SIGHTS
2 Brúarhlöð

ACTIVITIES, COURSES & TOURS
3 Arctic Rafting

SLEEPING
4 Buubble
5 Geysir Hestar
6 Hotel Gullfoss

EATING
7 Gullfoss Panorama Restaurant & Cafe
see 6 Hotel Gullfoss Restaurant

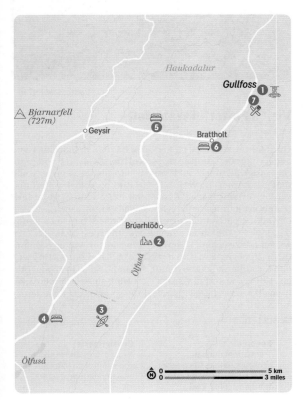

WITGOAWAY/GETTY IMAGES ©

Gullfoss waterfall

WHERE TO EAT NEAR GULLFOSS

Gullfoss Panorama Restaurant & Cafe
This restaurant a short walk from the waterfall is popular with tour groups and adjacent to a souvenir shop. Views are nice, but the cafeteria-style restaurant doesn't directly overlook the waterfall. Try the traditional Icelandic lamb stew or the mushroom soup. €€

Hotel Gullfoss Restaurant
The restaurant is the shining star at this hotel near the waterfall. It's known for serving up beautifully plated Icelandic salmon, chunky lamb stew and colourful beet salads. €€

Visit a Powerful Waterfall

HEAR THE FALLS THUNDER

One of three key stops on the Golden Circle sightseeing route and a staple of tour itineraries, **Gullfoss** is always a magnificent waterfall to see, but if you visit during the summer you'll find it at its most powerful. Translating as 'golden waterfalls', Gullfoss offers plenty of opportunities for visitors to get intimately acquainted with its nooks and crannies via the 3.2km of walking paths that surround it. If you're here on a sunny day, look for the water pouring over the rocks that take on a golden-brown colour. If you're visiting during winter, be mindful of slippery steps. And if you're worried about getting wet, don't. Unlike Skógafoss (p129), Seljalandsfoss (p131) and others, this is a waterfall visitors view from above. It's more likely you'll see a rainbow than feel the spray of the mist here.

 WHERE TO STAY NEAR GULLFOSS

Hotel Gullfoss
Clean rooms and comfortable beds as close to the waterfall as you can get. €€

Buubble
Transparent bubble accommodation; sleep under the stars and wake up to the Northern Lights. €€€

Geysir Hestar
A rustic guesthouse and a collection of private cottages on a working horse farm. €

Gullfoss is one of Iceland's best-known tourist attractions, but in 1907, it almost became a hydroelectric dam. One local fought to stop it from happening. Sigríður Tómasdóttir, a young woman with no formal education, made several arduous journeys to Reykjavík to argue for the preservation of the falls. The attention she generated led to plans for the hydroelectric plant being cancelled. The Icelandic government eventually bought the waterfall, which sat on land owned by Tómasdóttir's father and it became a national landmark in 1979. Her lawyer, Sveinn Björnsson, was later elected the first president of Iceland.

There's a small memorial to Tómasdóttir at Gullfoss.

Go White-Water Rafting

ENJOY THE SCENIC RIDE

Iceland may not be the first place you think to go white-water rafting, but rafting here is an experience you're guaranteed never to forget. Ride the Hvítá river through a majestic canyon just below thundering Gullfoss. The glacier river's name means 'white river', a reflection of the white caps rafters will find here. The canyon has been sculpted by the river, and its clear blue water flows from Langjökull, Iceland's second-largest glacier. This is a place where giant rock walls seem to softly rise out of the water and may be one of the most picturesque rafting locations in the world.

The rapids are suitable for first-time rafters and considered a Class II, which is typically a signal to expect waves, splashes and at least a little thrill, especially if you're new to rafting.

It's only warm enough to go rafting here between May and September. Tour companies provide life jackets, helmets and wetsuits, but rafters must be at least 11 years old and know how to swim. A base camp offers showers, saunas, changing rooms, a restaurant and a bar.

WHITE-WATER RAFTING COMPANIES

Arctic Adventures
Small group tours with a focus on sustainability and respecting nature.

Arctic Rafting
A local company that's been leading river rafting tours here since 1985.

Hike Breccia Rock Formations

EASY HIKING TRAIL, UNREAL VIEWS

Brúarhlöð canyon is an overlooked spot where the voluminous Hvítá river cuts through extraordinary breccia rock formations. Sharp cliffs rise from glacial water running through this narrow gorge, showing off hints of blue and green as it flows. The best views of this unique canyon are from above and don't require an arduous hike to access. The trail is under 1.5km each way with an elevation gain of just 9m. Expect it to take between 15 and 20 minutes each way and to be tempted by the peaceful picnic spots you pass on the way.

GETTING AROUND

A rental car will give you the most flexibility to visit the sights surrounding Gullfoss. All Golden Circle tours stop at the waterfall.

Public buses will take you as far as Flúðir, where you'd need hire a taxi to get to the waterfall.

Langjökull

Gullfoss

Faxafoss

Hraunalaug

Beyond Gullfoss

Glide across a magnificent glacier on a snowmobile. Fish for salmon, or enjoy the silence of a secluded hot spring.

The area surrounding Gullfoss is ripe for adventures on water and on ice. Climb onto a snowmobile to speed across a seemingly endless glacier and feel like you're speeding across the moon. Stop to explore ice formations, visit a remarkable ice cave and marvel at the many shades of blue you'll encounter on the journey. For a warmer adventure in this area, fish for salmon and gigantic sea trout on one of the country's most popular fishing rivers. Or watch fish move through a fish ladder as they make their seasonal journeys. Whatever you choose, there may be few better places to relax than a tiny secluded hot spring worlds away from the crowds.

TOP TIP

Even if you aren't fishing, stop at Faxafoss to watch jumping salmon navigate a fish ladder as they're swimming upstream during summer.

ANDRIY BLOKHIN/SHUTTERSTOCK ©

Fishing near Faxafoss (p110)

Snowmobiling, Langjökull

Snowmobile on a Glacier
SPEED ACROSS AN ICE CAP

There's no feeling quite like whizzing across a glacier on a snowmobile. **Langjökull**, which means 'long glacier', offers 935 sq km of pure adventure. This glacier is 50km long, almost 20km wide, and nearly 609m deep at its thickest point, and its highest point is almost 1.5km above sea level. Langjökull sits on top of two volcanic systems and several mountains, the tops of which sometimes peek through the ice. This is as close to the moon as you'll get on Earth. And if you're already in Gullfoss, you're almost there.

Langjökull's Klaki base camp can only be accessed by a 4WD vehicle. It's about three hours from Gullfoss by F road. Tour companies run monster-truck tours from here, adding a rough ride through the Icelandic highlands to an already unforgettable adventure. It's often possible to combine snowmobiling with other glacial adventures, such as hiking or exploring unreal natural ice caves. These tours are great for independent travellers on road trips without monster trucks. You will need a driver's licence to operate a snowmobile, and tour operators provide thermal suits and helmets. Children over six can join as passengers.

LANGJÖKULL GLACIER TOUR OPERATORS

Mountaineers of Iceland
Mountaineers of Iceland has been running snowmobile, super-Jeep and ice-cave tours on Langjökull glacier for nearly 30 years. The most popular is a half-day snowmobiling tour from Gullfoss.

Sleipnir Tours Iceland
Forget super-Jeeps, this company will whisk you through the Icelandic highlands in style in custom-made monster trucks. Spend a few hours snowmobiling on Langjökull glacier with the option to add a Golden Circle tour.

 WHERE TO EAT IN FLÚÐIR

Restaurant Minilik
This colourful Ethiopian restaurant is a pleasant surprise, with authentic food and a welcoming vibe. €€

Fish & Chips
Stop at this food stand for a quick road-trip meal or pick up picnic provisions. €

Restaurant Mika
Everything from bread to sauces and chocolate is made from scratch at this family-run restaurant. €€

Hrunalaug Hot Spring

RULES OF THE ROD

Southern Iceland's rivers are known for their ample stocks of sea trout, salmon and Arctic char. There are several places to rent fishing gear in the area. If you bring your own equipment, you have to disinfect it before you can use it in Iceland.

You do need a permit for fishing here. For lake fishing, opt for an annual fishing pass. This **Fishing Card** (veidikortid. is) provides access to dozens of lakes across the country for an entire year for under 8900kr. Rivers issue a limited number of permits each day. You'll need to purchase in advance for a specific date and location.

Prime fishing season in this area is from July through September.

Soak in a Secluded Hot Spring

A REMOTE SPOT TO RELAX

The **Hrunalaug Hot Spring**, about a half-hour's drive from Gullfoss, is so far off the beaten path you might get it all to yourself. This tiny hot spring, just outside the town of Flúðir, has three small pools, each at a different temperature. The third pool is piping hot and perfect for soaking on a winter day. Admission operates on an honour system (it's privately owned by a local farmer); you'll need to pay the 1000kr entry fee in cash. That's a bargain compared with the Blue Lagoon and Sky Lagoon, but it comes with trade-offs. There are no saunas, steam rooms or cafes. There aren't even bathrooms or changing rooms, apart from an old sheep barn that doesn't offer much privacy. But you've got a better shot at getting this secluded spot to yourself, and that might just be priceless.

Fish for Salmon at Faxafoss

A WATERFALL ABUNDANT WITH FISH

Faxafoss is an underrated waterfall and just a 20-minute drive from its famous neighbour Gullfoss. What this waterfall lacks in height, it makes up for in width (79m) and with fish. It's located on the **Tungufljót**, one of Iceland's best-known rivers for catching sea trout. The sea trout can weigh up to 13.5kg, but these huge fish aren't the only draw in this stretch of river. During the season (late June through September), you'll also find a wide pool filled with salmon at the base of the 30m Faxafoss cascade. Fishing permits are required, with only fly-fishing allowed. Salmon measuring over 68.5cm must be released back into the water.

There's a fish ladder next to the waterfall and a boardwalk that provides easy access to its base.

GETTING AROUND

You can get around this area by bus, but it won't be convenient or quick. Rent a car instead or hire a car and driver for the most flexibility and range.

GRINDAVÍK

Grindavík ⊙REYKJAVÍK

This fishing town on Iceland's southern peninsula is where you'll find the Blue Lagoon, a silica-laden complex of geothermal baths that's become an icon of Nordic wellness. Grindavík traces its history to 934 when a pair of Viking settlers first arrived to the area. Nowadays, it's a hub for Icelandic saltfish production and home to a small but informative saltfish museum. There's a campsite in town and golf and horseback riding nearby. When it's time to eat, head to Bryggjan cafe for fresh lobster, traditional Icelandic lamb or hearty vegetable soup. Or try Icelandic staples like smoked salmon sandwiches, local trout or baked salted cod. After lunch, check out the remains of the *Hrafn Sveinbjarnarson III*, a fishing boat that ran aground in 1988 on the Hópsnes peninsula near Grindavík. Everyone on board survived, but the ship's wreckage – like the remnants of other ships that have crashed here – was never moved.

TOP TIP

The Blue Lagoon's world-famous silica may work wonders for your skin, but it isn't nearly as good to your hair. Wear a swimming cap or use a leave-in conditioner to keep your hair from getting stiff and feeling like straw for the rest of your trip.

ROBERTO LA ROSA/SHUTTERSTOCK ©

Blue Lagoon (p113)   111

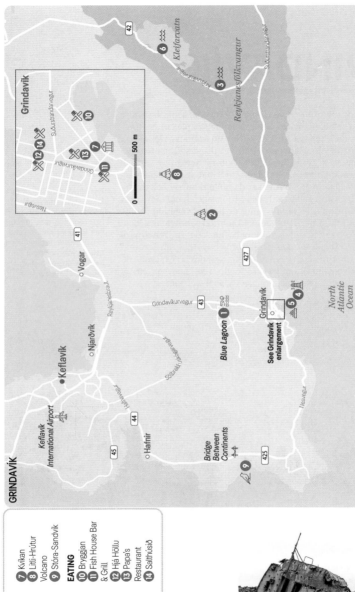

GRINDAVÍK

HIGHLIGHTS
1 Blue Lagoon

SIGHTS
2 Fagradalsfjall Volcano
3 Grænavatn
4 Hópsnes Lighthouse
5 Hrafn Sveinbjarnarson III
6 Indjánahöfði Natrure Reserve
7 Kvíkan
8 Litli-Hrútur Volcano
9 Stóra-Sandvík

EATING
10 Bryggjan
11 Fish House Bar & Grill
12 Hjá Höllu
13 Papa's Restaurant
14 Salthúsið

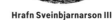

Hrafn Sveinbjarnarson III

Bathe in the Blue Lagoon
RELAX IN GEOTHERMAL WATER

The Blue Lagoon is one of Iceland's top sights – and for good reason. This oasis on the Reykjanes Peninsula is a place where steam rises from icy blue water surrounded by mossy green lava fields or snow-covered lava fields that resemble the moon, depending on the season. Walking through the sprawling geothermal bath complex is like walking through another world, especially on a snowy winter day.

The Blue Lagoon was initially a delightful curiosity, a pleasant byproduct of geothermal energy production. It has since become one of the most recognisable spas in the world. Take in unreal scenery while soaking in warm geothermal water that's bright blue because of the nourishing silica, algae and minerals it contains. Get a massage as you float in the water. Enjoy the calming effects of a facemask and a multi-step bathing ritual that makes the most of the lagoon's elements. Walk through three connected chambers, slathering your skin with silica in the first and algae in the second. The last step is to exfoliate with a scrub that's a mixture of local minerals.

The Blue Lagoon is designed for sustainability and is powered by the same geothermal energy that makes it possible. It's one of those places that almost feels natural but is human-made.

Spend a day here or settle in at one of two on-site hotels. Sample Michelin-starred Icelandic cuisine without leaving the property, and take a piece of this magical place home, with products from its skincare line.

If you're on a long layover and have time for just one thing, this is an excellent option.

Search for Shipwrecks
WRECKAGE WITH STORIES TO TELL

The Hópsnes peninsula near Grindavík is home to the rusting skeletons of several old ships. You'll find almost a dozen old shipwrecks scattered across the shoreline. These shipwreck sites show just how dangerous the water – and the fishing businesses that keep this town and much of Iceland going – can be. Most wrecks have signs that tell the ship's story, though salt has beaten down the text on some markers. One of the best-known shipwrecks in this area is the **Hrafn Sveinbjarnarson III**. This fishing boat ran ashore on a cold February morning in 1988 but all on board survived. The remains of the ship were never moved.

EXPLORE MORE ICELANDIC NATURE

The **Fagradalsfjall volcano** erupted in 2021, spewing lava for months. After six months, the lava stopped flowing, but it's still possible to hike the site. In 2023, the **Litli-Hrútur volcano** erupted and hiking paths were quickly established around the site.

It's possible to access the starting point of Litli-Hrútur's hikes by car, but a guided volcano tour is your best bet for exploring this area safely. Remember, volcano hikes are often hours-long experiences covering many kilometres.

For a less strenuous volcanic experience, drive around **Grænavatn**, a volcanic crater lake with a unique green tint caused by high sulphur levels. The **Indjánahöfði Nature Preserve** is a peaceful spot at the edge of this moody lake.

 CASUAL EATS IN GRINDAVÍK

Papa's Restaurant
A family-friendly quick-service restaurant that offers package deals on family meals. €€

Fish House Bar & Grill
A relaxed spot for fresh fish and creative crab dishes and a beer. €€

Bryggjan
A spacious harbourside restaurant best known for its lobster, lamb and vegetable soups. €€

WHERE TO EAT SALTFISH

Salthúsið
This quaint and cosy restaurant is dedicated to salted cod, the fish so important to the local economy it landed on the Icelandic coat of arms. The menu includes burgers, chicken sandwiches and vegetarian items.
€€

Hjá Höllu
A health-focused restaurant known for its harbour-fresh cod fillet served with peanut salsa. €€

While you're here, check out the bright orange **Hópsnes lighthouse**. You'll also find hiking and biking trails in this area. Pay attention to the signs, as you're going to get a better idea of the ships that sailed – and wrecked – here.

Cross Rare Species off Your List
LOOK FOR BIRDS

There's no shortage of **birdwatching** opportunities in Iceland, a country with few predators to eat endangered birds. Several excellent birdwatching spots are in this area, as Grindavík is one of the first destinations for lost US birds migrating from the west. Head to the shore or a nearby garden to look for gulls. If you're lucky, you may spot a rare gull, such as Ross's gull, Franklin's gull or Bonaparte's gull. Look for whooper swans, geese, ducks and red-necked phalaropes at the **Stóra-Sandvík** inlet. Or head to the **Reykjanes cape** to see the only Arctic tern colony located in a geothermal area. This picturesque spot is excellent for seabird watching. Fulmars, kittiwakes, razorbills and gannet can all be seen around here.

You'll find white-winged scoters, velvet scoters and large flocks of eiders in **Víkur**.

The best time for birdwatching here depends on what you want to see. If you're looking for breeding species, plan your trip between late May and June when migrant birds have arrived and are fighting for territory. To add rare species to your list, pack a raincoat and visit between September and November.

Learn about Iceland's Fish Traditions
SALTFISH SOUP, ANYONE?

Saltfish is an Icelandic tradition. This method of preserving cod in salt built the Icelandic economy in the late 19th and 20th centuries and continues to support the local financial industry. The **Kvíkan**, a saltfish museum, honours the tradition while bringing visitors up to speed on the practicalities of preserving fish and the huge effect it had on Iceland. Freshly caught cod is split, washed, beheaded and stacked in layers. Salt is placed between the layers and the fish are left to dry. Saltfish was a staple of Icelandic diets that has since become a sought-after delicacy in parts of the Mediterranean and Africa. It's often cooked in tomato broth or another type of soup.

This museum makes you feel like you're right there alongside the fishers and fish-farm staff doing this work. See what old farms looked like and how the process of making saltfish has evolved. It's an interesting peek into the work that's gone into making this region, and Iceland, what it is today, and an excellent introduction to Grindavík.

GETTING AROUND

Renting a car will give you the most flexibility to explore this area. There's bus service from Keflavík International Airport directly to the Blue Lagoon. Limited bus service is also available between the airport and Grindavík.

Beyond Grindavík

Keflavík
Njarðvík
Bridge Between Continents
Krýsuvík
Gunnuhver
Grindavík
Valahnúkamöl Brimetkill

A dramatic landscape of lava fields, towering cliffs and scenic viewpoints, where volcanic eruptions are common.

Volcanic activity isn't uncommon on the Reykjanes Peninsula, which has seen at least three volcanic eruptions since 2020. The Reykjanes Peninsula where Grindavík lies is an active volcanic zone and eruptions draw tourists from around the world. Vast lava fields stretch endlessly in the middle of nowhere, punctuated by bubbling geysers. Lighthouses, rugged cliffs and scenic viewpoints are features of the coastline.

This is the only place in the world where you can walk from Europe to North America. And, depending on your timing, you may be able to witness hot lava flowing from a fresh eruption. Check safetravel.is for safety information before attempting to explore eruption zones on your own.

TOP TIP

Flexibility is key to visiting volcanic eruption zones. Prepare to book last-minute and choose refundable flights for easy changes.

HANDMADEPICTURES/SHUTTERSTOCK ©

SAGAS, LEGENDS & FOLKLORE

Every natural wonder here has its legend in Iceland. Celtic fairy tales, Nordic sagas and stories from Christianity come together to explain a mysterious landscape where geology and science don't always deliver answers. Here, folklore is interwoven with history.

Legends have circulated here since at least the 12th century when they began appearing in Icelandic literature. One folktale suggests the majestic towering rocks at Reynisdrangar are the remains of trolls frozen in stone because they were out past sunrise.

These stories are believed to have been an effort to help children manage growing up in this rugged unforgiving landscape, and pretty much every spectacular natural formation in Iceland has a tale associated with it.

LOVISAFALS/SHUTTERSTOCK ©

Brimetkill

Discover a Hidden Lava Rock Pool
NATURE'S COASTAL CREATION

Few places in the world look more wild and idyllic than **Brimetkill**, the lava rock pool at the edge of the Atlantic Ocean on Iceland's southern coast. This spot is just a 10-minute drive from Grindavík. Go on a sunny day to see the rocks beneath the surface of the water and Brimetkill's full range of blues. This lava pool is so perfect it looks human-made, though nature is what has carved it into the rugged coastline. A walkway and viewing platform since 2023 have made this spot easier to find, but there's no pathway to the pool itself. The waves here can be powerful and fierce, so swimming, soaking, lounging and going beyond the bounds of the platform aren't allowed. It wouldn't be a pleasant experience anyway. Unlike the Blue Lagoon (p113) and Secret Lagoon (p100), which are filled with warm geothermal water, Brimetkill is filled with

 BEST RESTAURANTS IN KEFLAVÍK

Kef Restaurant
Inside Hotel Keflavík. Indulgent brunch on the weekends and fine tasting menus for dinner. €€

Fernando's
This spot is popular for both its lobster pizza and its lobster linguine. €€

Fiskbarinn
Inside Hotel Berg. Tasting menu with a romantic harbour view. Fine dining with huge flavour. €€€

icy cold Atlantic Ocean water. In the winter, this can be an excellent spot for aurora-borealis viewing when the conditions are right.

Smell the Geysers

THE MUDDY TOE OF REYKJANES

Driving up, the **Gunnuhver Geothermal Area** on Reykjanes Peninsula looks like any other collection of Icelandic geysers. But it soon becomes clear that it's not. Gunnuhver, about 15 minutes from Grindavík, is in the heart of the Reykjanes geopark where the North Atlantic Ridge rises from the ocean, creating craters, lava fields, bird cliffs and geothermal hot spots like this one. Gunnuhver is a geothermal area that engages all the senses. Smell the scent of sulphur lingering in the air. See steam rising from cracks in a landscape that looks almost like Van Gogh painted it. Hear bubbles and gurgles grow louder and quieter as you follow the wooden footpath through. You might want to stand still when the wind blows: shifting winds can quickly envelop you in steam. This is where you'll find Iceland's largest mud pool. The 20m mud pit boils vigorously and is impossible to miss. Mud pools form when steam from boiling geothermal water condenses and mixes with surface water and carbon dioxide and hydrogen sulfide, causing fresh lava rock to turn to clay. The springs here are constantly growing and evolving. The remnants of a previous platform, one the springs physically grew out of, are still here.

Walk from Europe to North America

A BRIDGE BETWEEN CONTINENTS

It's not often that one can walk from Europe to North America, but in this corner of Iceland it's easy to do – and in just a few minutes. The **Bridge Between Continents** is a 15m footbridge across the sandy rift that separates the Eurasian and North American tectonic plates. Fissures form as the plates move against one another. This bridge crosses a major fissure. A sign in the middle of the bridge marks the division between North America and Europe. The bridge, named **Leif the Lucky Bridge** after Icelandic explorer Leif Erikson, is surrounded by lava fields and small craters. Just 20 minutes from Grindavík, it feels like a bridge in the middle of nowhere and the landscape could almost fool you into thinking you're on the moon. On a clear day, you can see Eldey island – a sanctuary for thousands of seabirds – from here. Visit the Reykjanes Geopark visitor centre for a personalised certificate to commemorate your crossing.

WHERE TO RIDE ICELANDIC HORSES

Sólvangur Icelandic Horse Centre
A family-run stable with horseback riding suitable for beginners, near the town of Selfoss.

Bakkahestar Horse Riding Tours
Horseback riding on the beach with friendly horses and patient instructors.

 BEST BARS IN KEFLAVÍK

Library Bistro & Bar	**Brons**	**Paddy's Irish Pub**
This stylish cocktail bar and restaurant offers happy hour from 3pm to 7pm every day.	A local bar that specialises in darts and is spacious enough to accommodate large groups.	A dimly lit Irish pub where the bartenders know how to properly pour a Guinness.

DANITA DELIMONT/ALAMY STOCK PHOTO ©

Viking World

WHERE TO SHOP FOR WOOL

Þingborg Wool Shop, Selfoss
Shop here for handmade wool products made by a local collective of women in South Iceland. It specialises in farm-to-sweater clothing. Select from hats, socks, mittens, sweaters and more. Or pick up some yarn to take home.

Uppspuni Mini Mill, Hella
This gem in the Icelandic countryside is more than just a wool shop. The wool here is made from the farm's own sheep and processed in a mill downstairs. Check out the workshop before picking up some yarn for later.

Take in Epic Scenery

CLIFFS, CRASHING WAVES AND EUROVISION

Valahnúkamöl, a collection of giant rocks that rise from the sea about 20 minutes from Grindavík, is one of the most scenic parts of the southern Icelandic coast. This is where towering cliffs meet crashing waves, a place that can look wildly different depending on the season and time of day. Hike to the top of the hill for a bird's-eye view of this magical stretch of rugged coastline. Check out the bronze great auk sculpture, an ode to a now-extinct flightless bird that once nested here. These birds bred on isolated rocky islands and thrived, with easy access to the ocean and a steady supply of food, making Iceland an ideal nesting spot. The last two auks in the world are believed to have been killed in the mid-1800s on Eldey island, which sits about 16km off the coast. And get up close to the two red keyboards commemorating the filming of the Will Ferrell movie *Eurovision Song Contest: The Story of Fire Saga*. This is where the Volcano Man scene was shot.

WHERE TO STAY IN KEFLAVÍK

Hotel Berg
A modern boutique hotel with a dreamy rooftop pool minutes from Keflavík International Airport. €€

Hotel Keflavik
A recently renovated family-owned hotel with a gym, sauna, restaurant and bar in the building. €€

Diamond Suites
A hotel within the Hotel Keflavík, with over-the-top luxury suites and impeccable service. €€€

Rock 'n' Roll in Keflavík

AN ODE TO ICELANDIC MUSIC

If you're a fan of Björk, Sigur Rós or Of Monsters and Men, you won't want to miss the **Museum of Rock 'n' Roll** in Keflavík, a 20-minute drive from Grindavík by car or a 32-minute journey by bus. If you aren't a fan of these legendary Icelandic musicians, come here to discover what you're missing.

Just a short drive from the airport, this fun museum lays out Icelandic music history and has a sound lab where you can play electric drums, electric guitars or electric bass. There's also a karaoke booth to record your own music video.

The museum has a cavernous hallway where you can walk through music history. Documentaries about Icelandic musicians play all day long, and there are ample opportunities to learn how and why so many musicians from this tiny island nation have found global success through a collection that includes costumes, instruments and other Icelandic pop and rock memorabilia.

It may not look like much more than a warehouse on the outside, but don't let that fool you. This highly interactive museum is an excellent place to spend a few hours, especially in inclement weather.

Climb Aboard a Replica Viking Ship

TASTE VIKING LIFE

This architectural gem in Njarðvík, about 20 minutes by car from Grindavík, is a sight to behold. Designed by Iceland architect Guðmundur Jónsson, **Viking World** is a museum with walls of glass meant to reflect the beauty of Viking ships. It's the kind of structure you could stand and stare at for hours. You can see the main attraction, *The Icelander*, from the outside, but you'll want to go inside to board the ship. This replica Viking ship made of pine and oak sailed to New York in 2000 to commemorate Leif Eriksson's journey a thousand years earlier. The ship is made of 18 tonnes of wood, 5000 nails and a Danish sail. Take a look below the ship and get an idea of what it might have been like to sail the seas alongside Vikings.

Other exhibits tell the story of Norse seafaring and the settlement of Iceland.

This is a great option for escaping the airport for a couple of hours if your flight is delayed. It's about 25 minutes from the airport on the Line 1 public bus.

ABOUT GOLDEN CIRCLE TOURS

The Golden Circle is Iceland's premier route for sightseeing, and you don't need to rent a car to see it. Several companies offer Golden Circle tours that stop at Þingvellir National Park (p88), Gullfoss (p105) and the Geysir (p99) geothermal area. These tours can be done in a day, and some operators tack on things like ATV rides, horseback riding and glacial adventures. Some tours combine the Golden Circle with a visit to the Blue Lagoon (p113) or Sky Lagoon (p72). Others add sites, making the route more of a diamond than a circle. Some take you across this wild landscape in modified Jeeps and monster trucks. There's sure to be a tour here for you.

 BAKERIES & COFFEE

Kökulist Bakery
A broad variety of bakery items and lots of options for light breakfasts and lunches in Keflavík. €

Sigurjónsbakarí
A comfortable, welcoming spot for coffee and pastries near Keflavík International Airport. €

Blue Lagoon Cafe
The Blue Lagoon's most casual eating establishment. Come here for sandwiches, coffees and light meals. €€

ODDVAR ELGVIN/SHUTTERSTOCK ©

Krýsuvík

BEST CAFES IN KEFLAVÍK

Cafe Petite
An adorable place for a beer, a casual meal and a walk down memory lane.

Library Bistro Bar
A picturesque bistro with leather sofas, delicious meals and live music.

Explore Hot Springs & Mud Pools

BUBBLING SPRINGS SURROUNDED BY COLOUR

This colourful geothermal area in Krýsuvík is among the easiest to visit on the Reykjanes Peninsula. Wooden walkways cross the uneven earth and an abundance of signage explains where you are and what you're seeing. This is a landscape that looks like another planet. Steam rises from hot, icy blue pools in varying shades of orange and yellow earth. Listen for the bubbling of mud pools. Smell the sulphur in the air, and hear the hissing of vents in the mud in this other dimension, a place that looks like a painting, though the scent here will eventually bring you back to reality.

This geothermal area is an easy 25-minute drive from Grindavík.

GETTING AROUND

It's possible to get to the Blue Lagoon by bus, but you'll want to rent a car if you're planning to chase lighthouses or Northern Lights.

Public bus service is available through Strætó in Keflavík.

SELFOSS

REYKJAVÍK

Selfoss

Not to be confused with a northern waterfall of the same name, Selfoss is a college town and the largest residential area on Iceland's South Coast. It has a pedestrian-friendly town centre, several restaurants and a trendy food hall that opened in 2021 in a former dairy processing plant. There are a handful of hotels, guesthouses and vacation rentals in Selfoss as well as a few hostels and nearby camping areas. From Selfoss, it's a short drive to Kerið crater, one of Iceland's best-known and most striking craters and part of extended Golden Circle itineraries. Head to nearby Hella for waterfalls and caves. Check out an authentic turf farm. Visit the bubbling geysers at Hveragerði. Try fresh bread baked over a hot spring or try making your own steam-cooked eggs. The area surrounding Selfoss is home to several remote hotels perfect for late-night aurora borealis viewing and reconnecting with nature.

TOP TIP

Selfoss has been the heart of the Icelandic dairy industry since the 1930s. The town's historic Old Dairy has been transformed into a lively food hall and hotel complex that's a convenient stop for even the pickiest eaters on Ring Road trips around the country.

TOMSICKOVA TATYANA/SHUTTERSTOCK ©

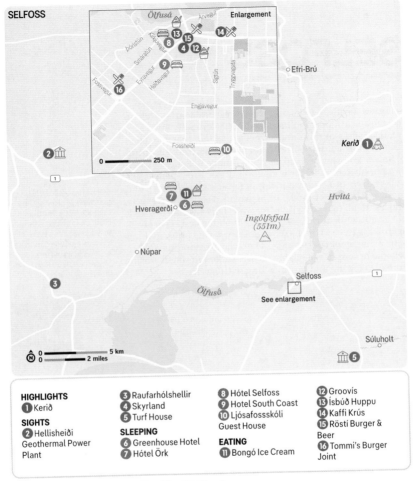

HIGHLIGHTS
1 Kerið

SIGHTS
2 Hellisheiði Geothermal Power Plant

3 Raufarhólshellir
4 Skyrland
5 Turf House

SLEEPING
6 Greenhouse Hotel
7 Hótel Örk

8 Hótel Selfoss
9 Hotel South Coast
10 Ljósafossskóli Guest House

EATING
11 Bongó Ice Cream

12 Groovís
13 Ísbúð Huppu
14 Kaffi Krús
15 Rösti Burger & Beer
16 Tommi's Burger Joint

Hike Kerið Crater

A COLOURFUL CRATER

One of Iceland's best-known volcanic craters is less than a half-hour's drive from Selfoss. Visiting Kerið feels like walking into a painting of a perfect aquamarine lake surrounded by a blanket of reds, greens and yellows. Kerið is the most striking of several crater lakes in Iceland's western volcanic zone and is

 BEST ICE CREAM IN SELFOSS & AROUND

Bongó Ice Cream
A gorgeous spot for delicious ice cream inside the Greenhouse Hotel in Hveragerði. €

Ísbúð Huppu
Tasty ice cream and even better milkshakes in Selfoss. Take a number and wait to be called. €

Groovís
If there's one thing that makes ice cream better, it's doughnuts. Stop by this place in Selfoss for both. €

believed to have formed when one of the earth's magma chambers depleted itself, caving in to create this colourful natural wonder. Most craters are the result of explosions.

Much of Kerið is made of rich red volcanic rock, but its least steep slope is a bed of mossy green during the summers. Hints of yellow are a reflection of the land's sulphur content.

Visitors can walk around the lake – Björk once performed a concert from a raft in the middle of it – in about 30 minutes or walk from the viewing platform down to the lake in about 15 minutes. There's a lakeside bench with epic sunset views at the bottom of the stairs. From here, it's easy to see the blue-green variations in the crystal-clear water and to the rocks at the bottom of the lake. The lake usually freezes during winter and comes to resemble an ice rink; the caldera isn't as colourful at this time, but there is something charming about seeing it covered in snow and icicles. There's a small fee to access the crater and a small car park outside but no restrooms or cafe.

Visit a Power Plant
AN UNUSUAL BUT POWERFUL EXPERIENCE

A working power station may seem like an odd place to visit on holiday, but this detour to **Hellisheiði Geothermal Power Plant** – located just past the Hveradalir Geothermal Area – is worth it, particularly for anyone interested in climate change and renewable energy. Nearly all of its power comes from renewable sources. More than 85% of Icelandic homes are heated by renewable sources, such as geothermal energy. Geothermal power supports nearly 30% of Iceland's energy needs, and a handful of geothermal power plants like this one are scattered across the country. A museum inside the power station brings sustainable energy to life, with exhibits on hydropower, geothermal energy and wind energy. Learn how water is used to generate electricity and how a power station works. The exhibit isn't huge, but it is free and insightful – for both kids and adults.

Wander Around a Turf House Farm
THE JEWEL OF ARCTIC ARCHITECTURE

You'll find one of Iceland's best-preserved turf farms just south of Selfoss. The Icelandic turf house is considered a jewel of Arctic architecture. These structures used soil as insulation from the elements, keeping early Icelanders sheltered from harsh weather. The exhibits here explain how turf houses were built and how they've evolved over time. This is a must-see for anyone interested in architecture and local storytelling from a

BEST PLACES TO STAY IN SELFOSS

Greenhouse Hotel
A comfortable hotel that looks and feels like a greenhouse. Enjoy the food hall downstairs. €€

Hotel South Coast
Offers comfortable rooms, exudes Nordic style. Expansive breakfast buffet and eight wheelchair-accessible rooms. €

Hótel Selfoss
A relaxing hotel with comfortable rooms, river views and a dreamy spa. €€

Ljósafossskóli Guest House
Former boarding school turned hostel, with single, double, family rooms and shared bathrooms. There's a laundry, sports court and playground. €

Hótel Örk
Stylish hotel with modern rooms. Has a hot tub, a geothermal sauna and an outdoor swimming pool with a water slide. €€

 CASUAL EATS IN SELFOSS

Kaffi Krús
A cute cafe for a casual lunch. It has an extensive and creative pizza list. €

Tommi's Burger Joint
Simple burgers with flavourful beef patties, and fries served in baskets. €

Rösti Burger & Beer
This restaurant is as straightforward as its gets. Come here for burgers, beers and views. €€

VISIT SKYRLAND

The Skyrland museum inside the Old Dairy Site is all about the world-famous Icelandic superfood: *skyr*. Learn how recipes were passed down through families for more than 1000 years. Begin to understand the role *skyr* played in the development of the Icelandic nation, and find out what goes into every delicious spoonful of this high-protein health food.

This museum speaks to each of the five senses, with opportunities to touch, see, hear, smell and taste the things that go into making *skyr*. Interactive exhibits are designed to keep kids entertained, and do a good job of entertaining adults as well. There's a tasting opportunity at the end of the tour and a *skyr* bar on-site.

Raufarhólshellir

proprietor who lived here as a child decades ago. There are several structures on the property, as well as a cafe and a playground. There's no better way to understand the challenges of living in Iceland than to step into one of these unique constructions.

Hike a Lava Tunnel

JOURNEY THROUGH MAGICAL ROCK FORMATIONS

Iceland is a country filled with lava tunnels, tubes and caves. This one is well worth a visit and can be a great spot to catch the Northern Lights if your timing is right. At almost 1.4km, **Raufarhólshellir** is one of the longest lava tunnels in Iceland. It's just 30 minutes outside of Reykjavík and walking into it is surreal. The tunnel was created by hot-flowing lava an estimated 5000 years ago. The lava bashed against the mountains here, creating falls and clearing a path that's up to 10m high and nearly 30.5m wide. The interior carries a red tint. A hole at the top of the tunnel allows light in during the day and occasionally lets in the Northern Lights on dark winter nights. There's no lava flowing here now, but walking through a tunnel carved by lava is still a powerful and thought-provoking experience. Expect to feel small against the forces of nature.

This tunnel can only be visited on guided tours. The standard tour includes a walk across a sprawling lava field, all the necessary equipment, and a chance to walk into this natural formation. A longer three- to four-hour tour option is available. That tour requires good balance and reasonable physical fitness. Both tours are best done in sturdy hiking shoes and a light jacket, even during the summer. Temperatures inside the tunnel are typically around 2°C. Helmets and headlamps are included with your visit.

This tunnel is just a half-hour's drive from Reykjavík, making it an easy option for a day trip from the capital. The area visited on the standard tour is wide and cavernous, so it's perfect for travellers looking to experience a lava tube without feeling like they're *in* a lava tube!

GETTING AROUND

Renting a car will give you the greatest flexibility to explore the surrounding area, but you can also take the number 51 bus from Reykjavík. There are 33 scheduled buses a week, and the ride takes about 50 minutes.

Hveragerði

Selfoss

Hella

Eyrarbakki

Hvolsvöllur

Beyond Selfoss

This region is home to charming fishing towns, pretty waterfalls, fresh lobster and a little bit of WWII history.

The area around Selfoss is one of the most interesting in Iceland. It includes remnants of the greatest lava flow on Earth since the Ice Age. See where the North Atlantic Ocean stopped the lava and the unique landscape that was left behind at Þjórsárhraun. Experience a mini-earthquake and learn about how volcanoes have shaped Icelandic life at the Lava Centre in Hvolsvöllur. Iceland's longest river, the Þjórsá, flows through this area, forming stunning waterfalls and picturesque views along the way. There are a handful of small heritage museums, such as the Eyrarbakki Maritime Museum, along the coastline and a half-dozen or so historic churches. Restaurants in coastal Eyrarbakki are known for their fresh, delicious lobster.

TOP TIP

Head inside the Sunnumörk Shopping Center in Hveragerði for a look between tectonic plates. The crack was discovered during construction.

THOMAS MARX/SHUTTERSTOCK ®

Church, Eyrarbakki

ARCTIC IMAGES/ALAMY STOCK PHOTO ©

Lava Centre

BEST PLACES TO STAY IN HELLA

Hotel Rangá
Icelandic luxury with fine dining and a backdrop of Northern Lights. €€€

Glass Cottages Iceland
These glass cottages in the middle of sprawling lava fields are every bit as magical as they look. Stay here to experience the Northern Lights without having to brave the cold. €€€

Stracta Hotel
This hotel oozes Nordic style at a good-value price. There's an on-site restaurant as well as saunas and outdoor hot tubs. €€

Walk Through an Earthquake

FEEL THE EARTH SHAKE

There may be no better place for a museum dedicated to the study of lava and volcanic activity. The **Lava Centre** in Hvolsvöllur, a 40-minute drive from Selfoss, sits in the shadows of several volcanoes, including the notorious Eyjafjallajökull, whose 2010 eruption caused the closure of large swaths of European airspace; Katla, one of Iceland's largest volcanoes; and Hekla, one of Iceland's most active volcanoes. It's also within a two-hour drive of Fagradalsfjall, the volcano that erupted in 2021.

This museum offers a hands-on geology lesson that fills in the backstory of Iceland's wildest landscapes. Interactive displays bring the wild south Icelandic terrain to life, explaining how volcanoes work and why there are so many of them here. Head into the museum to experience a few seconds of shaking and get an idea of what an earthquake would feel like at three different strengths. You can touch lava rocks and there's even an exhibit that looks almost like real, flowing lava. Don't leave before heading to the building's roof to check out the

 WHERE TO EAT IN HVERAGERÐI ──────────

Ölverk Pizza & Brewery
Family-owned brewery powered by geothermal energy offers craft beer and wood-fired pizza. €€

Rósakaffi
Eating here feels like eating in a greenhouse. Stop for sandwiches, salads and snacks. €€

Greenhouse Food Hall
Tacos, noodles, ice cream and more under one roof. What more could you want? €

volcano views. On a clear day, you can see Hekla, Katla and Eyjafjallajökull and more from the roof.

Tour the Caves of Hella

FOUR CAVES, MANY MYSTERIES

This collection of caves opened to the public in late 2019. Visitors can go inside four of the 12 caves, including one believed to have been a chapel at some point. The four caves open to visitors on guided tours are sparsely decorated with crosses and ancient wall carvings. Beyond a small piece of rail track – a rarity in Iceland – there isn't much inside these caves. Still, the walls tell stories of being expanded and repurposed, giving hints as to who may have sought shelter here and why, while locking some secrets firmly into the past. Whisky tastings are occasionally hosted here, and the cave's chapel is a popular spot for weddings. The caves are located just off the Ring Road about a half-hour's drive or 45-minute bus ride from Selfoss, and a large sign makes the site easy to find. There's a small snack bar and a souvenir shop on-site and a collection of sheep in the grass by the car park.

Follow the Steam

COOK EGGS IN NATURE'S KITCHEN

Hveragerði, about 15 minutes' drive from Selfoss, is a small town that's big on hot springs and greenhouses. The town's first greenhouse was built in 1923. Horticulture has been a local pastime ever since. This is the northernmost place in the world where bananas grow. Tomatoes, flowers and cocoa plants are also grown here, and the greenhouses that house them really are green; like most of the town, they're heated by the hot volcanic spring water that runs beneath the surface of the ground. Students at a local horticultural school grow the crops and open their greenhouses to the public on the first day of summer every year.

This is the only place in Iceland where there are hot springs in the centre of town. Hveragerði even translates to 'the steam valley'. These hot springs aren't as active as they were before an earthquake in 2008 that caused several to dry up. Still, the spring water is hot enough to boil eggs and bake bread, and that's exactly what happens here. For about 600kr, visitors to this geothermal area can boil an egg in a hot spring and sample fresh bread that's been baked in lava instead of an oven. Hang around for a half-hour and you'll likely see at least one geyser erupt. Continue heading west on the Ring Road and you'll come across another geothermal area worth

BEST PLACES FOR SEAFOOD

Rauða Húsið Restaurant
You'll find this charming restaurant in an old house in Eyrarbakki, the village where lobster fishing began in Iceland in 1954. €€

Hafið Bláa Restaurant With A View
A beautiful restaurant in Þorlákshöfn with fresh lobster and ocean views. Even if you don't eat here, stop for a picture with the giant lobster outside. €€

Fjöruborðið
Head to nearby Stokkseyri, also an old fishing town, to feast on lobster soup and this restaurant's signature lobster tails. €€

 WHERE TO STAY BEYOND SELFOSS

Hótel Grímsborgir
A high-end, luxury hotel set across 16 buildings on an idyllic patch of nature. €€€

Hotel Vatnsholt
This countryside hotel offers family rooms, making it ideal for groups as well as families. €€

Art Hostel
Shared dorms or private en-suite rooms with perks such as kitchenettes, hangers and flowers. €

DENNIS JACOBSEN/SHUTTERSTOCK ©

Long-tailed duck

BEST CAFES & BAKERIES

Auðkúla Dome Cafe
This adorable cafe in Hella is set inside a clear dome that makes you feel like you're eating in a dreamy forest greenhouse. €

Almar Bakari
Stop here in Hveragerði for a quick lunch and to pick up some lava-baked bread for the road. €

GK Bakari
This Selfoss bakery has a huge selection of pastries and makes an Icelandic rye with cranberries and seeds. €

stopping for. With just a little bit of snow on the ground, this place might just convince you you've landed on the moon.

Look for Wetland Birds

ICELAND HAS MORE THAN PUFFINS

The **Flói Nature Reserve** is the hidden wetland attraction of Eyrarbakki, a tiny fishing village that's home to around 600 people. More than 70 types of birds have been spotted in the wetlands here. In spring and summer, greylag geese and white-fronted geese pass through, as do wigeon, tufted duck, and waders like snipe. During the winter, mostly gulls make their home here. Long-tailed duck and common eider make occasional appearances. This nature reserve encompasses the eastern bank of the Ölfusá river. These areas of marshlands, pools and ponds are internationally recognised bird sanctuaries.

GETTING AROUND

You'll need to rent a car to get around this area. Public buses don't run to the coastal towns here, but there is a bus between Selfoss and Hveragerði. Buses run about once an hour with some exceptions during the day. The journey takes about 15 minutes.

SKÓGAFOSS

REYKJAVÍK ⚙ Skógafoss

Skógafoss waterfall is located in Skógar, a tiny village at the southern edge of the Eyjafjallajökull glacier. Skógar is renowned for its waterfall, but in the summer it is a gateway to the majestic mountains and colourful valleys of the highlands. Let the sound of thundering water wake you in your cosy tent. Hike to the top of Skógafoss and, if you're ambitious, keep going. Follow a hiking trail past dozens of waterfalls on the Skógá river and continue on a multiday camping journey through the highlands.

Discover rural Icelandic history at the Skógar Museum, where visitors can wander through old turf houses, get up close to an old fishing boat and learn how transport across this vast, wild geography has changed over the decades. Nearby, put on a pair of crampons and set out on a magical guided glacial hike at Sólheimajökull (p143).

TOP TIP

Thanks in part to Justin Bieber and social media, the epic waterfalls here are popular. To avoid peak crowds during the summer, take advantage of the midnight sun by visiting in the late evening or early morning. It'll look like daytime, and your photos will have fewer people in them.

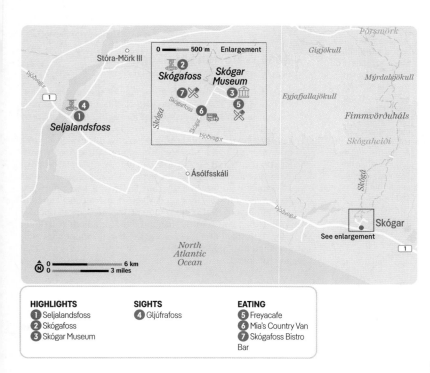

HIGHLIGHTS
1 Seljalandsfoss
2 Skógafoss
3 Skógar Museum

SIGHTS
4 Gljúfrafoss

EATING
5 Freyacafe
6 Mia's Country Van
7 Skógafoss Bistro Bar

CHENG YUAN/SHUTTERSTOCK ©

Seljalandsfoss waterfall

WHY I LOVE SKÓGAFOSS

Meena Thiruvengadam, writer

I'm a city girl who has spent most of the past 15 years living in New York, Chicago, London and Washington, DC. I've become adept at falling asleep to the sound of sirens and navigating chaotic crowded streets on foot.

Skógafoss is the opposite of all that. Stand at the base of Skógafoss and the sound of rushing water drowns out everything else. You can hear the power behind the water and feel a chill in the air, even during the summer when the bright green grass stands out against the midnight sun.

I'm not sure there's a more peaceful place in south Iceland to spend a late summer night.

Chase Waterfalls at Skógafoss

EXPERIENCE 25m OF CASCADING WATER

Skógar is built around Skógafoss, one of the largest waterfalls in Iceland. The 25m-wide waterfall is a popular filming location, so don't be surprised if it looks familiar. The *Secret Life of Walter Mitty* and *Eurovision Song Contest: The Story of Fire Saga* were both filmed here, and for good reason. This waterfall looks like something straight out of a postcard. Its width and 61m drop come together to create a powerful spray and unforgettable scene. There's a staircase on the eastern edge of the falls that leads to a sweeping view over the cascades. Experienced hikers may continue along toward Fimmvörðuháls (p135), one of Iceland's most popular hiking trails, and into the Icelandic highlands. If you're not up for that much of a hike, chase the two dozen or so waterfalls you'll find along the 8km stretch of the Skógá river that leads to Skógafoss.

 WHERE TO EAT IN SKÓGAR

Skógafoss Bistro Bar
A hotel restaurant with a varied menu built around fresh, locally sourced ingredients. €€

Freyacafe
A pretty cafe inside the Skógar museum serving up beautiful coffee drinks and excellent desserts. €€

Mia's Country Van
A food truck specialising in fish and chips, perfect for a road-trip lunch. €

Go Back in Time

A MUSEUM NOT TO MISS

Visit the **Skógar Museum** to learn about Icelandic history through the evolution of local architecture. Start at the old turf houses that anchor the museum. These basaltic rock structures from the mid- to late 1800s are roofed with turf, giving them the strength to withstand harsh Icelandic winters. The museum grounds are also home to the first wooden house built in Iceland. That house was built entirely of driftwood in 1878 and lived in until 1974. There's also a reconstructed elementary school from the early 1900s and a small hydroelectric power plant from 1929.

The museum opened in 1949 and was curated by the same person until 2013. It's home to more than 15,000 items and maintains a large collection of fishing artefacts, historic agricultural items, and household goods. Self-sufficiency was key in rural Iceland in the late 1800s and early 1900s, making for a particularly interesting collection.

Guided tours are available in English, German and Icelandic, but reservations are required. Tours may also be available in French, Spanish, Norwegian and Danish.

Walk Around the Famous Seljalandsfoss

ICELAND'S ONLY 360-DEGREE-VIEW WATERFALL

Unless you're planning to move here, there are many more waterfalls in Iceland than you'll have time to visit. **Seljalandsfoss** is worth your time and effort; it's one of Iceland's most famous waterfalls. Justin Bieber filmed a music video here. Shah Rukh Khan danced here with Kareena Kapoor in a Bollywood movie. There's a good chance you've seen this 61m beauty before, but there's still nothing like experiencing it for yourself.

One reason Seljalandsfoss is special is that you can walk all the way around it. This is the only opportunity you'll have to get a 360-degree view of a waterfall in Iceland, and you'll want to. The views from the sides and behind the falls are some of the best, but prepare to get wet; this area is always misty and walking paths can get slippery. The water leading into Seljalandsfoss comes from the Eyjafjallajökull glacier that sits on top of the volcano that erupted in 2010 and disrupted European air traffic.

A 2km trail connects Seljalandsfoss with **Gljúfrafoss**, a 40m waterfall too often overlooked on the South Coast. Peek at its magnificence through the cliffs that allow Gljúfrafoss to play peekaboo with visitors.

FILMED IN SOUTH ICELAND

Rogue One: A Star Wars Story
The first *Star Wars* spinoff was filmed on the southern coast of Iceland, which served as a substitute for Jordan in the 2016 science fiction movie.

Game of Thrones
You'll recognise black-sand Reynisfjara Beach and its towering basalt columns from season seven of this HBO series.

Star Trek: Into Darkness
Reynisfjara Beach played outer space in this 2013 *Star Trek* movie.

Dilwale
Parts of this 2015 Bollywood film were shot at Skógafoss and Reynisfjara Beach. At one point, Shah Rukh Khan emerges from a flock of birds near the Reynisdrangar rock formations.

GETTING AROUND

A rental car and willingness to hike short distances will give you the most flexibility and best scenery. You can also get from Reykjavík to Skógafoss by bus. The public bus operator Strætó operates two buses a day between

Reykjavík and the Skógar campsite: Route 52. Reykjavík Excursions runs a Highland Bus service between Reykjavík and Skógar during the summer.

Fimmvörðuháls

Vestmannaeyjar   **Skógafoss**

Heimaey

Beyond Skógafoss

From the magnificent Icelandic highlands
to the rugged Vestmannaeyjar and endless
picturesque waterfalls, there's lots to see here.

Skógar is a gateway to more than two dozen waterfalls, the
Icelandic highlands, and an island whose fate was forever
changed when a volcano erupted in 1973. Experienced hikers can begin the ambitious Fimmvörðuháls trail into the Icelandic highlands from the base of Skógafoss. Or turn back
around a few waterfalls into the hike and head for the coast.
Catch a ferry to Vestmannaeyjar, a collection of islands off
the southern Icelandic coast, and learn how residents in this
area quickly evacuated before it was blanketed in volcanic ash.
See how the island has developed amid the constant threat of
volcanic activity. There's also a beluga whale sanctuary and
several sites where puffins congregate.

TOP TIP

If puffins are a priority,
check schedules for park
closures during mating
season.

JAN JERMAN/SHUTTERSTOCK ©

Fimmvörðuháls (p135)

Tanginn, Vestmannaeyjar

Frolic with Beluga Whales

VISIT A BELUGA WHALE SANCTUARY

Meet Little Grey and Little White, a pair of Beluga whales who call the world's first **Beluga Whale Sanctuary** home. The sanctuary opened in the town of Vestmannaeyjabær, one hour and 15-minutes by car and ferry from Skógafoss, in 2019 and is open to visitors between April and October. The sanctuary is built around a huge natural bay where rescued beluga whales can swim, dive and explore in a more natural environment than their previous home. These playful whales travelled more than 9656km to get here from a Shanghai amusement park. Their epic journey required a flight, some driving, a lot of creativity, and a short ferry ride.

Beluga whales are an endangered species, and their population continues to decline as a result of pollution and human interference. The sanctuary has room for up to 10 of these magnificent creatures and hopes to relocate more of them in the future.

Born dark gray, these gigantic whales turn white in a process that can take up to eight years. They can grow up to 5m long, weigh over 1360kg and live for 50 years. They can also swim backward and change the shape of their forehead by blowing air around their sinuses.

BEST PLACES TO STAY IN VESTMANNAEYJAR

Hótel Vestmannaeyjar
This clean, comfortable hotel has single and double rooms perfectly located in the Vestmannaeyjar. €€

Hrafnabjörg Guesthouse
This picturesque B&B is the kind of place that will quickly make you feel at home. It's simple, well-located, and there's a laundry available on-site. €

Puffin Nest Capsule Hostel
If you're on a budget and just looking for a place to rest your head, consider this capsule hotel. Enjoy common spaces, including a kitchen and dining area, before retreating to your private capsule in the evening. €

WHERE TO EAT IN VESTMANNAEYJAR

Tanginn
Harbour views and a menu that includes reindeer steak, reindeer burgers and whale steak. €€

Slippurinn
Locally sourced Nordic cuisine in the hometown of head chef Gísli Matthías Auðunsson. €€€

Brothers Brewery
Take a brewery tour and have a beer flight at this small craft brewery. €€

Eldheimar museum

PUFFIN TOUR OPERATORS

Kayak & Puffins
Kayak across the Klettsvík Bay for up to two hours looking for puffins, eider ducks, and more in these rugged cliffs.

Eyjatours
This company combines puffin spotting with a trip into the Eldfell volcano and to the town where the island's first Viking family settled.

Ribsafari
See the millions of puffins that nest here every year from a speedboat off the coast of Heimaey.

Don't be surprised if you hear Little Grey and Little White when you visit. Beluga whales tend to be vocal animals.

Look for Puffins
THIS IS PUFFIN PARADISE

There may be no bird more closely associated with Iceland than the puffin. And there may be no better place to see these adorable orange-beaked birds than Vestmannaeyjar, an archipelago that's believed to be home to the largest Atlantic puffin colony in the world. **Heimaey**, the island where you'll find Vestmannaeyjar's key sites, is the easiest place to see them. Puffin season runs from April through August but can sometimes jut into September. August is prime time for baby puffins, so much so that the children living in the area are allowed to stay out late redirecting puffins who may be lost and need a hand making it into the wild.

Head to the island's western coast or southern tip for scenic puffin viewpoints. A lookout near **Stórhöfðaviti** is one of the best for spotting a large number of puffins in one place.

See a Volcanic Eruption Aftermath
A HISTORICAL ISLAND EVACUATION

A dramatic volcanic eruption in 1973 wiped out hundreds of homes on Heimaey island, about an hour and 20 minutes by car and ferry from Skógar. The **Eldheimar** museum offers a chance to walk around the ruins of one of them. This is some-

HISTORIC SITES IN VESTMANNAEYJAR

Skansinn
This fort from the 1500s was a British military base during WWII.

Landlyst Museum
This tiny wooden house was a maternity hospital. There's still 19th-century medical equipment inside.

Sagnheimar Museum
Learn about local puffin culture, the Turkish invasion and why the national festival is epic.

times called a Pompeii of the north, a place where life was going on as usual until it wasn't.

The catastrophic Eldfell eruption buried about 400 homes in volcanic ash. The 5300 residents had to evacuate the island in the middle of a cold January night. Many of them never saw their homes again. The museum tells their stories, explaining what happened after lava and ash covered 20% of the island's surface during an eruption that lasted five months. It helps visitors understand what it's like to live with the constant threat of a volcano eruption and how quickly life and landscapes can change, even in modern times. Emergency services were able to evacuate almost everyone in a matter of hours, although one person unfortunately died. Rescue workers stayed behind but most of the town was eventually destroyed.

A Desolate Black-Sand Beach

AN ESCAPE FROM EVERYTHING

This barren black-sand beach is where a US Navy plane ran out of petrol and crashed in 1973. All seven crew members walked away. For 50 years, the wreckage of this military transport plane sat here almost untouched. It became a popular photo spot, drawing visitors from around the world willing to make a one-hour trek to the site for the feeling of walking into a science-fiction film. The wreckage was moved in the summer of 2023 because tourist traffic was disrupting farm operations near the site, which is 10-minutes from Skógar by car. The walk from the car park is just over an hour each way.

Venture Into the Highlands

COLOURFUL MOUNTAIN-SCAPES

A 26km trail leads from Skógar into the Þórsmörk Valley in the Icelandic highlands. The **Fimmvörðuháls** trail is one of Iceland's most spectacular and challenging hiking routes. Some people complete the trail in seven to 10 hours. It cuts between the Eyjafjallajökull and Mýrdalsjökull glaciers, delivering epic scenery along the way. Or try the longer 55km **Laugavegur Trail** from Landmannalaugar in the Fjallabak Nature Reserve to the Þórsmörk Nature Preserve. From jagged canyons to volcanic moonscapes and gorgeous waterfalls, these trails offer a taste of all the dramatic scenery Iceland has to offer. You'll need to make these hikes during the summer and expect snow at the top, regardless of when you go. Visibility and wind conditions can make a big difference in how you experience these hikes, and hiking poles are recommended.

WHERE TO STAY OUTSIDE SKÓGAR

Umi Hotel
Every room at this boutique hotel has a mountain or ocean view and a private bathroom. €€

Seljalandsfoss Horizons
This collection of two-bedroom luxury cabins is perfect for groups of families travelling together. €€€

Paradise Cave Hostel
This property is far nicer than your average hostel. It offers private rooms, traditional hostel dorms and kitchen access near Seljalandsfoss. €

Skálakot Manor Hotel
This small hotel belongs on postcards. It has the feel of a lodge and specialises in horseback-riding tours. €€

GETTING AROUND

A car will give you the most flexibility in exploring this area. Public bus service connects Reykjavík to Skógar, where you can catch buses into the Icelandic highlands during the summer. A 45-minute ferry from Landeyjahöfn runs to and from Vestmannaeyjar several times a day. Bikes, cars and camper vans are allowed on the ferry, but you will have to check-in at least 30 minutes before departure.

VÍK

REYKJAVÍK

Vík

Vík is the southernmost village in Iceland. It's home to fewer than 1000 people and is the wettest place in Iceland, so don't forget your raincoat. Because Vík has several hotels and restaurants, a hostel and a well-equipped campsite as well as grocery stores and petrol stations, it's an ideal stop on an around-the-country road trip. The village sits in the shadow of the Mýrdalsjökull glacier, which is on top of the Katla volcano. Vík was blanketed with ash when Eyjafjallajökull erupted in 2010 and is a hub of volcanic research.

Head to the Vík í Mýrdal church for a bird's-eye view of Vík's black-sand basalt beach and Reynisdrangar, the carved rock formation forcing its way out of the ocean. You'll find another black-sand beach, Reynisfjara Beach, on the other side of Dyrhólaey. These beaches are great for birdwatching but not for swimming because the water can be dangerous.

TOP TIP

Reynisfjara is a striking but dangerous beach where deadly sneaker waves can come in at any time. They're called sneaker waves because they sneak up on people, powerful enough to sweep them away, and can reach far further ashore than anyone expects. This is no place for swimming or long walks.

MEDIAWORLDIMAGES/ALAMY STOCK PHOTO ©

Horse riding on black-sand beach

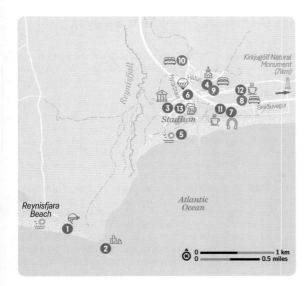

SIGHTS
1. Hálsanefshellir Cave
2. Reynisdrangar
3. Skaftfellingur Museum
4. Vík í Mýrdal Church
5. Víkurfjara Beach

ACTIVITIES, COURSES & TOURS
6. True Adventure
7. Vík Horse Adventure
see 6 Zipline Iceland

SLEEPING
8. Hótel Kría
9. Hótel Vík
10. Vík HI Hostel

DRINKING & NIGHTLIFE
11. Lava Bakery & Coffee
12. Skool Beans
13. Smiðjan Brugghús

Ride Horses on a Black-Sand Beach

CALM BEACH FOR HORSE RIDING

To ride horses along a black-sand beach without the threat of being washed away by a terrifying sneaker wave, head to **Víkurfjara Beach**. This beach is calmer than Reynisfjara, making it possible to ride horses here while taking in sweeping views of the Reynisdrangar rock formation from afar. It's also calmer than Kirkjufjara, the beach leading toward the Dyrhólaey rock formations that define the coastline.

This is one of those places that feels wild and free, especially when you're in the saddle. Víkurfjara Beach is an idyllic spot for enjoying Icelandic horses' unique *tölt* (running walk) gait, a relaxed pace that feels tailor-made for sightseeing in landscapes like these. Prefer a slower pace? **Vík Horse Adventure** has you covered with a stable about 100m from the beach. It offers half-hour and full-hour rides that are suitable for beginners, making it easy for just about anyone to tour this area with a four-legged guide.

BEST COFFEE SHOPS IN VÍK

Skool Beans
A micro roaster located inside an old yellow school bus. A great spot for creative coffee drinks and pastries.

Lava Bakery & Coffee
This minimalist cafe is a great option for a quick breakfast, lunch, or afternoon coffee and a snack.

 BEST HOTELS IN VÍK

Hótel Kría
Sleep in the shadows of mountains at this luxurious hotel near the beach. €€€

Hótel Vík
A sleek hotel with dreamy views, a restaurant and a bar minutes from the beach. €€

Vík HI Hostel
A small, friendly hostel with cosy dorms, breakfast and a comfortable vibe. €

BEST & ONLY BREWERY IN VÍK

Craft brewing doesn't have a long history in Iceland where it wasn't legal to brew full-strength beer until 1989. Beer was the last type of alcohol to be allowed in Iceland after prohibition. Because of beer's ties to Danish culture, beer was seen as an unpatriotic beverage around the time of Icelandic independence.

Smiðjan Brugghús opened in 2018, not far from the beach in Vík. The brewery is the only one in the village and specialises in hop-forward IPAs, robust stouts and crisp lagers. There are 10 craft beers on draught at any given time, so go ahead and sample a few. It also serves up ribs, burgers and other bar food.

See Giant Rock Formations & Caves

HUGE BASALT SEA STACKS

Reynisdrangar, Iceland's iconic basalt sea stacks that rise from the sea, are the stuff of Icelandic folklore. Tales suggest they may be the remains of trolls that were out too late and turned to stone as the sun came up.

These spiky cliffs soar more than 61m into the air, almost as if they're sharp old knives poking through the earth. The giant rocks are a favourite among nesting Arctic terns, puffins and fulmars. While they're not far from the main road, their magnificence is best experienced from afar because the waves here and on Reynisfjara Beach can be especially strong, unpredictable, and deadly.

The **Hálsanefshellir Cave** is just one example of how powerful the water can be here. This basalt sea cave has been sculpted by the pounding waves of the Atlantic Ocean. Over time, the soft volcanic rock here eroded, leaving behind a cave made of striking columns in a hexagonal pattern. The cave is believed to have offered respite to weary fishers in centuries past. Nowadays, it's better known for its unique acoustics and almost hand-carved look. Even from afar, this natural wonder is a work of art.

Zipline over a Canyon

EPIC SOUTH ICELAND VIEWS

Ziplining isn't just for lush tropical landscapes. In Vík, you can zipline over a river canyon and epic south Icelandic valleys. **Zipline Iceland**, the country's first zip-line operator, has a collection of four zip lines between 30m and 140m long. Getting to the zip-line platform requires a short car ride as well as a short hike. There's more hiking required to the platforms, but it passes by beautiful scenery. These views are worth the effort. Get a unique perspective as you go over Hundafoss, a gorgeous waterfall that's easy to miss when you're looking for it on foot but impossible not to see from above. If you think Icelandic scenery is unreal on the ground, just wait until you see these rocky cliffs and majestic flowing river from above.

Float over Beaches & Rock Formations

TAKE A TANDEM PARAGLIDE

Vík's black-sand beaches and magnificent rock structures are mesmerising just as they are. But you can take to the skies for a unique perspective on these natural wonders. After a

 KEY SITES IN VÍK

Vík í Mýrdal Church
An idyllic white church with a red roof and sweeping ocean views.

Kirkjugólf Natural Monument
A collection of basalt stone chunks that resembles a human-made floor.

Skaftfellingur Museum
Offers an introduction to a 100-year-old ship and the Icelanders who relied on it.

MICHAEL VER SPRILL/GETTY IMAGES ©

Hálsanefshellir Cave

DON'T CALL THEM PONIES

Icelandic horses have five gaits or paces. Most horses have three: walk, trot and gallop. Icelandic horses add *tölt*, a relaxed pace that's perfect for taking in the scenery; and flying pace, a faster, more adventurous full gallop – more commonly used with show horses.

As you're mounting your horse, you'll notice it's smaller than what you may be used to riding. Icelandic horses are shorter than most, coming in at around 1.3m to 1.4m when they're full-grown. For comparison, full-grown quarter-horses are generally between 1.5m and 1.6m while Clydesdales are around 1.8m in height.

Whatever you do, don't call these petite horses 'ponies'.

safety orientation, **paraglide** in tandem with a guide from **True Adventure** over this spectacular section of the South Iceland coast. You'll get a panoramic view of the Reynisdrangar basalt stacks as you soar over crashing waves, rugged cliffs and magnificent rock formations that rise mightily from the ocean. Feel the wind in your hair and the sun on your face as you take in the expansive lava fields, behemoth craters and broad swaths of vibrant green moss below. The only thing better than taking in these views without having to worry about sneaker waves might be the feeling of freedom you get while floating through the sky.

Paragliding tours range from one to two hours long and no prior experience is required. There's no need to jump off a cliff or mountain or out of an airplane. Just hang on as the pilot you're flying with begins down a slope and gets lifted in the air by the canopy. Expect a smooth, controlled, unforgettable ride. You'll spend 10 to 15 minutes in the air on a one-hour ride and use the rest of the time to prepare for the experience.

To paraglide, you'll need to be at least 12 years old and meet weight requirements, generally between 15kg and 135kg. You'll want to dress in layers and ensure your outerwear is suitable for rain. Wear a thin hat that'll slip under your helmet as well as gloves and hiking boots.

GETTING AROUND

It's possible to travel from Reykjavík, Selfoss and Skógar to Vík by using public buses.

For the greatest flexibility, you'll want to rent a car.

Beyond Vík

Discover small sleepy towns, scenic waterfalls and a magnificent natural canyon you won't need a 4WD to access.

Dyrhólaey · Vík · Gígjagjá

Vík, Iceland's southernmost village, is the only town within a 48km radius. Beyond Vík, you'll find magnificent glaciers, powerful volcanoes and unforgettable once-in-a-lifetime adventures. Snowmobile on a glacier or venture into an ice cave. Look for rock formations and caves, including one that really does resemble Baby Yoda from *Star Wars*. Check out the magnificent basalt columns at Dverghamrar, a scenic spot where you're not at risk of the ocean washing you away. Like the rest of Iceland, this area is dotted with churches, waterfalls and tiny towns. There are hotels, guesthouses and farms, but not much beyond the breathtaking scenery as you continue east on the Ring Road.

TOP TIP

The area surrounding Vík is ripe for exploration by geology buffs or anyone else looking to better understand natural wonders.

HECTOR KNUDSEN/GETTY IMAGES ©

Gígjagjá

Dyrhólaey

Natural Cave with a Familiar Look

STAR WARS–INSPIRED CAVE ENTRANCE

If you're a *Star Wars* fan, **Gígjagjá** is the Icelandic cave you can't miss. You don't even have to be a *Star Wars* fan for the Baby Yoda–shaped cave entrance to jump out at you. The cave makes for an excellent photo stop, but you will need to drive for about 20 minutes on a rough gravel road to get there. Rent a 4WD if this spot is on your wish list and head to the cave around sunrise or sunset. Go into the cave and look out for gorgeous views framed by Baby Yoda.

Hike the Highlights of Dyrhólaey

VOLCANIC ISLAND TURNED PENINSULA

Few places show Iceland's constant evolution like Dyrhólaey, a volcanic island that's since become a peninsula on the South Coast. This section of coastline – 20 minutes' drive from Vík – includes the southernmost point of the Icelandic mainland. It's best known for its soaring cliffs, coated in bright green in certain seasons, and an arch above that's large enough so a boat could pass through in calm seas.

This stretch of coastline makes for one of the most scenic drives in Iceland, and two car parks allow for closer access to this nature preserve. A hiking trail connects the black sands of Kirkjufjara Beach with the peak of Dyrhólaey. The nearly 5km hike is considered moderately challenging and hits all the highlights – the beach, the arch and the lighthouse.

There's an islet here that can be an ideal spot for puffin spotting, but it closes for just over a month every summer while the birds are nesting here.

WINTER'S SILVER LINING

There's a silver lining to visiting Iceland during winter when the darkness can stretch for as long as 19 hours a day. Long nights like these are when the aurora borealis emerges, dancing across the sky in shades of green, red and pink.

These dancing waves occur when electrons from space smash into the upper atmosphere of the Earth. Look for viewing spots with minimal light pollution, like Þingvellir National Park, Dyrhólaey or the Seltjarnarnes Peninsula. Several apps promise to help you find the best spots. Some tours drive the countryside looking for the Northern Lights and some hotels offer a wake-up service when it's spotted overhead.

 WHERE TO STAY NEAR VÍK

Hotel Katla
This modern hotel has comfortable rooms, rustic charm, an extensive breakfast buffet and few neighbours. €€

Black Beach Suites
Modern, well-equipped studio apartments. Wake up to water views through floor-to-ceiling windows. €€

Mið-Hvoll Cottages
Simple accommodation in a collection of cute cottages that feel like rustic log cabins. €€

PILAT666/GETTY IMAGES ©

MUNMEMORIES/GETTY IMAGES ©

Scan this QR code for more information on Katla Geopark.

Fjaðrárgljúfur canyon

TOP SIGHT

Katla Geopark

Katla is one of Iceland's fiercest and most striking volcanoes. It's surrounded by a UNESCO World Heritage geopark that accounts for nearly 10% of the land in Iceland. Katla makes it clear that Iceland truly is a land of fire and ice. Katla's last major eruption was in 1918. That eruption lasted 24 days, fortunately without loss of life.

DON'T MISS

Katla Visitor Center

Katla Ice Cave

Eyjafjallajökull

Sólheimajökull

Eyjarhóll, Pétursey

Dverghamrar

Fjaðrárgljúfur

Journey into an Ice Cave

Head underground and into the **Katla Ice Cave** to see black ash from centuries of eruptions encased in ice. Notice the older blue ice layers and trapped air bubbles as you move through this space underneath an offshoot of Iceland's fourth-largest glacier. The black-striped layers of ice you see are key for determining the age of glaciers like this one.

A few steps have been carved into the ice to make it easier to navigate. Otherwise, this ice cave remains in its natural state. Tours typically visit the oldest part of the ice cave where the ice can be clear blue.

Snowmobile on a Glacier

Go snowmobiling on top of **Mýrdalsjökull** glacier, the ice cap that tops Katla, Iceland's largest volcano. Mýrdalsjökull is Iceland's southernmost glacier and an estimated 250m deep.

Tours start with a briefing at Midgard base camp and include monster truck rides to the snowmobile site. This experience has to be booked with a tour company and cannot be done independently. You will need a driver's licence to drive a snowmobile. Tour operators provide thermal suits and helmets.

These are typically full-day excursions, so plan your time accordingly.

Go Glacier Hiking

Spend a half-day hiking on a small-group tour of **Sólheimajökull**, a massive chunk of the larger Mýrdalsjökull glacier. Sólheimajökull is between the volcanoes Katla and Eyjafjallajökull. It isn't surrounded by tall mountains like other glaciers and is a rare spot for landscape views from an ice cap.

Sólheimajökull is about 8km long and 1.6km wide. With its shades of white, blue and black, this is one of the most popular spots in Iceland for glacier hiking.

This glacial hiking experience is suitable for beginners and available year-round.

To get to the hike site, you'll have to walk across a field of ash and sand from the **Eyjafjallajökull** volcanic eruption in 2010. The glacier itself is retreating, and hiking it offers a fascinating geology lesson.

Hike a Magical Canyon

There's nothing like walking through a lush green fairy tale, and there may be no more fairy-tale place for a hike than **Fjaðrárgljúfur** canyon in the Katla Geopark. Even Justin Bieber has been captivated by this canyon, where he filmed a music video.

This is a canyon so majestic it doesn't even look real. It's just over 1.6km long and nearly 101m deep. This is a place where the crystal-clear Fjaðrá river twists and winds through what looks like a hand-carved piece of Earth.

The canyon's name translates to 'feather'. When looking down on the canyon from above, it's easy to see why. Anyone who doesn't speak Icelandic is likely to find hiking the marked trails here significantly easier than learning how to pronounce this nature reserve's name.

A 3km hiking trail through canyon landscapes leads to waterfall views and is popular among birdwatchers, hikers and runners. The trail is considered easy and takes about an hour to complete, though astounding canyon views are likely to slow you down. There's a campsite here with barbecue grills and a cosy cave perfect for candlelit dining.

GLACIER TOUR COMPANIES

Tröll Expeditions offers glacier and ice-cave tours from Vík. Southcoast Adventure runs South Coast ice-climbing, glacier-hiking and snowmobile tours. Katlatrack runs ice-caving and glacier tours, plus a Hidden Mountains from *Game of Thrones* tour from Vík.

TOP TIPS

- It's possible to walk on glaciers in Iceland year-round, but you shouldn't do this on your own.
- Professional guides know the terrain here well and provide necessary safety equipment, such as crampons and helmets.
- For glacier hiking, opt for a warm inner layer and a waterproof outer layer of clothing.
- Choose sturdy shoes to which you can easily attach crampons.
- Specially modified trucks that aren't available for rent are the only way to access these areas.
- Batteries drain faster in cold temperatures. Bring a power bank.

Above: Jökulsárlón (p160). RIght: Viking village film set (p167)

SOUTHEAST ICELAND

RAW GLACIAL BEAUTY, CHARMING HAMLETS

The mighty Vatnajökull ice cap dominates the Southeast, with its huge rivers of frozen ice cracking steep-sided valleys. Verdant farmsteads offer welcome sanctuary.

Blow your mind as you traverse the 200km stretch of Ring Road from Kirkjubæjarklaustur to Höfn, transporting yourself across vast deltas of grey glacial sand, past marooned-looking farms, around the toes of craggy mountains, through surreal lava fields (wait! Is that a troll on the move?) and by crackling glacier tongues and ice-filled lagoons. The only thing you won't pass is a town.

The giant Vatnajökull – Europe's most massive ice cap – dominates the region, its twisting tongues of frozen ice carving valleys opening at the sea. One of several glacial lagoons, Jökulsárlón is a photographer's paradise where wind and water sculpt calving icebergs into fantastical shapes and sweep them out to Fellsfjara where they sparkle in the sun.

The unfathomable coastal deserts of glacial sand are remnants of calamitous collisions between fire and ice. Further inland, the epicentre of Iceland's worst volcanic event, the Lakagígar fissures, make for galvanising hiking – up mountains, through lava-filled fissures. With so much austerity on display, it's not surprising that Skaftafell (the southern branch of the enormous Vatnajökull National Park) is such a popular oasis. This sheltered enclave between the glaciers and the sand deltas throbs with life and colour, and the footfalls of hikers.

North, as you edge toward the Eastfjords, the small seaside town of Höfn is a warming sight, offering the chance to dine on its famous langoustines and stroll its peaceful fishing harbour.

PRYSTAI/SHUTTERSTOCK ©

THE MAIN AREAS

SKAFTAFELL
Premier glacier and waterfall hikes.
p148

BEYOND SKAFTAFELL
Volcanic landscape and austere exploration.
p154

JÖKULSÁRLÓN
Glittering icebergs float to black-sand beaches.
p160

BEYOND JÖKULSÁRLÓN
From glacial lagoons to catch-of-the-day.
p161

Find Your Way

You'll need your own wheels or join a tour to explore the 200km of untouched volcanic wonderland from Kirkjubæjarklaustur to Höfn. Book well ahead to stay overnight..

Skaftafell, p148

Iceland's favourite national-park pocket is a resplendent area of green amid icy masses and vast sand deltas.

Jökulsárlón, p160

Admire the ever-changing ice sculptures at this bewitching lagoon that empties out on black-sand beaches.

Höfn, p166

Dine in the town's restaurants, sampling delicious seafood treats netted by the local fishing fleet.

CAR

By far the most convenient way to stop for photo ops and hikes, a car gives freedom. Fuel up frequently as petrol pumps are few and far between. Never drive on glaciers. Get groceries in Kirkjubæjarklaustur and/ or Höfn.

TOURS

Occasional buses and a multitude of tours drive the Ring Road, connecting Reykjavik and popular towns in Iceland's southwest with eastern destinations such as Jökulsárlón.

NORTH
ATLANTIC
OCEAN

Hvalnes
Lón
Stafafell
Ketillaugarfjall
(670m)
Geitafell
Stokksnes
Hoffellsjökull
Jökulsá í Lóni
Hornafjörður
Höfn
Heinabergsjökull
Fláajökull

Vatnajökull

Öræfajökull
(1522m)
Grímsvötn
(1719m)

Hali
Diamond
Breiðármörk
Beach
Jökulsárlón
Hrollaugseyjar
Fjallsárlón

Grænalón
Skaftárjökull
Hvannadalshnúkur
(2110m)

Tungnaá
Langisjór
Síðujökull
Þórðarfjall
(1090m)
Sléttaratangur

Laki
Lómagnúpur
(767m)
Foss á
Síðu
Gjátindur
(943m)
Blágil
Fagrifoss
Kirkjubæjarklaustur

Skaftáros
Fjaðrárgljúfur

Hólmsá
Hrífunes
Hörfursey
(582m)
Kúðafljót

NORTH
ATLANTIC
OCEAN

0   30 km
0   15 miles

ARCTIC IMAGES/ALAMY STOCK PHOTO ©

Super-Jeep tour (p152), Vatnajökull

Plan Your Time

How deep you dive in the timeless Southeast with its eons-old glaciers is up to you: from a quick awe-inspiring zip to plentiful activities including kayaking, ice caving, glacier walking and puffin viewing.

Pressed for Time

● If you really have to zoom through, then stop off at **Fjaðrárgljúfur** (p158) for a magnificent view of canyon and waterfalls. Get groceries in Kirkjubæjarklaustur or eat at excellent restaurant **Kjarr** (p155), then enjoy the otherworldly photo ops in the **sandar** (p156). Hike in **Skaftafell** (p148) on its vista-blessed heath before capping off the mammoth day at **Jökulsárlón** (p160) glacier lagoon.

Three Days to Explore

● With extra time, get off the Ring Road into more remote regions like spectacular **Laki** (p159) reserve. The family-friendly **puffin tour** (p155) to Ingólfshöfði is a gas. Or, tour one of the glacier lagoons (Jökulsárlón, Fjallsárlón or Heinabergslón) by kayak, amphibious boat or Zodiac. Join a **glacier walk** (p152) or **snowmobile tour** (p152), or ride in style up on the glacier in a **super-Jeep** (p152).

SEASONAL HIGHLIGHTS

SPRING	SUMMER	AUTUMN	WINTER
Glacier walks and snowmobiling are generally available year-round (weather permitting).	Puffins visit Ingólfshöfði from May to early August. Access roads to Lakagígar open mid-June.	Boat trips on Jökulsárlón generally run from May to October. Interior F roads close.	Winter sparkles with the Northern Lights and the chance to visit ice caves that form under the glacier edges.

SKAFTAFELL

REYKJAVÍK ✪

Skaftafell
National Park

The jewel in the crown of Vatnajökull National Park, Skaftafell encompasses a breathtaking collection of peaks and glaciers. It's the country's favourite wilderness: join the more than 500,000 visitors per year who come to marvel at thundering waterfalls, twisted birch woods, the tangled web of rivers threading across the sandar, and brilliant blue-white Vatnajökull with its lurching tongues of ice, festooning rugged mountainsides.

Skaftafell deserves its reputation, and few visitors – even those who usually shun the great outdoors – can resist it. In the height of summer it may feel like every traveller in the country is here. However, if you're prepared to get out on the more remote trails and take advantage of the fabulous hiking on the heath and beyond, you'll leave the hubbub behind. For example, you can find serenity by visiting the famous waterfall, Svartifoss, under the midnight sun.

TOP TIP

Skaftafellsstofa Visitor Centre (vjp.is) has helpful staff, maps, a summertime cafe and internet access. Follow the rules: all flora, fauna and natural features are protected, open fires prohibited and rubbish must be carried out. Stick to marked paths to avoid damaging plant life. Drones are prohibited without official park permission.

VADYM LAVRA/SHUTTERSTOCK ©

Skaftafellsjökull (p150)

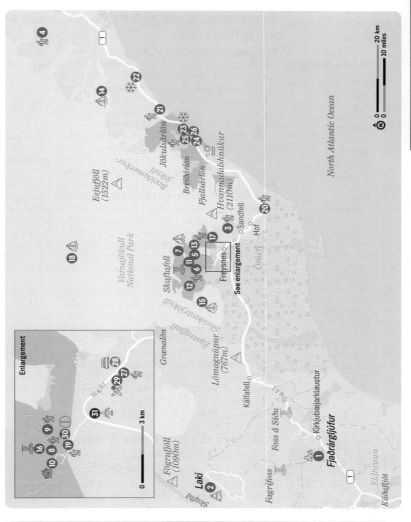

HIGHLIGHTS
1 Fjaðrárgljúfur
2 Laki

SIGHTS
3 Falljökull
4 Jökulfell
5 Kristínartindar Ridge
6 Morsárdalur
7 Morsárjökull
8 path S2
9 path S5/S6
10 Sel
11 Skaftafell
12 Skaftafellsfjöll
13 Skaftafellsjökull
14 Skalafellsjökull
15 Skeiðarárjökull
16 Svartifoss
17 Svínafellsjökull
18 Vatnajökull

ACTIVITIES, COURSES & TOURS
19 Arctic Adventures
20 From Coast to Mountains

21 Glacier Adventure
22 Glacier Jeeps
23 Glacier Journey
24 Glacier Trips
25 Ice Explorers
26 IceGuide
see 19 Icelandic Mountain Guides
27 Local Guide

SLEEPING
28 Hótel Skaftafell

EATING
29 Söluskálinn Freysnesi

INFORMATION
30 Skaftafellsstofa Visitor Centre

TRANSPORT
31 Atlantsflug

149

HIDDEN BIKE PATH

Styrmir Einarsson, a ranger at Skaftafell, has lived in Svínafell for 12 years. He shares his favourite new development in the park area.

In 2023 a bike trail between Skaftafell and Svínafell was made. Not many people know about it because the park has only just finished it and is setting out to publicise it. Really, almost no one has begun to use it yet and it's amazingly peaceful. There are two small hanging bridges over the rivers which give incredible views. It's about 7.5km each way, so a straightforward return trip, too.

Wonder at Vatnajökull & its Outlet Glaciers
WALK TO THE ICE FACE

Vatnajökull is the world's largest ice cap outside the poles. At 7800 sq km, it's more than three times the size of Luxembourg, with an average thickness of 400m to 600m (and a maximum of 950m). Under this enormous blanket of ice lie countless peaks and valleys, including a number of live volcanoes and subglacial lakes, plus Iceland's highest point – the 2110m mountain Hvannadalshnúkur (p156).

Huge outlet glaciers, pleated with crevasses, flow down from the centre of Vatnajökull to the lowlands. There are around 30 of them, with many visible (and accessible, to varying degrees) from the Ring Road (Rte 1) in the southeast.

A very popular trail offers an easy one-hour walk (path S1; 3.7km return) to **Skaftafellsjökull**, a relatively small glacier tongue that ends within 1.5km of Skaftafellsstofa Visitor Centre. The marked trail begins at the visitor centre and leads to the glacier face, where you can witness the bumps and groans of the ice (although the glacier is pretty grey and gritty here). It has receded greatly in recent decades so land along this trail has been gradually reappearing. Pick up the brochure describing the trail's geology.

Close to Skaftafell, companies guide glacier walks on tongues such as **Falljökull** (Icelandic Mountain Guides has a hut at the park). Between Jökulsárlón and Höfn, there are guided walks on famous beauty Breiðamerkurjökull, which crumbles into icebergs at the breathtaking Jökulsárlón lagoon (p162).

Heading east on the Ring Road from Skaftafell, a sign points the way to **Svínafellsjökull**. A gravel road near **Hotel Skaftafell** leads to a car park, from where it's a 500m walk to the northern edge of the glacier and fine photo ops. In summer 2018, geologists identified a huge risk of rock landslide here, so no one goes onto this glacier these days.

Svartifoss

Walking to the Svartifoss Waterfall
BASALT CASCADES AND HEATH-TOP VIEWS

Seek out your perfect view of famous Svartifoss (Black Falls), a stunning, moody-looking waterfall flanked by geometric black basalt columns. The relatively easy 1.8km trail leads up from the visitor centre via the campsite. To take pressure off the busy trail, park staff recommend an alternate path back. From the waterfall, continue west up the track to Sjónarsker, where a view disc names surrounding landmarks, plus an unforgettable vista stretches across Skeiðarársandur

VADYM LAVRA/SHUTTERSTOCK ©

 WHERE TO STAY & EAT IN & NEAR SKAFTAFELL

Ferðaþjónustan Svínafelli
Well-organised campsite with six basic cabins (sleeping four), and spotless amenities block at Svínafell, 8km east. €

Hótel Skaftafell
One of very few hotels, so in hot demand, despite being merely functional. It's 5km east, with a restaurant. €€€

Cafe Vatnajökull
Welcoming roadside eatery with fresh-made snacks and excellent coffee. Alternative to petrol-station dining. €

(p156). From here you can visit the traditional turf-roofed farmhouse **Sel**. This two-hour, 5.5km return walk (**path S2**) is classified as easy.

Or, for a challenging hike (**path S5/S6**), from Svartifoss head east over the heath to the viewpoint at Sjónarnípa, looking across Skaftafellsjökull. Allow three hours return (7.4km).

Hiking the Skaftafellsheiði Loop
EXPLORING THE GLORIOUS HEATH

On a fine day, tackle the five- to six-hour walk (path S3; 16.7km) around Skaftafellsheiði (Skaftafell Heath), a hiker's dream (except when it's closed during the spring thaw because you'd be knee-deep in mud). It begins by climbing from the campsite to Sjónarsker, continuing across the moor to 610m-high Fremrihnaukur. From there it follows the edge of the plateau to the next rise, Nyrðrihnaukur (706m), which affords a superb view of **Morsárdalur**, and **Morsárjökull** and the iceberg-choked lagoon at its base. At this point the track turns southeast to an outlook point, Gláma, on the cliff above Skaftafellsjökull. The route continues down to Sjónarnípa and then back to the campsite.

For the best view of Skaftafellsjökull, Morsárdalur and the Skeiðarársandur, it's worth scaling the summit of **Kristínartindar** (1126m). The best way follows a well-marked 2km route (classified as difficult) up the prominent valley southeast of the Nyrðrihnaukur lookout, and back down near Gláma.

Trekking Hills & Dales
MAKING THE MOST OF SKAFTAFELL'S TRAILS

Skaftafell is ideal for both day hikes and its longer treks through wilderness regions. Stop in to talk to the rangers at the visitor centre who are keen to help you prepare and inform you of potential risks. Pick up a good map outlining shorter hiking trails there, or one of the larger topo maps. Before embarking on more remote routes, enquire about river crossings along your way and leave a travel plan at safetravel.is.

Most visitors stick to popular routes on Skaftafellsheiði, and from mid-June to mid-August, rangers usually guide free daily interpretive walks from the visitor centre – a great way to learn about the area.

But hiking in areas like the upper **Morsárdalur** and Kjós valleys requires more time, motivation and planning. The seven-hour hike (20.9km return) from the campsite to the glacial lake in Morsárdalur is enjoyable. Alternatively, cross

BEST FOOD FOR THE PARK

Visitor Centre Cafe
In summer, this busy cafe sells sandwiches, cake and hiking snacks (*skyr* etc), plus hot food (soup, dish of the day) with some vegetarian options.

Glacier Goodies
The food truck near the visitor centre makes a small menu of well-executed dishes: lobster soup, fish and chips, baby back ribs.

Groceries
Get meals and a few supplies year-round at **Söluskálinn Freysnesi**, the petrol station opposite Hótel Skaftafell, 5km east of the park. Bring groceries from supermarkets in Kirkjubæjarklaustur or Höfn.

GUIDES AROUND SKAFTAFELL —

From Coast to Mountains
Owner Einar, Iceland's first ice cave guide, offers climbs of Hvannadalshnúkur peak, and cave and puffin tours (p156).

Local Guide
Family-owned and in the area for generations; first-rate local knowledge, year-round glacier hikes and ice climbs.

Glacier Horses
Short horse rides in view-blessed countryside, 9km east of the park. Bookings are essential.

SHIFTING SANDS OF HISTORY

The historical Skaftafell was a large farm at the foot of the hills west of the present campsite. Shifting glacial sands slowly buried the fields and the district came to be known as Hérað Milli Sanda (Land Between the Sands). After all the farms were annihilated by the 1362 eruptions, it became the 'land under the sands' and was renamed Öræfi (Wasteland). Cute Svínafell, just east, offers camping and lodging and was once home to Flosi Þórðarson, who burned Njáll and his family to death in Njál's Saga. It was also the site where Flosi and Njál's family were finally reconciled, thus ending one of the bloodiest feuds in Icelandic history. In the 17th century, Svínafellsjökull nearly engulfed the farm, but it has since retreated.

the Morsá river at the foot of Skaftafellsheiði and make your way across the gravel riverbed to the birch woods at Bæjarstaðarskógur. The complete walk to/from Bæjarstaðarskógur takes about five hours (15.8km return).

A long day hike beyond Bæjarstaðarskógur leads into the rugged **Skaftafellsfjöll**. Or, summit the 862m-high **Jökulfell ridge**, which affords a commanding view of the vast expanses of **Skeiðarárjökull**. Even better is an excursion into the Kjós dell.

Glacier Hikes & Ice Climbing
EXPLORING ON THE ICE

Strap on crampons and crunch your way around a glacier. One highlight of any visit to the southern reaches of Vatnajökull is a glacier hike. You can see waterfalls, ice caves, glacial mice (moss balls, not actual mice!) and different-coloured ash from ancient explosions. But – take note: as fascinating as the glaciers are, they are also riven with fissures and are always potentially dangerous, so do not stride out onto one without both guiding and the right equipment.

A number of authorised guides operate year-round in the area (and at lesser-visited glacier tongues further east, towards Höfn). The largest companies, **Icelandic Mountain Guides** (mountainguides.is) and **Arctic Adventures** (glacierguides. is), have information and booking huts beside Skaftafellsstofa Visitor Centre, where you can talk to experts and get kitted out for glacier walks (warm clothes are essential; waterproof gear and hiking boots are available for hire).

Locally owned companies throughout the Southeast, like excellent Glacier Adventure over on Breiðamerkurjökull (p163), also offer more challenging ice treks and ice climbs, or combos, such as a glacier hike plus a lagoon boat trip.

Getting up on the Vatnajökull Ice Cap
SNOWMOBILING, HIKING AND SUPER-JEEP JOYRIDES

Access to the bulk of Vatnajökull is only for experienced folks set up for a serious polar-style expedition: the ice cap is cracked with deep crevasses, made invisible by coverings of fresh snow, and there are often sudden, violent blizzards. You can travel way up into this ice wilderness on organised snowmobile or super-Jeep tours.

Companies lead activities on the broad glacial spur **Skálafellsjökull**, 840m above sea level and with spectacular 360-degree views. Most travellers choose to do an awesome snowmobile ride. You're kitted out with overalls, helmets, boots and gloves,

 GUIDES AROUND SKAFTAFELL

Tröll Expeditions
Offering glacier hikes, ice climbing and wintertime ice cave tours from its base 18km east near Hof.

Icelandic Mountain Guides
Family-friendly 'Blue Ice Experience' on the ice run from Skaftafell four to eight times daily year-round.

Glacier Adventure
Glacier walks plus winter ice-cave exploring from its base at Hali Country Hotel, 68km east.

then play follow-the-leader along a fixed trail – great fun. **Glacier Jeeps** and **Glacier Journey** both offer snowmobiling and super-Jeep tours. Glacier Jeeps also offers a glacier hike. Snowmobile drivers need a driving licence (passengers don't).

Glacial Ice Caves in Winter

MAGNIFICENT, SHIMMERING NATURAL PHENOMENA

Wonder at glorious dimpled caverns of exquisite blue light accessible (usually at glacier edges) only from around November to March. They can be viewed only in cold conditions, and become unstable and unsafe in warmer weather. Temporary ice caves are created anew each season by the forces of nature, and are scouted by local experts. They *must* be visited with guides, who will ensure safety and correct equipment. As with glacier hikes, tours generally involve getting kitted out (crampons, helmets etc), then driving to the glacier edge and taking a walk to the cave. Reasonable fitness and mobility are required.

With their rapid growth in popularity, the largest and most accessible ice caves become crowded when tour groups arrive (from as far afield as Reykjavík). Day tours from Reykjavík are not an especially good idea, due to travel time (four-hour drive, one way). Often these guided groups visit the same cave – it's disappointing to find queues to enter.

We recommend you go with a local company. **From Coast to Mountains** (fromcoasttomountains.com) and sister company **Local Guide** (localguide.is) are the regional experts on ice caves in the Southeast, and can get you to more remote, private caves if you have time, stamina and cash.

Other good, locally owned companies include **Glacier Adventure**, **IceGuide**, **Glacier Journey**, **Ice Explorers** and **Glacier Trips** (spot a trend in the names?). Some tours depart from Skaftafell, while most depart from the Jökulsárlón car park (57km east of Skaftafell) – check when booking.

SOARING OVER THE GLACIERS

Sightseeing flights by **Atlantsflug** (flightseeing.is) offer a brilliant perspective on all this natural splendour. They leave from the tiny airfield on the Ring Road, just by the turnoff to the Skaftafellsstofa Visitor Centre. Choose between tour options, with views over Landmannalaugar, Lakagígar, Skaftafell peaks, Jökulsárlón and Grímsvötn.

If you love a thrilling scenic overflight, you can pair your glacier flight with a helicopter ride over scintillating Askja at highland farm Möðrudalur (p305).

FOR LODGING IN THE SOUTHEAST

Inside the park, the only option is to camp. There's very little accommodation nearby, and hotels in the Southeast book up. Bring either a tent or a firm hotel booking. For other places to stay see page 150.

GETTING AROUND

All visiting vehicles must pay for parking at Skaftafell (if you go to Jökulsárlón in the same day, then you'll pay 50% of the rate there – and vice versa). Signs indicate rates and how to pay (input your licence plate number via a website, the Parka app, kiosks at the lot, or screens inside the visitor centre). The fee is for one day, and is valid until midnight each day.

Skaftafell is a stop (in front of the visitor centre) on the Reykjavík–Höfn Strætó bus route 51, and Reykjavík–Jökulsárlón excursion buses (icelandbybus.is) stop here.

Skaftafell
Laki
Skeiðarársandur   Hvannadalshnúkur
Kirkjubæjarklaustur   Ingólfshöfði
              Landbrotshólar
Eldhraun

Beyond Skaftafell

Glaciers lord over lava fields, waterfalls and the largest sandy glacial outwash plains in the world.

Glittering glaciers and brooding mountains line the eye-popping stretch of the Ring Road between Skaftafell and little Kirkjubæjarklaustur hamlet in the east and the iceberg-filled lagoon Jökulsárlón in the west. The unfolding landscape, from lava fields to pseudocraters, torquing glaciers to waterfall-laden escarpments, makes it difficult to keep your eyes on the road – come with an empty data card in your camera, you'll use it all.

Towards the coastline, the Ingólfshöfði reserve is visited by guided tour only, but offers an expansive view on land and sea, with puffins to boot. And inland, the Lakagígar (Laki crater row) makes for secluded, magnificent hiking, while Hvannadalshnúkur, Iceland's tallest mountain, is the province of the pros.

TOP TIP

Limited food and sleeping options in the Southeast don't meet demand. Book very early, self-cater and know that you'll be paying inflated prices.

LINDA_K/SHUTTERSTOCK ©

Hvannadalshnúkur (p156)

Ingólfshöfði

Peep Puffins on a Historic Headland
TRACTOR RIDE TO INGÓLFSHÖFÐI

While everyone's gaze naturally turns inland in this spectacular part of Iceland, there are reasons to look offshore too – in particular to the 76m-high **Ingólfshöfði** (pronounced in-golvs-huv-thi) promontory, rising from the flatlands like a strange dream.

In spring and summer, this beautiful, isolated nature reserve is visited by nesting puffins, skuas and other seabirds, and you may see whales offshore. It's also of great historical importance – it was here that Ingólfur Arnarson, Iceland's first settler, stayed the winter on his original foray to the country in 874 CE.

The reserve is open to visitors on tours with local farmer, climber and photographer Einar on the Ingólfshöfði Puffin Tour (puffintour.is). Tours begin with a fun and spectacular ride across 6km of shallow tidal lagoon in a tractor-drawn wagon. After a short but steep sandy climb, there's a 1½-hour guided walk round the headland. The emphasis is on

WINTER AROUND SKAFTAFELL

Winter travel in the region is booming, with the strong draws of the Northern Lights and ice caves (p153). These caves form within the ice of a glacier and become solid and safe for visiting only in the coldest months. You can also still do glacier walks in winter – and the glaciers look more pristine, taking on the iridescent blue hue so beloved by photographers. In the right conditions, Svartifoss freezes in January to February (on the flip side, in winter the falls are not always accessible, due to slippery, unsafe tracks). Between December and March, access to trails is weather-dependent, and some may require crampons. There are also restricted daylight hours, so always talk to park staff about your best options.

 WHERE TO EAT IN KIRKJUBÆJARKLAUSTUR

Kjarr
Mod new bistro at the foot of the Systrafoss with superb Arctic char and other fresh, seasonal fare. €€

Systrakaffi
This busy restaurant gets slammed in summer, but has a wide-ranging menu from burgers to lamb. €€

Hótel Klaustur Restaurant
Popular sunny, enclosed dining terrace and bar featuring local produce (Arctic char, slow-cooked lamb shank etc). €€

birdwatching, with stunning mountain backdrops to marvel over on clear days. The puffins usually appear sometime in May and leave Iceland around mid-August.

Go for a post-tour (excellent) coffee or cake at welcoming Cafe Vatnajökull, just up on the Ring Road.

Hit Iceland's Highest Peak
CLIMBING HVANNADALSHNÚKUR

Iceland's highest mountain, **Hvannadalshnúkur** (2110m), pokes out from Öræfajökull, an offshoot of Vatnajökull. This lofty peak is actually the northwestern edge of an immense 5km-wide crater – the biggest active volcano in Europe after Sicily's Mt Etna. It erupted in 1362, firing out the largest amount of tephra in Iceland's recorded history.

Einar, the owner of From Coast to Mountains, holds the record for ascents of Hvannadalshnúkur (over 300!) and his grandfather was on the team that first ascended it. His stepson Aron, who owns Local Guide, also takes groups up, as does Icelandic Mountain Guides.

Driving Through Prehistory
WORLD'S LARGEST GLACIAL PLAIN

The sandar are fantastically flat sweeps of sand sprawling along Iceland's southeastern coast. High in the mountains, glaciers scrape up silt, sand and gravel that is then carried by fast-flowing grey-brown glacial rivers, or (more dramatically) by glacial bursts, down to the coast and strewn in huge, barren plains. The sandar here are so impressive that the Icelandic word (singular: *sandur*) is used internationally to describe these glacial outwash plains.

Immediately to the west of the world's largest sandur, **Skeiðarársandur**, a precipitous 767m-tall palisade of cliffs known as **Lómagnúpur** towers over the landscapes, begging to be photographed. It's the inspiration for many legends, and looks particularly good as a backdrop to the turf-roofed farm at Núpsstaður where buildings date back to the early 19th century, and the idyllic chapel is one of the last turf churches in Iceland.

Inland Núpsstaðarskógar, a beautiful low-growing woodland area on the slopes of the mountain Eystrafjall, is best explored on a tour (due to the perils of crossing the Núpsá river). In July and August, Icelandic Mountain Guides runs a guided five-day (65km) backpacking hike through Núpsstaðarskógar, over to Grænalón (an ice-dammed marginal lake), across the glacier Skeiðarárjökull and then into Morsárdalur in Skaftafell.

JÖKULHLAUP!

The section of Ring Road that passes across Skeiðarársandur was the last bit of the national highway to be constructed, in 1974 (until then, folks from Höfn had to drive to Reykjavík via Akureyri). Long gravel dykes have been strategically positioned to channel floodwaters away from this highly susceptible artery. They did little good, however, when within a few hours in late 1996 the Grímsvötn (or Gjálp) eruption created a massive *jökulhlaup* (glacial flood) releasing up to 3000 billion litres of water and dragging icebergs the size of three-storey buildings – three Ring Road bridges were washed away like matchsticks. There's a memorial of twisted bridge girders and an information board along the Ring Road just west of Skaftafell.

 WHERE TO STAY NEAR KIRKJUBÆJARKLAUSTUR

Magma Hotel
Winning hearts with beautiful design, peaceful surrounds and friendly staff, by a lake with lush views. €€€

Iceland Bike Farm
Stay in a countryside 'glamping hut' and take fat-tyre mountain bike rides (also available to nonguests). €€

Kirkjubær II Campground
Good kitchen, paid showers and laundry. €

Lómagnúpur

Do not drive off-road in these expanses. It is illegal and hugely destructive to the fragile environment.

This 70km stretch has very little by way of traveller facilities. The few accommodation options in pretty green oases include Dalshöfði Guesthouse on a remote, scenic farm 5km north of the Ring Road, and Lækjaborgir Guesthouse, a cluster of sweet, high-quality studios and cottages. There are no shops – BYO groceries if you are overnighting.

Exploring the Twin Falls at Kirkjubæjarklaustur

A PEACEFUL OASIS IN THE VOLCANIC SOUTHEAST

Many a foreign tongue has been tied in knots trying to say Kirkjubæjarklaustur. It helps to break it into bits: *Kirkju* (church), *bæjar* (farm) and *klaustur* (convent). Otherwise, do as the locals do and call it 'Klaustur'.

Klaustur is tiny, even by Icelandic standards – a few houses and farms scattered across a brilliant-green backdrop. Still, it's the only real service town between Vík and Höfn, and it's a major crossroads to several dramatic spots in the interior, including Landmannalaugar and Laki.

At the western end of the village, the lovely double waterfall, **Systrafoss**, shimmers down the cliffs and a sign outlines three short walks in the pretty wooded area (Iceland's tallest

WHY I LOVE SKEIÐARÁRSANDUR

Alexis Averbuck, writer

Wild Skeiðarársandur is the largest sandur in the world, covering 1300 sq km. As you drive from the south, up the east coast, you pass lava fields and pseudocraters, and emerge into this moody glacial outwash plain stretching 40km between ice cap and coast (from Núpsstaður to Öræfi). Mists swirl down off the glaciers which are just becoming visible in the distance, and the vibe is absolutely one-of-a-kind. Since the Settlement Era, Skeiðarársandur continues to grow, swallowing farmland. The region used to be relatively well-populated (for Iceland), but in 1362 the volcano beneath Öræfajökull (known as Knappafellsjökull) erupted and the *jökulhlaup* (flooding caused by volcanic eruption beneath ice) laid waste. The area was renamed Öræfi (Wasteland).

 WHERE TO WALK AROUND LAKI

Crater Row
Gentle 500m walk through craters from Laki parking and ranger hut. A brochure (on park website) explains its history.

Tjarnargígar
Relatively easy trail to the Tjarnargígar crater lake; extend to 1½ hours through lava channel Eldborgarfarvegur.

Fagrifoss
A short walk to magnificent, usually deserted falls; the parking turnoff is 24km along Rte F206 to Laki.

SERGEY DZYUBA/SHUTTERSTOCK ©

THE GUIDE

SOUTHEAST ICELAND BEYOND SKAFTAFELL

FJAÐRÁRGLJÚFUR

The verdantly twisting picturesque Fjaðrárgljúfur canyon, topped by waterfalls and carved out by the Fjaðrá river, has been well and truly discovered, thanks to Instagrammers and one Justin Bieber (who filmed a video clip here). Park at the top to reach the metal-barriered overlook with the best views. Or follow the well-maintained walking trail down its southern edge with plenty of places to gaze into the gorge's gorgeous rocky, writhing depths and emerald-green surrounds. It's a couple of kilometres down to the larger car park (rumoured to be getting a cafe soon).

The canyon is just west of Kirkjubæjar-klaustur, 3km north of the Ring Road via Rte 206.

trees grow here!). The lake, Systravatn, reached by a leisure-ly climb up steps cut into the hill beside the falls, was once a bathing place for nuns. A marked 2.5km walking path leads from the lake to descend near the basalt columns of Kirkju-gólf (Church Floor), and takes in glorious views.

Look out for local Arctic char (trout) on menus – it comes from pure water directly under the nearby lava field – like at the excellent bistro Kjarr, at the foot of the falls.

Stop by the helpful tourist office inside the visitor centre for good local information and a short film on the Laki erup-tion, plus coverage and exhibitions on Katla Geopark and Vatnajökull National Park. This is the base for the lesser-visited western pocket of the national park, best accessed from the Fjallabak Route (Rte F208), which connects to pop-ular Landmannalaugar and arcs up from the western side of the Skaftá river, between Vík and Kirkjubæjarklaustur. It's only accessible by 4WD or super-bus.

Witness Iceland's Largest Pseudocrater Field & Lava Flows

THE SURREAL MOUNDS OF LANDBROTSHÓLAR

West of the village of Kirkjubæjarklaustur and south of the Ring Road, the vast, dimpled, vivid-green pseudocrater field **Landbrotshólar** undulates into the distance. It's the larg-est in Iceland at about 50 sq km. Pseudocraters form when hot lava pours over wetlands. The subsurface water boils and steam explodes through to make these barrow-like mounds – not real craters. The origin of the lava of Landbrotshólar has been a matter for debate, but it's now believed to be the 10th-century Eldgjá eruption. To the west, they give way to eerie lava field **Eldhraun**, averaging 12m thick, that appears to alter as light conditions change. It contains more than 15 cu km of lava and covers an area of 565 sq km, making it the world's largest re-corded lava flow from a single eruption (Laki).

You'll emerge in the west near Hrífunes (pronounced something like ri-voo-ness), a perfectly placed hamlet, in the peaceful and impossi-bly green surrounds of Skaf-tártunga, with many excellent guesthouses.

FOR WATERFALL LOVERS

Foss á Síðu, 11km east of Kirkjubæjarklaustur on the Ring Road, is a head-turning cascade. During especially strong winds, however, it actually goes straight up! For another great waterfall, visit **Aldeyjarfoss** (p253).

WHERE TO STAY IN HRÍFUNES

Glacier View Guesthouse
In clear weather, see Vatnajökull and Mýrdalsjökull from the lounge. €€

Hrífunes Guesthouse
Stylish farmhouse, cosy lounge and stunning photos by local photographer who runs tours (phototours.is). €€

Hrífunes Nature Park
Enjoy stellar views, Northern Lights in winter and an outdoor wood-fired hot tub with modern small houses. €€

The Austere Crater Rows of Lakagígar

HIKE MOUNTAINS, CRATERS, VOLCANO LAKES AND LAVA FIELDS

It's almost impossible to comprehend the immensity of the Laki eruptions, one of the most catastrophic volcanic events in human history. Nowadays the smoothly variegated scree hills and twisted lava fields covered with delicate green moss bely the apocalypse that spawned it some 235 years ago. It's a fascinating place to visit and hike, with relatively few visitors.

Always stick to marked paths and roads in this ecologically sensitive region – part of Vatnajökull National Park. Your footsteps and tyre tracks remain for generations. The narrow track through the reserve is a loop: drive it counterclockwise to avoid encountering an oncoming vehicle and damaging the landscape. Rangers staff a hut with excellent information at the Laki car park when the road to Laki is open (usually mid-June until early September).

Although **Laki** (818m) peak did not erupt, it loaned its name to the 25km-long Lakagígar Crater Row, which stretches northeastwards and southwestwards from its base. Scramble up a steep path for 40 minutes to one hour from the parking area. From the top, exhilarating 360-degree views encompass the fissure, undulating lava fields, lakes and glinting glaciers in the distance.

The crater row itself is fascinating to explore, with multicoloured dunes, lava tubes and unusual wildlife like the Arctic fox and snow bunting. At the foot of Laki, marked paths lead through the two closest craters.

An absolute highlight of the Laki experience, Fagrifoss (Beautiful Falls) exceeds its name. One of Iceland's most bewitching falls, it has rivulets of water shimmering over immense black rocks.

Visiting the area requires a large, robust Jeep and four-wheel driving experience (rivers must be forded). If you don't meet these requirements, join a tour. Family-owned Secret Iceland in Kirkjubæjarklaustur offers excellent super-Jeep tours that get you to the crater field first-thing so you hike Laki mountain completely alone, then return, stopping for wonderful little-known hikes, with knowledgeable guides who provide informative geological and historical commentary along the way.

BYO lunch (there's no food for sale). Camping is forbidden within the reserve. The nearest campsite, operated by the national park, with hut facilities, toilets and showers, is at Blágil, about 11km from Laki, off Rte F207.

THE LAKI ERUPTION

In the summer of 1783, a vast set of fissures erupted, forming around 135 craters. The Laki craters fountained molten rock 1km into the air for eight months, spewing out over 15 cu km of volcanic material, creating the lava field **Eldhraun**, covering 565 sq km. Far more devastating were the hundreds of millions of tonnes of ash and sulphuric acid that poured from the fissures. The sun was blotted out, grass died off, and around two-thirds of Iceland's livestock perished from starvation and poisoning. Some 9000 people – a fifth of the country's population – were killed and the remainder faced the Móðuharðindin (Hardship of the Mist), a famine that followed. Across the northern hemisphere, clouds of ash blocked the sun. Temperatures dropped and acid rain fell, causing devastating crop failures.

GETTING AROUND

Kirkjubæjarklaustur is a stop on the Reykjavík–Vík–Höfn bus route. Buses stop at the N1. Buses travelling east call at Skaftafell and Jökulsárlón. Super-Jeep trips using the Fjallabak Route (F208) to Landmannalaugar or going to Laki leave from here.

JÖKULSÁRLÓN

Spectacular, luminous-blue icebergs drift through Jökulsárlón (p162; pronounced yokul-sar-lon) glacier lagoon, right beside the Ring Road between Höfn and Skaftafell. About a million people per year make the pilgrimage to visit this wonder.

The icebergs calve from Breiðamerkurjökull, an offshoot of Vatnajökull, crashing down into the water and drifting towards the Atlantic Ocean. They can spend up to five years floating in the 25-sq-km-plus, 250m-deep lagoon, melting, re-freezing and occasionally toppling over with a mighty splash, startling the birds. They then move on via Jökulsá, Iceland's shortest river, out to sea at Fellsfjara. Although it looks as though it's been here since the last ice age, the lagoon is only about 80 years old. Until the mid-1930s Breiðamerkur-jökull reached the Ring Road. It's now retreating rapidly (up to a staggering 500m per year), and the lagoon is con-sequently growing.

REYKJAVÍK ⊛   ● Jökulsárlón

TOP TIP

Countless tours take in Jökulsárlón, a true Iceland highlight. With summer's plentiful light, visit in early morning or late evening to avoid crowds. Follow rules: flora, fauna and natural features are protected, drones and fires prohibited and rubbish must be carried out. Stick to marked paths to preserve delicate terrain.

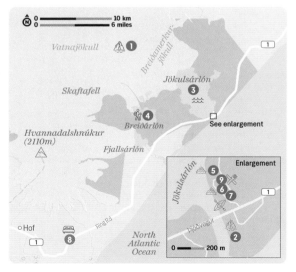

SIGHTS
1 Breiðamerkurjökull
2 Fellsfjara (Diamond Beach)
3 Jökulsárlón

ACTIVITES, COURSES & TOURS
4 Breiðárlón
5 Glacier Lagoon
6 Ice Lagoon Zodiac Boat Tours
7 IceGuide

SLEEPING
8 Fosshotel Glacier Lagoon

EATING
see 9 Heimahumar
9 Jökulsárlón Cafe
see 9 Nailed It
see 9 Sweet & Savory

Beyond Jökulsárlón

Djúpivogur •

Fláajökull
Heinabergsjökull • Hólmur • Lón
Skálafellsjökull • • Höfn

● Jökulsárlón
Fjallsárlón

Glacier lagoons, ice tongues and ice caves emerge at lush lagoons and dramatic mountain ranges with activities throughout.

TOP TIP

See our Skaftafell (p148) and Beyond Skaftafell (p154) sections for more tours getting out in the icy wonderland. In summer: glacier walks, kayaking, snowmobile and super-Jeep tours. In winter: ice caves.

Just southwest of Jökulsárlón, another wonderful and less-visited glacier lagoon, Fjallsárlón beckons. Then, the heavenly 80km stretch of Ring Road between Jökulsárlón and Höfn is dotted with about 20 rural properties (many with glaciers in their backyards) offering accommodation, activities and occasionally food. North of Höfn, the land softens into generous bird-filled lagoons and wetlands before spiring into sheer scree hills and merging into the Eastfjords.

Gentle, family-friendly lures include a quality museum and outdoor hot-pots. But those looking for a little more exertion will find walks to (or on) glacier tongues, visits to wintertime ice caves, snowmobile safaris, glacier lagoon kayaking and horse riding in natural splendour.

TOMAS WOLESCHLAGER/SHUTTERSTOCK ©

FEDERICO NERI/SHUTTERSTOCK ©

> Scan this QR code for parking rates at the lagoon and trail maps.

Amphibious tour, Jökulsárlón

TOP SIGHT

Jökulsárlón & Fellsfjara

Which is best? In the wee hours, alone, with light shifting on ice forms? Or during the day? When you can not only admire the wondrous glinting ice sculptures in the lagoon and on the beach – some of them striped with vivid ash layers from volcanic eruptions – and scout for seals, but also take a thrilling lagoon boat trip.

DID YOU KNOW?

Vatnajökull is Iceland's largest ice cap.

Around its edges, slow-moving rivers of ice – glaciers – flow down the mountainsides.

Glaciers carry stony sediment, which they dump in the moraines that surround Jökulsárlón.

On the Water

In summer, the lagoon is a hub for boat tours and some kayaking – a chance to get out among the bergs. Check in 30 minutes before to avoid missing the boat (as it were).

Amphibious Boat Tours

Take a memorable 40-minute trip with **Glacier Lagoon** (ice lagoon.is) in an amphibious boat, which trundles along the shore like a bus before driving into the water. On-board guides regale you with factoids about the lagoon, and you can taste 1000-year-old ice. Trips run from May to October (sometimes longer) out of the eastern car park – up to 40 a day in summer. Prebook online.

Zodiac Tours

Glacier Lagoon and **Ice Lagoon Zodiac Boat Tours** (ice lagoon.com) offer Zodiac tours of the lagoon. The one-hour experience has a maximum of 10 passengers per boat and travels at speed up near the glacier edge (not done by the amphibious boats) before cruising back at a leisurely pace. Book ahead online. Glacier Lagoon's minimum age is 10 years and 1.3m height; Ice Lagoon Zodiac Boat Tours' is six years or 1m height.

Kayaking

The chance to get out among the icebergs in a quiet kayak woos nature lovers. **IceGuide** (iceguide.is) leads hour-long paddles from May to September from their van on the eastern car park. Prebook online – minimum age 14, maximum weight 120kg (265lbs).

Walking the Lagoon

Lagoon boat trips are excellent, but you can get almost as close to those cool-blue masterpieces by walking along the shore, and taste ancient ice by hauling it out of the shallows. On the Ring Road west of the car park, there are designated parking areas where you can visit the lake at less-touristed stretches of shoreline. And the national park has set up walking routes with information detailing geological features, and rangers lead daily tours mid-June to mid-August from their hut in the car park. Consult the maps on the park website for a series of trails from easy to challenging, such as route B1 from the car park to the glacier ridge, **Helguhóll**.

A favourite, longer route, the **Breiðármörk Trail**, connects the western car park at Jökulsárlón to the lagoons **Breiðárlón** (10km one way) and Fjallsárlón (15.3km; p164). It's classified as challenging (at least five hours with no water along the route), though much of it is over level ground and there are no rivers to ford. The visitor centre at Skaftafell sells a trail map. Ice Explorers and Glacier Adventures guide glacier hikes on **Breiðamerkurjökull**.

Fellsfjara

Cross from the lagoon car parks underneath the Ring Road bridge out to the mouth of the Jökulsá river. Tourists dubbed the site '**Diamond Beach**', and the name has stuck on marketing brochures. You'll see why: ice boulders and bergs glittering photogenically on the black-sand beach as part of their final journey into the ocean.

Eating at the Lagoon

Year-round **Jökulsárlón Cafe** in the lagoon eastern car park offers basic snacks but is usually overwhelmed. Better bets are food trucks **Heimahumar** (warm up with lobster bisque, a lobster roll or hot dog), **Nailed It** (fresh fish and chips) and **Sweet & Savory** (crepes and pancakes).

JÖKULSÁRLÓN ON FILM

A natural film set, Jökulsárlón masqueraded as Siberia in *Lara Croft: Tomb Raider* (2001) – the amphibious boats were painted grey and used as Russian ships. For James Bond *Die Another Day* (2002) the lagoon was specially frozen and six Aston Martins were destroyed on the ice.

TOP TIPS

- Look for approaching traffic plus distracted drivers on the single-lane Ring Road bridge.
- Two large car parks on the ocean side of the Ring Road (signposted Eystri- and Vestri-Fellsfjara) are best for campers. Walk under the bridge to the lagoon.
- In June and July, avoid nesting and dive-bombing Arctic terns near the lagoon's eastern car park.
- Closest accommodation east: around Hali (13km; no camping; next campsite is in Höfn), or west: **Fosshotel Glacier Lagoon** (28km), camping at Svínafell (52km) or Skaftafell (60km).

ZACK FRANK/SHUTTERSTOCK ©

Fláajökull

Floating Fjallsárlón Glacier Lagoon
SAND PLAINS AND INTIMATE LAGOON VIBES

The easternmost part of the large sandar region (p156), Breiðamerkursandur is backed by a sweeping panorama of glacier-capped mountains, some of which are fronted by deep lagoons. **Fjallsárlón** is one such lagoon, and it's a popular smaller (around 3 sq km) alternative to busy, larger (25 sq km) Jökulsárlón, 10km further east. Breiðamerkursandur is one of the main breeding grounds for Iceland's great skuas. Thanks to rising numbers of these ground-nesting birds, there's also a growing population of Arctic foxes. Historically, Breiðamerkursandur also figures in *Njál's Saga*, which ends with Kári Sölmundarson arriving in this idyllic spot to 'live happily ever after' – which has to be some kind of miracle in a saga.

A sign off the Ring Road indicates Fjallsárlón, where icebergs calve from Fjallsjökull and Zodiac tours cruise among the bergs. Among the walking paths here is Breiðármörk Trail (p163), which connects to Jökulsárlón (in the national park). The visitor centre is home to Frost, a cafe with hot

WHERE TO STAY IN THE JÖKULSÁRLÓN COUNTRYSIDE

Hrafnavellir Guest House
Seven small cabins about 25km east of Höfn on a super-peaceful patch with views across the river delta. €€

Kálfafellsstaður Guesthouse
Embrace the farmstay experience within a 20-minute drive of the glacier lagoon. €€

Lambhús
Ducks and horses, plus 11 cute, compact self-catering cottages (sleeping four to five) 31km from Höfn. €€

dishes, soups, salad and snacks. Fjallsárlón Glacial Lagoon Boat Tours (fjallsarlon.is) depart for 45-minute Zodiac trips among lagoon icebergs (April to October; minimum age 5). The trail to the boat's departure point at the lagoon shore is gently intrepid, and there's also an intimacy to a tour on this lagoon – you don't have to travel far to reach the glacier snout and the lack of huge crowds is grand.

Get Your Glacier On

EXPLORING VATNAJÖKULL'S EASTERN GLACIER TONGUES

Kvíárjökull glacier snakes down to the Kvíá river and is easily accessible from the Ring Road; look for the sign for Kvíármýrarkambur just west of the bridge over the river. Leave your car in the small car park and follow the path into the scenic valley.

Vatnajökull National Park authorities are working with landowners between Ingólfshöfði and Höfn to gain public access to areas of raw natural beauty (and take pressure off popular Skaftafell in the face of rising tourist numbers). These areas are signed off the Ring Road – for now, they are not especially well known, so you stand a good chance of finding yourself a tranquil pocket of glaciated wonder.

Uniquely, three glacier tongues – **Skálafellsjökull** (p152), **Heinabergsjökull** and **Fláajökull** – converge on the Hjallanes and Heinaberg area. A fourth, Hoffellsjökull, lies further east, closer to Höfn. Remarkable walking trails and scenery include glacier lakes and moraines.

Heinabergsjökull is 8km off the Ring Road on a gravel road (signposted east of Guesthouse Skálafell). Walking trails from Guesthouse Skálafell include the 8km Hjallanes loop or a 7.5km hike to Heinabergslón (the icy lagoon at the foot of Heinabergsjökull). From Heinabergslón an 8.3km trail leads to Fláajökull. Brilliant kayaking trips on Heinabergslón are operated by IceGuide.

Hoffellsjökull is accessed from the road to Hoffell guesthouse. A signed, 4km gravel road (which washes out in heavy rain) leads to the glacier, which calves into a small lake. This is a good glacier to walk to from the guesthouse; upon your return, you can soak in the hot-pots there.

Stop by the visitor centres in Skaftafell or Kirkjubæjarklaustur, or the ranger hut at Jökulsárlón, to ask about road conditions, find out if any areas are newly accessible, and buy the *Heinaberg, Hjallanes, Hoffell* map. Or visit the Jökulsárlón and Heinaberg sections of the national park website (vjp.is).

BEER IN THE SOUTHEAST

Look out for Vatnajökull Beer: marketed as 'frozen in time' beer, it's brewed from 1000-year-old water (ie Jökulsárlón icebergs), flavoured with locally grown Arctic thyme. You'll find it in restaurants around the Southeast (though it's brewed in Selfoss).

Fabulous farmhouse restaurant Jón Ríki at **Hólmur** is something of a surprise, with funky decor, a small in-house brewery, and beautifully presented, high-quality dishes. Book ahead for grilled langoustine, avocado chips and panna cotta for dessert. Sourdough pizza goes well with super-interesting house brews like the mango IPA or the jalapeno-and-pumpkin ale.

Seljavellir Guesthouse
Superb spot with 20 smart, minimalist rooms – all with splendid views – about 6km from Höfn. €€

Dynjandi
Cosy three-room guesthouse on a photogenic horse farm at the foot of mountains about 9km from Höfn. €€

Guesthouse Skálafell
Friendly working farm with a handful of agreeable rooms in the farmhouse and in motel-style units and cottages. €€

Celebrating a Local Writer & Arctic Char

FEED YOUR MIND AND YOUR BELLY

Cleverly crafted museum **Þórbergssetur** (thorbergur.is; its inspired exterior looks like a shelf of books) pays tribute to the most famous son of this sparsely populated region – writer Þórbergur Þórðarson (1888–1974). Þórbergur was a real maverick (with interests spanning yoga, Esperanto and astronomy), and his first book *Bréf til Láru* (Letter to Laura) caused huge controversy because of its radical socialist content.

It's in the Hali Country Hotel, 13km east of Jökulsárlón, and is also home to a quality restaurant specialising in Arctic char.

Höfn's Seafood Scene

FINE DINING HARBOURSIDE

Although it's no bigger than many European villages, the Southeast's main town feels like a sprawling metropolis after driving through the emptiness on either side. Its setting is stunning; on a clear day, wander the waterside, find a quiet bench and just gaze at Vatnajökull and its guild of glaciers.

Höfn simply means 'harbour', and is pronounced like an unexpected hiccup (just say 'hup' while inhaling). It's an apt name – it relies heavily on fishing and fish processing, and is famous for its *humar* (often translated as lobster, but technically it's langoustine). In recent years the catch has been scarce so commercial fishing has been halted at the time of writing. Every year in late June or early July, Höfn's **Humarhátíð** festival honours this tasty crustacean, however, those on the menu these days are imported. Nonetheless, the good restaurants in the town have some of the best food (and seafood, in particular) on this coast.

Stroll off your meal on Ósland promontory, about 1km beyond the harbour with a walking path round its marshes and lagoons full of seabirds.

Swim it off at Sundlaug Hafnar, the town's popular outdoor swimming pool with water slides, hot-pots and a steam bath. Or shop it off at handiwork store Handraðinn.

Most Ring Road travellers stop to use the town's services, so prebook accommodation, especially in summer.

Strolling Sandy Spits

LÓN'S SEABIRDS AND SOARING MOUNTAINS

The name **Lón** (Lagoon; pronounced 'lone') describes this shallow bay enclosed by two long spits between the sheer mountains Eystrahorn and Vestrahorn. The best access for

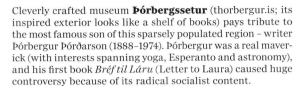

BEST RESTAURANTS IN HÖFN

Otto Matur & Drykkur
Oldest house in Höfn (1897), now an elegant space high on Nordic style and delicate dishes. €€

Pakkhús
Boisterous harbourside warehouse with high-level kitchen creativity. Wait for a table in its downstairs bar. €€

Hafnarbúðin
Tiny old-school diner with big breakfasts, fast-food favourites and fine langoustine baguette – for a (relative) bargain of 2500kr. €

Íshúsið Pizzeria
Family-friendly thin-crust, stone-baked pizzas right by the harbour. €€

Kaffi Hornið
Casual log-cabin bar and restaurant with varied menu plus, of course, local seafood. €€

 WHERE TO STAY IN HÖFN

Old Airline Guesthouse
Central and sparkling, with five rooms (shared bathrooms), plus a large lounge and guest kitchen. €€

Guesthouse Dyngja
Pristine, six-room guesthouse in a prime harbourfront locale, with self-service breakfast and an outdoor deck. €€

Milk Factory
Renovated dairy factory with 17 modern, hotel-standard rooms, including two with disabled access. €€

strolls on the sandy eastern spits is via Eystrahorn. Like other precipitous peaks in the region, this batholithic mountain was formed as a subsurface igneous intrusion, gradually revealed through erosion.

At the western end of Lón, the commanding Vestrahorn and its companion Brunnhorn form a cape between Skarðsfjörður and Papafjörður. Travel down the signposted road to Stokksnes to explore this striking area, known as Horn – the Viking Cafe is here, as is a farm-owner charging for car-park camping and land access to a black-sand beach with an old **Viking village film set**, where seals laze and the backdrop of Vestrahorn creates superb photos.

To the northwest an enormous colony of swans nests in spring and autumn in the delta of Jökulsá í Lóni river.

Exploring Wild Coast from Höfn to Djúpivogur

DRIVING OR HIKING RAW LANDS

Prepare yourself. The 105km stretch between Höfn and Djúpivogur is yet another impossibly scenic stretch. You'll curve past a handful of wee farms backed by amazingly precipitous peaks and austere scree hills in colours ranging from sienna to ebony. Mawing valleys open inland, seeming as if a dinosaur might be just around the bend. Black-sand beaches and bird-filled wetlands add plenty of 'oooh' moments.

In the middle of nowhere, Stafafell farm is a good hiking base for exploring Lónsöræfi as is Brekka í Lóni Farmstay. Among the day hikes in the hills and valleys north of Stafafell is a well-marked, 14.3km, four- to five-hour return walk to Hvannagil, a colourful rhyolite canyon on the eastern bank of the Jökulsá í Lóni river. Get a route description online at stafafell.is.

A trio of brothers owns Stafafell farm; one operates a hostel while another runs a basic campsite. There are no stores – bring picnic supplies from Höfn or Djúpivogur.

LÓNSÖRÆFI NATURE RESERVE

Get in touch with your inner hermit in remote, rugged nature reserve Lónsöræfi. Hiking this 320-sq-km protected wilderness with its colourful rhyolite mountains, inland from Stafafell, is challenging and only for experienced hikers (some trails require substantial river crossings). Although Lónsöræfi isn't in Vatnajökull National Park, the website (vjp.is) details hiking trails, and visitor centres at Skaftafell and Skriðuklaustur (in the east) advise and sell topo maps. Stay at campsites in the reserve or mountain huts (ferdaf. is) along the Snæfell–Lónsöræfi hike. It's a minimum 1½ to two days to reach the first hut unless you have someone to drive you partway. Or go with a guide from Icelandic Mountain Guides or South East Iceland.

GETTING AROUND

It's easiest to see the region with your own wheels. But if you're bussing, timetables may refer to Höfn as Höfn í Hornafirði (meaning Höfn in Hornafjörður) to differentiate it from all the other *höfn* (harbours) around Iceland. Höfn has a small airport serving Reykjavík's domestic airport.

One notable road in the area, 4WD track F985, branches north from the Ring Road, about 35km east of Jökulsárlón and 45km west of Höfn, to the broad glacial spur

Skálafellsjökull. This 16km-long track is practically vertical in places, with iced-over sections in winter, so best visited on tours with Glacier Jeeps and Glacier Journey (snowmobile or super-Jeep up on the glacier).

Don't even think of attempting to drive Rte F985 in a 2WD car – you'll end up with a huge rescue bill. F roads are only for heavy-duty 4WD vehicles. People in small 4WD cars, or inexperienced 4WDers, should likewise not attempt this route.

WEST ICELAND

A MICROCOSM OF ICELANDIC ELEMENTS

West Iceland offers everything from windswept beaches and historic villages to awe-inspiring volcanic and glacial terrain in one neat little package.

Geographically close to Reykjavík yet far, far away in sentiment, West Iceland (known as Vesturland; west.is) is a splendid blend of Iceland's offerings. Yet the larger masses of tourists have missed the memo, and you're likely to have remote parts of this wonderful region to yourself at times. Two of the best known Icelandic sagas, *Egil's Saga* and *Laxdæla Saga*, took place along the region's brooding waters, marked today by haunting cairns and an exceptional museum in lively Borgarnes.

The diverse and fascinating landscape of the long arm of 100km Snæfellsnes Peninsula is a favourite for its glacier, Snæfellsjökull, and the area around its national park is tops for birding, whale watching, lava-field hikes and horse riding. The harbour village Stykkishólmur makes an ideal base with some tempting restaurants and the ferry out to Flatey island and the Westfjords beyond.

Inland beyond Reykholt you'll encounter lava tubes and remote highland glaciers, including enormous Langjökull with its unusual ice cave; all added enticements. The coast and rolling meadows of the Dalir region are even less visited still, and have remote windswept promontories calling for exploration.

Good roads and regular buses mean that the features of the West are an easy trip from Reykjavík, offering a cross-section of the best Iceland has to offer in a very compact region.

THORSTEN HERBOLD/SHUTTERSTOCK ©

THE MAIN AREAS

BORGARNES
Saga-soaked
waterfront town.
p172

STYKKISHÓLMUR
Quaint harbour,
Snæfellsnes base.
p180

**SNÆFELLSJÖKULL
NATIONAL PARK**
Gorgeous glacier-
topped reserve.
p187

PX MEDIA/SHUTTERSTOCK ©

Above: Rauðfeldsgjá (p192). Left: Lighthouse, Súgandisey (p182)   169

Find Your Way

Buses serve the region's main villages, but to reach the furthest corners, wheels or a tour are necessary. The Baldur car ferry connects Stykkishólmur on Snæfellsnes Peninsula and Brjánslækur in the Westfjords, via Flatey island.

0 N

0   20 km
0   10 miles

CAR

Roads are largely excellent and easy to navigate in western Iceland. The rugged dirt roads are few, with only a handful of F roads off-limits for 2WD. Most villages have petrol stations.

BUS

Because of the good bus services passing through Borgarnes, you can reach many destinations in the West using Strætó (straeto. is) buses. Reykjavík to Akureyri routes run through Borgarnes, Bifröst and Staðarskáli, so it's simple to continue onwards toward the north.

Stykkishólmur, p180

Wander past charming chocolate-box houses in this buzzy harbour town with super eating and ferries to Flatey.

Borgarnes, p172

Step back into Saga times at the impressive Settlement Center in this fun-loving town.

Snæfellsjökull National Park, p187

Tramp through crunchy lava fields, along wind-swept coastlines and over Snæfellsjökull, the icy heart of this magical park.

Church, Ingjaldshóll (p193)

Plan Your Time

A tidy package of wild Iceland, the West makes for several simple loops: oft-forgotten Hvalfjörður, into the upper valley to the west of Borgarnes (called Borgarbyggð) and out along the Snæfellsnes Peninsula.

Pressed for Time

● Start your time in West Iceland at the **Hvammsvík Hot Springs** (p177) in Hvalfjörður to soak in the warm pools and cold-plunge in the ocean before driving on to the Snæfellsnes Peninsula. In a major hurry, you can circle the tip of the peninsula, through **Snæfellsjökull National Park** (p187), gawping at the cliffs and waterfalls, the ice cap and the craters, before dining in **Stykkishólmur** (p180).

Three Days to Explore

● Hike into the canyon **Rauðfeldsgjá** (p192) or up the **Saxhóll Crater** (p189) and hop a whale- and puffin-watching boat tour. Continue on to the Dalir, visiting **Eiríksstaðir** (p184) for saga stories and **Erpsstaðir** (p184) for ice-cream confections. Then go inland for activities on **Langjökull** (p179) or caving at **Víðgelmir** (p179), overnighting in **Húsafell** (p178).

SEASONAL HIGHLIGHTS

SPRING	SUMMER	AUTUMN	WINTER
Iceland awakes from winter. Mountain roads slowly become passable again and puffins arrive in May.	Lots of daylight, activities and mountain roads open. Hikers welcome; puffins leave by mid-August.	Breezier weather, optimal visiting conditions for those who prefer solitude as the tourist season begins to wind down.	Long nights with likely Northern Lights viewings and ice activities from snowmobiling to ice caving.

ANGELIKA HÖRSCHLÄGER/GETTY IMAGES ©

BORGARNES

REYKJAVÍK

Unassuming Borgarnes has got it going on. For such a tiny place, it bubbles with local life. One of the original settlement areas for the first Icelanders, it is loaded with history and sits on a scenic promontory along the broad waters of Borgarfjörður. Zip past the busy petrol stations and go into the old quarter to encounter the fun small-town vibe and one of Iceland's best museums, the Settlement Center. There you can learn about the establishment of human civilisation in Iceland, plus the dramatic antics of poet-warrior Egill Skalla-grímsson. His homestead and sites from the saga describing his life dot the town.

The laid-back vibe and cheerful, excellent restaurants and bar, welcoming guesthouses and top-notch geothermal pool make Borgarnes a good base before exploring further afield.

TOP TIP

West Iceland's main tourist information centres are in Borgarnes at Ljómalind craft co-op and the national park offices in Malarrif and Hellissandur. Read up in advance to enjoy the saga-soaked region: *Egils' Saga, Laxdæla Saga, Heimskringla, Eyrbyggja Saga, Saga of Erik the Red* and *Saga of the Greenlanders*, to name a few.

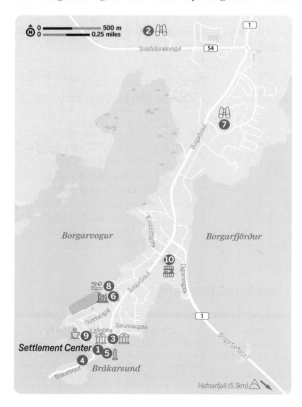

HIGHLIGHTS
1 Settlement Center

SIGHTS
2 Borg á Mýrum
3 Borgarfjördur Museum
4 Brákarsund
5 Brákin
6 Skallagrímsgarður
7 Viewing Disc

ACTIVITIES, COURSES & TOURS
8 Borgarnes Swimming Pool

DRINKING & NIGHTLIFE
9 Blómasetrið–Kaffi Kyrrð

SHOPPING
10 Ljómalind

Skallagrímsgarður cairn (p174)

FOR SPIRITS LOVERS

Crystalline Reyka vodka, found across Iceland, is produced in Borgarnes at Iceland's first distillery. For more on Icelandic drink, see page 34.

The Swashbuckling Poet of Egil's Saga

EXCELLENT MUSEUM AND SAGA LANDMARKS

Egil's Saga starts by recounting the tale of Kveldúlfur, grandfather of the warrior-poet Egill Skallagrímsson, who fled to Iceland during the 9th century after a falling out with the king of Norway. Kveldúlfur grew gravely ill on the journey, and instructed his son, Skallagrímur Kveldúlfsson, to throw his coffin overboard after he died and build the family farm wherever it washed ashore – this happened to be at Borg á Mýrum, a local farmstead. Egill Skallagrímsson grew up to be a fierce and creative individual who killed his first adversary at the age of seven, went on to carry out numerous raids on Ireland, England and Denmark, and saved his skin many a time by composing eloquent poetry.

HILLTOP VIEWS

The dramatically sheer mountain **Hafnarfjall** (844m) rises south across the fjord from Borgarnes. It's approximately – give or take a millennium or two – four million years old. You can climb it (7km) from the trailhead on Rte 1, near the southern base of the causeway into Borgarnes. There's a small birch wood at the base. Be careful of slippery scree cliffs once you ascend – you'll get sweeping views from the top. If that's a bit much, head to the much lower **Viewing Disc**, a small disc on the hill just northeast of the campsite, which labels the peaks all around.

WHERE TO SLEEP IN BORGARNES

Bjarg
This attractive series of linked cottages 1.5km north of Borgarnes overlooks the fjord and mountains. €€

Helgugata Guesthouse
Friendly Ludmila keeps this tidy guesthouse, perched on the cliff overlooking the twinkling fjord beyond. €€

Kría Guesthouse
Kría's two rooms have great water views in a private home on a quiet residential street. €€

Learn about him at Borgarnes' excellent **Settlement Center**, housed in an imaginatively restored warehouse by the harbour. The museum is divided into two fascinating exhibitions; each takes about 30 minutes to visit. The Settlement Exhibition covers the discovery and settlement of Iceland. Egil's Saga Exhibition recounts the amazing adventures of Egill and his family. It also has a top-notch restaurant.

To go deep into how the saga ties to the landscape around Borgarnes, download the detailed Locatify SmartGuide app and load the 'Egils Saga, Borg on the Moors' tour, which tells the stories of local landmarks from the tale. The Settlement Center has marked eight of the sites with cairns, including **Brákin**, **Borg á Mýrum** and **Skallagrímsgarður**, the burial mound of Skallagrímsson's father and son.

The Borg á Mýrum farm is named for the large rock (*borg*) behind the farmstead (private property); you can walk up to the cairn for views all around, and visit the small cemetery, which includes an ancient gravestone marked by runes.

Þorgerður Brák was Egill's nursemaid, and thought to be a Celtic slave. In one of the more dramatic moments in *Egil's Saga*, she heroically saves Egill's life, then dies in the strait, between Borgarnes and the islet offshore, named **Brákarsund** after her. The town celebrates an annual festival, Brákarhátíð, in her honour.

Embrace Town Culture
GEOTHERMAL POOL, CAFE CULTURE, SHOPS AND MORE

The charm of Borgarnes lies in its zippy daily life. Start at beautiful **Borgarnes Swimming Pool** (borgarbyggd.is), with hot-pots and steam room, all part of a large fjordside sports complex. This is a wonderful place to relax with views of the sea just offshore.

Seek refreshment at **Blómasetrið–Kaffi Kyrrð**, the quaint flower and gift shop that is also a cosy cafe with hot drinks, beer and snacks. Or, sleep over at the family's guesthouse. Browse **Ljómalind** crafts co-op and farmers market, a long-standing collaboration between local producers. It stocks everything from fresh dairy products from Erpsstaðir (p184) and organic meat to locally made bath products, handmade wool sweaters, jewellery and all manner of imaginative collectables.

The small municipal **Borgarfjörður Museum** has engaging exhibits, from the story of children in Iceland over the last 100 years to contemporary art shows.

BEST PLACES TO EAT IN BORGARNES

Bara
This welcoming bar serves Icelandic craft brews and some of the best fish and chips in Iceland, with a fun, friendly vibe. €€

Englendingavík
Casual, with a wonderful waterfront deck, Englendingavík serves tasty homemade dishes, from cakes to full meals of roast lamb or fresh fish. It has an attached guesthouse with good bay views. €€

Settlement Center Restaurant
This light-filled eatery built into the rock face is one of the region's best bets. Choose from traditional Icelandic and international eats (lamb, fish stew etc). The lunch buffet is very popular. €€

GETTING AROUND

Borgarnes is the major transfer point between Reykjavík and Akureyri, Snæfellsnes and the Westfjords. The bus stop is at the cluster of petrol stations (N1, Orkan). All services are reduced in winter.

Beyond Borgarnes

Fecund farms with deep history leading to powerful stone-strewn lava tubes and highlands, the gateway to the ice caps beyond.

As you head inland from buzzy Borgarnes and its broad Borgarfjörður up the river-twined valleys, you'll find more sites rich in early settlement lore, such as Reykholt, home to historian and chieftain Snorri Sturluson. Húsafell is the jumping-off point for activities on and in (!) Langjökull ice cap, plus has a hot springs and peaceful vibes. The nearby lava fields networked with underground tubes call to spelunkers, and spots like an idiosyncratic Icelandic goat farm and well-regarded horse farms call to animal lovers. Just south, generous Hvalfjörður is home to both the hike to Glymur waterfall as well as an inviting hot springs experience; a dreamy way to wrap it all up.

TOP TIP

This region of the West is especially fine for taking your time. The slow pace and varied landscape invite continued exploration.

JAIMIE TUCHMAN/SHUTTERSTOCK ©

Snorralaug (p178)

GLYMUR WATERFALL HIKE

At the head of Hvalfjörður, and up Botnsdalur valley, lies Glymur, Iceland's second-highest waterfall (198m). From the trailhead, it'll take a couple of hours to reach the cascade's viewpoints on rough, slippery trails. A log is placed to bridge the river only in summer. At the trailhead there's a good map with instructions. Reach the trailhead by following the turnoff on Rte 47 to Botnsdalur.

Bring water shoes for fording the river if you plan to cross and return on the west side, or retrace your steps on the east side. Try to visit after heavy rains or snow-melt for full effect. Note: there is no camping allowed around the trailhead.

Hvalfjörður Hot Springs & Hiking
POSH SPA AND WILDERNESS WALKS

Hvalfjörður (pronounced *kval*-fyur-thur) and the surrounding area feels suddenly pastoral despite being a mere 30-minute drive from the capital. Although lacking the majesty of the Snæfellsnes Peninsula further on, the sparkling fjord with shimmering waterfall Glymur offers excellent day-trip fodder. Those in a hurry to get to Borgarnes and beyond should instead head straight through the 5.7km-long tunnel beneath the fjord. Cyclists aren't permitted in the tunnel.

Interestingly, during WWII the fjord contained a submarine and warship station; over 20,000 American and British soldiers passed through. Learn more at the War & Peace Museum.

Today, though, the highlight is the Hvammsvík Hot Springs.

 WHERE TO STAY BEYOND BORGARNES

Steindórsstaðir
Set on a farm 2km from Reykholt proper; offers clean, cosy rooms with countryside views, and a hot tub. €€

Fossatún
Family-friendly spot with a guesthouse, hotel, cottage and camping huts next to a roaring waterfall, plus restaurant. €€

Hótel Glymur
On the northern side of Hvalfjörður with contemporary amenities, giant windows, hot-pot and restaurant. €€

As you round the north side of the fjord, keep your eyes peeled for the Saurbæjarkirkja, the church at the Saurbær farmstead. It's worth a look for its beautiful stained-glass work by Gerður Helgadóttir. It is named for Reverend Hallgrímur Pétursson, who served here from 1651 to 1669 and composed Iceland's most popular religious work, *Passion Hymns*.

On the southern side of Hvalfjörður you'll find dramatic **Mt Esja** (914m), a great spot for wilderness hiking. The most popular trail to the summit begins at Esjustofa Hiking Center (with a cafe), just north of Mosfellsbær. There are several routes up the mountain, but most people hike 2.8km to the viewpoint at Steinn. The trail gets much more technical after that.

Hvanneyri's Wool & Waffles

VISITING A QUIET FJORDSIDE HAMLET

Find your way to off-the-beaten-path village Hvanneyri, 12km east of Borgarnes, and in among fjordside homes you'll find the Agricultural Museum of Iceland complex with the fantastic wool centre, Ullarselið (ull.is). Handmade sweaters, scarves, hats and blankets share space with skeins of beautiful hand-spun yarn, and interesting bone and shell buttons. Plus there are needles and patterns to get you started. Skemma Cafe (Skemman Kaffihús) has a sunny deck and soups, waffles, cakes and coffee.

Historic Reykholt's Museum, Pool & Church

GOING DEEP ON SNORRI'S SAGA

Reykholt is a sleepy outpost (just a few farmsteads really) that on first glance offers few clues to its past as a major medieval settlement. It was home to one of the most important medieval chieftains and scholars, Snorri Sturluson, who was killed here, and today the main sights revolve around him. The interesting medieval study centre Snorrastofa is devoted to him and is built on his old farm, explaining Snorri's life and accomplishments, including a 1599 edition of his *Heimskringla* (sagas of the Norse kings).

At the age of 36, Snorri was appointed *lögsögumaður* (law speaker) of the Alþingi (Icelandic parliament). In the following decades he endured heavy pressure from the Norwegian king to promote the ruler's interests but, instead, Snorri busied himself with his writing until the unhappy Norwegian king Hákon finally snapped and issued a warrant for his capture

BEST HOT SPRINGS IN THE WEST

Deildartunguhver
Find Europe's biggest hot spring about 5km west of Reykholt, just off Rte 50, near the junction with Rte 518. Look for billowing clouds of steam, which rise from scalding water bubbling from the ground (180L per second and 100°C).

Krauma
Bathing complex at Deildartunguhver offering sleek hot pools, a cold pool and two steam rooms. There's also a restaurant and food truck.

Hvammsvík Hot Springs
Book ahead to soak in these fjord-front hot-pots and then cold plunge just offshore if you dare.

Canyon Baths
Húsafell's fabulous wilderness hot-pots newly opened only for pre-booked visits.

Dive into the Icelandic sagas

WHERE TO RIDE HORSES BEYOND BORGARNES

Hestaland
Ride fields and fjord shores with this top-notch horse farm. You'll get a short lesson in the arena before heading out.

Oddsstaðir
Guides multiday riding tours throughout West Iceland with a large team of horses.

– dead or alive. Snorri's political rival and former son-in-law Gissur Þorvaldsson saw his chance to impress the king and possibly snag the position of governor of Iceland in return. He arrived in Reykholt with 70 armed men on the night of 23 September 1241 and hacked the historian to death in the basement of his farmhouse.

The most important relic of Snorri's farm is **Snorralaug** (Snorri's Pool), a circular, stone-lined pool fed by a hot spring that may be the oldest handmade structure in Iceland. The stones at the base of the pool are original 10th-century, and it is believed that this is where Snorri bathed. A wood-panelled tunnel beside the spring (closed to the public) leads to the old farmhouse – the site of Snorri's gruesome murder.

The quaint old church dating from 1896 is open to the public; a 1040–1260 cistern for a smithy was found beneath it in 2001 – look for the viewing glass in the floor.

Icelandic Goat Centre
GABBING WITH THE GOATS

Farm workers walk you through pretty fields with endangered Icelandic goats. The farm's most famous resident, Casanova, a bright-eyed goat who had a starring turn in *Game of Thrones* (running from a dragon), passed away some years ago, but many charming ruminates remain and the gift shop is full of goodies, goat-related and otherwise. Find the farm, Háafell, on dirt road Rte 523, northeast of Reykholt. Coffee or tea included.

Húsafell Recreation Base
PLAYING IN THE HIGH COUNTRY

Tucked into an emerald, river-crossed valley, with the Kaldá river on one side and a dramatic lava field on the other, Húsafell, with its encampment of summer cottages, campsite, bistro and geothermal swimming pool, and hot-pots with mountain views, is a popular outdoor retreat for Reykjavík residents, and the main access point for nearby Langjökull glacier. The star of the show in the Húsafell holiday village is the chic Hótel Húsafell, offering spacious, comfortable rooms. Art is the original work of local artist Páll Guðmundsson, and the restaurant is one of the best in the region. It's also the base for Canyon Baths hot springs (p177) and Into the Glacier.

Nearby Gamli Bær guesthouse, in a quaint, renovated 1908 farmhouse, is full of charm and with country views and a hot-pot, run by jovial Sæmi.

GO BEYOND HÚSAFELL

If you've got a large 4WD that's insured for F roads, it's possible to continue from Húsafell into the interior along Rte F578 beyond Surtshellir, through the lakes at Arnarvatnsheiði, and on to Hvammstangi. Note that Rte F578 is usually only open seven weeks a year; check road.is.

Hraunfossar

Getting out onto Langjökull & the Kaldidalur Corridor

ICE-CAP ACTIVITIES AND REMOTE ROADWAYS

Southeast of Húsafell, the extraordinary Kaldidalur valley skirts the edge of a series of glaciers, offering incredible views of the Langjökull ice cap (the second-largest glacier in Iceland) and, in clear weather, Eiríksjökull, Okjökull and Þórisjökull. Do not attempt to drive up onto the glacier yourself. Tours depart from Reykjavík or Húsafell for the **Into the Glacier** ice cave, a major tourist attraction. This enormous (300m-long) human-made tunnel and series of caves heads into the glacier at 1260m above sea level. It contain exhibitions, a cafe and even a small chapel. Mountaineers of Iceland and Tröll Expeditions offer snowmobiling on the ice cap, but check which side they are leaving from (sometimes it is over by Gullfoss in the Golden Circle, p105).

The Kaldidalur Corridor, also simply known as unsurfaced Rte 550, is slow but dramatic going (mountain ice, barren rock), and is often fogged in in summer. It links south to the Golden Circle, offering the option to create an extended loop from Reykjavík. Access to Rte 550 is limited to sanctioned vehicles – ask your rental outfit before setting off.

BEST LAVA FEATURES

The name of spectacular **Hraunfossar** waterfall, west of Húsafell, translates to 'Lava Field Waterfall' because the crystalline water streams out from below the lava field all around. Walk a little further on the marked trail to reach Barnafoss, another churning chute. East of Húsafell, along Rte 518, the vast, barren lava flows of **Hallmundarhraun** make a wonderful eerie landscape dotted with gigantic lava tubes. These long, tunnel-like caves are formed by flows of molten lava beneath a solid lava crust, and it's possible to visit the 1100-year-old, 1.5km-long **Víðgelmir** – the Cave – on a tour. Or, if you have caving gear (helmet, torch etc), **Surtshellir**, along Rte F578 (rental cars not allowed), is a dramatic, 2km-long tube connected to **Stefánshellir** which is about half the size.

GETTING AROUND

Borgarnes is a major transit hub for Strætó buses throughout the region and to the Westfjords and North Iceland. From

September to May, bus 81 runs inland to Reykholt. Using your own wheels is easier by far for freedom from schedules.

STYKKISHÓLMUR

Stykkishólmur

✪
REYKJAVÍK

The charming town of Stykkishólmur (visitstykkisholmur.is), the largest on the Snæfellsnes Peninsula, is built up around a natural harbour tipped by a basalt islet. It's a picturesque place with a laid-back attitude and a sprinkling of brightly coloured buildings from the late 19th century. With a comparatively good choice of accommodation and restaurants, and handy transport links, Stykkishólmur makes an excellent base for exploring the region and the national park.

Several artists have small galleries with ceramics, woollens and other crafts, so it's a good place to look for local handmade wares. There's also free wi-fi throughout the whole town. What's not to love?

The Baldur car ferry crosses Breiðafjörður, stopping in Flatey for five minutes. From early July to early August, when there are two boats per day, you can take the first ferry to Flatey, then the second ferry onward or back to Stykkishólmur.

TOP TIP

In addition to its more formal sit-down restaurants, Stykkishólmur is great for casual eats. There's everything from food trucks on the harbour (fish and chips, ice cream) to inland hot-dog wagon, Meistarinn, and a pizzeria and burger joint, Skúrinn.

MIHAI.ANDRITOIU/SHUTTERSTOCK ©

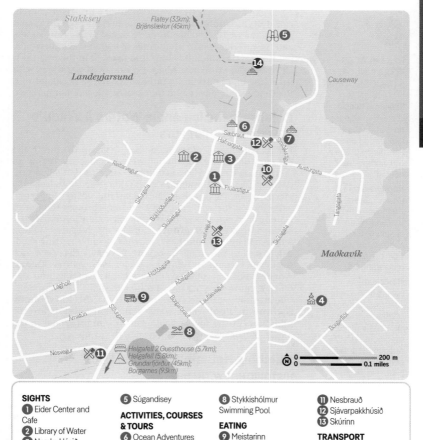

SIGHTS
1. Eider Center and Cafe
2. Library of Water
3. Norska Húsið
4. Stykkishólmskirkja

5. Súgandisey

ACTIVITIES, COURSES & TOURS
6. Ocean Adventures
7. Seatours

8. Stykkishólmur Swimming Pool

EATING
9. Meistarinn
10. Narfeyrarstofa

11. Nesbrauð
12. Sjávarpakkhúsið
13. Skúrinn

TRANSPORT
14. Baldur Car Ferry

Strolling Through Town & History
MUSEUM, CHURCH AND BRILLIANT FJORD VIEWS

Stykkishólmur's quaint maritime charm comes from the cluster of wooden warehouses, shops and homes around the town's harbour. Most date back about 150 years. One of the most interesting (and oldest) is the **Norska Húsið**, now the regional museum. Built by trader and amateur astronomer Árni Thorlacius in 1832, the house has been skilfully restored and displays a wonderfully eclectic selection of local antiquities. On the 2nd floor you visit Árni's home, an upper-class 19th-century residence decked out with his original wares.

For duck aficionados, head just behind to the **Eider Center and Cafe** which explains everything you need to know about duck farming and duvet making in this, the centre of eider farming.

BEST PLACES TO EAT IN STYKKISHÓLMUR

Sjávarpakkhúsið
Old fish-packing house transformed into a wood-lined fine-dining eatery with harbourfront outdoor seating. €€

Narfeyrarstofa
Book a table on the 2nd floor for the romantic lighting of antique lamps and harbour views from this excellent restaurant. €€

Nesbrauð
Bakery on the road into town, to stock up on sugary confections such as *kleinur* (traditional twisty doughnuts) or *ástar pungur* (literally 'love balls'; fried balls of dough and raisins). €

You can't miss spotting Stykkishólmur's futuristic church, called **Stykkishólmskirkja**, with its sweeping bell tower that looks like a whale vertebra. It was designed by Jón Haraldsson, and the interior features hundreds of suspended lights and a painting of the Madonna and child floating in the night sky.

Cap off your stroll at the basalt island of **Súgandisey** with its scenic lighthouse and grand views across Breiðafjörður. Reach it via the causeway at the tip of Stykkishólmur harbour.

Celebrate the Icelandic Waters & Wildlife
BOAT TOURS AND HOT-POTS

For relaxing views of town and bay, head up the hill to the **Library of Water**. This window-lined space showcases an installation by American artist Roni Horn (b 1955). Light reflects and refracts through 24 glass pillars filled with Icelandic glacier water. There's also a chess set if you feel like lingering.

Get out on the water with a boat tour through the fjord's islands, bird colonies (puffins from spring until August) and basalt formations. **Seatours** runs its much-touted 'Viking Sushi', a one-/two-hour boat ride that includes netting shellfish to devour raw. It partners with Reykjavík Excursions for Reykjavík pick-up and children under 15 travel free. **Ocean Adventures** lets you try your own hand at angling and also offers a puffin-viewing tour. Both are based at the harbour.

To actually get *in* the water, head inland to **Stykkishólmur Swimming Pool** where water slides and hot-pots are the highlights at the town's geothermal swimming pool in the municipal sports complex alongside the campsite.

Climbing Helgafell for Good Luck
HISTORIC HILL WITH LORE

The holy mountain Helgafell (73m), about 5km south of Stykkishólmur proper, was once venerated by worshippers of the god Þór. Although quite small, the mountain was so sacred in Saga times that elderly Icelanders would seek it out near the time of their death. Today locals believe that wishes are granted to those who climb the mount.

In the late 10th century, Snorri Goði, a prominent Þor worshipper, converted to Christianity and built a church at the top of the hill; its ruins still remain. The nearby farm of the same name was where the conniving Guðrun Ósvífursdóttir of *Laxdæla Saga* lived out her later years in isolation. Her grave marks the base of the mount.

Stay at wonderful **Helgafell 2 Guesthouse** if you want to overnight on the lambent pond alongside the mountain.

GETTING AROUND

You can get to Reykjavík (2½ hours) by changing in Borgarnes. Buses run out of the peninsula to Hellissandur via Vatnaleið (crossroads of Rtes 54 and 56), Grundarfjörður, Ólafsvík and Rif. All services are greatly reduced in winter.

The Baldur car ferry (seatours.is) runs between Stykkishólmur and Brjánslækur in the Westfjords (2½ hours) via Flatey (1½ hours). Book ahead to bring your car or camper.

Beyond Stykkishólmur

Gentle Grundarfjörður and its iconic mountain Kirkjufell, windswept island Flatey, plus saga country make for super exploring

After you leave Stykkishólmur, on the Snæfellsnes Peninsula's populated northern coast, and move west you'll pass rugged lava fields to reach smaller townships, including charming Grundarfjörður with its famous mountain Kirkjufell and accompanying resplendent waterfalls. Between Stykkishólmur and the Westfjords, the rolling fields of the Dalir, one of Iceland's bread baskets, are also home to two fascinating saga sights focussing on Erik the Red (Eiríkur Rauðe) and Leifur Eiríksson. The Erpsstaðir dairy farm is also a perfect pit stop for refreshments.

Across the broad Breiðafjörður (that's what the name means: broad), tiny Flatey island, an idyllic windswept isle, calls out for a serene overnight.

TOP TIP

No cars are allowed on Flatey, so for those travelling with a car, it is possible to send it on across (no additional charge) while you stay behind in Flatey.

IRINA KORSHUNOVA/SHUTTERSTOCK ©

Hiding Out on Peaceful Flatey Island
SOJOURN OR STAY BETWEEN THE WEST AND WESTFJORDS

Of Breiðafjörður's innumerable islands, little Flatey (literally 'Flat Island'; flatey.com) is the only one with year-round inhabitants. In the 11th century Flatey was home to a monastery, and today the appealing island is a popular stopover for travellers heading to (or from) the Westfjords, as well as filmmakers: several movies and series have been shot here. Push the slow-mo button on life, and enjoy a windswept afternoon amid brightly coloured houses and swooping Arctic terns.

Hótel Flatey, which is open from the last week in May until the end of August, has some of the most charming, nook-like vintage rooms in Iceland, and the on-site restaurant is fantastic as well. On some summer evenings, slip down into the basement bar for live music. One of the island's farms, about 300m from the pier, Krákuvör (438 1451) offers camping on a meadow sweeping to the shore.

The Baldur ferry (p182) serves Flatey, which can be visited as a day trip in summer when there are two boats a day.

Following in the Footsteps of Erik the Red
THE SAGA-FILLED DALIR DISTRICT

The scenic corridor of rolling fields and craggy river-carved buttes between West Iceland and the Westfjords is known as Dalir. It served as the setting for the *Laxdœla Saga*, the most popular of the Icelandic sagas. The story revolves around a love triangle between Guðrun Ósvífursdóttir, said to be the most beautiful woman in Iceland, and the foster brothers Kjartan Ólafsson and Bolli Þorleiksson. In typical saga fashion, Guðrun had both men wrapped around her little finger and schemed until both were dead. Most Icelanders know the stories by heart and hold this area in great esteem.

Also, the farm **Eiríksstaðir** was home to Eiríkur Rauðe (Erik the Red), father of Leifur Eiríksson, the first European to visit America. Although only a ruin of the original farm remains, a fascinating reconstructed turf house built using only the tools and materials available at the time is an excellent blast into the past. Period-dressed guides show visitors around, explaining interesting details of Settlement Era living and also telling the story of Erik the Red, who went on to found the first European settlement in Greenland. His exploits were captured in *Saga of Erik the Red* and *Saga of the Greenlanders*.

Founded as a cargo depot in Saga times, the pin-sized town of **Búðardalur** (pronounced boo-thar-dalur) occupies a pleas-

---

ERPSSTAÐIR DAIRY FARM TREATS

When the peanut gallery starts moaning, 'Are we there yet?', you know it's time to head to Erpsstaðir, the perfect place to stretch your legs. Like a mirage for sweet-toothed wanderers, this dairy farm on the gorgeous Rte 60 (between Búðardalur and the Ring Road; with high mountain valleys, streams and waterfalls) specialises in delicious homemade ice cream. You can tour the farm, greet the buxom bovines, chickens, rabbits and even guinea pigs, then gorge on a scoop. The farm also sells *skyr* (yoghurt-like dessert) and cheese; try the rocket-shaped *skyr-konfekt* (meant to look like an udder), a delicious dessert made with a hard white chocolate shell encasing thick *skyr*. It'll blow you away. Want to stay? There is a rental house, too.

 WHERE TO STAY BEYOND STYKKISHÓLMUR

Kirkjufell Guesthouse
Modern, well-equipped guesthouse with a top waterfall-filled fjord setting just outside Grundarfjörður. €€

Sauðafell Guesthouse
This lovely farmhouse has peaceful views over the valley. Five comfy bedrooms share three bathrooms. €€€

Dalahyttur
Three tiny cottages (each sleeping four) with sweeping views of Hólsfjall mountain and beyond. €€

Eiríksstaðir

WEST ICELAND EXPLORATION

Noel Bas Barrera, chef of Sjávarpakkhúsið, shares his tips for how to get out into the raw open spaces of West Iceland.
@noel_brx
@sjavarpakkhusid

I feel like the west of Iceland is one of the most beautiful and quiet places. Close to Reykjavík, small towns, cosy, no stress. Living in the middle of nature. If I am not working, I'll go somewhere, always. Kayak in Stykkishólmur with Kontiki. Glymur waterfall. I go in my camper and try to discover new places.

The whole Snæfellsnes Peninsula is fantastic: Hellnar with its really nice cafe, tiny and in front of the ocean...one of my favourites. I love the lonely road through the Berserkjahraun (Berserkers' lava field). Go by bicycle or go with a car, about 15km west of the intersection of Rte 54 and Rte 56.

ant position looking out over **Hvammsfjörður**, at the mouth of the Laxá river. A current claim to fame is its dairy, which produces most of the cheese in Iceland. The local supermarket carries a good sample. If time permits, add in a stop at Leifsbúð. Downstairs, its little cafe near the water offers cakes, soup and salad, and upstairs a multimedia exhibition focuses on Leifur Eiríksson and exceptional Guðríður Þorbjarnardóttir (p191).

Before leaving town, swing into Bolli Craft (facebook.com/bollicraft) for cool local arts and crafts including handmade sweaters, sheep-horn buttons and charming elves.

Just north of the spot where Rte 590 heads west off Rte 60 you'll find the encampment at **Laugar**, the birthplace of *Laxdæla Saga* beauty Guðrun Ósvífursdóttir. Historians believe they've found Guðrun's bathing pool (Guðrúnarlaug): the hot pool is well marked above the entrance to Dalahótel, a fine place to overnight, and has a small changing kiosk. Tungustapi, in the distance, is a large elf cathedral.

✄ WHERE TO EAT & DRINK IN GRUNDARFJÖRÐUR

Bjargarsteinn Mathús	**Valeria Coffee**	**Meistarinn**
Superb waterfront restaurant creating Icelandic dishes, with an emphasis on seafood and everything fresh. €€	Who better than a friendly Columbian expat to import, roast and serve some of the best coffee in Iceland?	Hot-dog and sandwich wagon with items named after Danish royal family members. Also in Stykkishólmur. €

ROUTE 590

The dramatic coastline of the oft-forgotten peninsula between the Snæfellsnes Peninsula and the Westfjords is traced by the 85km track Rte 590 (OK for 2WD; along Rte 60 look for the turnoff at Fellströnd). Windswept farmsteads lie frozen in time, and boulder-strewn hills, crowned with flattened granite, roll skyward. Keep an eye out for white-tailed eagles.

Near the beginning of the track, the farm at Hvammur produced a whole line of prominent Icelanders, including Snorri Sturluson of *Prose Edda* fame. You can spend the night at remote, lovely Guesthouse Nýp. If you can't get in there, try Vogur Country Lodge or the campsite, Á, just before Skarð – a lonely farm that has remained in the hands of the same family for over 1000 years.

Loving Grundarfjörður's Carved Terrain
BEHOLDING KIRKJUFELL AND FJORDSIDE FALLS

Spectacularly set on a dramatic bay, little Grundarfjörður is backed by waterfalls and surrounded by ice-capped peaks often shrouded in cottony fog. More prefab than wooden, the town feels like a typical Icelandic fishing community with a great vibe. The surrounding landscape can't be beaten, with its iconic **Kirkjufell** (463m), guardian of the town's northwestern vista. It's said to be one of the most photographed spots in Iceland, appearing in *Game of Thrones* and on everyone's Instagram. Ask staff at the Saga Centre (a tourist information centre, library, internet point and small museum rolled into one) if you want to climb it; they may be able to find you a guide. Two spots involving a rope climb make it dangerous to scale when wet or without local knowledge. Kirkjufell is backed by the roaring waterfalls, Kirkjufellsfoss; more camera fodder.

Understanding the Greenland Shark
VISITING THE SHARK MUSEUM

The farmstead at **Bjarnarhöfn** is the region's leading producer of *hákarl* (fermented shark meat), a traditional Icelandic dish. The museum has exhibits on the history of this culinary curiosity, along with the family's fishing boats and processing tools. A video explains how the Greenland shark, which is used to make *hákarl*, is poisonous if eaten fresh; fermentation neutralises the toxin. Note that Greenland shark is classified as near threatened, and is the longest-living vertebrate on the planet, with some living over 500 years.

Each visit to the museum comes with a bracing nibble of *hákarl*, accompanied by Brennivín (aka 'black death') schnapps. Ask about the drying house out the back. You might find hundreds of dangling shark slices drying, the last step in the process.

Find the museum off Rte 54 on a turnoff from Rte 577, on the fjordside, northeastern edge of Bjarnarhafnarfjall (575m).

GETTING AROUND

Strætó bus 59 services Borgarnes–Bifröst–Búðardalur–Skriðuland–Króksfjarðarnes–Hólmavík. It has connections to Reykjavík from

Borgarnes. Bus 57 Reykjavík–Akureyri runs through Bifröst and Staðarskáli (to Reykjavík or to Akureyri).

SNÆFELLSJÖKULL NATIONAL PARK

Snæfellsjökull NP wraps around the glacier Snæfellsjökull (sneye-fells-yo-kutl). Around its flanks lie lava tubes, protected lava fields, which are home to native Icelandic fauna, and prime hiking and bird- and whale-watching spots.

When the fog around the glacier lifts, you'll see the mammoth ice cap, which was made famous when Jules Verne used it as the setting for *Journey to the Center of the Earth*. Among certain New Age groups, Snæfellsjökull is considered one of the world's great 'power centres'.

TOP TIP

Malarrif and Hellissandur each have a national park visitor centre. The park's online map is excellent and rangers have a summer programme of free park guided tours – check online or on its Facebook page.

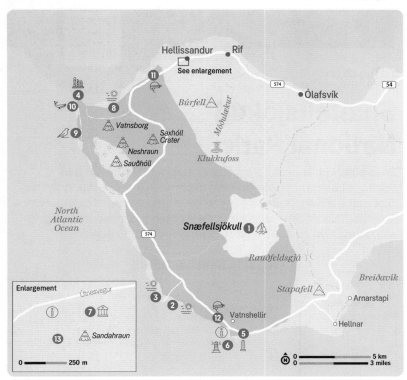

HIGHLIGHTS
1 Snæfellsjökull

SIGHTS
2 Djúpalónssandur
3 Dritvík

4 Fálki
5 Lóndrangar
6 Malariff Lighthouse
7 Sjóminjasafnið
8 Skarðsvík

9 Svörtuloft Lighthouse
10 Þúfubjarg Bird Cliffs

ACTIVITIES, COURSES & TOURS
11 Öndverðarnes

12 Summit Adventure Guides
13 Vatnshellir

Scan this QR code for hiking trail maps and wildlife guides.

Djúpalónssandur

TOP SIGHT

Snæfellsjökull National Park

Snæfellsjökull National Park is abundance. Stay on the park's edges (it has no accommodation or camping) and make forays in. Distances are short so it's easy to get a smorgasbord of experience quickly. Malarrif and Hellissandur are home to visitor centres that sell maps, give advice and offer free guided tours in summer.

DON'T MISS

Öndverðarnes

Saxhóll Crater

Snæfellsjökull

Djúpalón Beach & Dritvík

Malarrif rock stacks

Djúpalón Beach & Dritvík

On the southwest coast, Rte 572 leads off Rte 574 to wild black-sand beach **Djúpalónssandur**. It's a dramatic place to walk, with rock formations (an elf church and a kerling – a troll woman), two brackish pools (for which the beach was named) and the rock-arch Gatklettur. Some of the black sands are covered in pieces of rusted metal from the English trawler *Eding*, which was shipwrecked here in 1948. An asphalt car park and public toilets allow tour-bus access, and crowds. Down on the beach you can still see four lifting stones where fishing-boat crews would test the strength of aspiring fishermen. A series of rocky sea stacks, some of which are thought to be a troll church, emerge from the ocean up the coast as you tramp north over the craggy headland to reach the black-sand beach at **Dritvík**. From the 16th to the 19th century Dritvík was the largest fishing station in Iceland, with up to 60 fishing boats, but now there are only ruins near the edge of the lava field.

Snæfellsjökull

It's easy to see why Jules Verne selected Snæfell for *Journey to the Center of the Earth*: the peak was torn apart when the volcano beneath it exploded and then collapsed back into its own magma chamber, forming a huge caldera. Today the crater is filled with the Snæfellsjökull ice cap (highest point 1446m) and is a popular summer destination.

Saxhóll Crater & Sauðhóll

About 11.5km north of the Djúpalón exit, on Rte 574, follow the marked turnoff to the roadside scoria Saxhóll Crater, which was responsible for some of the lava in the area. There's a drivable track leading to the base, from where it's a 300m climb for magnificent views over the enormous **Neshraun** lava flows. Or trek south into the greener crater Sauðhóll.

Vatnshellir

The 8000-year-old Vatnshellir lava tube with multiple caverns lies 32m below the earth's surface, 1km north of Malarrif. The car park is visible from Rte 574, and the tube can only be visited by guided tour with **Summit Adventure Guides**.

Öndverðarnes

At the westernmost tip of Snæfellsnes, Rte 574 cuts south, while Rte 579, a tiny gravel and occasionally surfaced track, heads further west across an ancient lava flow to the tip of the Öndverðarnes (pronounced und-ver-thar-nes) peninsula, which is great for whale watching.

Exploring a Golden Beach

As the paved road winds through charcoal lava cliffs you'll pass **Skarðsvík**, a golden beach with basalt cubes. A Viking grave was discovered here in the 1960s; it's easy to see why this was a favoured final resting place.

The Point

After Skarðsvík the track is unpaved and bumpier (though still manageable for a 2WD). Park at the turnoff (left side) to walk through craggy lava flows to the imposing volcanic crater **Vatnsborg**, or continue driving straight on until you reach a T-intersection. One kilometre to the left lie the dramatic Svörtuloft bird cliffs (Saxhólsbjarg), with excellent walkways, and the tall, orange **Svörtuloft lighthouse**. To the right, a bumpy track runs parallel to the sea 1.9km to a squat, orange lighthouse. From its parking area, you can walk to the very tip of the peninsula, for whale watching, or walk 200m northeast to **Fálkí**, an ancient stone well that was thought to have three waters: fresh, holy and ale!

MALARRIF & LÓNDRANGAR

Malarrif lighthouse and visitor centre are about 2km south of Djúpalónssandur. A trail leads 1km east along cliffs to rock pillars at **Lóndrangar**, which surge into the air in surprising pinnacles. **Þúfubjarg bird cliffs** lie further east. Lóndrangar and Þúfubjarg are also accessible from Rte 574.

TOP TIPS

- The best way to reach the glacial summit is to take a tour with Summit Adventure Guides or Glacier Tours. These companies approach the peak from the south, on Rte F570.
- Rte F570's northern approach (near Ólafsvík) is frustratingly rutty (4WD needed) and frequently closed due to weather-inflicted damage.
- Even the well-trained and outfitted are not allowed to ascend the glacier without a local guide; contact the national park visitor centre in Hellissandur or Malarrif for more information.

Beyond Snæfellsjökull National Park

Adventure around sparkling fjords, dramatic volcanic peaks, sheer sea cliffs, sweeping golden beaches and crunchy lava flows.

To the east of Snæfellsjökull National Park, coastal Rte 574 passes the hamlets of Hellnar and Arnarstapi, with their glacier tour companies and interesting sea-sculpted rock formations. It continues east along the broad southern coastal plain, hugging huge sandy bays such as Breiðavík on one side, and towering peaks with waterfalls on the other. This stretch has some super horse riding, especially out on the beaches with crags towering inland.

Delve into the seafront portion of Hellissandur on the northern edge of the park and you'll find a series of old warehouses and utility buildings covered in brilliant graffiti – definitely worth a stroll.

TOP TIP

With the 2023 opening of the park visitor centre in Hellissandur, infrastructure is growing here, including yummy cafe Gilbakki.

KARIN DE JONGE-FOTOGRAFIE/SHUTTERSTOCK ©

Breiðavík (p192)

Arnarstapi

Walking Between Hellnar & Arnarstapi

COASTAL FORMATIONS AND LAVA FIELDS

Bárður, the subject of Bárðar saga *Snæfellsáss*, was part giant, part troll and part human. He chose an area near **Hellnar**, a picturesque spot overlooking a rocky bay, as his home (called Laugarbrekka). Towards the end of his intense saga, he became the guardian spirit of Snæfell. Today Hellnar is a tiny fishing village (once huge) where the shriek of seabirds fills the air and whales are regularly sighted.

Bárðarlaug, up near the main road, was supposedly Bárður's bathing pool, though the pond is no longer hot. Down on the shore, the cave Baðstofa is chock-a-block with nesting birds. Nearby is the head of the 2.5km walk to/from **Arnarstapi**. This slender trail follows the jagged coastline through a nature reserve, passing lava flows and eroded stone caves. During tumultuous weather, waves spray through the rocky arches; when it's fine, look for nesting seabirds. Ancient, velvety moss-cloaked lava flows tumble east through the Hellnahraun. Fjöruhúsið is tops for a seafront soup or cake.

GUÐRIÐUR ÞORBJARNAR-DÓTTIR: THE FAR TRAVELLER

Guðriður Þorbjarnardóttir was among Iceland's most celebrated explorers, and surely earned her nickname the 'Far Traveller'. Born in Hellnar before the year 1000 (a small sculpture marks the site of her family's farm at Laugarbrekka), Guðriður had a serious case of wanderlust. Not only was she one of the first Europeans to reach Vinland (thought to be Canada's Newfoundland), she bore a child while she was there: the first European born in North America! Later, Guðriður converted to Christianity and embarked on an epic pilgrimage to Rome, where some say she met the pope and recounted her experiences.

For more about Guðriður, read *Saga of Erik the Red* (p184), *Saga of the Greenlanders*, *The Far Traveler* by Nancy Marie Brown and *The Sea Road* by Margaret Elphinstone.

 WHERE TO EAT NEAR SNÆFELLSJÖKULL NATIONAL PARK

Fjöruhúsið	**Samkomuhúsið**	**Reks**
Renowned fish soup in beauty by the bird cliffs at the trailhead of the scenic Hellnar–Arnarstapi path. €	Arnarstapi's tried-and-true old-school eatery for Icelandic specialties like lamb soup and fish and chips. €€	Serves up reliable fish of the day and Icelandic staples in a cosy atmosphere in Ólafsvík. €€

GOING BERSERK

According to *Eyrbyggja Saga*, a farmer grew weary of having to walk around the jagged lava flows to visit his brother in Bjarnarhöfn (p186). He brought two berserkers – insanely violent fighters who were employed as hired thugs in Viking times – to work on his farm. To his dismay one of them took a liking to his daughter. He turned to local chieftain Snorri Goði for advice, but Snorri had a crush on the farmer's daughter too. He recommended setting the berserker an impossible task: promise him the daughter's hand in marriage if he cleared a passage through the lava field. To the horror of both, the berserkers ripped a passage straight through. The farmer trapped the berserkers in a sauna and murdered them, allowing Snorri to marry his daughter.

Today, a path through Berserkjahraun remains, and a grave was discovered containing the remains of two large men.

Canyons & Coastline

GLORIOUS RAUÐFELDSGJÁ AND WINDSWEPT BREIÐAVÍK

Just northwest of Arnarstapi on Rte 574, a small track branches off to the stunning **Rauðfeldsgjá** (pronounced roith-felds-gyow), a steep, narrow cleft that mysteriously disappears into the cliff wall. Birds wheel overhead, a stream runs along the bottom of the gorge, and you can slink between the sheer walls for quite a distance. The gorge figures in a dramatic part of the local saga of Bárður, described on a sign at the parking area.

East of Rauðfeldsgjá, Rte 574 skirts the edges of an enormous sandy bay at **Breiðavík** (pronounced bray-tha-veek). The windswept coast, with its yellow expanse of sand, is wonderfully peaceful, though tricky to access. The pasture-filled region running along the coastal mountains from here east to Vegamót is considered one of the best places in Iceland for horse riding.

On the eastern edge of Breiðavík, look for the placard telling the grisly tale of Axlar-Björn, Iceland's notorious 16th-century serial killer, who made his living in lean times by murdering travellers here.

The deserted farmstead at Ytri-Tunga, just east of Hof, occasionally has a colony of seals offshore, best seen in June and July.

Just where Rte 54 curves between the Snæfellsnes Peninsula and the mainland, you'll find the dramatic basalt towers of Gerðuberg rising from the plain.

Horse Riding & Hot Springs

ENJOYING THE ROLLING COASTLINE OF SOUTHERN SNÆFELLSNES

Embrace the open air and relaxation of the quiet southern coast of Snæfellsnes. Family-run Stóri Kambur offers one-to two-hour rides on the beach, some with a historical saga theme, and all with glacier views when it's clear, plus short kids rides. It has cottages to let, too. Equine enthusiasts can also try friendly horse farm Lýsuhóll, which also has a guesthouse and cottages.

FOR CANYON LOVERS

Deep Rauðfeldsgjá with its spiring seabirds is just one of many Icelandic canyons. Others worth checking out include **Fjaðrárgljúfur** (p143) and **Ásbyrgi** (p260).

WHERE TO STAY ON THE SOUTHERN SNÆFELLSNES PENINSULA

Miðhraun – Lava Resort
Sprawling and family-friendly with cottages, restaurant, geothermal baths, playground and farm animals. €€

Fosshotel Hellnar
Sun-filled, comfortable rooms and a good restaurant; run with sustainability in mind. €€€

Hótel Búðir
Windswept inn on a gorgeous, remote coastline – room 28 has the best views (and a teeny balcony). €€€

Nearby, the geothermal source for Lýsuhólslaug pumps carbonated, mineral-filled waters in at a perfect 37°C to 39°C. Don't be alarmed that the pool is a murky green: the iron-rich water attracts some serious algae.

Búðir & Búðahraun's Lonesome Loveliness
WALKS AMID LAVA AND ITS FLORA

Búðir has a lonely church and a hotel, but there is no sign of its former fishing village along its craggy, mossy inlets. A walking trail leads across the elf-infested nature reserve, **Búðahraun** lava field. The ancient lava field is protected; if you look down into its hollows and cracks you'll find flourishing flowers and ferns, many of them protected native Icelandic species. The path also leads to the crater Búðaklettur. According to local legend, a lava tube beneath Búðahraun, paved with gold and precious stones, leads all the way to Surtshellir in upper Borgarfjörður. It takes about three hours to walk to the crater and back.

Small Towns, Curious Church & Waterfalls
TEENY ÓLAFSVÍK AND RIF

Quiet, workaday **Ólafsvík** won't win any hearts with its fish-processing plant. Although it's the oldest trading town in the country (it was granted a trading licence in 1687), few of the original buildings survive. For visitors it's best as a jumping-off point for whale watching – the waters offshore and west to the tip of the peninsula are the region's best for whale sightings. Blink-and-you'll-miss-it **Rif** is a harbour hamlet that makes Ólafsvík look like a teeming metropolis. Dramatic waterfall Svöðufoss, with its barrelling cascades and dramatic hexagonal basalt, rockets along in the distance.

Between Rif and Hellissandur, spot the lonely church (built 1903) at **Ingjaldshóll**, the setting of *Víglundar Saga*. If the church doors are open, you can see a painting depicting Christopher Columbus' possible visit to Iceland in 1477; it's thought he came with the merchant marine and enquired about Viking trips to Vinland.

The Freezer Hostel has the best nightlife around: check online for its music and theatre programme.

WHALE WATCHING & PUFFIN-SPOTTING

Láki Tours has excellent fishing, puffin-spotting and whale-watching trips from Grundarfjörður (p186) or Ólafsvík. Whale-watching tours from Ólafsvík (mid-February to September) cover the area's best cetacean habitat – orca, fin, sperm, blue, minke and humpback are all possibilities.

Puffin tours (June to late August) from Grundarfjörður go to wonderful basalt island Melrakkaey, with puffins, kittiwakes and other seabirds. Cute and endearingly comic, the puffin (*Fratercula arctica*, or *lundi* as they're called in Icelandic) is one of Iceland's best-loved birds. It's a member of the auk family and spends most of its year at sea. For four or five months it comes to land to breed, generally keeping the same mate and burrow from year to year.

GETTING AROUND

Strætó bus 82 runs from Stykkishólmur around the peninsula's western tip to Hellissandur four days per week (no bicycles allowed).

There is no public transport along the peninsula's southern side. Private wheels are best.

JAN JERMAN/SHUTTERSTOCK ©

Above: Hornbjarg cliff (p216). Right: Icelandic sheep

THE WESTFJORDS

OFFBEAT ICELAND

On Europe's westernmost tip, stoic puffins watch the sunset from the edge of a cliff, as if posing for the postcards: Greetings, from the Democratic Republic of the Westfjords.

The people of northwest Iceland – known as Vestfirðingar – have over the years threatened to secede from the rest of the country by establishing the Democratic Republic of the Westfjords. It is, thankfully, a joke, but it's telling: the massive northernmost peninsula, home to only 7000 people, does feel like a land of its own.

On a map of Iceland, the Westfjords region is already in juxtaposition – the coastline appears to be drawn with a shaky hand, shaped by fjord after fjord after fjord: the Nordic word for narrow inlets with deep sea and steep mountains. The difference has to do with geological age. The land is Iceland's oldest and resembles that of neighbouring Greenland in many ways.

The natural curves make driving full of twists and turns. Consider this for scale: the region itself is merely one-fifth of Iceland's size but its circular drive covers some 950km altogether, known as the Westfjords Way. It's a commitment; only about 20% of Iceland's visitors see the region, excluding the great deal of cruise ship passengers stopping in Ísafjörður, the cosmopolitan capital.

More than any other region in Iceland, the Westfjords is a summer destination. The birds of Látrabjarg, nesting in millions on Europe's westernmost tip, at least, agree summer is the best time to enjoy the rugged wilderness of narrow fjords and steep cliffs.

MARTIN GILLESPIE/SHUTTERSTOCK ©

A photographer's guide to the Westfjords

THE MAIN AREAS

ARNARFJÖRÐUR	LÁTRABJARG PENINSULA	ÍSAFJÖRÐUR	HORNSTRANDIR PENINSULA	HÓLMAVÍK
Dynjandi waterfall and quirky museums. **p200**	Yellow beach and bird cliffs. **p205**	The largest town by far. **p209**	Multiday hikes and Arctic foxes. **p215**	Folklore heritage and whale watching. **p216**

Find Your Way

A vast size and small population set the Westfjords up as the ultimate road-trip destination, more about the journey than the must-sees. We've picked the places that capture its natural landscape and culture.

Denmark Strait

Ísafjörður, p209
A colourful community in bright tin-clad buildings, hemmed in on all sides by towering peaks and the dark waters of the fjord.

Arnarfjörður, p200
Home to two museums – the Icelandic Sea Monster Museum and Samúel Jónsson's Art Farm – that subtly capture the isolation of the 'Westfjords Alps'.

Látrabjarg Peninsula, p205
Sharp cliffs the length of a town, occupied by Mr Puffin and his seaside friends. Welcome.

Aðalvík
Búrfe (497m)
Grænah

Skálavík
Bolungarvík
Suðureyri ○
Önundarfjörður
Tungudalur
Ingjaldsandur
Ísafjörð
Suðavík

Núpur ○ ○ Skrúður
Svalvogar ○
Dýrafjörður
Þingeyri
Lambadalsfja (957m)

Lighthouse
Kaldbakur (998m)
Hrafnseyri
Sjónfríð (920m)
Grænahlíð
Arnarfjörður
Dynjandi

Pollurinn
Kollsvík ○   Hænuvík ○
Tálknafjörður
Vatnsfjörður Nature Reserve
Breiðavík ○   Hnjótur ○   Patreksfjörður
Foss
Flókalundur
Hellulaug
Hvallátur
Bjargtangar   *Sauðlauksdalur*
Krossholt ○   Brjánslækur
Ferry
Kleifaheiði
Barðaströnd

Flat

Breiðafjörður

0 ────── 20 km
0 ────── 10 miles

Hornstrandir Peninsula, p215
Be among the small but steady number of travellers trekking to Hornbjarg, the iconic cliff that most people will only see on postcards.

Greenland Sea

Hólmavík, p216
The second-largest industry in Hólmavík – after fishing – is studying and sharing stories from the past: residents thrive on folklore.

CAR
Hire a car to explore the wild landscape of the Westfjords, preferably a 4WD. Expect gravel outside the main Westfjords Way – the loop connecting most towns and villages – and take care over winter.

FERRY
The only way to reach the Hornstrandir Peninsula, a remote nature reserve without a road. Scheduled departures leave from Ísafjörður, June to September. In Breiðafjörður, the Baldur car ferry sails year-round between the southern Westfjords and Snæfellsnes Peninsula.

PLANE
Icelandair flies between Ísafjörður Airport, 5km south on the fjord, and Reykjavík's domestic airport twice a day. Hire a car at the airport or take the shuttle into Ísafjörður. Norlandair flies from Reykjavík to Bíldudalur and Strandir a few times a week.

Plan Your Time

Quick visits to the Westfjords hardly exist, unless you arrive by plane to Ísafjörður. Allow at least several days for the circular drive known as the Westfjords Way.

Pressed for Time

● Take Iceland's westernmost detour with a long, winding drive to **Látrabjarg Peninsula** (p205), some five hours from the Ring Road. From June to mid-August, the peninsula tip is one of Europe's liveliest bird cliffs, with puffins hanging out by the car park, fish in their mouth. Overnight in **Patreksfjörður** (p205), the only sizeable settlement beyond **Ísafjörður** (p209). Eat and drink at **Flak** (p205).

● The next day, take the mountain road to **Arnarfjörður** (p200). The people of the Westfjords forbid anyone from leaving without seeing **Dynjandi waterfall** (p201).

KARSTEN WROBEL/ALAMY STOCK PHOTO ©

Krossneslaug (p219)

See more of the Westfjords online

SEASONAL HIGHLIGHTS

Summer is the time to visit Hornstrandir, Látrabjarg, Mt Bolafjall and Strandir. Darkness and snow bring the action to Ísafjörður – skiing, concerts and hot baths.

JANUARY
In Ísafjörður, the first rays of sun rise above the mountain ridge and touch parts of town after weeks of absence.

FEBRUARY
Off-piste skiing in the 'Westfjords Alps' near Flateyri and Þingeyri; cross-country tracks from Ísafjörður.

APRIL
Music festival **Aldrei fór ég suður** (over Easter weekend) attracts many of Iceland's best musicians and a devoted crowd.

MUMMI BJARNI/GETTY IMAGES ©, CAVAN IMAGES/GETTY IMAGES ©, PEOPLEIMAGES.COM · YURI A/SHUTTERSTOCK ©

Five Days to Travel Around

● Bring swimsuits and dive about shoulder-deep into local leisure life at **Pollurinn** (p208), a geothermal hot-pot in **Tálknafjörður** (p208). Celebrate local legends at the **Icelandic Sea Monster Museum** (p203) and drive the foggy **Arnarfjörður** (p200) road to colourful sculptures made by naivist **Samúel Jónsson** (p203).

● Set up base at the cosmopolitan capital **Ísafjörður** (p209). Wander past timber houses and fishing heritage, in time for the buffet at **Tjöruhúsið** (p212).

● Travel one-lane mountain tunnels for lunch at **Vagninn** (p212) in **Flateyri** (p212) and, through another set of tunnels, to the **Bolafjall platform** (p212).

A Week or More

● Catch a scheduled boat to **Hornstrandir** (p215), Iceland's majestic reserve on the Arctic edge. Return, back to the grid, with tired legs and the memory of seeing **Hornbjarg** (p216), the iconic cliff.

● Reap another reward for the far-traveller at **Krossneslaug** (p219), a geothermal swimming pool located where the road ends on the Westfjords' eastern spine known as **Strandir** (p218). Linger in the up-and-coming **Hólmavík** (p216) for peculiar museums, **Galdur Brewery** (p218) and whale watching without the crowds.

● Rent a bicycle at the atmospheric cafe **Simbahöllin** (p202) and ride to the lighthouse at **Svalvogar** (p202), a journey favoured by the growing number of cyclists pedalling the **Westfjords Way** (p202).

MAY

Scheduled boat tours to Hornstrandir begin at the end of the month. Temperatures remain cold for camping.

JULY

Temperatures up to 20°C; excellent for hiking and cycling. The cycling tournament, Westfjords Way Challenge, takes place.

AUGUST

Pufflings – the baby puffins – prepare to leave their burrows at Látrabjarg Peninsula.

OCTOBER

The tourist season dies down, earlier than in other regions, with some cafes and museums shut as early as September.

ARNARFJÖRÐUR

Arnarfjörður

REYKJAVÍK

There was a time Arnarfjörður had its own currency, Péturs-króna, issued by the largest company in the fjord's settlement Bíldudalur. Fish was caught in its calm waters, sheltered by many inlets and creeks, and exported directly to Spain. Trade within Iceland, however, had alpine barriers: the largest of mountains in the mountainous Westfjords sealed off the area. That spell of isolation wasn't entirely broken until 2020 with the opening of the Dýrafjarðargöng, mountain tunnels connecting Arnarfjörður to the northern part of the Westfjords. Dynjandi waterfalls, the icon of the Westfjords, can now be visited and admired year-round.

Driving – or, as some prefer, cycling – along the foggy coast of Arnarfjörður may inspire the sight of something mysterious in the distance, as in the past when Iceland's greatest gallery of sea monsters inhabited the fjord.

TOP TIP

Around 23km southeast of Bíldudalur, the runoff water of a hot spring warms the fjordside concrete pool Reykjafjarðarlaug to about 34°C. Less visible is a riverbed further behind the locker rooms – follow the path for 30m. This natural, turf-fringed bath – always open but prettiest at sunset – is over 40°C.

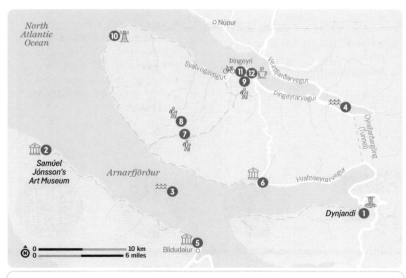

HIGHLIGHTS
1 Dynjandi
2 Samúel Jónsson's Art Museum

SIGHTS
3 Arnarfjörður
4 Dýrafjörður
5 Icelandic Sea Monster Museum
6 Jón Sigurðsson Memorial Museum
7 Kvennaskarð
8 Mt Kaldbakur
9 Sandafell
10 Svalvogar Lighthouse
11 Þingeyri

EATING
12 Simbahöllin

NICK FOX/SHUTTERSTOCK ©

Dynjandi waterfall

Iceland's Greatest Waterfall?

SOOTHING WATERFALL WATCHING

The Westfjords' best-known site, the **Dynjandi waterfall** is in fact a cascade of six falls in the *river* Dynjandi. But the grand and picturesque Fjallfoss on top tends to steal the limelight from its smaller siblings below; they're worth checking out as you walk the path (about 15 minutes) up to the main vista.

Fjallfoss is neither powerful nor tall by Icelandic waterfall standards – and that makes its popularity even more special. Many seasoned travellers regard it as a favourite, and one reason may be proximity. The water spreads wide without a splash, allowing visitors to get close without soaking in spray. It is immersive and overwhelming, but watching the water crawl down the cliffs is also soothing and calm.

Camping is no longer allowed at Dynjandi, despite good bathroom facilities. Drones are forbidden during the nesting season, from May to September.

THE WESTFJORDS LEGEND

Jón Sigurðsson, the architect of Iceland's independence, was born on 17 June 1811, at Farmstead Hrafnseyri. The interesting, modern **Jón Sigurðsson Memorial Museum** outlines his life and has a reconstruction of his turf house, a 19th-century church and a small cafe. Arrive on Iceland's National Day (on Jón's birthday!) for a free cake and serious speeches on sovereignty and strength.

Free cake or not, Jón himself preferred life on the banks of Copenhagen's canals. He left Iceland at the age of 22 and never returned, pushing against Iceland's loyalty to the Kingdom of Denmark with legal arguments, not the romantic nationalism of the freedom fighters before him.

WHERE TO STAY IN ARNARFJÖRÐUR

Harbour Inn
Smart and modern rooms with a guest kitchen and comfortable dining room. Good breakfast. €€

Bíldudalur Campground
Grassy, fjordside campsite next to the sports centre (no pool), with a playground and bouncing pillow. €

Hotel Sandfell
The only hotel option between Þingeyri and Patreksfjörður – friendly with simple-styled rooms. €€

Svalvogar lighthouse

JUST LIKE THE ALPS?

The people of the Westfjords have a humble way of describing the region. Ísafjörður on a sunny day? Ibizafjörður. The sharp summits towering over Dýrafjörður on both sides? The Westfjords Alps.

Dýrafjörður sure is stunning. Hike to **Sandafell** (367m) above Þingeyri for a fantastic view. The quickest route takes approximately 1½ hours round-trip, from the car park marked 'Sandafell bílastæði' on Google Maps.

The tallest mountain among the peaks (and in all of the Westfjords) is **Mt Kaldbakur** (989m). With an SUV, drive to **Kvennaskarð**, between Arnarfjörður and Dýrafjörður, and allow four hours, round-trip.

Cycling Tours
QUIET ROADS AND INCREDIBLE PATHS

The Westfjords' entire coastal loop – 960km of winding roads and steep mountain passes – is (to some people) a splendid cycling path. Every year, some one hundred cyclists complete the loop in just five days as part of the **Westfjords Way Challenge** (cyclingwestfjords.com), along with many more independent travellers touring the Westfjords on a bike for up to two weeks.

Part of the Westfjords' appeal as a cycling destination is what sets its roads apart from the rest of Iceland: less busy, with long stretches of wild, unspoiled scenery.

The best of the Westfjords Way is arguably the route between **Arnarfjörður** and **Dýrafjörður** via Svalvogar. The 49km circuit starts in the village of **Þingeyri**. The trip is strenuous, but on reasonably even ground. Experienced cyclists can loop the peninsula in about six hours to eight hours. For a less-demanding ride, ride the first half to the orange **Svalvogar lighthouse** and then backtrack to Þingeyri. Fat bikes are available at the coffee house Simbahöllin (simbahollin.is) and prices follow the route plan, starting at 12,500kr.

The Sea Monster Capital
ARNARFJÖRÐUR'S SOLE SETTLEMENT

Bíldudalur, the only settlement in the vast Arnarfjörður, has one of the finest fjordside positions in the country. Arriving by road from either direction, you're treated to spectacular views. The settlement dates back to the 16th century, when it was a trading hub for Danish merchants. It peaked

 WHERE TO EAT IN ARNARFJÖRÐUR

Hrafnseyri Cafe
Serves traditional Icelandic pastry, on the property of Iceland's independence hero. Open June to September. €

Vegamót
Cheery little grill with a view over the harbour in Bíldudalur, and a good mini-market too. €

Simbahöllin
Landmark coffee house in Þingeyri (on the other side of the tunnel) with Belgian waffles and tasty soups. €€

in size during the early industrialisation of Iceland's fishing fleet to a whopping population of 350 people, compared with 290 residents today.

The town's name is still associated in Icelandic culture with green peas: for much of the 20th century the village ran Iceland's largest cannery. The old cannery, opposite the church, is now occupied by monsters. Yes, monsters.

The **Icelandic Sea Monster Museum** (Skrímslasetrið) celebrates Bíldudalur's legacy of spotting freaky creatures spying from sea and occasionally crawling on land. The exhibition goes beyond folkloric anecdotes by giving visitors a sense of how these stories came to be. Ocean and isolation have historically defined life in the Westfjords and the strange creatures portrayed in the museum translate that reality into a vivid story. The shapeshifting Nykur, for instance, looks like a grey horse but the hooves face backwards. Check before jumping on an Icelandic horse, as the Nykur is primed to sprint to water and drown the rider.

Valleys of Surprise
SAMÚEL JÓNSSON'S ART FARM

The drive out to the tip of Arnarfjörður, along Rte 619 beyond Bíldudalur, is absolutely magnificent. The tiny track rims soaring mountains, lush pastured valleys collectively known as Ketildalir and untouched beaches, and looks onto the churning fjord and the incredible landscape on its northern side. Towards sunset and on partly cloudy days, the light shifts continually, and rainbows often form.

Where the road ends, the art show begins at **Samúel Jónsson's Art Museum**. Selárdalur valley is where the farmer from Brautarholt, named Samúel Jónsson, made his mark on Iceland's popular art history. Jónsson has been described as the 'artist with the infantile heart' but his life story certainly lacks the elements of innocence: his three children all died young and his sculptures and paintings received little attention. He went twice to Reykjavík over his lifetime, and was exposed primarily to art and architecture through books and postcards.

Age 72, he displayed his art to the world by spending his pension on the construction of a colourful church with an onion dome – the regional church some 2km up the road had refused to accept an altarpiece he made – and a flamboyant home to showcase his work. Outside are naive sculptures, including a Lions Court created from a postcard Jónsson saw of the Alhambra in Spain.

HIKING IN THE WESTFJORDS

Halla Mía, a journalist in Ísafjörður, shares her recommendations for hikes in the Westfjords. @hallamia

Naustahvilft – The Troll Seat
A steep, short hike. Legend says it was formed by a female troll who sat down to wash her feet in the fjord. Offers great views over the town of Ísafjörður and the fjord. Allow 1½ hours.

Óshlíð
Used to be the road to the remote fishing village of Bolungarvík. After it got replaced by a tunnel, the road is slowly being reclaimed by nature. A beautiful path for walking but also biking and running. Allow 3 hours.

Hornstrandir Nature Reserve
Take a boat to Veiðileysufjörður, hike to Hornvík and spend a day in Hornbjarg. Then walk to Hlöðuvík and from there to Hesteyri. A challenging but unique experience. Allow four days.

GETTING AROUND

With the 2020 opening of the Dýrafjarðar tunnels, starting some 9km from the waterfall, the sight is accessible year-round. The notorious mountain road to Bíldudalur, known as Dynjandisheiði, was at the time of writing being paved (due for completion in July 2024). The passage will remain challenging over winter, if not closed completely.

Beyond Arnarfjörður

A truly wild-feeling area, where white, black, red and pink beaches meet shimmering blue water, and towering cliffs and stunning mountains cleave the fjords.

Arnarfjörður ●

Tálknafjörður
Patreksfjörður ●

● Látrabjarg Cliffs

Rauðisandur

By some standards, the beach of Rauðisandur exists on the wrong latitude. If it was located, say, 20 degrees further south on the globe, colourful towels and sun umbrellas would line the 10km beach of reddish sand that is uniquely tropical-looking for Iceland. Sunbathing is possible on a bright summer day but most visitors come wearing walking shoes; the area is excellent for long and short hikes. Further on the peninsula is the region's most popular destination, Látrabjarg – a 14km stretch of cliffs that is home to thousands of nesting seabirds in summer.

Accommodation options are rich thanks to big-town Patreksfjörður with a population of 700 people – and, like it or not, rising with every new fish farm.

TOP TIP

Vatnsfjörður Nature Reserve is a pristine place along the winding Westfjords' south coast. Paths lead from Hótel Flókalundur.

PERSZING1982/GETTY IMAGES ©

MARTI BUG CATCHER/SHUTTERSTOCK ©

Church, Rauðisandur

Westernmost Detour

SANDY BEACHES WITH PUFFIN CLIFFS

The steep and narrow drive to **Rauðisandur** is an experience in itself. And please enjoy the view; from above, the 'red beach' may not look red at all – the sun often makes it seem yellow or even black. The sandy colour comes from pulverised scallop shells, spoiled elsewhere by volcanic eruptions. Once at sea level, the road reaches a junction: for a 1.5km walking path to the beach, turn right to Saurbær. For drive-in access to the beach, turn left to Melanes campsite.

Further down the road from Saurbær – the black wooden church – is a small white house hosting Franska Kaffihúsið (facebook.com/franskakaffihusid). The name translates as The French Cafe and sure enough their French flan is delicious. Open from June to August.

Heading further on Rte 612, to the tip of the peninsula, are one of Europe's largest bird cliffs. The **Látrabjarg Peninsula** – also the westernmost point of the European continent – are the place to watch puffins, razorbills, guillemots, cormorants and other seabirds from June to mid-August. The cliffs

BEST PLACES TO EAT & DRINK IN PATREKSFJÖRÐUR

Flak
Unpretentious craft pub with a minimal menu: soup, fish or vegetables. Lunch and dinner. €€

Stúkuhúsið
Cool eatery with friendly staff serving succulent fish fresh from the fjord outside the window – the cod with hints of wasabi is superb. €€

Albína Bakery
Lunch place with pizzas and sandwiches, plus a decent selection of cakes and pastries. Attached to a convenience store. €

 WHERE TO STAY AROUND ARNARFJÖRÐUR

Melanes
Adorable hobbit-sized, two-person wooden pods beside the sweeping Rauðisandur cove. Camping available. €€

Fosshótel Westfjords
A historic Patreksfjörður building renovated into this super-sleek, stylish hotel with modern rooms. €€€

Hótel Látrabjarg
On the Látrabjarg Peninsula, this small hotel has 13 rooms with private bathrooms. €€€

205

ROAD TRIP

The Westfjords Way

Entering the Westfjords is a 950km commitment; a loop zigzags the fjord landscape along the Westfjords Way. Sure, there are big-name attractions, but more than anything the journey is about exploring the wild subarctic landscape and small-town coastal life. Lie in moss at the side of a river, meet an eccentric traveller in a camper van, or attend the concert of a local pop band on a bright summer night.

1 Hellulaug

There are several pools in the Westfjords, and Hellulaug is distinctive for being right on the beach, offering a view of the freezing ocean while being shielded from the road. It is a breeze to access from the main road while still feeling private, so you can easily hop in for a dip while watching the fjord waters. At high tide, do as the locals do and jump in the frigid sea, then run back to the big toasty rock pool (38°C) to warm up.

The Drive: The car park above the pool is large but poorly marked; it is about 500m east of Hótel Flókalundur on Rte 62. Ignore the Google Maps (incorrect) marker west of Flókalundur.

2 The Abandoned Barn Fossfjörður

The old, A-shaped barn – with a rusting roof and a perfect silver-grey frame – has become an Instagram delight. The image captures the silence of the landscape and the loss of scale against the wide open fjord. Is the abandoned farm small, or surprisingly big? Maybe both. Nearby is

PAUL MAYALL ICELAND/ALAMY STOCK PHOTO ©

Skrúður

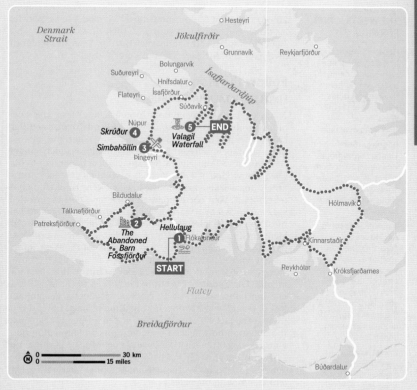

a great, illustrated lesson in the Icelandic language: 'foss' means waterfall and 'á' means river and from the small bridge over Fossá is a waterfall named Foss – the Waterfall in Waterfall River.

The Drive: The barn and Foss waterfall are only 1km apart on Rte 63. Search 'Abandoned Barn in Fossfjörður' to locate online.

3 Simbahöllin

Simbahöllin is a cool cafe in a restored 1915 general store with friendly staff serving tasty Belgian waffles during the day and hearty lamb tagines at night. Outdoor seating in an old bus, fjord views and a cosy vibe ensure this is one of the Westfjords best boltholes. Open from June to September.

The Drive: Take the Dýrafjarðargöng mountain tunnels, open since 2020, to reach the tiny village of Þingeyri. The landmark green house on the main street is hard to miss.

4 Skrúður

One of Iceland's oldest botanic gardens sits on the lower slopes of the fjordside valleys on Dýrafjörður's northern edge. Teeny Skrúður was established as a teaching garden in 1909. You'll see arched whalebones at one entrance.

The Drive: Just off Rte 624, signposted, with free entry.

5 Valagil Waterfall

A gigantic gorge with cascading waterfalls, revealed after a mellow walk along a lush valley. The trail is about 4km, round-trip, at the landward end of Álftafjörður.

The Drive: The marked trail starts at a small car park about 9km south of Súðavík; the tallest waterfall is visible throughout the walk.
Continue the loop, back to Hellulaug.

THE WESTFJORDS FOR KIDS

Haukur Sigurðsson, a photographer in Ísafjörður and father of two, shares his recommendations for family fun in the Westfjords. @haukursigurdsson

Raggagarður
This huge playground in Súðavík, 20km from Ísafjörður, is joyously attractive, with picnic and barbecue facilities.

Samúel Jónsson's Art Museum
Jónsson's naive animal sculptures capture the imagination of children. The drive from Bíldudalur is stunning and most of the museum (p203) is outdoors by a stony beach.

Holtsfjara
I have been to some great sandcastle competitions on this quiet beach in Önundarfjörður. (Marked on Google Maps as 'Önundarfjörður Pier'.)

stretch for about 14km in total, with the longest trail (about 20km) reaching Rauðisandur beach. It's best to visit in the evening, when the birds return to their nests.

On the way back, the shipwreck *Garðar BA* is an Instagram favourite and, fun fact, Iceland's oldest steel ship.

Follow the Money
FIND LITTLE TÁLKNAFJÖRÐUR

As the euphemism goes, odour from fish factories is the 'smell of money' in coastal communities. **Tálknafjörður** is different: money trickles down from the fjord's horizon. Six fish pens, farming hundreds of thousands of salmon and trout, put the scale of Iceland's lucrative aquaculture boom on full display. In a village of 250 people, it is all hands on deck and at lunchtime workers head to the low-key joint Hópið for a buffet (2700kr). Your correspondent came for a *plokkfiskur* (fish stew), followed by a warm *grjónagrautur* (porridge), and almost accepted a job in road construction on the way out. (For local cuisine prepared with considerably more attention to detail, Cafe Dunhagi delivers a true taste of the Westfjords.)

Meet with Tálknafjörður locals, once again, in the evening sun over the geothermal hot-pot **Pollurinn**. While the name means 'The Puddle', this hot-pot highlight of the Westfjords is essentially a natural bath created with lots of cement and lots of runoff water from a 1977 drilling project. Enter day or night – the lockers are always open and admission is paid at the donation box. Backed by mountains and sweeping fjord views, locals often kick back with a beer in the evening; but cans only, no glass. To get here, take Rte 617 some 3.5km beyond Cafe Dunhagi – the hot-pot is signposted with a tiny white sign with black lettering.

To bathe in warm and clean water, however, visit the **Tálknafjörður Swimming Pool**. Its green water slide and shallow leisure pool make a great choice for kids. The pool in neighbouring Patreksfjörður is a firm recommendation, too, with excellent views.

GETTING AROUND

The pitted roads in this sparsely populated region are rough and driving is slow. The pot-holed gravel road to Rauðisandur and Látrabjarg is a summer road, accessible for 2WDs in dry conditions. At the time of writing the mountain road to Arnarfjörður, known as Dynjandisheiði, was being paved. Expect challenging conditions in snow.

The Baldur car ferry (seatours.is) connects the southern Westfjords to Stykkishólmur on the Snæfellsnes Peninsula, departing from Brjánslækur terminal twice per day over summer, with a stop at Flatey island. The trip takes 2½ hours and costs about 13,000kr for

two adults; driving the same distance takes about four hours and costs a little less for two people.

Norlandair (norlandair.is) offers daily flights between Reykjavík and Bíldudalur (40 minutes). The airport has car rental (hertz. is) and a shuttle to and from Patreksfjöður (call ahead, 893-2636). Bus 62 with Strætó drives between Patreksfjörður and Ísafjörður five times a week via the Brjánslækur ferry terminal. The bus stops at Dynjandi waterfall (around midday) but there's no other service from there to nearby settlements.

ÍSAFJÖRÐUR

Ísafjörður

REYKJAVÍK

After a time spent travelling in the Westfjords, Ísafjörður feels like a bustling metropolis with hip cafes, authentic gift shops, fine restaurant choices and even a cinema open most nights. With a growing population of 2700 people, Ísafjörður is by far the largest settlement in the region and a hub of Westfjords adventure tours. There is hiking in the hills around the town and skiing in winter, and regular summer boats ferry hikers across to the remote Hornstrandir Peninsula.

The centre of Ísafjörður is a charming grid of old timber and tin-clad buildings, hemmed in on all sides by towering peaks and the dark waters of the fjord. Beyond the harbour, dense with cafes and small shops, it helps to have a car to explore the outbacks of town and neighbouring Bolungarvík, Flateyri and Þingeyri – all accessible within a 20-minute drive thanks to a series of tunnels.

TOP TIP

From Ísafjörður, tour operators sail to the island of Vigur, home to an incredible number of Arctic terns and coastal birds over the summer. The island, once farmed, has a cute cafe and enough to do to sustain a lovely afternoon. The sailing takes an hour, usually in calm seas, as the inlet is sheltered from the open ocean.

GESTUR GISLASON/SHUTTERSTOCK ©

ÍSAFJÖRÐUR

North
Atlantic
Ocean

Galtarviti
Lighthouse

Ísafjarðardjúp

Bolungarvik

Suðureyri

Syðridalsvatn

Hnífsdalur

Ísafjörður — Museum of Everyday Life

Westfjords
Heritage
Museum

Flateyri

Önundarfjörður

Súðavík

Vestfjarðarvegur

0 ——— 6 km
0 ——— 3 miles

HIGHLIGHTS
1 Museum of Everyday Life
2 Westfjords Heritage Museum

SIGHTS
3 Bolafjall Platform
4 Bolungarvik
5 Flateyri
6 Hnífsdalur
7 Holtsfjara
8 Ísafjarðardjúp
9 Naustahvilft
10 Önundarfjörður
11 Ósvör Maritime Museum
12 Raggagarður
13 Skálavík Beach
see 1 Tangagata Street
14 Tungudalur

Ísafjörður Now & Then

HISTORY MANIFESTED IN OLD HOUSES

In the unconventional love story *The Bridge Over Tangaga-ta* – more than anything an ode to the author's hometown – Eiríkur Norðdahl writes that Ísafjörður gets its name from Danish merchants who were unable to pronounce 'Skutuls-

 WHERE TO STAY IN & AROUND ÍSAFJÖRÐUR ────────

Ísafjörður Hostel
Luxury hostel with pristine four-bed dorms, on a residential street in the old part of town. €

Tungudalur Campground
Camping in a green valley just outside Ísafjörður, with good vibes at the kitchen-dining hut. €

Hótel Ísafjörður (Torg)
Beats the other Hótel Ísafjörður building (Horn); business-style rooms with the best views from the top floors. €€€

fjörður' – the name of the fjord Ísafjörður stands by, on an arcing spit that extends into the unpronounceable fjord.

True or not, the remote Westfjords' capital has long been shaped by incoming ships. Up until the early 20th century, Ísafjörður was Iceland's third-largest settlement, and timber houses from the merchant era define the central part of town; unlike Akureyri and Reykjavík, the old town never suffered major fires that wiped out densely populated homes such as the charming and aforementioned **Tangagata Street**.

Today, however, some 70% of harbour revenue in Ísafjörður comes from tourism, and it is Iceland's third-busiest port of call for cruise ships. Furthermore, the University Centre of the Westfjords attracts many international students seeking a graduate degree in coastal and marine management.

But to find out about the days the young flocked to Ísafjörður to learn how to haul fish, head to the old wooden houses on the harbour tip, which house the **Westfjords Heritage Museum**. It's crammed with fishing and nautical exhibits, tools from the whaling days and old photographs of sun-drying fish, tall ships and more fish.

In contrast to the heritage preservation of old items and visual documentation, the **Museum of Everyday Life** explores the magic of the mundane, with crafty, poetic storytelling. Curated by two local anthropologists, the personal narratives and story fragments draw from such exhibition items as shoes, books and mini-films.

Climb to the 'Troll Seat'

OUTDOOR ACTIVITIES

Locals in Ísafjörður value their outdoor escapes; the town is well-known for hosting tournaments in everything from cross-country skiing to cycling.

Within walking distance from the town's western edge, the valley of **Tungudalur** has a 9-hole golf course and a skiing area, along with walking and bike paths.

For a scenic hike, head to **Naustahvilft** above the road from the airport – about 150m uphill to a massive 'bowl' in the mountain ridge known as the 'troll seat'. It's a short but challenging climb, taking about 30 minutes.

Mountain biking has a strong following, with paths for all difficulty levels. Check out a trail map on the website Mountain Bike Ísafjörður (mtbisafjordur.is). Bikes are available for rent at Borea Adventures (boreaadventures.com), offering guided cycling tours several times a week, suitable for beginners. For those in shape for six hours of cycling we recommend the 'fjord hopping' tour, which crosses mountains over to Bolungarvík.

THE PATH TO ÓSHLÍÐ

Two of Westfjords' largest towns, Ísafjörður and Bolungarvík, are just a 10-minute drive apart via the 5.4km mountain tunnel, open since 2010. Cyclists, runners and hikers have taken over the old road, around Mt Óshlíð. The small track, about 8km, is wonderfully scenic; outside of summer, seek local advice as the hill is prone to rockfalls and avalanches. Arriving in Bolungarvík, sweat or not, it's worth knowing that the swimming pool Sundlaug Bolungarvíkur beats the (indoor) pool in Ísafjörður.

The small village between Ísafjörður and Bolungarvík is **Hnífsdalur**, home to a large fish factory and a hundred-something people. There's no shop or service here, beyond several Airbnbs.

Old Bookstore
Antique furniture and wooden floors above the landmark bookshop in Flateyri. €€€

Korpudalur HI Hostel
Wonderfully located, on a farm in Önundarfjörður, some 20 minutes from Ísafjörður. Suited to families. €€

Einarshúsið Guesthouse
Eight lovely rooms in a turn-of-the-century heritage home near the harbour in Bolungarvík. €€

The calm fjords make Ísafjörður and the wider Djúpið (shorthand for the fjord system known as Ísafjarðardjúp) especially popular for kayaking. Tours are available with Bore and West Tours (westtours.is) and range from two hours to several days, sleeping on a remote beach somewhere in the company of seals and seabirds. People have compared the activity to attending a yoga retreat; the mind switches gear and time spools slowly, one paddle at a time. The Westfjords, if anything, are not about speed.

The Westfjords View
THE BOLAFJALL PLATFORM

It is now possible to walk – safely – beyond the edge of Bolafjall mountain by standing on a massive platform made from 60 tonnes of steel. Completed in 2022, the ambitious **Bolafjall platform** offers the ultimate Westfjords views at 638m and is likely to send butterflies straight to your stomach. The panorama extends over to the Hornstrandir Nature Reserve (p215) and the fjord system of **Ísafjarðardjúp**. Some people claim to see Greenland!

Look behind you, at the black basalt cliffs…and a giant radome – Bolafjall is a defence site, too. Hence the barbed wires and metal gates. The radar station is one of four NATO monitors in Iceland scanning the Atlantic airspace.

From June to early September, it is possible to drive all the way to the mountaintop, some 9km from the town of **Bolungarvík** that is paying, in part, for the 200 million króna construction of Bolafjall platform. In light snow, the road remains open most of the way, with the remaining 3.5km a modest walk. But bear in mind the mountain is notoriously windy.

From summit to sea, further west on Rte 630, the road ends at **Skálavík beach**. The stony creek, with pockets of soft sand, is favoured by locals for family fun and a cold swim.

On the way back to Ísafjörður, just before entering the tunnel separating the twin towns, is the atmospheric **Ósvör Maritime Museum**, a replica of a fishing station from the 19th century.

Fish & Books by the Kilo
A VISIT TO FLATEYRI

Part of the Ísafjörður municipality, **Flateyri** is a village on a sandbar in the stunning **Önundarfjörður** that has successfully blended its seafaring heritage with tourism. As elsewhere in the Westfjords, developments in Iceland's fishing industry have devastated small-scale operations. Local fishers have instead turned to sea angling and made Flateyri into a lead-

 WHERE TO EAT IN & AROUND ÍSAFJÖRÐUR

Tjöruhúsið
Ambitious, rustic seafood place. Serve-yourself buffet of hot skillets and lively hosts. €€

Heimabyggð
A local favourite with an excellent lunch menu, coffee and sourdough pizzas. €€

Vagninn
Plokkfiskur (fish stew) with rye bread or spicy fish soup brightens the day. In Flateyri. €€

The Old Bookstore

ing base for sea-angling tours. Iceland Pro Fishing (iceland protravel.com) occupies the harbour with a row of cottages where guests overnight between sea-angling tours, hauling big species like cod and haddock.

Walking around Flateyri, note the adorable street art all over town – 12 species of migratory birds, painted by local artist Jean Larson. Flateyri residents are seasonal too as many houses are in fact summer cottages and Airbnbs.

The newest building in Flateyri is the 2023 campus for Flateyri Folk High School, a non-formal residential school based on a Nordic model teaching life skills and community work to gap-year youth.

But intellectual institutions are not new around here: founded in 1914, **The Old Bookstore** (Gamla Bókabúðin) claims to be 'the oldest store in Iceland still in traditional operation'. Today's merchandise is, appropriately, very nostalgic: classic children's books, vintage housewares and colourful analogue cameras. The English selection covers a wide range of translations by Icelandic authors – set in the Westfjords, a trilogy by Jón Kalman begins with the title *Heaven and Hell*.

FLATEYRI'S PAINFUL PAST

In 1995 a major avalanche changed the fate of Flateyri overnight: 20 residents died when the snow wiped out 33 houses. The tragedy came on the heels of an another major avalanche in Súðavík just seven months earlier, which killed 14. What was said to be a once-in-a-century event then happened again in 2020 when two avalanches caused destruction to the harbour area in Flateyri. Avalanche barriers shielded homes, some of which were inhabited by Syrian refugees at the time. The barriers have expanded further in recent years, visible in the mountain hills. By the church is a memorial honouring the 20 people who died in 1995; to this day it's the deadliest natural disaster in Iceland's modern history.

GETTING AROUND

Arriving in Ísafjörður from the southern Westfjords is somewhat of an experience through the one-lane Vestfjarðargöng Tunnel. Completed in 1996, the 9km-long Ísafjörður–Suðureyri–Flateyri tunnel beneath the mountains becomes an unusual one-lane tunnel in parts of the 6km stretch from Ísafjörður to Flateyri. In the middle of the mountain it branches, and a 3km section of the tunnel shoots off to Suðureyri. Worry not: pullovers throughout allow oncoming traffic to alternate as you ride through the damp chutes.

Most places of interest within Ísafjörður are accessible by foot. To reach the Tungudalur

valley, hop on a local bus at Pollagata. Strætisvagnar Ísafjarðar, as the municipal bus network is known, also runs to Flateyri, Suðureyri and Þingeyri. There's no public transport to Bolungarvík.

Strætó buses travel from Aðalstræti 7 in Ísafjörður from June to August – with no winter service – to Hólmavík (Route 61) and Patreksfjörður (Route 62). From there it's possible to get on another bus to Reykjavík – Route 62 stops at Brjánslækur for the ferry to Stykkishólmur (p180). Alternatively, try carpooling at samferda.net for long rides.

Hornstrandir
Nature Reserve • Hornbjarg Cliff

Hesteyri •
Veiðileysufjörður

Norðurfjörður

Ísafjörður

Djúpavík •

Hólmavík •
Drangsnes

Beyond Ísafjörður

Every direction is a journey. The watery borders
of Ísafjörður lead to a remote peninsula and road
along the longest fjord to a witchcraft village.

The largest of the region's fjords, 75km-long Ísafjarðardjúp takes
a massive swatch out of the Westfjords' landmass and the watery
borders of inhabited and unpopulated land. Across from Ísafjörður's
side is the Hornstrandir Nature Reserve, accessible only by ferry.
With barely a phone signal and not one road, the pristine peninsula
is a hiking destination. The road down Djúpið, as Ísafjarðardjúp is
casually called, winds in and out of a series of smaller fjords, making the drive from the bustling city of Ísafjörður to Hólmavík like
sliding along each tooth of a fine comb. North of Hólmavík, continue up the magnificently peaceful Standir coast until the track
suddenly ends in Norðurfjörður, the capital of Iceland's smallest
municipality, with a population of 44 and one trillion Arctic terns.

TOP TIP

An hour's drive from
Ísafjörður, Litlibær is one
of the Westfjords' most
atmospheric eateries
inside a turf-roofed hut
that's crammed with family
photos and memorabilia.

ZDENEK KAJZR/GETTY IMAGES ©

WIRESTOCK CREATORS/SHUTTERSTOCK ©

Arctic fox, Hornstrandir Nature Reserve

The Wildest Corner

NO-ROAD HIKING DESTINATION

The northernmost tip of the Westfjords, accounting for 0.6% of Iceland's land mass, is one of Europe's last wildernesses. **Hornstrandir Nature Reserve** is a breathtaking beauty of soaring mountains and precipitous cliffs. A small but steady number of travellers make the journey, moving from one fjord to the next, taking anywhere from two nights to a week. Travellers are guaranteed fickle weather and a sighting of the Arctic fox in its brown summer coat. The foxes living in remote Hornstrandir seem oblivious to the fact that almost everywhere else humans hunt them: some even approach people, eating from the palm of their hand. The last full-time human resident of the rugged area moved away in 1952 – it never was an easy place to farm – but many descendants have turned family farmsteads into summer getaways. And the former doctor's house at Hesteyri now serves coffee and cake.

To get to Hornstrandir, you must first head to a harbour; there are no roads. Ísafjörður has daily departures with Borea (boreaadventures.com) and West Tours (westtours.is) from June

WHY I LOVE HORNSTRANDIR

Egill Bjarnason, writer

On my first trip to the Hornstrandir as a reporter, I interviewed summer residents at Hesteyri petitioning to declare the remote peninsula a 'digital-free zone'. At the time, government officials wanted to raise a cell tower but everyone I spoke with unanimously favoured a carefree life over the safety of phones.

The spirit of the Westfjords – radical for the modern age – is to preserve a frontier for real adventures. On assignment for this book, I sailed once again to Hornstrandir. Two bars. One bar. Closing in on Veiðileysufjörður, a short inlet with a long name, mountains shrugged off the faint signal on my phone. Zero.

 WHERE TO STAY BEYOND ÍSAFJÖRÐUR

Heydalur
Quirky farmstay with a picturesque pool inside a greenhouse, and Kobbi, a talking parrot. €€

Hótel Laugarhóll
One of the Westfjords most appealing retreats with a gorgeous geothermal hot-pot and pool. €€

Hótel Djúpavík
Landmark hotel originally built for seasonal workers during the herring boom in Djúpavík. €€

THOMAS H. MITCHELL/GETTY IMAGES ©

Whaling station ruins, Hesteyri

WAS THAT A POLAR BEAR?

Since 2008, five polar bears have travelled from northeastern Greenland to Iceland, all but one over summer, when the lack of sea ice pushes bears to leave their usual territory in search of food. Most have arrived at Hornstrandir. The government policy is to kill them, claiming they are weak and aggressive after swimming hundreds of kilometres.

Walruses have been spotted every two years. In the last few years, however, they have frequented random harbours across Iceland in greater numbers – a total of five times in 2023.

The Sheep Farming Museum in Hólmavík has a slideshow on polar bears arriving from Greenland.

to mid-August. Hornvík and Hesteyri are the two base camps, staffed by a lone ranger, and most hikes are tailored around the landmark **Hornbjarg cliff**. The most popular hike is four to five days, known as the Royal Horn (Hornleið), from **Veiðileysufjörður** to **Hesteyri** via the northern strip. Day tours from Ísafjörður to Hesteyri are available in July and August, with West Tours, altogether some five hours. The Hornstrandir Visitor Center on the main square in Ísafjörður offers practical travel information and a small exhibit on the Arctic fox.

To see Hornbjarg without a multiday hike, book a boat with Strandferðir (strandferdir.is) departing from Strandir (p218) on the eastern end of the Westfjords, a four-hour drive from Ísafjörður.

The Capital of Folklore
WITCHCRAFT IN HÓLMAVÍK

Hólmavík is traditionally a fishing village and a service town for the Strandir region. In more recent years, however, the town has reinvented itself by telling stories from the past. Folklore is a major industry.

The Folklore Institute at the University of Iceland, on main street Höfðagata, bestows a significant sense of authority upon the village of folklore. Recent studies have explored the life of

 WHERE TO STAY BEYOND ÍSAFJÖRÐUR

Malarhorn
In Drangsnes, the guesthouse has a seaside restaurant and a boat taking people to Grímsey island. €€

Urðartindur
One of two guesthouses in Norðurfjörður, with modern rooms and private bathrooms. €€

Reykjanes tjaldsvæði
Grassy campsite between Ísafjörður and Hólmavík with good facilities and a pool on Hótel Reykjanes' property. €

THE ROYAL HORN IN FOUR DAYS

Sail from Ísafjörður to **1 Veiðileysufjörður**, one of the local *jökulfirðir* (glacier fjords), for this four-day hike. From the bottom of the fjord, follow a cairn-marked trail up the slope and through the mountain pass. From the pass you can descend the mountain on either side until you reach **2 Hornvík**. The hike from Veiðileysufjörður to Hornvík can take anywhere between four and eight hours. There's a ranger station at the campsite in Hornvík (located at a creek named Höfn), so feel free to get the latest weather forecast and information about trail conditions. Use your second day to visit **3 Hornbjarg**, one of Iceland's most beautiful bird cliffs with diverse flora and fauna. Spend another night at the campsite. Day number three is a hike from Hornvík to **4 Hlöðuvík**. The partly marked trail goes through a moun-

tain pass and is relatively easy to find. At Hlöðuvík, the campsite is situated next to Hlöðuvíkurós (the mouth of the Hlöðuvík river). Like Hornvík, Hlöðuvík faces north – it's the perfect place to watch the spectacular midnight sun. Figure around six hours to reach Hlöðuvík. On the final day, hike through Kjarnsvíkurskarð (a mountain pass) and Hesteyrarbrúnir pass to **5 Hesteyri** (figure around eight hours). Hesteyri is an old village that was abandoned around the middle of the 20th century. There are still several well-kept houses amid the fields of angelica. Ruins of a turn-of-the-century whaling station are found near the village. The coffee shop in Hesteyri is a good place to stop at the end of your hike – you can wait here for your prebooked ferry back to Ísafjörður, or enjoy an extra night to explore the area.

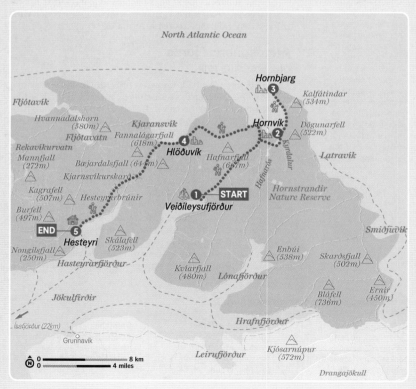

NECROPANTS

Of all the mystical displays at the Museum of Icelandic Sorcery and Witchcraft, perhaps the most bizarre is a plastic replica of legendary 'necropants' – trousers made from the skin of a dead man's legs and groin. It was commonly believed that if a donor made a verbal agreement, his corpse could be skinned upon his death and the resulting necropants would produce money when worn (with the scrotum always full of coins). In order for this to work, the skinned portion of the corpse had to be without holes; the sorcerer had to put the necropants on immediately; then a coin stolen from a poor widow had to be placed in the necropants' scrotum.

peasant farmers through 19th-century diaries and the outrageous, bizarre and brief Witchcraft Era. Over a 30-year period, from 1654, 100 people were burned alive for supernatural practices. Unlike the witches of New England's Salem trials, most of Iceland's convicted 'witches' were men. Often 'occult practices' were simply old Viking traditions or superstitions, but hidden *grimoires* (magic books) full of puzzling runic design were proof enough for the local witch hunters (the area's elite) to burn around 20 souls (mostly among the poor) at the stake.

The **Museum of Icelandic Sorcery and Witchcraft** serves as a form of restitution for the victims of that dark era. Through narratives and recreation of artefacts, the museum commemorates the art of witchcraft. Don't miss the detailed descriptions of the spells and the startling 'necropants'. It is open year-round, with a restaurant attached.

The year 2022 marked a major event for Iceland's way of living: sheep no longer outnumbered the national population. For one thousand years, the stoic, resilient animal kept the nation alive with its meat, milk and wool. The **Sheep Farming Museum**, located a 10-minute drive from Hólmavík, tells the surprisingly complex and layered history of Icelandic sheep. Lambs roam the backyard, and visitors can sometimes feed them with milk from a bottle.

The final folkloric offspring is the taproom of **Galdur Brewery** (facebook.com/witchcraftbeer), where ales are coded with runic witchcraft. Open most afternoons.

Atmospheric Fjords
ONE-WAY SIDE TRIP

The road less travelled, known as **Strandir**, is the eastern spine of the Westfjords. Indented by a series of bristle-like fjords and lined with towering crags, the drive north of Hólmavík, the region's only sizeable settlement, is rough and incredibly rewarding.

Across Steingrímsfjörður from Hólmavík, **Drangsnes** (pronounced *drowngs-ness*) is a remote little town with views across to North Iceland and the small uninhabited island of Grímsey (not to be confused with the larger Grímsey north of Siglufjörður), only 10 minutes by boat from the Drangsnes dock. Guests walk the island for about two hours and, from June to mid-August, puffins are a promise: the island is estimated to nest 1% of Iceland's entire puffin population – somewhere around four million in total size.

Just as the stoic puffin stares at the ocean from the edge of a cliff, so do people at the Drangsnes Hot Pots. The three tubs,

WHERE TO EAT BEYOND ÍSAFJÖRÐUR

Cafe Riis
Landmark cafe in Hólmavík with pizzas, burgers, colourful cocktails and late-night opening hours. €€

Kaffi Norðurfjörður
Fantastic establishment overlooking Norðurfjörður's tiny harbour; open from lunch to dinner in summer. €€

Steinshús
A perfect stop for a coffee and meat soup between Ísafjörður and Hólmavík. Summer only. €

MENNO SCHAEFER/SHUTTERSTOCK ©

Drangsnes Hot Pots

WHALE WATCHING IN HÓLMAVÍK

Hólmavík offers whale watching without the crowds; the calm waters of Steingrímsfjörður are ideal for people prone to seasickness. Humpback whales and white-beaked dolphins are the most common sight. In 2023, a blue whale was spotted once. Láki Tours (lakitours. is), the sole operator at the harbour in Hólmavík, offers daily departures from June to October, lasting about two hours (an hour shorter than the average tour elsewhere in Iceland). The whales often feed close to shore, offering some of the best land-based sightings in Iceland, too. Locals often know where the whales are residing on a given week – but a good place to start is Rte 68 by the Sheep Farming Museum. Keep an eye out for the spouts or the fin of a humpback. If nothing else, the walk along the beach is lovely.

planted by the sea after the discovery of hot water, are a local hangout, and are always open. Shower across the road *before* dipping in and contribute to the donation box.

Djúpavík is a holiday village, Westfjords-style, capturing the calm energy of Strandir. When a herring boom went bust in the 1950s, the settlement revived as a holiday home. Hotel Djúpavík, founded in 1985, was originally built for seasonal workers – mostly women – in fish processing. And the herring factory that was once the largest concrete building in Iceland is a rustic gallery space, The Factory art exhibition, with an international reach. Take in the scenery with a 5km loop trail with a view from the mountain above the village. Kayaks and mountain bikes are available to rent at the hotel.

Norðurfjörður is the capital of the municipality known as Árneshreppur (population 42). It has the food shop Verzlunarfjelag Árneshrepps, the restaurant Kaffi Norðurfjörður with a delightful view over the harbour, and two guesthouses: Urðartindur and Bergistangi. It's a capital, alright! Nearby Gjögur Airport has weekly flights to Reykjavík.

Some 3km up a dirt track beyond Norðurfjörður the road ends at **Krossneslaug**, a geothermal (infinity) pool and hotpot that shouldn't be missed. Walk down to where it sits at the edge of the universe on a wild black-pebble beach. It's an incredible place to watch the midnight sun flirt with the roaring waves. Admission is 1100kr and despite having official opening hours, the pool is accessible night and day via machine payment.

GETTING AROUND

Hire a car – or hitchhike – to explore Strandir. Over summer, bus 61 with Strætó runs between Hólmavík and Ísafjörður twice a week, in sync with bus 59 connecting Hólmavík to western Iceland via Borgarnes.

Norlandair (norlandair.is) flies (a very small plane) between Reykjavík's domestic airport and the airstrip at Gjögur (50 minutes, twice a week), 16km southeast of Norðurfjörður.

NORTH ICELAND

THE LAND OF FORCE

Boiling mud pits, frozen lakes and mesmerising Northern Lights. The north is a place of extreme force.

Icelandic author Hallgrímur Helgason once observed the allure of Siglufjörður as the power of the outpost: the last latte this side of the North Pole.

The mammoth north carries an atmosphere that is difficult to define. The ocean does it best. One day, the waters outside are calm and reflective like a painting. The next, tall waves break violently on the shore.

Life is tied to the ocean, with towns entirely established out of nautical convenience. Changes in fish stock and fishing policies have forced many to reinvent themselves, for better or worse. Siglufjörður, once among Iceland's largest towns during the herring heyday, welcomes more cruise ships than trawlers nowadays.

The region's top natural sights are variations on a couple of themes: the grumbling, volcanically active earth, and water and ice coursing towards the broad coast. There are endless treats to discover: little Akureyri, with its surprising moments of big-city living; windy fjordside pastures full of stout Viking horses, and ice fishing in the winter landscape of Lake Mývatn.

Prepare to be enticed by offshore islands populated by colonies of seabirds and a few hardy locals; lonely peninsulas stretching out towards the Arctic Circle; white-water rapids ready to deliver an adrenaline kick; national-park walking trails to reach unparalleled views; unhyped and underpopulated ski fields; and underwater marvels that woo divers into frigid depths.

FOMINAYAPHOTO/SHUTTERSTOCK ©

THE MAIN AREAS

Above: Hofsós Swimming Pool (p228). Left: Dimmuborgir lava field (p255) 221

Greenland Sea

Akureyri, p235

Look for the Northern Lights over the snow-capped mountains of Iceland's northern capital, known for a subarctic botanical garden and an enticing public pool.

Skagafjörður, p226

Jump on a horse and get close to a lively countryside where people pride themselves on once harbouring Grettir the Strong.

Sandvík

Flatey

Siglufjörður   Siglunes   Gjögurtà

○ Hraun   *Fljótakív*   Hólsfjall

Framnes   *Aravatn*   Ólafsfjörður

Kálfhamarsvík   Hvalnes   *Mánney*   ○ Hrísey

Þórðarhöfði   Dalvík   Grenivík

Skagheidi   Reykir   *Hofsós Swimming Pool*   *Svarfadardalur*

Grettislaug

Húnaflói   Skagaströnd   Saudarkrókur   ○ Viðvík   Heljarfjall (1289m)

Molduxi (706m)   Hólar ○   *Myrkarjökull*   Strýta (1456m)   Akurey

Húnafjörður   Reynisstaður ○   Hofstaðir ○

Illugastaðir   Blönduós   Varmahlíð   *Háafjall (1188m)* ○ Háls   *Súlur (1213m)*   Hrafnag

Hvítserkur   Húnavellir   Glaumbær   *Öxnadalur*

Borgarvirki   *Hóp* ○ Þristapar   *Svínavatn*   *Hellufell (908m)* ○ Vindheimamelar

Miðfjörður   *Vesturhópsvatn*

Hvammstangi ○   ○ Viðigerði   Hof ○   *Blanda*   *Heradsvötn*

Laugarbakki ○   *Kolugljúfur*   *Kjölur Route (4WD Only)*   *Torfufell (1241m)*

○ Reykjaskóli   *Þristikla*

Vatnsdalsa

Austari-Jökulsa

Find Your Way

Where you go, and how, is relative to the sun. Raft glacial rivers and catch a ferry to an offshore island in the summer, round up horses in autumn and ski from mountain summits over winter. Spring? Pleased to meet you, Mr Puffin.

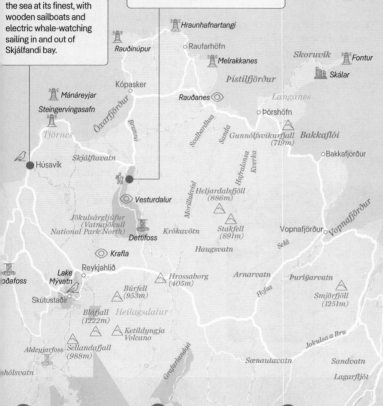

Húsavík, p249
Small-town Iceland by the sea at its finest, with wooden sailboats and electric whale-watching sailing in and out of Skjálfandi bay.

Jökulsárgljúfur Canyon, p258
Bring a raincoat for a close – and wet – view of the captivating Dettifoss waterfall and hiking shoes for the pristine 'Canyon Trail' along Iceland's second-longest river.

Greenland Sea

Hraunhafnartangi

Rauðinúpur

○ Raufarhöfn

Melrakkanes

Skoruvík   Fontur

Skálar

Kópasker

Pistilfjörður

Langanes

Rauðanes ◎

Mánáreyjar

Steingervingasafn

Öxarfjörður

Brúna

○ Þórshöfn

Gunnólfsvikurfjall (719m)   *Bakkaflói*

Tjörnes

Skjálftavatn

○ Bakkafjörður

● Húsavík

Svalbarðsá

Sanda

Hafralónsá

Kverká

Morituláreist

Heljardalsfjöll (886m)

○ Vesturdalur

Jökulsárgljúfur (Vatnajökull) National Park North

Krókavötn

Stakfell (891m)

Vopnafjörður ○   *Vopnafjörður*

Dettifoss

Haugsvatn

Selá

◎ Krafla

Reykjahlíð   Hrossaborg (405m)   *Arnarvatn*

Þuríjarvatn

○ðafoss

Lake Mývatn

Búrfell (953m)

Hófsá

Smjörfjöll (1251m)

Skútustaðir

Bláfjall (1222m)   *Heilagsdalur*

Ketildyngja Volcano

Jökulsá á Brú

Aldeyjarfoss   *Sellandafjall (988m)*

Grafarlandaá

Sænautavatn   *Sandvatn*

ðhólsvatn

Lagarfljót

CAR
Hire a car to explore the wild northern landscape, preferably a 4WD. Gravel roads are common along the northern coast, and outside of summer drivers need to follow the weather forecast with care.

BUS
Strætó (straeto.is) is the public service network across Iceland, as well as within Akureyri. Over summer, buses depart twice a day between Akureyri and Reykjavík via Skagafjörður. Buses to Húsavík, Mývatn and Siglufjörður go from Akureyri.

PLANE
Akureyri Airport is undergoing massive expansion, due for completion in 2024, reflecting local ambition to compete with Keflavík. EasyJet and Edelweiss already offer directs flights from London and Zürich, respectively.

Plan Your Time

Iceland is, as they say, a road-trip destination. Northern Iceland, however, defines roads more broadly: sailing routes, horse tracks, glacial rivers and frozen lakes.

Mývatn Nature Baths (p257)

If You Only Do One Thing

● Rent a car for the day or join an organised tour and head for the pompously branded route **Diamond Circle** (p253) to smell the muddy hot springs of magnificent **Lake Mývatn** (p255); set sails on a wooden boat from charming **Húsavík** (p249) to look for whales; and stretch your legs with a walk to the mighty Dettifoss waterfall on top of the **Jökulsárgljúfur Canyon** (p258). Lunch at the harbour in Húsavík, have coffee and cake at **Vogafjós** (p256) or picnic at **Vesturdalur** (p260). Relax at the atmospheric **Mývatn Nature Baths** (p257), ideal in any weather.

SEASONAL HIGHLIGHTS

Northerly winds bring cold air from Greenland's ice cap, pushing against the balmy Gulf Stream from the south. So if you don't like the weather, just wait a minute.

JANUARY

The chance to try *súrsaðir hrútspungar* (pickled ram's testicles) with jolly, drunk Icelanders celebrating the heathen Þorrablót festivities.

MARCH

Ice fishing at the **Mývatn Winter Festival** and the first whale-watching tour of the season. Peak off-piste skiing.

MAY

Potato farmers take a risk planting in May – but temperatures can still drop below zero at night.

Three Days to Travel Around

● Delve into modern life at the Arctic edge with a stroll around **Akureyri** (p237), the northern capital. The **Akureyri Museum** (p238) and the **Herring Era Museum** (p245) help you understand the region – and Icelanders – a little better.

● Drive **Eyjafjörður** (p241), Iceland's longest fjord, for fabulous restaurants and cafes in small-town Iceland, only mildly touched by tourism. Circle back via the stunning **public pool in Hofsós** (p228).

● From September to April, look for the **Northern Lights** (p242) over the snowcapped mountains of the north.

One Week or More

● More days allow for new modes of transport. Jump on a horse in **Skagafjörður** (p227) and then, if you will, into frigid diving waters at the underwater geothermal chimney **Strýtan** (p248). Pace the flat island of **Hrísey** (p247) to break in the hiking shoes, before embarking on the **Canyon Trail** (p262) from Dettifoss to Ásbyrgi.

● The region rewards coastal detours. Take foggy **Vatnsnes Peninsula** (p234) to the iconic sea stack **Hvítserkur** (p234), as part of the 900km Arctic Coast Way to **Langanes peninsula** (p265).

● Unwind, at last, with a warm bath at the fancy **Forest Lagoon** (p239) and the view-blessed **GeoSea** (p251).

JULY

Compared to the rest of Iceland, summers are dry in Akureyri, Mývatn and Jökulsárgljúfur. Expect record temperatures, Iceland scale.

SEPTEMBER

The Northern Lights appear. (Always there, just too bright to tell.)

OCTOBER

Bad weather can shake things up but heavy snowfall is rare. Bargain hotel prices.

DECEMBER

Beware: winter roads. Check weather forecasts and road conditions, particularly on Holtavörðuheiði and Öxnadalsheiði.

SKAGAFJÖRÐUR

● Skagafjörður

REYKJAVÍK
✪

The bloodiest battles in Iceland's history were fought over Skagafjörður, in a wicked era of heavy swords and axe assassins riding at night. The land remains a rich ground for wealth, home to bands of horses and people who like horses.

Many Ring Road travellers pass through Skagafjörður, maybe with a stop at the petrol station in Varmahlíð. This little-known fjord, sure enough, does not offer the stunning vistas of its neighbours and big-name attractions are Saga Age references, not necessarily visceral wonder.

It's a destination for new knowledge and surprising stories. Glaumbær, the 18th-century turf-farm museum, is the best of its kind in northern Iceland. Horse farms in the area often host hour-long shows that showcase the five gaits of the Icelandic horse, and detail the breed's history.

TOP TIP

Fosslaug hot spring and Reykjafoss waterfall cascades are little-known gems just 10km from Varmahlíð. The riverside Fosslaug bath, the size of a large Jacuzzi, is fed by a hot spring and is around 36°C to 40°C over summer; balmy over the colder months. Without swimsuits, Reykjafoss' small waterfalls make for a lovely Ring Road detour.

HIGHLIGHTS
❶ Hofsós Swimming Pool

SIGHTS
❷ 1238 The Battle of Iceland
❸ Drangey
❹ Glaumbær
❺ Grettislaug
❻ Icelandic Emigration Center
❼ Varmahlíð

Skagafjörður 76

❸ Hofsós ❶❻
Hofsós
*Hofsós
Swimming Pool*

🔥❺

745

748

73

🏛❷ Sauðárkrókur
75

767

76

75

🏛❹

❼

Ⓝ 0 ——— 10 km
0 ——— 6 miles

752   1

ARCTIC-IMAGES/GETTY IMAGES ©

Icelandic horses, Skagafjörður

Rider's Stronghold
GET CLOSE TO NATURE

The proper way to travel around Skagafjörður is on the back of an Icelandic horse, a small and stocky breed serving Icelanders since Viking days a millennium ago. Import of foreign horses is strictly forbidden by law, in order to protect these hardy animals from disease, but due to their unique features many are exported, from the breeding farms in Skagafjörður. Hólar University – which teaches equine science, among other subjects – is located here, and will host the biennial National Icelandic Horse Competition in 2026 (the 2024 tournament takes place in Reykjavík).

Experienced riders can join multiday tours, lasting four to seven nights, costing around 300,000kr per person. Short tours (one to three hours) follow a beginner rhythm, however, with variations of pace towards the tour's second half. Lýtingsstaðir (lythorse.is) and Syðra-Skörðugil (sydra skordugil.is) have a range of options, and farmstay accommodation. Langhús Horse Tours (icelandichorse.is), located towards Siglufjörður, offers special experiences for children who are too young for tours.

RIDE THE GLACIAL RIVERS

The area around Varmahlíð is home to northern Iceland's best white-water rafting. Trips run from around May to September on the high-octane Austari-Jökulsá (East Glacial River, Class 4+ rapids) and the more placid, family-friendly Vestari-Jökulsá (West Glacial River, Class 2+ rapids). Bakkaflöt (bakkaflot. is) and Viking Rafting (vikingrafting. is) run a range of rafting options, plus white-water kayaking. The rivers have long stretches of calm, providing a balanced diet of action and nature watching.

 WHERE TO STAY IN SKAGAFJÖRÐUR

Hofsstaðir
Modern country hotel with 30 rooms, all with terrace, on a farm property some 20km from the Ring Road. €€

Guesthouse Gimbur
North of Hofsós, this small family-run guesthouse offers a warm welcome and spacious rooms with seafront views. €

Hotel Tindastoll
By Main St in Sauðárkrókur, the hotel – Iceland's oldest – dates back to 1884. Rooms are humble in size. €€

KAVRAM/SHUTTERSTOCK ©

Glaumbær museum

HOFSÓS SWIMMING POOL

One of Iceland's youngest public pools, Hofsós Swimming Pool is a striking piece of modern Icelandic architecture. Overlooking the fjord, it offers a deceptive view where the fjord almost looks like an extension of the 25m swimming pool. Expect crowds on warm, sunny days or wait until winter when it returns to its regular role as a hub for local life in Hofsós, a village of 190 people.

Horses are still used for traditional sheepherding work, and some farms offer (paying) travellers to join the four-day mission of collecting sheep from the mountains each autumn. The sheep are then rounded up and sorted by farms in events known as *réttir*, taking place all over Iceland. Less common are *stóðréttir* horse round-ups practiced in Skagafjörður, when free-roaming horses are gathered from summer pastures. Watch hundreds of horses being herded and sorted in a paddock called a *rétt*. Three of the best-known round-ups are Laufskálarétt, Víðidalstungurétt and Skrapatungurétt, held in late September to early October (search '*stóðhestaréttir*' at bbl.is).

Saga Island
OFF-SHORE DRANGEY

Iceland's legendary anti-hero Grettir the Strong went to exile in the dome-shaped island of **Drangey**, according to the medieval saga chronicling his life, after arson and retributions for the death of his brother. Thankfully, only one part of his biography inspires people to action nowadays: the 7km swim to the mainland. Twenty people have completed the cold endeavour since Grettir's alleged 1030 escape – most recently

✕ WHERE TO EAT IN SKAGAFJÖRÐUR

Sauðá
The finest restaurant in Sauðárkrókur. Pan-fried cod and lamb ribeye, locally sourced. €€

Sauðárkróksbakarí
The local bakery in Suðárkrókur has an ambitious selection and comfy seating. Great rye bread. €

Retro Mathús
Travellers in Hofsós praise this lovely location for wholesome food and competitive prices. €€

in 2017, when friends Harpa Berndsen and Sigrún Geirsdóttir finished within four hours. **Grettislaug**, a well-maintained geothermal pool with 2000kr admission, marks the other end of the swim, as Grettis soothed his aching bones in an inviting spring. (The attached campsite is a superb location.)

For the rest of us, Drangey Tours (drangey.net) offers daily four-hour tours from Sauðárkrókur to the island from 1 June to 20 August. The company has been running for three generations, with skipper Helgi Hrafn at the helm of the small fishing boat bringing people to the island's tiny harbour. Passengers spend two to three hours on the island, walking and observing puffins and seabirds. Expect to hear many (unbelievable) stories of Grettir.

The Story of Grettir the Strong, along with a medieval literature genre of 38 separate family stories known as Sagas of the Icelanders, were penned in the 1200s to bolster the authority of ruling chieftains, as Iceland had neither a king or a central government. The Sturlunga Era, as the period is known, marked the nation's first and only civil war. Stories of these battles and brutality are told at the **1238 The Battle of Iceland** exhibition in Sauðárkrókur. The exhibition tries hard to be digital and interactive, with mixed results – it's well worth the stop for Viking enthusiasts. Tourist Information is located by the exhibition entrance.

Turf House Drama
LIFE IN A TRADITIONAL FARMHOUSE

The 18th-century turf-farm museum **Glaumbær** (glaumbaer. is) is the best museum of its type in northern Iceland. The traditional Icelandic turf farm was a complex of small separate buildings, connected by a central passageway. Here you can see this style of construction, with some building compartments stuffed full of period furniture, equipment and utensils. It gives a fascinating insight into the cramped living conditions of the era – beds, for one, did not allow people to sleep laying flat. Modern-day health and safety laws don't allow the full experience: houses like these used to be full of smoke from cooking and heating.

The farm is an informal backdrop to the **Icelandic Emigration Center** exploring the reasons behind Icelanders' mass emigration to North America, from 1870 to 1914, uprooting a shocking one-fifth of the country's population.

VARMAHLÍÐ

Varmahlíð (pronounced var-ma-leeth) is a village on the Ring Road junction in Skagafjörður. The service centre, not quite a town, is a base for white-water rafting and horse riding. The village rests on a hill, with an excellent campsite on top. Travellers with tents and camper vans are much better served staying here than in Sauðárkrókur. Although lacking the charm of other neighbouring public pool rivals, Sundlaugin Varmahlíð has a water slide, outdoor hot-pots and a steam room. Hotel Varmahlíð (hotelvarmahlid.is) has a restaurant with a pizza oven, beating the fast food at the massive Olís service station.

GETTING AROUND

Compared to other areas in Iceland with a population of 3000 people, Skagafjörður has a strong network of public buses. Strætó bus 57 travels twice a day to and from Reykjavík and Akureyri, from Olís in Varmahlíð and N1 in Sauðárkrókur. There's no bus to Hofsós; hire a car or hitchhike.

Rte 744 from Sauðárkrókur to Skagaströnd and Blönduós is wide and paved; a quiet alternative to the Ring Road.

Öxnadalsheiði, the mountain pass between Skagafjörður and Akureyri, frequently closes over winter. Check road conditions (road.is).

Offbeat Northern Coast

Traffic jams: sheep crossing the road. Yellow light: a lighthouse. Driving the northern coast is the alternative to the Ring Road, from Hvammstangi to the tip of Langanes Peninsula. But there's no A to B; come and go as you please. The road fluctuates between gravel and asphalt; drive slowly and take in the ocean view. At the edge of the Arctic, time spools slowly...slowly.

1 Skagaströnd

The village of Skagaströnd has one restaurant (Harbour), one guesthouse (Salthús) and two psychics who happen to be neighbours (Museum of Prophecies). All of these businesses have materialised in the last decade, which may explain why the village still feels like an unspoiled secret in charming flux: the old fish factory is now home to the art residency, NES (neslist.is). Cape Spákonuhöfði is a wonderful walk.

The Drive: Skagaströnd is 20km north of the Ring Road, on Skagi peninsula. For a shortcut to the town of Sauðárkrókur, take Rte 744 instead of going around the peninsula.

2 Hofsós Swimming Pool

The sleepy fishing village of Hofsós (population 190) has been a trading centre since the 1500s, but is now on the map for its spectacular fjord-front swimming pool. Open since 2010, the pool is integrated into the landscape with an infinity view over the fjord.

JOAN GIL/ALAMY STOCK PHOTO ©

Gannets, Langanes Peninsula

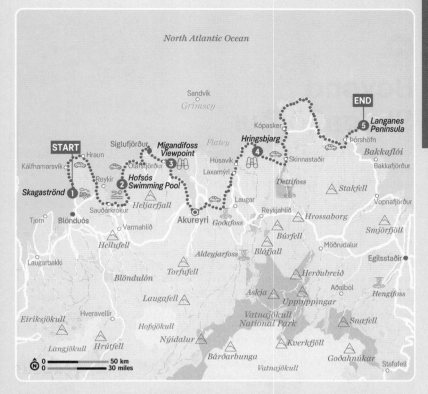

The Drive: The road to Hofsós is paved from the west; the (dramatic) drive to Siglufjörður is partly gravel and includes a one-lane mountain tunnel.

3 Mígandifoss Viewpoint

On the eastern end of Múlagöng (also called 'Ólafsfjarðargöng') is a rest area facing north towards Mígandifoss, an unexpected ocean-plunging waterfall, with a view of Grímsey island on clear days. This is an excellent spot for stars, Northern Lights and midnight sun.

The Drive: Take the two mountain tunnels between Siglufjörður and Ólafsfjörður and then Múlagöng (3.4km) east of Ólafsfjörður; the viewpoint is about 1.5km further down Eyjafjörður.

4 Hringsbjarg

Stop at the cliff-edge viewing platform Hringsbjarg for an amazingly broad horizon and maybe a resting puffin. Driftwood

is the first thing a driver sees when the car winds down the steep Tjörnes Peninsula to the flat black beach of Öxarfjörður.

The Drive: Hringsbjarg is along Rte 85. The name itself is not signposted, but its large car park makes it an obvious vista some 34km beyond Húsavík.

5 Langanes Peninsula

Shaped like a goose with a very large head, foggy Langanes Peninsula is one of the loneliest corners of Iceland. At Skoruvíkurbjarg is a rare view of a gannet colony. Over summer, the bumpy road to Fontur on the narrow tip of Langanes Peninsula is accessible for 4WDs, passing stony beaches with driftwood and random ocean debris.

Skagafjörður
Blönduós
Vatnsnes
Peninsula • Hvítserkur
Þrístapar
Hvammstangi

Beyond Skagafjörður

Small-town Iceland, knitted together by the Ring Road, dots the northwestern coastline with textile museums and knitting co-ops.

Back on the Ring Road, finding attractions along the northwestern drive takes some work: neither villages or nature will woo you off the road with splashy phenomena. Look out for seals along Vatnsnes Peninsula, Ethiopian scripture on a restaurant sign in Blönduós, a warehouse in Hvammstangi manufacturing wool wear, a road sign pointing to Hvítserkur, the Kolugljúfur canyon (once home to a 'beautiful' female troll), a monument honouring the victims of Iceland's last death penalty, a stony fortress that may or may not have been a Viking-era battlefield, farms offering horse rides and well-priced accommodation, and the village of Laugarbakki where musician Ásgeir grew up. Without taking your eyes off the road, please.

TOP TIP

From June to September, the Blanda river (starir.is) is a prominent place to go fly-fishing for salmon, with gorgeous pools.

TYPO GRAPHICS/GETTY IMAGES ©

Seals (p234), Vatsanes Peninsula

Blönduós

The Blönduós Stop

A RIVER TOWN SHAPED BY DRIVERS

Blönduós (population 900) is a default stop along the Ring Road, with services positioned along the highway, at the edge of the settlement itself. Roadside food options are BS (one of the places is named B&S Restaurant) and...Ethiopian. Teni, named after the owner's Ethiopian mother, is a delightful surprise inside a tiny shopping centre housing the Kjörbúðin supermarket, Vínbúðin liquor store and the clothing and pet food shop This and That. Alternatively, picnic at the small island **Hrútey**, with paths leading from a footbridge near the campsite.

The churning Blanda river divides the town in half, with sharp architectural contrast, hence the two churches in town: super old and super modern. Wooden houses form the traditional 'downtown Blönduós' on the western side, with charming guesthouses and Hótel Blönduós. Vintage coffee shop Apótekarastofan and restaurant Sýslumaðurinn are part of the hotel establishment, bringing a delightful old street to life. Boutique guesthouse Brimslóð Atelier (brimslodguesthouse.is) serves a fabulous three-course dinner every night for 8000kr and offers, by appointment, workshops in New Nordic cooking and Icelandic food heritage – owners Inga and Gísli have authored several cookbooks, including *Into the North: Live Well, Eat Well – The Icelandic Way.*

WHY I LOVE VATNSNES PENINSULA

Egill Bjarnason, writer

The most simple travel advice I can give, for anyone embarking on a grand Icelandic tour, is to follow the Ring Road through the scenic south and the coastline elsewhere, especially north. The 900km coastal drive from Hvammstangi to Þórshöfn, known as the Arctic Coast Way, begins on the Vatnsnes Peninsula. The peninsula tip is entirely gravel, and pot-holed in places, making it impossible to go fast. In fog – there is always fog! – the rocky shoreline is mystic and full of petrified trolls, or whatever Hvítserkur really is. When the sun breaks through, these very same rocks are hangouts for ringed seals, just chilling in the ocean breeze.

 QUICK STOPS ALONG THE RING ROAD

Kolugljúfur
A scenic waterfall at an enchanting canyon that legend has it was once home to a troll beauty.

Borgarvirki
Good views from a 177m-high basalt fortress 'restored' in the 1950s to resemble an alleged Viking defence site.

Þingeyrarkirkja
A precious stone church – a rarity in Iceland – sitting quietly and photogenically beside Hóp lagoon.

LOWE99/GETTY IMAGES ©

Hvítserkur

1828 MURDER MYSTERY

Residents on Stapakot were jolted awake on 14 March 1828, when a woman from a neighbouring property burst in to tell them that a fire was raging and two men were trapped inside. It was a lie. The men were already dead – clubbed with a hammer and stabbed 12 times before the house was set ablaze with shark oil. Despite the passing years, it's a crime that Icelanders have never forgotten, as the convicted killers were the last people ever executed – they were beheaded at **Þrístapar** by the Ring Road between Blönduós and Hvammstangi. The case has sparked endless speculation, a feature film, a pop song and at least 10 books, including the bestselling *Burial Rites* by Hannah Kent.

Another town expert, Elín Sigurðardóttir runs the **Textile Museum** (textile.is) in a head-turning modern building on the north bank. This attractive museum displays contemporary textile art, painstakingly intricate embroideries from the museum's collection and early Icelandic costumes. Next door is the **Icelandic Textile Centre** (textilmidstod.is), which hosts the festival Iceland Knit Fest in June and the textile residency 'Ós'.

When it is time to leave, know that driving the highway at 100km/h can set you back 20,000kr in fines. The Blönduós police district is famously diligent in traffic surveillance. (At 110km/h, the fine is 50,000kr.)

Trolls & Seals
NEIGHBOURS ON VATNSNES PENINSULA

Legend has it that Hvítserkur was a troll caught by the sunrise while attempting to destroy the monastery at Þingeyrar. True or not, **Hvítserkur** is a 15m-high sea stack. From the car park, a short walk leads to a viewing platform overlooking Hvítserkur, and in the other direction a path goes down to a scenic black-sand beach with views of a large seal haul-out site. Seals tend to hang out by Sigríðarstaðavatn lake, south along the beach.

The entire Vatnsnes Peninsula is a place to watch harbour seals all year round. **Illugastaðir**, a farm 20km north of **Hvammstangi**, has a seal-watching hut for bad weather, about 900m from the car park. In fact, the primary attraction in Hvammstangi is the harbourfront Icelandic Seal Centre (selasetur.is) where you can learn about their conservation and folkloric fame.

GETTING AROUND

Outside summer, check the weather forecasts and road conditions before driving over Holtavörðuheiði, the mountain road marking the border of northern Iceland to the west.

The Arctic Coast Way, threading the coastline from Vatnsnes Peninsula, is only for snowless conditions.

AKUREYRI

Akureyri stands strong as Iceland's second city, but a Melbourne, Manchester or Montreal it is not. And how could it be? There are only 22,000 residents! Despite its diminutive size, expect cool cafes, quality restaurants and something of a late-night scene on the Hafnarstræti pedestrian street – a far cry from other towns in rural Iceland.

Akureyri sits at the head of Eyjafjörður, Iceland's longest (60km) fjord, at the base of snowcapped peaks. In the early days, Danish merchants shaped its character by promoting the planting of trees in well-tended gardens, laying the foundation for the Scandi-style public parks at Kjarnaskógur and Lystigarður. The harbour is the second-busiest port of call for cruise ships, just a stone's throw from the Arctic Circle. Lively winter festivals and some of Iceland's best skiing provide plenty of off-peak (and off-piste) appeal.

TOP TIP

Gilið, the steep street extending from the heart of Akureyri (there is literally a heart sculpture), hosts the Akureyri Art Museum, Fróði Bookstore and Deiglan gallery. Linger at cafe Ketilkaffi inside the art museum.

ATTILA JANDI/SHUTTERSTOCK ©

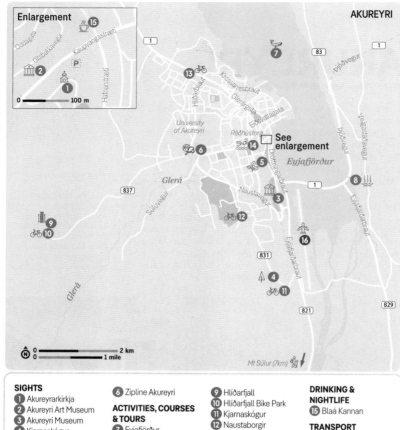

SIGHTS
1. Akureyrarkirkja
2. Akureyri Art Museum
3. Akureyri Museum
4. Kjarnaskógur
5. Lystigarðurinn

6. Zipline Akureyri

ACTIVITIES, COURSES & TOURS
7. Eyjafjörður
8. Forest Lagoon

9. Hlíðarfjall
10. Hlíðarfjall Bike Park
11. Kjarnaskógur
12. Naustaborgir
13. Skíðaþjónustan
14. Sundlaug Akureyrar

DRINKING & NIGHTLIFE
15. Blaá Kannan

TRANSPORT
16. Akureyri Airport

Central Akureyri

MODERNIST CHURCH, POST-MODERN RAVINE

Central Akureyri is defined by a church, **Akureyrarkirkja**, just as Reykjavík is defined by Hallgrímskirkja – and it so happens that the two church icons were both designed by Guðjón Samúelsson, the first Icelander to be educated in architecture. Guðjón became the 'State Architect of Iceland', a

 WHERE TO STAY IN AKUREYRI

Hótel Akureyri
Boutique-style hotel with well-equipped rooms (the front ones have fjord views). €€

Hamrar Campground
Family favourite, with a playground operated by the local scout group. €

Sæluhús
Mini village of modern studios, perfect for a few days' rest and relaxation. €€€

AKUREYRI WALKING TOUR

The walk begins outside the round-shaped **1 Hof Culture House**, where cruise ships dock and buses depart for Reykjavík. The building is home to the North Iceland Symphony Orchestra, and a tourist information desk in summer. Cross the only four-lane road in Akureyri, over to the rather joyless town square **2 Ráðhústorgið** – contrary to robust **3 Hafnarstræti**, a main shopping street only 200m long, with mostly restaurants, hotels and souvenir shops (locals seem to favour shopping at the town's mall). At **4 Eymundsson** bookshop, cross the road and take the 96 steps up to **5 Akureyrarkirkja** church. About 600m further onwards is the **6 Lystigarðurinn** botanical garden, a delightful spot for a fragrant wander. The wealth of plant life on display is truly astonishing considering the garden's proximity to the Arctic Circle; you'll find examples of every species native to Iceland, as well as a host of high-latitude and high-altitude plants from around the world. Akureyri is famously sunny and, assuming that is the case, walk the tree-lined Spítalavegur downhill to the **7 Brynjuís** ice-cream shop, a landmark in the old part of town known as Innbærinn. The wooden houses – the oldest being Laxdalshús from 1795 – used to stand by the shoreline, before the time of landfills. The ice-cream shop tends to be busy regardless of the weather, and don't worry if the day is cold and grey – just have the liquorice flavour to match the sky's colour. Extend the old-town walk, if you will, with a stroll along Aðalstræti ('Main Street') that is today a leafy residential street leading to the Akureyri Museum.

diligent go-to guy for new public buildings and institutions in the early years of Iceland's independent statehood. When a town needed a new church, or the country a National Theatre, Guðjón was off to the drawing board. Completed in 1940, the church was among Guðjón's later works and is styled more like a 1920s US skyscraper than its Reykjavík sibling, although the basalt theme connects them.

The church contains a large 3200-pipe organ and a series of rather untraditional reliefs of the life of Christ. There's also a ship suspended from the ceiling, reflecting an old Nordic tradition of votive offerings for the protection of loved ones at sea. Perhaps the most striking feature is the beautiful central stained-glass window above the altar, which originally graced Coventry Cathedral in England. The church admits visitors most days; it tends to be closed on weekends over the summer.

Post-modernism, however, rules the neighbouring **Gilið** ('The Ravine'), the road where galleries and craft shops centre on the **Akureyri Art Museum**. The ambitious museum is by far the best art museum outside of Reykjavík. At the time of writing, Ragnar Kjartansson's *The Visitors* – a worldwide, 21st-century triumph – was among the exhibits. The museum covers four floors and showcases classic and contemporary art, from photography to performance pieces; Icelandic to international. There are guided tours every Thursday (in English) at 12.30pm.

The Town of Trade
AKUREYRI THROUGH MUSEUMS

To understand the character of Akureyri a little better, consider this list of (mediocre) museums in and around town: The Industry Museum, Motorcycle Museum of Iceland, The Icelandic Aviation Museum, The Ystafell Auto Museum, The Toy Museum and The Sundry Collection.

Not on the list: a maritime museum. The heritage of Akureyri is transportation and trade, moving things and stuff around to the rest of Iceland and the outside world, ever since the days of 17th-century Danish merchants. The town's position, at the bottom of Iceland's longest fjord, is suited to transport, not fisheries.

Akureyri Museum, the best artefact museum by far, overlooks a beautiful garden by the old Aðalstræti (Main Street), a 30-minute walk from today's central part of town. Start in the basement, where the pride of Akureyri as the bourgeoisie northern capital is on full display: the shiny gifts Frederik VIII of Denmark brought with him on a visit in 1907; black-

---

BEST PLAYGROUNDS

Birkivöllur
A wooden playground wonderfully positioned in the woods of Kjarnaskógur with a nearby maze, four volleyball courts and a large jumping pillow. BBQ facilities (bring your own coal) and public toilets.

Sundlaugagarðurinn
Several swings, a blue castle and two rainbow-coloured jum-ping pillows. Enter from the car park at Sundlaug Akureyrar, next to the World Class gym. With a public toilet.

Naustaskóli
Playgrounds outside schools and kindergartens, such as this impressive suburban location, are open spaces on weekends and over the summer break from mid-June to mid-August.

 WHERE TO STAY IN AKUREYRI

Berjaya Iceland Hotels
Rooms are compact but well-designed, showcasing Icelandic art. €€

Hótel Kjarnalundur
Large 66-room hotel at the base of Kjarnaskógur public park. €€

Hafnarstræti Hostel
Capsule beds in mixed dorms on the main pedestrian street. €

Timber church outside Akureyri Museum

and-white pictures of garden parties; and wooden snow sledges to slide down the countless hills.

The museum garden became the first place in Iceland to cultivate trees when a nursery was established here in 1899. Next door is a tiny, black-tarred timber church and Nonni's House, the 19th-century home of children's writer Jón Sveinsson. His books are rather dated for today's youth – kids, nowadays, don't relate to the act of fleeing a migrating polar bear on sea ice – but the house itself gives a glimpse of the life of middle-class Akureyri at the time, far from the rural turf-house existence of most Icelanders.

Forest Bathing in a Calm Lagoon
TAKE A RELAXING PLUNGE

What could this cold northern region possibly do with all that abundant hot water? Take a bath, relax. Contemplate the answer, and life.

Some years ago, during the building of the Vaðlaheiðar Tunnel on Akureyri's outskirts, the construction crew was struck by a stream of hot water midway into the 7km mountain dig. Fast forward five years, and the result of that discovery is the **Forest Lagoon**, open since 2022. The luxury bath resort is located on the nearby green hill, with a view over Akureyri from two overlapping baths of varying temperature.

A faint smell of burning wood from the fireplace inside fills the calm outdoor scene. The Finish dry sauna is superb, and some guests move ritually in and out of the cold plunge pool. Compared to the neighbouring GeoSea in Húsavík (p251) and Mývatn Nature Baths (p257), the Forest Lagoon leans towards

BEST PLACES TO SIT WITH A BOOK

Stu Ness, the co-owner of Fróði bookshop, recommends places to relax with a book, be it cold or warm outside.

Lystigarðurinn
The botanical garden in Akureyri is the perfect place to settle down on a bench, or patch of grass, and lose yourself in a good book.

Bláa Kannan
This turret-topped old building on Hafnastræti is both eye-catching with its dark blue exterior, but also a real treat inside. A classic coffee house with homemade bakes and perfect corners to sit in. Watch the world go by and delve into a good book.

Kjarnaskógur
This nearby forest is a great escape from the bustle of downtown Akureyri, with secret glades that are the ideal location to hide away on a sunny day.

🍸 WHERE TO DRINK IN AKUREYRI

Græni Hatturinn
An intimate venue: the best place to see live music – and one of the best in Iceland.

R5 Micro Bar
Sample seasonal ales and the best of Iceland's craft-brew scene at Akureyri's most ambitious bar.

Götubarinn
The locals' favourite drinking spot, with a downstairs piano for late-night singalongs.

Hlíðarfjall ski resort

WAYS TO REACH THE SKY

Zipline Akureyri
(ziplineakureyri.is) Five zip lines run through a rustling river and steep cliffs at the Glerá river in town, suitable for thrill-seekers of all ages.

Mt Súlur
A pleasant but demanding day hike leads up the Glerárdalur valley to the summit of Mt Súlur (1213m). The trail begins on Súluvegur, just before the Glerá bridge. Allow six hours unless, of course, you are a participant in the ultra trail run Súlur Vertical (sulurvertical.is), held every August.

Circle Air
(circleair.is) Helicopter tours departing from Akureyri Airport for scenic tours over Askja, Lake Mývatn, Troll Peninsula and Grímsey.

relaxation rather than Iceland's pool culture of socialising; the atmosphere is maintained by high admission costs (6600kr) and a policy on children – not allowed after 6pm.

Meanwhile, children have their own stronghold in Akureyri. The **Sundlaug Akureyrar public pool** is a national favourite – confirmed in a 2022 survey! – designed for the little people and their pool guardians. The outdoor area has three water slides (for the crazy) and five hot tubs (for the lazy). The taller water slides are limited to 120cm in height. No one appears to go there to swim laps, but in any case there are 10 lanes in total.

Winter Action
WHEN SNOW FINALLY FALLS

Winter turns the region in and around Akureyri into one big playground. The skiing season may last from mid-November to as late as mid-June.

Hlíðarfjall in Akureyri is the largest resort, with seven lifts, including a four-person chairlift. The longest slope is 2.3km, with groomed pistes for alpine skiing and snowboarding. Rental gear (hlidarfjall.is/ski-rental) is available at the base and so are day passes (adult 5500kr). The 5x5 Ski Pass (skiiceland.is) gives you five days at the five major resorts in North Iceland: Akureyri, Sauðárkrókur, Siglufjörður, Ólafsfjörður and Dalvík.

WHERE TO EAT IN AKUREYRI

Eyja
Wine bar and bistro with three-course options and a fish-of-the-day main. €€

Kaffi Ilmur
In a charming historical building (once a saddlery), this cafe offers tasty breakfast and lunch options. €

Bautinn
Pronounced *b-oi-t-in*, this landmark restaurant offers a menu that's safe in the burger and pizza territory. €€

Service for cross-country skiing has improved, along with its popularity. Akureyri has slopes at Hlíðarfjall and inside the Kjarnaskógur forest. Some are lit up, but fortunately not all, as darkness brings out the Northern Lights. Sometimes there are tracks in Skíðadalur near Dalvík (no charge). Courses are offered in Ólafsfjöður and Siglufjörður. Rental gear is available at Skíðaþjónustan (skidathjonustan.com).

While the resorts and slopes are certainly fun they don't merit comparison to famed ski destinations in Europe. But off-piste mountain skiing, practised at both sides of Eyjafjörð, is unique. The towns of Siglufjörður and Grenivík are the primary base camps for summit-to-sea rides, either by a snowcat or a helicopter, usually sliding down Mt Múlakolla and Mt Kaldbakur respectively. Tour operators Arctic Freeride (facebook.com/arcticfreeride), Kaldbaksferðir (kaldbaksferdir.com) and Arctic Heli Skiing (articheliskiing.com) offer multiday packages.

The Whales of Eyjafjörður

NARROW FJORD WITH CALMER WATERS

Whale watching is a fast-growing operation in Akureyri, and Eyjafjörður more widely, thanks to an increased number of humpback whales in recent years. Sailing conditions in the narrow and long fjord tend to be smoother than at most other whale-watching destinations in Iceland. And shorter – about two hours over summer. It is therefore a good option for children and those prone to seasickness.

Expect to see humpbacks and minke whales; the number of species swimming into Eyjafjörð are far fewer than in neighbouring Skjálfandi bay near Húsavík (p249), where people have a real chance of seeing a blue whale. Elding Whale Watching (elding.is) dominates the Akureyri market with large steel ships offering indoor and outdoor viewings, departing from behind the Hof Culture House. Keli Sea Tours (keliseatours.is) operates a single oak boat with morning and afternoon tours.

Before purchasing a ticket, it is worth asking where in Eyjafjörð the whales have been spotted in recent days. In winter especially, the whales tend to move towards the northern end of the fjord, creating time pressures for Akureyri tours. Tour operators from Hjalteyri (northsailing.is), Hauganes (whales.is) and Dalvík (arcticseatours.is), located towards the middle of Eyjafjörð, can be a safer option considering the location of whales in the past.

BIKERS TAKE THE SKI LIFT

Akureyri has a growing network of paths connecting the lower ends of Eyjafjörður. The best trails for cycling (and running) are at **Kjarnaskógur** and **Naustaborgir**. Racer cyclists (the people wearing Lycra) ride along the flat coastline, with a smooth 14km path from Hof Culture House to the village of Hrafnagil. On the other side of the fjord, a forest path leads to Vaðlaheiði mountain via the Forest Lagoon. The Hlíðarfjall skiing resort keeps one of its chairlifts open over summer to shuttle mountain bikers up to the **Hlíðarfjall Bike Park** (hlidarfjall. is) from mid-July to September. Bikes are available to rent at **Skíðaþjónustan** (skidathjonustan.com).

GETTING AROUND

Stræto city buses in Akureyri are free for everyone, but do not service the airport. Call 461 1010 for a taxi. To pay for parking in Akureyri, it can save time to download EasyPark or Parka for mobile payments. Free parking is widely available, such as by the public pool. To locate and rent a scooter, download the Hopp app –

expect to pay around 1000kr for rides within the downtown area.

Runners and cyclists will enjoy the smooth 14km path between Hof Culture House to Hrafnagil. Tourist information is located inside Hof Culture House, with public toilets in the basement.

EVRENKALINBACAK/SHUTTERSTOCK ©

Scan this
QR code for the
Icelandic aurora forecast.

TOP SIGHT

The Northern Lights

There is a science to predicting the phenomena, but ultimately catching the Northern Lights comes down to a mix of luck and effort. North Iceland offers good chances – just as Iceland in general – with the added bones of a snowy winter landscape.

PLAN AHEAD

Choose when to go

Find a base

Follow the aurora forecast

Escape city lights

Avoid challenging road conditions

Plan outdoor adventures to fill the time

When to Go

There is a reason September is the third-most-visited month in Iceland: nights turn dark enough to see the Northern Lights while winter storms of road-shutting, plan-altering magnitude are rare. The forces creating the spectacular streaks of colours are active year-round; we just don't see them during bright summer nights. If catching them is a primary goal, visit during the darkest months, from November to February. By mid-April the nights are too bright.

Contrary to the name, the Northern Lights do not brighten with every northern latitude. They appear, instead, on top of the globe like a doughnut, known as the aurora oval. Middle-of-the-aurora-belt Iceland is a prime location throughout; North Iceland has the benefit of shorter daylight hours – about one hour less in December, compared to Reykjavík – which is a minuscule benefit in scientific terms, really. The North, however, has the added benefit of being popular for plenty of outdoor adventures like hikes and skiing, so you will have plenty to fill your time when you're not chasing auroras, plus a range of quality country accommodation, away from city lights.

Find a Base

Many visitors lack the experience and expertise to handle Iceland's wintry road conditions. It doesn't help that in the north the sun can rise as late as 11.39am and set as early as 2.43pm, meaning drivers spend most of their day driving in the dark. From November to February, a good base to spend several days will make travel safer and more relaxed, by searching on foot or with an organised tour. All you need is a dark spot. And this is easy in small-town North Iceland. In Akureyri, where public buses are free, the hills of Hlíðarfjall and Kjarnaskógur forest are free of city lights.

Follow the Forecast

The Northern Lights are caused by solar activity. A flow of charged particles from the sun, called the solar wind, slams into the Earth's magnetic field and causes atoms in the upper atmosphere to glow. The lights appear quite suddenly, their intensity varying – scientists do a daily forecast based on solar winds in the previous three days to predict aurora strength. The Icelandic Met Office (vedur.is/weather/forecasts/aurora) publish this forecast, with a nine-scale activity range. (The scale deviates from a normal curve, usually hovering around level three, while any strength beyond level five indicates a rare solar storm.)

Make a Travel Plan

Going with a tour operator provides a good structure to the experience, and a chance to try something new like dog sledding (snowdogs.is), boat cruising (elding.is), cruising in a super-Jeep or snowmobiling (myvatnsnowmobile.is). The best places for winter activity in the north are Akureyri, Mývatn and Siglufjörður. Guides will also have the resources and experience to help track the forecasts and seek out the lights. And they'll often know the best viewing spots and will have back-up spots if the weather isn't cooperating.

AURORA PHOTOGRAPHY

The Northern Lights are photographed at shutter speed of five to 20 seconds. A tripod is an absolute must for a strong picture; better yet, invest in a remote shutter release. The newest smartphones are still able to capture surprisingly good footage, but are hardly promising enough to make your work shine in the competitive field of #auroras.

TOP TIPS

- Prepare like you're going to a mountain summit, with no trees or buildings sheltering you from the cool wind. Searching for the auroras is a waiting game – and success can come down to that extra layer you thought was unnecessary. Invest in a thermal underlayer that will retain heat.
- Some people put too much emphasis on escaping city lights. It's enough to just leave immediate light pollution like street lights and houses to get a clear view of darkness. Venturing 500km off the grid won't make a difference.

243

Grímsey •

Siglufjörður
•
Ólafsfjörður •   Hrísey
Dalvík • • • Grenivík
• Árskógssandur
Svarfaðardalur

Akureyri ●

Beyond Akureyri

Cruise coastal towns and villages, less than 30
minutes apart, along Iceland's longest fjord.

The sizeable towns beyond Akureyri were established out of
nautical convenience with limited transportation between
them. Siglufjörður and Ólafsfjörður, separated by two mountain ranges on the Troll Peninsula, were a day trip apart before the opening of Héðinsfjarðargöng Tunnel in 2010. The
15-minute drive today reveals the uneven fate of northern
coastal communities: Siglufjörður has reinvented itself as
a destination known for a splendid herring museum, a Moroccan restaurant and lavish skiing weekends at Hótel Sigló.
Other traditional fishing communities – such as the villages
of Hjalteyri, Árskógssandur and Hauganes – are following
the lead.

TOP TIP

Often overlooked, Grenivík
is the sole town on the
eastern side of Eyjafjörður
with fantastic outdoor
activities and high-class
accommodation.

GESTUR GISLASON/SHUTTERSTOCK ©

Herring Era Museum

If You Are Going to Siglócisco

BE SURE TO WEAR A HAT

Siglufjörður owes its fortune of colourful timber houses to herring – the small, silvery fish that move in massive schools. In its heyday Siglufjörður was home to thousands of workers and fishing boats crammed into the small harbour to unload their catch for the waiting women to gut and salt. For years, the export accounted for 20% of Iceland's entire foreign-trade revenue. An influx of foreign ships and sailors fuelled the boom, as well as the many saloons and cinemas in town. On idle days, when ships had to stay in harbour to wait off a storm, the streets of Siglufjörður bustled.

But herring wander the northeast Atlantic with no respect for the human desire for economic predictability. By 1969, they were gone completely. **Herring Era Museum**, set in three buildings that were part of an old Norwegian herring station, does a stunning job of recreating the enormous era, and the struggles that followed. The award-winning museum – lauded by the European Museum Forum – is hands down the most

SIGLUNES RESTAURANT

Siglufjörður's herring boom was prompted by Norwegian fishers and, to this day, newcomers continue to shape the remote settlement. Moroccan chef Jaouad Hbib prepares delicious, from-scratch Moroccan cuisine for the wood-lined Siglunes Restaurant at Hótel Siglunes. Tajines sizzle with heat, both in the temperature and flavour sense, and starters are a well-conceived blend of delicate salads and exquisite homemade cheese. Top it off with crème brûlée for dessert. Book ahead.

HIGH-END HOTELS IN SIGLUFJÖRÐUR & BEYOND

Sigló Hótel
Smart rooms, plus an elegant restaurant and bar, suspended over water, stylish lounge and waterside hot-pot. €€

Deplar Farm
Two helipads and a yoga room, with salmon fishing, kayaking and heliskiing at this stunning location in Fljót valley. €€€

Sóti Lodge
Boutique country hotel offering tailor-made hiking and skiing tours on the Troll Peninsula. €€€

GRÍMSEY ISLAND

Best known as Iceland's only true piece of the Arctic Circle, the remote island of Grímsey, 40km from the mainland, is a serene little place where birds outnumber people by about 10,000 to one. The island is small (5 sq km), but the welcome is big and the relaxation deep. The Grímsey Ferry Sæfari departs daily (three hours, 4000kr), making the voyage a mission by itself. It is possible to catch the ferry back the same day – after five hours on the island – but spending the night is recommended: reaching the *Orbis et Globus* artwork that marks the Arctic Circle takes at least three hours there and back. The 7980kg concrete sphere by Kristinn Hrafnsson moves every year as the Arctic Circle moves with the wobble of the Earth's tilt.

intriguing heritage museum in northern Iceland and beyond.

While today's population of Sigló (as the kid's call it) is about 1200 people – a third of the herring-era size – local entrepreneurs have successfully reversed a sorry housing market into a fun place to wander. The Icelandic Poetry Center (Ljóðasetur Íslands), Herhúsiðartist's residence and the Icelandic Folk Music Centre would arguably not exist without the can-do spirit of bringing new life into old houses. Micro-brewery Segull 67 and landmark restaurants Kaffi Rauðka and Torgið all occupy former warehouses.

Murder mysteries have helped too! *Trapped,* the Icelandic TV series created by Baltasar Kormákur, was filmed largely in Siglufjörður and the bestselling *Dark Iceland* crime series by Ragnar Jónasson is currently being adapted for TV by Warner Bros in Germany.

Ólafsfjörður, the sister settlement of Siglufjörður thanks to 11km of mountain tunnels, is beautifully locked between sheer mountain slopes. Lacking the same charm and urban planning, it offers an excellent swimming pool.

Straeto bus 78 departs from Akureyri morning, noon and afternoon (Sunday to Friday) to Siglufjörður and Ólafsfjörður.

Seafront Settlements
FROM AKUREYRI TO SIGLUFJÖRÐUR

Sleepy villages, at the very least, offer a good night's rest; the coastal settlements along Rte 82 to Siglufjörður are fun to varying degrees. **Dalvík**, the region's largest, is in a snug spot between breezy Eyjafjörður and the rolling hills of **Svarfaðardalur**, a valley home to the Bakka brothers of folkloric fame for stupid solutions to simple problems. Cafe Gísli, Eiríkur, Helgi honours the dubious trio with a friendly setting decked out in timber, vintage bric-a-brac and mismatched china. Fish soup and homemade cake – this might just be the perfect small-town cafe.

Another fun eatery is Baccalà Bar in the village of **Hauganes** close to Dalvík. *Baccalà*, a Portuguese culinary term, is a salty version of cod and it so happens that the local fish factory is a major exporter. Outside seating is on a patio the shape of a Viking longship, with whalebone decor, and portions are generous. Work up an appetite with a swim in the sea in the sandy creek of Hauganes Hot Tubs (adult/children 2000/1000kr, open until 8pm), next to a campsite well-suited to trailers and vans.

At **Árskógssandur** the largest employer is the craft brewery Kaldi, open Monday to Friday, with a hospitality side

---

 WHERE TO EAT IN SIGLUFJÖRÐUR

Fiskbúð Fjallabyggðar	**Frida Chocolate**	**Aðalbakarí**
The fishmonger in Siglufjörður serves fish and chips inside the fish shop, as a reputable side business. €	Handmade artisanal chocolate in a local artist's gallery – what's not to like? €€	On main street Aðalgata; with pastries, sandwiches and a cold draught from the local Segull 67 microbrewery. €

Baccalà Bar, Hauganes

SOUTH OF AKUREYRI

Eyjafjarðarsveit is the valley south of Akureyri, accessed by Rtes 821 and 829. Its largest resident is *Edda*, a giant metal sculpture of a cow made by local artist Beate Stormo, commissioned by the community. The tallest structure, however, is the yellow water slide at Sundlaugin Hrafnagili, a delightful public pool without crowds. Turn the trip into an *ísbíltúr* – the Icelandic word for 'driving around to get ice cream' – with a visit to the ice-cream shop at Holtsel (holtsel. is) dairy farm. Over winter, the Christmas Garden (instagram/jolahusid) brings the festive spirit with hot chocolate and fire-baked marshmallows on a property of gingerbread houses selling food and Christmas decorations.

show: Bjórböðin ('The Beer Spa') is an extremely awkward 'wellness' experience taking place inside a windowless room with a wooden bathtub smelling of beer and a bottomless beer pump. Drinking, for the next half-hour, is a 'treatment'.

Perhaps appropriately the only community without cars (more or less) is connected to Árskógssandur via the Hrísey Ferry Sævar, reaching **Hrísey** island within 15 minutes, at least seven times daily year-round. The name Hrísey comes from the Icelandic word for dwarf birch (*hrís*), which covered the island when Iceland was settled. Statistically speaking, the island is Iceland's second-largest offshore island (after Heimaey) but in reality a vast number of houses have seasonal residency; some are listed for rent at visithrisey.is. Spend a leisurely half-day walking to the birdwatching cabin (*fuglaskoðunarhús*) and enjoying the fjord panoramas the island has to offer. Restaurant Verbúðin 66 specialises in fish and chips and the convenience store Hríseyjarbúðin sells supplies.

Straeto bus 78 from Akureyri stops at Hauganes, Árskógssandur and Dalvík en route to Siglufjörður. There are three daily departures from Sunday to Friday.

BEST SUMMER FESTIVALS IN AKUREYRI & BEYOND

Akureyri Art Summer	**The Great Fish Day**	**Folk Music Festival**
(listasumar.is) A long-standing festival held through July with events for all ages and appetites, mostly free.	Fish, fireworks and Icelandic pop bands on an outdoor stage in Dalvík on the second Saturday in August.	Folk-music aficionados will enjoy this relaxed five-day affair in early July at the Folk Music Centre in Siglufjörður.

Underwater Geothermal Chimney
STRÝTAN THE DIVING DYNAMO

Thoughts of scuba diving usually involve sun-kissed beaches and tropical fish, so perhaps it's surprising that some of the world's most fascinating diving lies within Iceland's frigid waters. Most divers flock to crystalline Silfra (p90) near Þingvellir in the south, but the real diving dynamo, known as Strýtan, lurks beneath Eyjafjörður.

Strýtan, a giant cone (55m) soaring up from the ocean floor, commands a striking presence as it spews out gushing hot water. This geothermal chimney – made from deposits of magnesium silicate – is truly an anomaly. The only other Strýtan-like structures ever discovered were found at depths of 2000m or more; Strýtan's peak is a mere 15m below the surface.

In addition to Strýtan, there are smaller steam cones on the other side of Eyjafjörður. Known as Arnanesstrýtur, these smaller formations aren't as spectacular, but the water bubbling out of the vents is estimated to be 11,000 years old. The water is completely devoid of salt, so you can put a thermos over the vent, bottle the boiling water and use it to make hot chocolate back at the surface!

Browse the range of tour options at Strytan Divecentre (strytan.is), based in Hjalteyri, about 20km north of Akureyri.

Straeto bus 78 runs between Akureyri and Hjalteyri every day except Saturday.

The Peninsula of No Name
EMERGING GRENIVÍK

Grenivík, the sole settlement on the eastern side of Eyjafjörður, sits on a peninsula with no name. Juxtaposed against the Troll Peninsula on the other side, it is perhaps no wonder this tiny fishing village is overlooked. Not for much longer. Luxury hotel Höfði Lodge (hofdilodge.com), set to open in 2024, will include horse stables and two helicopter pads for off-piste mountain skiing.

Several multiday hiking trails lead from Grenivík along the coast known as Látraströnd and Fjörður. SUVs can drive the peninsula all the way to Flateyjardalur, with several small rivers to ford.

BEST TOUR OPERATORS IN GRENIVÍK

Polar Horses (polarhestar.is) Horse farm Grýtubakki offers one- to three-hour riding tours that cross small rivers and explore the surrounding fjord vistas.

Cape Tours (capetours.is) Kayak tours of varying lengths and difficulty; with luck the whales of Eyjafjörður will join the tour.

Kaldbaksferðir (kaldbaksferdir.com) Reach the summit of Mt Kaldbakur in 45 minutes on a snow cat from January to spring. Walk, slide or ski back to Grenivík.

GETTING AROUND

Beyond the Ring Road, the drive is relatively quiet and smooth; the only gravel parts are east of Siglufjörður via Strákagöng tunnel to Hofsós. Take extra care in winter, and follow road conditions at road.is.

Vaðlaheiðar Tunnel connects Akureyri to the northeast region and is the default Google Maps route to Húsavík and Lake Mývatn. Over summer, it's possible to skip the tunnel for road 84, adding about 15 minutes to the trip.

The tunnel is currently the only toll road in Iceland, with a fee of 1700kr, payable online only.

Tickets for the passenger ferry from Árskógssandur to Hrísey (1800kr) are sold on board, without prebooking. The Grímsey Ferry Sæfari (samskip.is/saefari) departs from Dalvík – arrive 30 minutes early. The ferry can take 108 passengers and may sell out around summer solstice.

HÚSAVÍK

Húsavík

REYKJAVÍK

Húsavík, Iceland's whale-watching capital, has become a firm favourite on travellers' itineraries. With its colourful houses, unique museums and stunning snowcapped peaks across the bay, it's easily the northeast's prettiest fishing town. The town feeds a balanced diet of excitement and quiet energy. Beyond the busy harbour – bustling with fishers at work, whale-watching passengers and outside dining – are relaxing outdoor baths and green paths through ambitious forestry projects. The tree cover harmonises with the red-and-white wooden church, built in 1907 from Norwegian timber, defining the image of Húsavík to this day. But what is that smoke? Burning coal from the massive silicon metal-production plant PCC, the single largest employer since the days of dwindling revenue for remote fishing communities. Times are changing. Nearly one-fourth of the town's workforce is foreign born, owing to labour demand and lure, reshaping modern life on the northern edge.

TOP TIP

Among Eurovision fans, Húsavík is known for its starring role in the Netflix comedy *Eurovision Song Contest: The Story of Fire Saga*. Bar-pizzeria Jaja Ding Dong, named after the film's silliest song, honours Húsavík's role in the film by blasting the Oscar-nominated song 'Husavik (My Hometown)' by Molly Sandén and Will Ferrell.

Whale watching, Húsavík 249

SIGHTS
1 Húsavík Whale Museum
2 Skrúðgarður Húsavíkur

ACTIVITIES, COURSES & TOURS
3 Botnsvatn
4 Gentle Giants
5 GeoSea
6 Húsavík Mountain
7 Húsavík Swimming Pool
8 North Sailing
9 Yltjörn

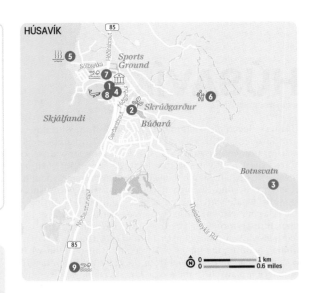

HÚSAVÍK

LOCAL BUSINESSES IN HÚSAVÍK

Húsavík Öl
A craft brewery with colourful ales inside Húsavík's former dairy plant. The taproom is next to the N1 petrol station.

Kaðlín
This shop operated by a local hand-knitting co-op sells just about everything made from Icelandic wool.

Hérna
A small coffee shop with homemade pastries, locally sourced tomato soup and Icelandic newspapers.

The Whale Residents of Skjálfandi Bay

CHOOSE A WHALE-WATCHING TOUR

It's easy to spot the number-one activity in Húsavík: the charming harbour is lined with schooners and wooden boats boarding passengers fwor the next whale-watching tour.

All whale-watching tours from Húsavík essentially do the same thing: sail into Skjálfandi bay and look for whales. The season extends from March to November and the range of species vary somewhat over the months: blue whales are most common in summer while orcas can be spotted during spring and autumn.

The 'classic' whale-watching tour lasts three hours and takes place on an old wooden ship operated by either **North Sailing** (northsailing.is) or **Gentle Giants** (gentlegiants.is). Passengers stay out on the deck the entire time, but warm overalls are provided.

To take this nautical experience to another level, the schooner tours by North Sailing take passengers sailing. One of the vessels – The Opal – has an electric engine, keeping both noise and carbon emissions to a minimum. Sails are typically raised on the way back to harbour.

WHERE TO EAT FISH IN HÚSAVÍK

Naustið
Wins wide praise for its super-fresh fish and simple skewers of fish and vegetables, grilled to order. €€

Gamli Baukur
Among shiny nautical relics, timber-framed Gamli serves spaghetti with shellfish and cod with green pesto. €€

Fish & Chips
The menu is in the name! Fresh ling, competitively priced, in generous portions. Closed over winter. €

For speed, Rigid Inflatable Boats (RIBs) move twice as fast as the other vessels. RIBs are a good choice when the whales are far out, but less so in high waves, as searching for whales requires a good view over the surface. Small boats are not allowed to motor any closer to whales than others – they must keep at least a 50m distance.

A three-hour tour costs around 11,000kr, but most hotels in the region have their own promotion code for online bookings. Over summer, tours depart every second hour, give or take, always with some same-day availability. Boats also run frequently in April, September and October, but drop way off in March and November. There are no tours from December to February.

When booking, it's worth enquiring about how big the boat is and how many passengers may be on it. Bus groups tend to favour 10am and after lunch. The evening tours over the brightest months of summer are a delightful choice, sailing into the resting sun with few other boats around.

Yoga studio Spirit North (spiritnorth.is) hosts gong mediation sessions on the electric Opal several times each summer. Another exclusive experience is a trip to the abandoned Flatey island (two hours) at the mouth of Skjálfandi. Contact Gentle Giants for a group offer.

Hot Húsavík

GEOTHERMAL SEAWATER AND THE GOLDFISH POND

Sjóböðin á Húsavík, branded in English as **GeoSea**, is a hot bath and a selfie.

The cliff-edge infinity pool merges with Skjálfandi bay and the mountain ridge of Víknarfjöll. It begs for a great holiday photo, drink in hand. Spectators may wonder if smartphones survive as bath items and evidently many are now waterproof – although maybe not tested in salty, geothermal seawater.

The GeoSea exists thanks to a geothermal drillhole that got tainted with seawater, pumping up salty water of bathing temperature, unfit for other purposes. There's no chlorine – hence, the algae growing on the grey concrete and the signpost urging all visitors to shower.

The baths are frequented by socialising locals – as annual membership is a bargain compared to the 5500kr single admission – and are busiest in the evening sun.

Húsavík Swimming Pool, the public pool in Húsavík, is another (less expensive) option after a cold day at sea. Here, you'll find a steam bath, three hot tubs and a water slide named Anaconda.

WHALE-WATCHING CODE OF CONDUCT

Whales rely more on hearing than sight and researchers have little doubt that noise causes them stress – measured by their level of cortisol, the stress hormone, in areas of increased maritime traffic and behaviour towards aggressive whale-watching boats. These findings, however, are sometimes forgotten in the competitive business of watching whales, especially since Iceland has no official penalties for bad behaviour. Passengers themselves can hold companies to account by knowing the industry 'codes of conduct' agreed to by all major operators in Iceland: no vessel is allowed to chase whales at full speed. At a 300m distance, boats should slow to 5 knots (jogging speed) and stop entirely at a 50m distance (the whale may still swim closer, as is often the case). The guidelines also advise a limit of three boats when encountering 'a situation'.

 TOURS WITHOUT WHALES

Saltvík Horse Farm
(saltvik.is) Two-hour coastal rides with glorious views over Skjálfandi bay. No special riding experience required.

Travel North
(travelnorth.is) Local tourist agency, with day tours to Askja and Mývatn, as well as guided birding and geology trips.

Húsavík Jet Ski
(husavikjetski.is) Cruise the coastline with local guides who love the sea and powerful engines.

Goðafoss waterfall

THE GUIDE

...Whale
...m (whale
...eum.is) provides
...you need to
...how about the
...mpressive creatures
that visit Skjálfandi
bay. Housed in an
old harbourside
slaughterhouse, the
museum interprets the
ecology and habits of
whales, conservation
and the history of
whaling in Iceland
through beautifully
curated displays,
including several
huge skeletons
(they're real) soaring
high above and a
mind-blowing blue
whale skeleton. Note
the narwhal tusk
and the (newest)
room dedicated to
plastic pollution and
the environmental
challenges facing
whales around the
globe.

Kids also enjoy a dip into the lukewarm **Yltjörn**, a natural pond some 2km south on the main road to Akureyri, known less formally as the Goldfish Pond. Watch long enough from the banks and you will see some handsome yellow gold fish going about their day, unaware of their incredible subarctic survival. The forefathers of these fish arrived around 2001 when warm runoff water from a geothermal electricity project warmed the natural pond to about 15°C to 20°C. At the time, a movement among locals wanted to import crocodiles but Iceland's Minister of Agriculture pointed out the potential harm for Húsavík's population: they can eat people alive. Case closed, for now.

Húsavík's Backyard
LAKESIDE LOOP AND MOUNTAIN PATH

Húsavík's ocean front can get busy over summer, when whale-watching boats depart every hour, but getting away from the crowds is an easy inland walk. Head through the public park known as **Skrúðgarður Húsavíkur**, where the trail continues for 3km to **Botnsvatn** lake (also accessible by car). The little-known lake is a 5km loop, favoured by local residents. **Húsavík Mountain**, with rolling blue-purple hills of lupine, is about a two-hour walk, round-trip. Start at Auðbrekka, leading from the public pool, for an easy to moderate path to the top. North E-Bike (northebike.is) explores the territory on electric mountain bikes.

GETTING AROUND

Eagle Air (eagleair.is) flies from Reykjavík's domestic airport to Húsavík six days a week, year-round. Húsavík Airport is 13km from town.
The longest possible distance in Húsavík – from one end of town to the lighthouse by

GeoSea – is roughly 2km. Locals like to drive, but you are welcome to walk, or grab a green Hopp scooter (hopp.bike) somewhere on the pavement.

THE DIAMOND CIRCLE DRIVING TOUR

Rise and shine with a three-hour hike around eastern Mývatn and take in a smorgasbord of geological anomalies at **1 Dimmuborgir**, **2 Hverfjall** and **3 Grjótagjá**. Lunch at Fish and Chips in the tiny village of **4 Reykjahlíð**. Drive to the stinky **5 Hverir** hot-spring area and hike to the Námafjall mountain for a view of the steaming landscape. Take a detour to the **6 Krafla power station** for a look down the turquoise Víti crater. Wrap up the first day with an evening session at the Mývatn Nature Baths, the northern version of the Blue Lagoon. The next morning, make your way to Húsavík. A good time to go whale watching is early morning and late evening; sailing in the evening sun is lovely and the waters much less busy. Take the paved Rte 862 along the Jökulsárgljúfur canyon. Check out the roar of thunderous

7 Dettifoss, the 'most powerful' waterfall in Europe. Picnic at **8 Hljóðakletar** and walk among the canyon walls of **9 Ásbyrgi**. On the way to Húsavík, during puffin season, take a short walk to the **10 Tjörnes Lighthouse** west of Mánárbakki. The area is known for fossil-rich coastal cliffs (the oldest layers dating back about two million years). In **11 Húsavík** swing by the Húsavík Whale Museum for a bit of background information, then hop aboard a whale-watching tour. Back on land, get dinner at the harbour restaurant Gamli Baukur. Finish the circle at the heavenly waterfall **12 Goðafoss**, named after an event in history when pagan carvings of the Norse gods were tossed away to usher in the era of Christianity. With a 4WD, Aldeyjarfoss is a spectacular waterfall some 40km south of Goðafoss.

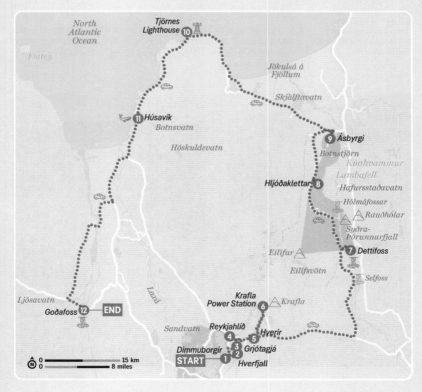

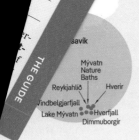

Mývatn
Nature
Baths

...avík

Reykjahlíð   Hverir

Vindbelgjarfjall

Lake Mývatn ●●● Hverfjall
Dimmuborgir

Beyond Húsavík

Move from Húsavík's ocean breeze to the
mountain air. Lake Mývatn is a destination for
all seasons.

TOP TIP

The 250km loop connecting
Húsavík, Mývatn and
Jökulsárgljúfur canyon
is known as the Diamond
Circle, a pompous name
juxtaposing South Iceland's
'Golden Circle'.

Lake Mývatn is Iceland's coldest winter settlement, edging the
uninhabited highlands, yet one of the most desired whereabouts
in the north. Its hotels, after all, can offer an otherworldly backyard: spluttering mud pots, weird lava formations, steaming
fumaroles and volcanic craters, set around a bird-filled lake.

Mývatn (pronounced *mee*-vaht) is a destination defining the
north; the postcard picture of Iceland over winter: white ground
surrounded by mountains, steaming with hot springs. When
spring arrives and the lake thaws, a gazillion migratory birds settle in with an apocalyptic swarm of black flies. Western Mývatn
offers some of the best birdwatching in Iceland, while the other
half is only home to the legendary *hverafugl* ('hot spring bird').

DANITA DELIMONT/SHUTTERSTOCK ©

Hverfjall crater

FOTOFANATIC.NL/SHUTTERSTOCK ©

Grjótagjá cave

Lakeside Lava
EASTERN MÝVATN

The features along Mývatn's eastern lakeshore are linked together with roads and paths, altogether a three-hour hike.

Reykjahlíð (population 300) is the main village and an obvious base. There is little to it beyond a collection of hotels and basic services, with a well-marked track to **Grjótagjá**, a gaping fissure with a 45°C water-filled cave. *Game of Thrones* fans may recognise this as the place where Jon Snow is, ahem, deflowered by Ygritte.

Dominating the lava fields on the eastern edge of Mývatn is the classic tephra ring **Hverfjall** (also called Hverfell). This near-symmetrical crater appeared 2700 years ago in a cataclysmic eruption. Rising 452m from the ground and stretching 1040m across, it is a massive and awe-inspiring landmark in Mývatn.

Some 2km towards the lake from Hverfjall is the giant jagged lava field at **Dimmuborgir** (the 'Dark Castles'). It is commonly believed that Dimmuborgir's strange pillars and crags were created in an eruption 2000 years ago when the lava formed a

ÞEISTAREYKIR ROAD

Driving between Húsavík and Mývatn, take the road less travelled via Þeistareykir. The mountain area, with a paved road to Mývatn, has hot springs rarely visited by tourists. Completed in 2022, the paved road was built to improve access to the Þeistareykir Power Plant, the fourth-largest geothermal energy source in Iceland. Avoid Þeistareykir Road over winter and drive instead via Laugar.

The hot springs of Þeistareykir are next to the A-shaped hut visible from the road. Without paths and fences, it is important to watch your step.

 WHERE TO STAY BEYOND HÚSAVÍK

Original North
Glamping in white tents with made-up beds and central heating on the banks of the glacial Skjálfandafljót river. €€

Langavatn Guesthouse
Friendly, good-value farmstay; one of many rural options in the area between Húsavík and Mývatn. €€

Dimmuborgir Guesthouse
A block of simple en-suite rooms overlooking Lake Mývatn, plus a smattering of timber cottages. €€

Hverir

...andic
...ce
...tters
...d to Father
...as, they are
...rded to the
...e post office in
...eykjahlíð, Mývatn.
...n the spirit of today's global outsourcing economy, Father Christmas' Icelandic colleagues have taken on the responsibility of replying to letters – 13 mischievous troll brothers, called the Yule Lads, come down from their mountain cave 13 days before Christmas to herald the holidays, and frighten children! Fortunately the letters are not delivered to the Yule Lads' home, where they might be stolen by their evil mother, Gryla, said to be a 600-year-old woman who eats children. The family even has a 'Christmas Cat', a giant feline with a habit of eating children too. The local theatre club performs as the Yule Lads in Dimmuborgir (jolasveinarniri dimmuborgum.com) every weekend in December, but don't expect English!

lake over marshland. The water of the marsh started to boil, and steam jets rose through the molten lava and cooled it, creating the pillars. As the lava continued flowing towards lower ground, the hollow pillars of solidified lava remained.

A series of non-taxing, colour-coded walking trails runs through the landscape. The most popular path is the easy Church Circle (2.3km).

Birder's Paradise

COUNTING TO 115 SPECIES

Western Mývatn offers some of the best birdwatching in Iceland, with more than 115 species recorded in the area. Fifteen species of ducks breed regularly – such as the tufted duck, greater scaup, Eurasian wigeon and common scoter – but altogether 28 duck species have been recorded. The banks of Laxá river (one of Iceland's most expensive salmon rivers) are prime habitat for harlequin ducks and Barrow's goldeneye in Iceland. Also watch out for gyrfalcons on the hunt.

For superb birdwatching background, visit **Sigurgeir's Bird Museum** (fuglasafn.is), housed in a beautiful lakeside building that fuses modern design with traditional turf house. Inside you'll find an impressive collection of taxidermy birds (more than 180 types from around the world), including every species that calls Iceland home (except one – the grey phalarope). The menagerie of stuffed squawkers started as the private collection of a local named Sigurgeir Stefansson.

WHERE TO EAT IN MÝVATN

Vogafjós
Memorable restaurant with a window separating the dining area from the farm's dairy where cows are milked. €€

Fish and Chips
Lakeside Reykjahlíð is perhaps an odd place for seafood but this takeaway is good value; opposite Kjörbúðin. €

Eldey Resturant
Stylish and well-regarded dining inside the high-end Hótel Laxá. €€€

Tragically, Sigurgeir drowned in the lake at the age of 37 – the museum was erected in his honour. Unrelated to birds, in a small pool of lake water, are *marimo balls:* bizarre little spheres of green algae that are thought to grow naturally in colonies in only a handful of places in the world (including Mývatn and Lake Akan in Japan).

For a bird's-eye view of western Mývatn, the steep but relatively straightforward climb up 529m Vindbelgjarfjall (also known as Vindbelgur) has a rewarding view over the lake and its alien pseudocraters.

Boiling Mud

MUD CAULDRONS AND PIPING FUMAROLES

Northern Mývatn's collection of geological gems lie along the Ring Road (Rte 1) as it weaves through the harsh terrain. There are plenty of paths for exploring the area on foot.

The magical, ochre-toned world of **Hverir** (also called Hverarönd) is a lunar-like landscape of mud cauldrons, steaming vents, radiant mineral deposits and piping fumaroles. Belching mud pots and the powerful stench of sulphur may not sound enticing, but Hverir's etheral allure grips every passer-by. A walking trail loops from Hverir to Námafjall ridge. This 30-minute climb provides a grand vista over the steamy surroundings. Avoid when slippery in wet conditions. Sadly, landowners now charge 1200kr parking fees, for limited infrastructure.

Steaming vents and craters await at **Krafla**, an active volcanic region 10km north of Hverir. Its most impressive – and, potentially, most dangerous – attraction is the Leirhnjúkur crater and its solfataras. In 1975 the Krafla fires began with a small lava eruption at Leirhnjúkur, and after nine years of on-and-off action, Leirhnjúkur became the ominous-looking, sulphur-encrusted mud hole that tourists love today.

On the other side of Krafla power station is the volcanic explosion crater Víti from 1724. There is a circular path from the car park around the 300m-wide rim.

Time for a bath? The powder-blue **Mývatn Nature Baths** (myvatnnaturebaths.is) is the northern answer to the Blue Lagoon, blessedly smaller and more low-key, although at the time of writing a major renovation was taking place, set to finish in 2024. Arrive early or late to avoid tour groups.

EXPLORE NATURE IN ACTION

Original North E-Bike Tours (originalnorth.is) Ride a mountain e-bike on forested paths to Ullarfoss waterfall.

Mýflug Air (myflug.is) The airline at Mývatn Airport specialises as a nationwide air ambulance, but the experienced pilots also offer a range of sightseeing tours.

Mývatn Activity (myvatnactivity.bokun.website/) Cycling is a wonderful way to travel along Lake Mývatn thanks to a cycle path from Reykjahlíð to Skútustaðir.

GETTING AROUND

Most of Mývatn's points of interests are linked by the lake's 36km loop road. The wonderful hiking trails, however, are not all connected. Without wheels you may find yourself on long walks along the busy lakeshore road – with an expanding path for cycling and walking.

All buses pick up and drop off passengers at Reykjahlíð; Route 56 with Strætó travels to Akureyri and Egilsstaðir. The only way to get to Mývatn on a bus from Húsavík is via Akureyri.

During winter, take Route 845 via Laugar village. The shortest default Route 87, from Húsavík to Mývatn, is difficult – if not closed – in snow.

...ULSÁRGLJÚFUR ...NYON

...man in Icelandic geology, the age of the Jökulsárgl-...anyon appears unbelievably young – only 4000 years ...ive or take. The river has an average discharge of one ...mpic-sized swimming pool every 13 seconds – impressive, ...r sure – but hardly the force to carve out the cathedral cliffs defining the landscape. Jökulsárgljúfur means 'Glacial River Canyon': it was formed by the melting of the mighty Vatnajökull, the largest glacier in Europe with many of Iceland's most-active volcanoes underneath the ice cap. 'Superfloods' the size of four Amazon rivers have scrubbed the cliffs, with entire basalt blocks flowing down like cork. Dettifoss, the captivating waterfall on top of the canyon, paints the picture.

Downstream from Dettifoss, travellers can escape the crowds. Hikes, long and short, await in Ásbyrgi, Vesturdalur and Hólmatungur.

Jökulsárgljúfur
Canyon

REYKJAVÍK
✪

TOP TIP

Hiking maps are available online (vjp.is) and at the Gljúfrastofa Visitor Centre in Ásbyrgi. The 33km Dettifoss to Ásbyrgi Canyon Trail is accessible for all levels of fitness, and with shorter variations. Trail run Jökulsárhlaup (jokulsarhlaup.is) in early August completes the trail in several hours.

SAM SPICER/GETTY IMAGES ©

Dettifoss (p260)

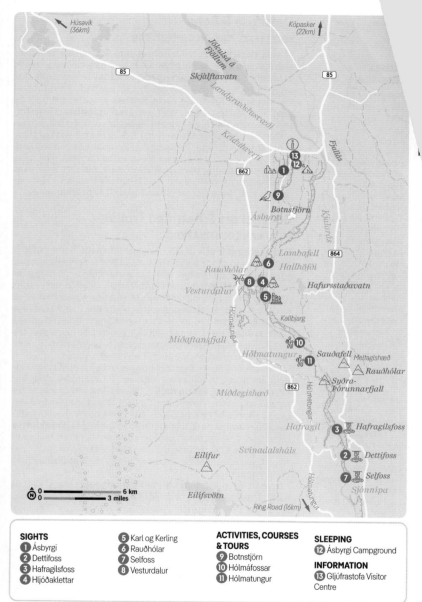

SIGHTS
1 Ásbyrgi
2 Dettifoss
3 Hafragilsfoss
4 Hljóðaklettar
5 Karl og Kerling
6 Rauðhólar
7 Selfoss
8 Vesturdalur

ACTIVITIES, COURSES & TOURS
9 Botnstjörn
10 Hólmáfossar
11 Hólmatungur

SLEEPING
12 Ásbyrgi Campground

INFORMATION
13 Gljúfrastofa Visitor Centre

...oad from ...market ...Ásbyrgi is ...plant that ...vented from ...ring the national ...rk by rangers armed with lawnmowers. The blue Nootka lupine, native to North America and a familiar sight in flower gardens there, has spread wildly in Iceland since its introduction in the late 1970s to halt soil erosion. But the experiment blew up in Iceland's face and left a permanent purple mark. Considered an invasive plant today, the lupine threatens not only the existing flora but also the barren volcanic interior. And the threat is growing. Encouraged by the warming atmosphere, lupine is spreading beyond Iceland's relatively temperate coastal areas and into the interior, previously thought too dry and cold to support the plant.

Dettifoss & Sons
WATERFALL TRIO ON CANYON TOP

Mighty **Dettifoss** truly is nature at its most spectacular. A massive 400 cu metres of water thunders over its edge every second in summer, creating a plume of spray that can be seen from 1km away – in other words, from the distant car park. The burble of running water is actually a trio. **Selfoss**, a smaller cataract extending from the walking trail, and **Hafragilsfoss**, a little further downstream by car, tend to be victims of waterfall-fatigue.

The falls can be seen from either side of the canyon but there is no bridge at the site. The easiest option is Rte 862 – the 'Dettifoss Route' – paved and open for much of the year. The main downside of taking the gravel alternative Rte 864 is missing west-bank-only Vesturdalur and Hljóðaklettar. Both sides require a walk from the car park of around 15 to 20 minutes.

Sunseekers & Petrified Trolls
WEST BANK DESTINATIONS

Lush **Ásbyrgi** is practically one giant sun patio thanks to 50m cliffs keeping out the wind. The Iceland Forest Service has made a mark on the landscape, with birch and pine trees lining the path to **Botnstjörn**, a small bird-friendly pond at the head of Ásbyrgi. The walls echo beautifully, and this was once used as a concert venue by the avant-garde Sigur Rós. For a bird's-eye view take the trail to Eyjan (3km) or Klappir (6km) from the Gljúfrastofa Visitor Centre (vjp.is), which has maps and toilets. The fabulous Ásbyrgi campground is popular among sunseeking Icelanders with trailers and camper vans.

The rays of sun are a deadly kiss for trolls – petrified by daylight according to folklore – with several examples along the western banks at **Vesturdalur**. The pristine valley marks the second half of the Canyon Trail (p262) from Dettifoss to Ásbyrgi. The series of weaving trails are excellent for shorter walks too. From the car park, a 3km trail goes around **Hljóðaklettar** (Echo Rocks), where basalt swirls create acoustic effects that make it impossible to determine the direction of the roaring Jökulsá river. If you have enough time, continue to the **Rauðhólar** (Red Hills) crater row.

On a bank on the 8km trail to **Hólmatungur** stand Karl og Kerling, two rock pillars believed to be petrified trolls. Hólmatungur can be done as a detour along the Dettifoss drive. The most popular walk here is the 5km loop to **Hólmáfossar** via Katlar.

GETTING AROUND

Rte 862 – paved from the Ring Road to Ásbyrgi – connects the area with Mývatn and Húsavík. It makes Dettifoss waterfall an easy Ring Road stop. Check conditions in winter as ploughing is not a priority. On the eastern banks of Jökulsá, the gravel Rte 864 is closed over winter.

Jökulsárgljúfur has well-maintained trails. Hiking maps are available online (vjp.is) and at the Gljúfrastofa Visitor Centre in Ásbyrgi.

There is also a designated cycling path. The trail to Hafragil lowlands, the most demanding hike within the park, can be difficult to locate without a guide.

To avoid backtracking the Canyon Trail, shuttle service is available through Nordic Natura (nordicnatura.is) and Hótel Skúlagarður (skulagardur.com). Prices start at 5500kr per person but are negotiable, based on group size.

Rifstangi
Rauðinúpur   Raufarhöfn   Skoruvíkurbjarg
Cape
Rauðanes   Langanes
Þórshöfn

Jökulsárgljúfur
Canyon

Beyond Jökulsárgljúfur Canyon

Don't trip over a puffin burrow, and bring a stick – or sacrifice your tallest travel companion – to fool angry Arctic terns. Even the birds around here are not expecting a visitor.

The northeastern coastal drive is an alternative to the direct road from Mývatn to Egilsstaðir, taken by a small but steady number of travellers.

The drive from Ásbyrgi starts with green fields and red-roof farms; a familiar countryside scenery preceding a rugged coastal land where driftwood is the tallest tree. The fog is stubborn and the feeling of 'remoteness' central to the experience. No? Continue to Fontur, the lighthouse on the tip of Langanes Peninsula.

But make no mistake: people do live here and the fishing villages Kópasker and Þórshöfn are doing quite well, thank you. They take pride in Iceland's legacy of sheep and fish, and embrace travellers the old-fashioned way: with openness and hospitality.

TOP TIP

Skoruvík on Langanes Peninsula has a rare gannet colony, visible from a cliff-edge viewing platform.

IMAGEBROKER.COM GMBH & CO. KG/ALAMY STOCK PHOTO ©

The Canyon Trail

The Canyon Trail from Dettifoss to Ásbyrgi is arguably Iceland's best two-day hike outside the highlands. Starting in Dettifoss, the 33km trail descends gradually from 370m to sea level and is accessible for all levels of fitness. The trail is divided broadly into three legs, of different tone and terrain: stony and black, lush and green, volcanic and red. Overnight in Vesturdalur.

1 Dettifoss

The Canyon Trail bypasses Dettifoss itself; take the 1km loop towards the waterfall spray before heading in the opposite direction – north. The first stop is just over the parking hill where you'll find drinking water and a sign pointing left to Vesturdalur (18.2km). Note the unmarked trail on the right, along the canyon cliffs, leading to the spectacular Hafragil lowlands. The lowland trail is not suitable for untrained hikers, people who are afraid of heights, or

those carrying a large backpack. Whether you go left or right, the next stop is Hólmatungur after 10km to 12km.

The Hike: Arrive at Hólmatungur after 10km or 12km (three to four hours, depending on the route), marking the first half of day one. The terrain is rocky but with the greatest views.

2 Hólmatungur

Lush vegetation, tumbling waterfalls and an air of tranquillity make the Hólmatungur area one of the most beautiful in the park. We recommend walking along

STEFAN WILLE/SHUTTERSTOCK ©

Ásbyrgi canyon

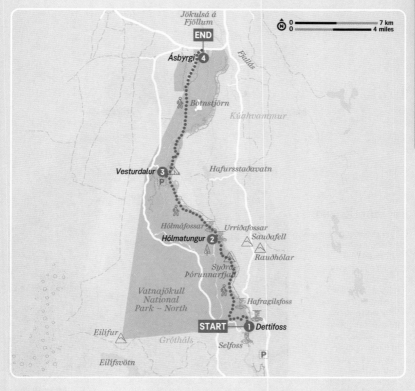

Jökulsá (ie not the path along the spring river Hólmá) for a view of Katlar. The two paths unite at the cascading Hólmárfossar. Look out for Karl og Kerling, the troll-like stacks, 1km before Vesturdalur.

The Hike: The path to Vesturdalur (8km, two hours) has an uphill section midway and at the spring river Stallá it is time to go barefoot and wade. The river is shallow but cold – a memorable part of the hike.

3 Vesturdalur

Sleep next to a spring river in the pristine Vesturdalur valley. Bring a portable stove but forget the towel: the basic campsite (for tents only) has no showers, only toilets and running water.

The Hike: Start the next day at Hljóðaklettar (p260), the main site at Vesturdalur, on the pleasant 12km path to Ásbyrgi. Travellers without the time for a two-day hike tend to opt for this section as the terrain is soft and flat and the scenery diverse.

4 Ásbyrgi

Arrive via the path to Klappir and you are suddenly confronted with a rewarding view over the entire shoe-shaped Ásbyrgi canyon (separated from the Jökulsárgljúfur canyon). Walk along the cliffs to Tófugjá, using rope and stairs, to the canyon floor. The finish line is at Ásbyrgi's Gljúfrastofa Visitor Centre. Good to know: there is a small public pool at Lundur (a 10-minute drive away), which is open from June to August.

Some argue the journey is more rewarding the other way, ending with the highlight Dettifoss – the trail is more uphill if you start at Ásbyrgi.

BEACH CLEANING

Every kilometre of coastline in Iceland is littered with about one tonnage of washed-up rubbish. Langanes Peninsula, a trap for litter with a stony beach, is shocking visual evidence of the amount of fishing gear, plastic bottles, plastic containers – plastic, plastic, plastic, plastic – polluting the North Atlantic and hurting wildlife. Ocean Missions (oceanmission.org), an NGO based in Húsavík, hosts weekly beach cleaning events along the northeastern coast. World Ocean Day – on 8 June – draws the largest crowd of volunteers.

Arctic Henge

Arctic Fox Plain
NORTHERNMOST DETOUR

The freedom to roam – the general public's right to access privately owned land for recreation and exercise – is important on the northeast corner. Sights lack tourism infrastructure, some at the preference of landowners, but everyone is free to roam on foot, no matter the font-size of 'PRIVATE' on any given sign. So, keep calm and carry on to **Rauðinúpur Cape**, 28km north of Kópasker village, with an offshore gannet colony and puffins stoically watching the open sea.

The cape is on the western end of Melrakkaslétta (Rte 870), a magnificent 55km old coastal road between Kópasker and

---

WHERE TO STAY BEYOND JÖKULSÁRGLJÚFUR CANYON

Melar Guesthouse
Renovated seaside home in Kópasker with a good atmosphere and hot tubs (1000kr for nonguests). **€€**

Hótel Norðurljós
Bright rooms with private bathrooms by the harbour in Raufarhöfn. **€€€**

Grásteinn Guesthouse
Get away from it all at these boutique cottages on a remote sheep farm 14km southwest of Þórshöfn. **€€**

Raufarhöfn. The road passes driftwood, rolling fields, ponds and marshes of the Northeast Iceland Birdtrail (birdingtrail. is). **Rifstangi**, the northernmost point of Iceland, is a 10km hike from the road and the round-shaped mountain Gefla (180m); a pleasant walk with a view. Note: Rte 85 is the main road between Kópasker and Raufarhöfn and is certainly more accessible.

Distant **Raufarhöfn** is Iceland's northernmost mainland township, struggling for the past decades to revive itself after an illustrious past as a herring port. The village has a beautiful natural harbour, guarded by an orange lighthouse. It is best known for the **Arctic Henge**, a human-made stone circle on the hill, set to celebrate Norse mythology and the midnight sun. In autumn 2024, folk-metal band Skálmöld has scheduled a giant outdoor concert at the henge.

The Lighthouse at the End

REMOTE PENINSULAS

There's excellent hiking on Þistilfjörður at **Rauðanes** headland, where a 7km marked walking trail leads to bizarre rock formations, natural arches, caves and secluded beaches, plus great birdlife (including puffins). The turn-off to Rauðanes is between Raufarhöfn (42km) and Þórshöfn (32km). Look for a small sign – the road leads 1.5km to an information board with walking trail details and a small car park.

Þórshöfn (population 380) is the region's largest settlement, and a base to explore the Langanes Peninsula.

Shaped like a goose with a very large head, foggy **Langanes peninsula** is one of the loneliest corners of Iceland. The peninsula's flat terrain, cushioned by mossy meadows and studded with crumbling remains, is an excellent place to break in your hiking shoes and find solitude.

Sealed Rte 869 ends at Sauðneshús, the old vicarage on the church estate, 7km north of Langanes. The museum, open in July and August, provides insights into how locals lived a century ago. The rutted track continues 50km along the Langanes Peninsula. On the beach by the signposted road to Ytra Lón Retreat are skeletons of pilot whales that got stranded here en masse in 2019. Further onwards, the drive to Skoruvík is bumpy but easy to navigate. Stop at **Skoruvíkurbjarg**, a cliff-edge vista, overlooking a rare colony of gannets, the largest seabird in the North Atlantic, known for thunderous diving. Suitable SUVs can continue to **Fontur**, the lighthouse at the tip of the peninsula, and the old fishing station at **Skálar**.

THE LEADER-SHEEP CENTRE

Of Iceland's 266 museums and exhibitions open to the public, the Study Centre on Leader-sheep (forystusetur.is) is perhaps the most peculiar and telling of Iceland's remote northeast corner. And you may ask, what exactly is a leader-sheep? A kind of superhero sheep – considered a subpopulation within the Icelandic sheep group – with the navigation skills to lead 'ordinary sheep' in bad weather and challenging conditions. They are usually larger than average, black and grey. Based on a study, published in the nature journal *Náttúrufræðingurinn*, the breed has existed in Iceland since settlement, for 1100 years, but suffered a major decline in the last decades. By latest accounts, there are 1422 individual leader sheep, some widely known by name.

 GETTING AROUND

Travelling the northeast coast in a 4WD offers more freedom, without being essential. Over summer, Melrakkaslétta (Rte 870) is accessible for 2WDs but as the road is poorly maintained, it is worth checking the latest condition. The rocky road on Langanes Peninsula is free of mud and rivers, but be wary of your tyres and windshield along the way.

Above: Stöðvarfjörður (p278). Right: Icelandic woollen sweater (p282)

EAST ICELAND

AS FAR FROM REYKJAVÍK AS POSSIBLE

Characterised not only by deep fjords, towering mountains and wild nature, this remote region may surprise you with its unique history, culture and wildlife.

Heading east on Ring Road 1 along the southern coastline, after leaving the glacial wonders of the southeast behind, you're soon greeted by awesome, rugged, multi-layered mountains. Here you'll find some of the oldest – and most colourful – rock in Iceland; about 13 million years old (ancient, yet infant on a global scale). These mountains have magnified storms, isolated communities, blocked out the sun, caused mudslides and avalanches, but also provided shelter, food and joy. Another telltale sign that you've entered the East: reindeer. In winter and spring, they come to the lowlands for grazing and can sometimes be sighted amid sheep and horses. Off the shore is the formerly inhabited island Papey, known for its rich birdlife, its name a reference to Irish monks believed to have preceded the Norse settlers. Centuries later, in 1802, Iceland's first documented black settler found freedom and respect in Djúpivogur. One hundred years on, as activities of foreign fishers in Icelandic waters were peaking, French sailors had a hospital built in Fáskrúðsfjörður – today a hotel and museum. During WWII, allied troops set up camp in the Eastfjords, and their presence is still palpable. The East remains a melting pot of cultures, most prominently the artsy community of Seyðisfjörður. You're as far from Reykjavík as you can get. Expect colour, creativity and tranquillity alongside resourceful and welcoming people.

MARIDAV/SHUTTERSTOCK ©

THE MAIN AREAS

FLJÓTSDALUR
Waterfalls, history and wilderness.
p270

SEYÐISFJÖRÐUR
Art, design and adventurous hiking.
p280

Find Your Way

East Iceland has very diverse nature and experiences that are all located at a relatively short distance from each other. We've picked some of the highlights that make a good base for further exploration.

Fljótsdalur, p270

Sheep-farming hub along lake Lagarfljót, marking the eastern border of Vatnajökull National Park. Hengifoss waterfall among many attractions.

Seyðisfjörður, p280

The region's culture capital is a 30-minute drive from Egilsstaðir. Superb shopping, tasty local food and pristine nature.

CAR

Car hire provides you with freedom and flexibility when exploring Iceland. Hire a 4WD for winter conditions and gravel roads. Find car rentals in larger towns, or arrive by ferry and bring your own.

BUS

There are sporadic public bus services in East Iceland. For fans of slow travel, this is an opportunity for a greener commute and in-depth discovery of each place. Ask locals or visit east.is for more information.

Reindeer

Plan Your Time

To discover every nook and cranny of the eastern region, you'll need plenty of time – especially when planning long hikes – while the highlights can be covered in a few days.

If You Only Do One Thing

● **Seyðisfjörður** (p280) is the vibrant beating heart of East Iceland, engaging through art and surrounded by stunning scenery. Listen to music and taste the best sushi in Iceland. Walk the rainbow street to the blue church, browse around in **Blóðberg** (p282), invest in a hand-knitted *lopapeysa* (Icelandic woollen sweater), then walk up to sound sculpture **Tvísöngur** (p281) and take in the view.

If You Have More Time

● Join a reindeer-sighting tour in **Breiðdalsvík** (p278), marvel at Petra's stone collection in **Stöðvarfjörður** (p278), learn about the French history of **Fáskrúðsfjörður** (p285), camp out in **Hallormsstaðaskógur forest** (p276), watch puffins in **Borgarfjörður Eystri** (p284), and hike up to **Hengifoss** (p272) in Fljótsdalur. From **Laugarfell** (p275), adventure into the wild.

SEASONAL HIGHLIGHTS

SPRING	SUMMER	AUTUMN	WINTER
Cool and unreliable weather; migrant birds arrive. Fewer tourists but some services are closed.	Height of the tourist season and the hottest weather. Best conditions for hiking, biking and horse riding.	Stunning foliage in Hallormsstaðaskógur. Dark nights and Northern Lights come out.	List í Ljósi art festival is held in Seyðisfjörður. Ski areas open, snowfall permitting; frozen landscapes glitter.

FLJÓTSDALUR

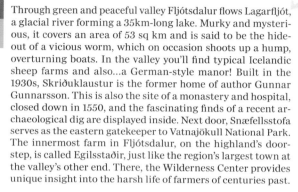

Fljótsdalur ●

✪ REYKJAVÍK

Through green and peaceful valley Fljótsdalur flows Lagarfljót, a glacial river forming a 35km-long lake. Murky and mysterious, it covers an area of 53 sq km and is said to be the hideout of a vicious worm, which on occasion shoots up a hump, overturning boats. In the valley you'll find typical Icelandic sheep farms and also...a German-style manor! Built in the 1930s, Skriðuklaustur is the former home of author Gunnar Gunnarsson. This is also the site of a monastery and hospital, closed down in 1550, and the fascinating finds of a recent archaeological dig are displayed inside. Next door, Snæfellsstofa serves as the eastern gatekeeper to Vatnajökull National Park. The innermost farm in Fljótsdalur, on the highland's doorstep, is called Egilsstaðir, just like the region's largest town at the valley's other end. There, the Wilderness Center provides unique insight into the harsh life of farmers of centuries past.

TOP TIP

Entrance to Snæfellsstofa is free. More than an information centre about Vatnajökull National Park, it's also a museum about its flora and fauna where you're invited to touch and feel the objects on display. Ask about road conditions, hiking routes and guided tours, and a fun family orienteering game around Fljótsdalur.

ARCTIC IMAGES/ALAMY STOCK PHOTO ©

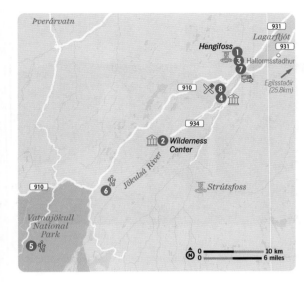

HIGHLIGHTS
1 Hengifoss
2 Wilderness Center

SIGHTS
3 Litlanesfoss
4 Skriðuklaustur

ACTIVITIES, COURSES & TOURS
5 Snæfell
6 Waterfall Circle

EATING
7 Hengifoss Food Truck
8 Klausturkaffi

THE GOOD SHEPHERD

Gunnar Gunnarsson's novella *The Good Shepherd* (1938) features fearless shepherd Fjalla-Bensi and his two four-legged friends who battle a snowstorm while searching for lost sheep in the wilderness during Advent.

Readings from *The Good Shepherd* are organised at Skriðuklaustur in many different languages on the third Sunday of December. See skriduklaustur.is for more information and events.

Unearthing Skriðuklaustur's Secrets

MONASTERY AND CULTURE CENTRE

Secrets lay buried here for centuries. The exact location of the Skriðuklaustur monastery, which was in operation 1493–1550, had been forgotten, too. In 2000, after some digging around, archaeologist Steinunn Kristjánsdóttir and her team struck gold and their excavation project began. In the following 12 years they found evidence of buildings – a church, monastery and hospital – measuring 700 sq metres. In a forgotten graveyard, they uncovered the remains of almost 300 individuals. Thousands of artefacts were discovered, including a gold ring and statuette of St Barbara, indicating how grand the monastery had been and how well-connected Iceland was with the outside world at that time. Although the names of the people buried at Skriðuklaustur are unknown, their bones have revealed some things about their identities and sufferings. Many were riddled with syphilis, including a young woman, whose face – and horrific facial wounds – was digitally reconstructed by 3D designer Cícero Moraes as part of a larger study, as reported by *Science Daily* in 2022.

Included in the entrance fee is a guided tour of the museum at Skriðuklaustur. Learn about the excavation and its

 WHERE TO EAT IN FLJÓTSDALUR

Hengifoss Food Truck
Serving homemade soups, waffles and ewe's milk ice cream. Irresistible after a hike to Hengifoss. €

Klausturkaffi
Delicious lunch buffet, highlighting local ingredients. Gluten-free and vegan options. Save room for cakes! €€

Wilderness Center
Try typical Icelandic farm fare; whatever is on today's menu – perhaps lamb, trout, rhubarb pie. €€

THE FORGOTTEN AUTHOR

Gunnar Gunnarsson was born on Valþjófsstaðir, the farm next to Skriðuklaustur, in 1889 as a poor farmer's son with literary aspirations. He studied in Denmark and released his first novel, *Guest the One-Eyed*, in Danish in 1912. His books became popular, particularly in Denmark and Germany, and were translated into many different languages. The first ever Icelandic motion picture, *Sons of the Soil,* released in 1920, was based on Gunnar's debut novel.

In 1939, Gunnar moved back to his home turf and had German architect Fritz Höger design Skriðuklaustur as his country manor. However, in 1948 he decided to relocate to Reykjavík and donated his manor to the Icelandic state.

BORCHEE/GETTY IMAGES ©

Litlanesfoss waterfall

findings. Then you can walk around the excavation site and afterwards journey into the past through a virtual reality tour of the church and monastery.

The museum at Skriðuklaustur is not only dedicated to the monastery but also to the life and work of author Gunnar Gunnarsson (1889–1975). The **Gunnar Gunnarsson Institute** was established here in 1997 to support literary projects and serve as a residence for artists, writers and scholars. Diverse cultural events are held here, including concerts and readings.

Hiking Hengifoss

ICELAND'S THIRD-HIGHEST WATERFALL

Lace up your boots for the 40- to 60-minute hike to **Hengifoss**, which at 128m is Iceland's third-highest waterfall. The path is partly steep but well maintained. Just take it easy and enjoy the view of Fljótsdalur, which becomes more spectacular the higher you go: the green valley, the massive lake and the sprawling forest on the other side.

As a special reward – and somewhat of a surprise – is another waterfall, **Litlanesfoss** (or Stuðlabergsfoss), midway. It's smaller than Hengifoss but also quite magnificent, as it's framed with columnar basalt. Continue your walk into the Hengifossárgil gully and, soon, Hengifoss comes into view in all its glory. It tumbles down a spectacular layered cliff; these layers tell the story of different volcanic eruptions from the Tertiary period when Iceland was created.

 BEST HIKES IN FLJÓTSDALUR & BEYOND

Hengifoss
Waterfall right off Rte 931. The 2.5km route is a little steep but fairly easy.

Waterfall Circle
Accessible by Rte 910, this 8km route leads past five waterfalls and one ravine.

Snæfell
Snæfell (1833m high) requires 4WD access along Rte F909. Experienced hikers only. Open in summer.

On the Highlands' Doorstep

TRAVEL BACK TO THE 1940s

As soon as you enter the gravel road that leads to **Egilsstaðir**, the innermost farm in Fljótsdalur, you get the feeling that time has slowed down. Welcome to the **Wilderness Center**, on the doorstep of Europe's most expansive highlands.

The stately farmhouse that greets you was built in 1940 and has been meticulously renovated in its original style. Fourteen siblings grew up here – and nine of them lived here their entire adult lives. They were known for their handicraft, resourcefulness and their close relationship with nature and the wilderness.

The Wilderness Center is an example for slow tourism. Here, you can wind down and listen to stories over a cup of coffee and a slice of homemade *hjónabandssæla* (rhubarb oat cake), sleep in a crowded but cosy *baðstofa* (old-fashioned Icelandic living room), soak in a hot spring with stacked stone walls, listen to birdsong and gaze up into the sky. In winter you might even catch the Northern Lights.

In an unassuming building you'll find a fascinating exhibition about the wilderness, humankind's relationship with the wild and the hardship of farmers past. Highlands' travel stories come to life through photos, videos and audio, along with an inventive set design, including an old-fashioned tent.

There are literary references to books by Gunnar Gunnarsson and Halldór Laxness. In Laxness' *Independent People*, the main protagonist Bjartur rode on a reindeer bull. The scene was actually inspired by a true story of a farmer from Fljótsdalur who tried to kill a sleeping bull but ended up trapped on its back.

To completely immerse yourself in nature, take long or short walks, with or without a guide, or better yet – discover nature from horseback. Longer tours go up to highlands' retreat Laugarfell (p275) – or even deeper into the wilderness.

How do you cross a wild glacial river, rushing through a deep gorge, without a bridge? Try the old-fashioned cableway – a short walking distance from the Wilderness Center – where you pull yourself across in a wooden box. It's great adrenaline-infused family fun and at the same time an insightful learning experience.

AUTHENTIC COUNTRY CELEBRATION

Jóhann Þórhallsson and **Sigrún Ólafsdóttir**, farmers in Fljótsdalur, discuss the highlight of the sheep farming calendar.

We have around 300 sheep but there are 4600 in the valley. In the summer they graze in a vast territory in the highlands, which stretches all the way to Vatnajökull glacier. It takes a few days and at least 30 people to round them up in the autumn. We travel by horses, six-wheelers and dirt bikes, track them down – sometimes using drones – and with the help of sheepdogs and leader sheep bring them back home. We have the largest *rétt* (sheep pen) in East Iceland, and the final day of roundup is a big country celebration.

GETTING AROUND

It's best to hire a car for travelling in and around Fljótsdalur. Hengifoss is only 30 minutes from Egilsstaðir and many of the main attractions are close by. A paved road (Rte 910) leads to Laugarfell on the edge of Vatnajökull National Park. Rte 931 leads you around lake Lagarfljót to Hallormsstaðaskógur forest. Rte 95 is a shortcut to Breiðdalsvík and Stöðvarfjörður. Rte 939 – a scenic mountain road that is only open in summer – goes to Djúpivogur.

Egilsstaðir

Hallormsstaðaskógur

Fljótsdalur

Stöðvarfjörður

Laugarfell   Breiðdalsvík

Djúpivogur

Beyond Fljótsdalur

What's your fancy? Hunting for waterfalls, getting lost in a forest, soaking in hot and cold water or dining out?

East Iceland is an incredibly diverse region where you can have varied experiences in a relatively compact area. The vast expanses of the highlands are a short drive from Fljótsdalur. On the other side of Lagarfljót lake lies Iceland's largest forest. Drop by organic barley and vegetable farm Vallanes to have a taste of the produce in its cafe, made with wood from Hallormsstaðaskógur. Thirty kilometres away, Egilsstaðir, the region's service centre, welcomes you with a selection of restaurants, cafes, bars – and Vök Baths. Drive southwards on Rte 95 and Rte 939 (closed in winter) for about an hour and you'll end up in scenic seaside villages. You can have a different kind of adventure every day.

TOP TIP

Travelling with kids? The Reindeer Park and Finnsstaðir farm have animals for petting. Horseback riding is for ages 10 and up.

OLEKSANDR KORZHENKO/ALAMY STOCK PHOTO ©

Hallormsstaðaskógur (p276)

Kirkjufoss waterfall

Highway to the Highlands
WATERFALLS AND OTHER WONDERS

The controversial Kárahnjúkar hydropower plant opened in 2007, resulting in a paved road, Rte 910, leading from Fljótsdalur to the eastern highlands. **Laugarfell** is a highland retreat on the borders of Vatnajökull National Park. It takes about 30 minutes to drive there from Snæfellsstofa Visitor Center in Fljótsdalur on Rte 910 (only the last stretch is unpaved). You need your own vehicle. In summer, you can camp at Laugarfell, and the mountain lodge offers rustic accommodation, hearty breakfasts, lunches and dinners, and lunch packs for your hike.

The 8km waterfall trail is fairly easy and extremely rewarding. It takes you to five different waterfalls on a round trip from Laugarfell, including the roaring 40m double waterfall **Kirkjufoss** in river Jökulsá í Fljótsdal. After your hike, relax in one of Laugarfell's two hot springs. According to legend, the water has healing powers.

The paved Rte 910 leads onwards to Kárahnjúkar (about one hour from Laugarfell). From there Iceland's largest dam, Hálslón, can be viewed. When it fills up and overflows in late summer, massive waterfall Hverfandi appears on its western end and cascades 100m down into Hafrahvammagljúfur canyon.

TOURS ON HORSEBACK, WHEELS OR FOOT

Laugarfell has partnered up with the Wilderness Center (p273), offering a range of tours in different seasons. If you haven't seen enough waterfalls already, walk the waterfall trail along **Jökulsá í Fljótsdal** where you'll see a total of 15 waterfalls! Experience nature from the back of an Icelandic horse, or rent a mountain bike.

There's also the 10- to 12-hour **Wonders of the Wilderness super-Jeep tour**, which is available in summer and winter. Highlights include **Hafrahvamma- gljúfur canyon** with spectacular vertical cliffs, **Stuðlagil canyon** with its distinct columnar basalt, and the geothermal waterfall in **Laugarvalladalur**, a natural hot spring shower.

 WHERE TO EAT IN EGILSSTAÐIR

Tehúsið
This hostel, bar, music venue, cafe and restaurant serves homemade soups, delicious cakes, hearty breakfasts. €

Eldhúsið
The restaurant at Lake Hotel Egilsstaðir has a selection of tempting courses, highlighting farm-fresh produce. €€

Nielsen Restaurant
In Egilsstaðir's oldest house, a Michelin-starred chef gets creative with local ingredients in seasonal dishes. €€€

FOREST FESTIVALS

The Icelandic Forest Service and the Association of Forest Farmers in East Iceland organise two major annual events.

Skógardagurinn mikli (The Great Forest Day) is held around Midsummer's Day in June with a family-friendly programme, games/challenges for kids, music and entertainment. Cattle farmers serve a whole roasted ox and sheep farmers serve grilled lamb. Other treats include grilled sausages, *lummur* (small pancakes), special kettle coffee and 'worm bread' made by foresters. The highlight is a lumberjack competition.

Jólakötturinn (named after the gruesome Yule Cat) is a Christmas market in mid-December. It's usually held at Valgerðarstaðir in Fellabær outside Egilsstaðir. In addition to Christmas trees, a range of local delicacies and handicraft are available.

If you're up for a challenge, hike **Snæfell** (1833m), Iceland's highest mountain outside glacial regions; it requires experience and preparation. Rte F909 leads from Rte 910 to the Snæfell lodge, where there's a campground and sleeping bag accommodation. It's only accessible in summer by 4WD vehicles. Rangers are happy to assist (call +354 842 4367 or email snaefellsstofa@vjp.is). After a successful mission, add your name to the list of conquerors at the lodge.

Lose Yourself in Hallormsstaðaskógur
ICELAND'S LARGEST FOREST (A SURPRISE)

Have you heard the joke that goes: 'What do you do if you get lost in an Icelandic forest? Stand up!' The myth that Iceland is basically treeless is shattered as you enter Hallormsstaðaskógur, Iceland's largest forest, covering 740 sq km on the banks of Lagarfljót. From Snæfellsstofa Visitor Center in Fljótsdalur it takes about 15 minutes to drive to the forest on Rte 931. Hallormsstaðaskógur has been a reserve since 1905 and includes 85 tree species from around the world. Most of them you can admire in the arboretum, including Swiss pine, mountain hemlock, subalpine fir, western red cedar and European aspen.

Through the forest lies 40km of paths for walking or biking. The longest leads up a mountain with a splendid view all the way to the highlands. Seven types of berries grow in the forest, and so it's a popular activity among locals to go berry picking in late summer. When the foliage takes on its fiery autumnal costume, walking through the forest becomes an entirely different experience. In winter, when the frost glitters and a blanket of snow covers the ground and branches, it turns into a winter wonderland. In summer, native tourists 'chasing after the sun' (a special kind of Icelandic hobby) flock to Hallormsstaðaskógur to camp in the woods.

Culture Cradle & Haute Cuisine
BASE FOR EXPLORING THE EAST

Centrally located in East Iceland and at a 30-minute driving distance from Snæfellsstofa Visitor Center in Fljótsdalur on Rte 931, **Egilsstaðir** functions as the region's service centre. It has the highest number of inhabitants, most shops and restaurants. It's also where the domestic airport is based, with regular flights to and from Reykjavík that take about 50 minutes. Given the convenient location, Egilsstaðir and the surrounding areas are a good base for exploring the East. Accommodation options range from a campsite and hostels to high-end hotels.

 WHERE TO SLEEP IN EGILSSTAÐIR

Hótel Edda	Gistihúsið – Lake Hotel Egilsstaðir	Hérað – Berjaya Iceland Hotels
Simple, comfortable and centrally located, this is among the least expensive options for a double room. €€	Family-run example of farming culture and hospitality, on the banks of Lagarfljót. €€€	Charming and quirky, Hérað highlights chic design and comfort with Eastern flair. €€€

ANNA WATSON/ALAMY STOCK PHOTO ©

Vök Baths

The town itself has many attractions, including **Selskógur** (a small forest perfect for walks and outdoor recreation such as cross-country skiing in winter) and a swimming pool with Jacuzzis and a slide.

The heritage museum features interesting exhibitions on reindeer and the self-sufficiency of farmers in past centuries.

Iceland's Only Floating Pools

SUBLIME SURRENDER, UNIQUE BATHING EXPERIENCE

Pay close attention or you might miss it. The grass-roofed building on the bank of Urriðavatn lake blends elegantly in with the surrounding landscape. **Vök Baths** are at a 30-minute driving distance from Snæfellsstofa Visitor Center in Fljótsdalur on Rte 931 and a few minutes from Egilsstaðir.

A special take on Icelandic bathing culture, Vök Baths offer relief from life on the road. The name *vök* references the holes that formed in the frozen Urriðavatn in winter, hinting at the geothermal activity. The hot water is used for heating houses in Egilsstaðir – and now also for bathing.

There are four pools with different temperatures, two of which float in Urriðavatn lake – Iceland's only floating infinity pools. There's also a sauna and a cold mist tunnel. Order a smoothie, a beer or glass of wine at the swim-in bar and enjoy the view.

ABSOLUTE TRANQUILLITY

Bergrún Arna Þorsteinsdóttir, assistant forest ranger in Hallormsstaðaskógur, provides an insight into her life and work.

I manage operations related to the forest, the outdoor recreation areas, the campsites in Atlavík and Höfðavík and organising events and activities.

There are more local than foreign tourists. The forest surprises them: 'Is this possible here?' they say. It's a totally different feeling, standing on sand, in a forest or on a glacier.

I'm also the co-owner of **Holt og heiðar**; we make syrup, jam, and other forest products. I collect the birch sap myself. My favourite thing in the forest is to wake up early and stand among the birch trees in spring. There's a feeling of absolute tranquillity.

 SPECIAL SOAKS BEYOND FLJÓTSDALUR

Laugarfell
Two natural hot pools, open in summer. The water is said to have healing powers.

Vök Baths
Iceland's only floating infinity pools, filled with geothermal water from Urriðavatn lake.

Stöðvarfjörður Pool
Tiny public swimming pool with one hot tub and mountain view. Open in summer only.

UNIQUE GEOLOGY

East Iceland's mountains are formed predominantly from lava flows that piled up in volcanic eruptions over millions of years. The gradual burial of older flows under newer ones caused the buried rock to heat up. Heated groundwater, which filled cracks and holes in the lava, dissolved the rock, transported the solutes, and precipitated them to form new minerals. When the Ice Age glacier tore through layers of rock, creating fjords and valleys, the minerals became visible. The glaciers dug deeper in East Iceland than most other parts of Iceland, so the quantity and diversity of minerals is greater, too, as explained by María Helga Guðmundsdóttir, geologist at the University of Iceland's Research Centre in Breiðdalsvík.

Quirky & Curious Seaside Villages

UNWIND IN DJÚPIVOGUR AND BREIÐDALSVÍK

While **Djúpivogur** is an almost three-hour drive from Snæfellsstofa Visitor Center in Fljótsdalur on Rte 1, there's a shortcut you can take in summer. If you take Rte 95 from Fljótsdalur and then Rte 939, the scenic gravel road across Öxi mountain pass, you can get there in 1½ hours. About 40 minutes eastwards on Rte 1 lies **Breiðdalsvík**. If you want to drive there directly from Snæfellsstofa, take Rte 95, a gravel road through Breiðdalur, which is open in summer. It takes approximately 1½ hours (30 minutes quicker than along the coast on Rte 1).

Djúpivogur became the first town in Iceland to become a member of the Cittaslow movement in 2013. In short, it focuses on environmental protection and protecting cultural heritage, local food culture and production, friendliness and hospitality. As you enter the town, you're greeted by beautifully renovated old houses. In Langabúð, the village's oldest house, which dates back to 1790, you can fill up on hearty homemade soup and take a look at the heritage and sculpture museum. At the harbour you'll find *Eggin í Gleðivík*, egg sculptures by Sigurður Guðmundsson, one for each of the 34 birds that nest in the area. At Búlandsnes, you can stroll along the shore and scout the different species from birdwatching huts.

As you enter Breiðdalsvík, you're greeted by Kaupfjelagið, a charming store and cafe. It's maintained as a museum but operated as a store, still carrying products that were sold when it opened over 60 years ago. It also facilitates the Breiðdalur Geology Centre and the Drill Core Library (DCL) of the Icelandic Institute of Natural History, with an impressive collection of kilometres of drill cores.

At Hótel Breiðdalsvík, you can taste local food and Beljandi, the beer brewed across the street. The brewery's bar is open in summer. Family-run travel company Tinna Adventure offers nature exploration and reindeer-sighting tours, always with a focus on slow travel, mindfulness and local hospitality.

Fascinating Finds in Stöðvarfjörður

STONES AND OTHER CURIOSITIES

Stöðvarfjörður is another unassuming seaside village worthy of exploring. The driving distance from Snæfellsstofa Visitor Center in Fljótsdalur is approximately 1½ hours, regardless of whether you take Rte 95 through Breiðdalur (open in summer) or Rte 1 along the coast.

 BEST ROCK MUSEUMS ALONG THE COAST

Auðunn's Stone & Mineral Collection
Check out polished rainbow-coloured rocks and other minerals.

Teigarhorn
Between Djúpivogur and Breiðdalsvík lies Teigarhorn, one of the most renowned zeolite spots in the world.

Petra's Stone & Mineral Collection
Packed with colourful samples discovered in the mountains around Stöðvarfjörður.

Petra's Stone & Mineral Collection

The village's greatest attraction is **Petra's Stone & Mineral Collection**, an eccentric local woman's house turned museum dedicated to her and her husband's passion for collecting rocks. It's the largest of its kind in Europe. Petra's favourite pastime was walking out her front door, up the hills and to the mountains above, keeping an eye out for something unusual and sparkly. The house and garden are absolutely packed with colourful stones of various shapes and sizes, and it's amazing to think that almost all of them were collected by one woman. Petra passed away in 2012 but her children manage the museum.

But there are other interesting things about Stöðvarfjörður, too. Nowhere else in Iceland can you sleep in a church – **Kirkjubær** is a lovely, old, deconsecrated church that now serves as a hostel. In a defunct freezing plant, artists get creative in the **Mupimup** workshop. A three-hour hike through Jafnadalur leads to giant boulder **Einbúi**. In the valley is also a spectacular stone arch. Outside the village, by farm Lönd, is a unique **sea geyser** called Saxa.

ICELAND'S OLDEST IMAGE?

During an ongoing excavation at Stöð in Stöðvarfjörður, ancient sandstone with an image of a ship carved into it was discovered in June 2023. Such images have been found in the other Nordic countries but never before in Iceland. Archaeologist Bjarni Einarsson, the principal investigator on-site, said in an interview with mbl.is that it may be the country's oldest image. It was discovered inside the wall of one of two longhouses, which predate the official settlement of Iceland and may have served as the seasonal residence of a foreign chieftain. He appears to have been wealthy and to have operated a whaling station and whale-oil processing plant from Stöð.

GETTING AROUND

In summer, it's tempting to take shortcuts between Rte 931 and coastal towns Djúpivogur (via Rte 95 and Rte 939) and Breiðdalsvík (via Rte 95). If you do, make sure you have a 4WD. Check the weather and road conditions on safetravel.is before heading off, and drive carefully. The longer, winding coastal road (Rte 1) – which is paved all the way – is enjoyable too.

TRABANTOS/SHUTTERSTOCK ©

SEYÐISFJÖRÐUR

Seyðisfjörður

Getting here is a bit of a fairy tale on its own. Up in the Fjarðar-heiði pass you're surrounded by mountains and the view is incredible. As you snake your way down, you drive past the spectacular Gufufoss waterfall, and then the town of Seyðis-fjörður – with its colourful houses, rainbow street and blue church – gradually appears, huddling between the shore of the narrow fjord and steep mountains. No wonder that winding road inspired a scene in Ben Stiller's *The Secret Life of Walter Mitty*. At certain times, the MS *Norröna* ferry also docks in Seyðisfjörður, dwarfing the charming wooden houses around the harbour. Stroll the rainbow street and browse the stores. Blóðberg, with the black and white mural, carries Icelandic de-sign; and Handverksmarkaður, in a red house across the street, stocks hand-knitted *lopapeysa* (sweaters) and other crafts. Get ready to discover the magic that surrounds this place.

✪ REYKJAVÍK

TOP TIP

Seyðisfjörður is Iceland's only international ferry port. The MS *Norröna* ferry, operated by Smyril Line (smyril-line.com), sails between Hirtshals in Denmark to Tórshavn in the Faroe Islands and onwards to Seyðisfjörður from April to October with one weekly departure in winter and two in summer. Bring your own vehicle or book travel packages.

SERENA BAGNOLI/SHUTTERSTOCK ©

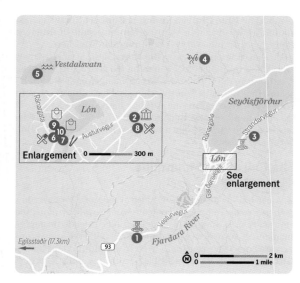

SIGHTS
1. Gufufoss
2. Skaftfell Art Center
3. Tvísöngur
4. Vestdalur
5. Vestdalsvatn

EATING
6. Kaffi Lára – El Grilló Bar
7. Norð Austur Sushi & Bar
8. Skaftfell Bistro

SHOPPING
9. Blóðberg
10. Handverksmarkaður

Tune into Seyðisfjörður's Artistic Vibe

CREATIVE COMMUNITY

That stately white timber building from 1907 is **Skaftfell Art Center**. This is the regional visual art centre for East Iceland, focusing on contemporary art. In addition to rotating exhibitions and regular cultural events, Skaftfell has an artist residency and a bistro, serving filling food, sweet treats, proper coffee and fine wine. The bistro was designed in honour of Swiss artist and Seyðisfjörður regular Dieter Roth by his son, Björn Roth, and Skaftfell's art library includes many of his books.

Take the 15- to 20-minute walk up to **Tvísöngur**. On a hill overlooking the town you'll find a sound sculpture by German artist Lukas Kühne, consisting of five concrete domes. Each has a frequency that represents one tone in the traditional Icelandic singing style *fimmundarsöngur* and is meant to amplify that particular tone.

The **List í ljósi** festival is held in February, towards the end of the darkest period, to illuminate Seyðisfjörður with glowing artwork and genuine joy. In July, the weeklong **LungA** celebrates creativity through workshops, lectures and varied

SKIING IN STAFDALUR

At a 10-minute driving distance from Seyðisfjörður is a superb skiing and snowboarding area with two disk lifts, one children's lift and slopes for snow-sport enthusiasts of all levels. Cross-country skiing tracks are made when possible. At the ski lodge, you can rent equipment and buy refreshments. Open daily December to May, weather permitting.

 BEST PLACES TO EAT IN SEYÐISFJÖRÐUR

Norð Austur Sushi & Bar
Japanese cuisine meets Icelandic fishing culture. Taste the freshest fish possible and Iceland's finest sushi. €€

Kaffi Lára – El Grillo Bar
Juicy burgers, flavourful salads and fresh fish, but the lamb is the star of the menu. €€

Skaftfell Bistro
Warm and welcoming bistro, serving seasonal dishes with a French and Mediterranean twist. €€

events. The **Blue Church Summer Concert Series** is held annually with Icelandic and foreign musicians of different genres performing every week throughout summer.

For shopping enthusiasts, **Blóðberg** design store carries everything from Sætt & Salt handmade chocolates from the Westfjords to the popular woollen garments from Icelandic label BAHNS, well suited for the whimsical Icelandic weather. In **Handverksmarkaður** you can buy handknitted *lopapeysa* sweaters in all shapes, colours and sizes made by enthusiastic locals. You can also buy unique jewellery made from ram's horns and seashells.

WHO WAS THE MOUNTAIN LADY?

The mysterious person whose remains were found in Vestdalur in 2004 – dubbed Fjallkonan or the 'Lady of the Mountain' – is believed to be a young woman who lived between 900 and 950 CE. In the hollow where she was found, there were almost 600 glass pearls and five gold, silver and bronze brooches – a unique discovery in Iceland. Archaeologist Sigurður Bergsteinsson reasons in a 2015 interview on visir.is that, in light of comparable finds in Norway, the woman may have been a sorceress.

The Call of the Mountains

HIKING TO HEAVEN

If you'd like to discover the natural side of Seyðisfjörður, there are many different ways to do so. The walk up along the Fjarðaá river is among the easier options. It leads through a small forest, to an area where blueberries, bilberries and crowberries grow (they're usually ripe from mid-August) and to **Gufufoss** waterfall. It's possible to continue along a marked path on the river's southern bank to further waterfalls and a memorial at a height of 300m. You'll be rewarded with an incredible mountain view.

Vestdalur is a valley and nature reserve on the western side of the fjord, known for unique vegetation and cultural relics. It used to be one of the main mail and trade routes in East Iceland and remnants from the route can still be seen. The 6km trail leads past waterfalls to a small lake, **Vestdalsvatn**, and a hollow where human remains from the Viking era were found in 2004.

Experienced mountaineers may be up for the **Seven Peak Challenge**. Ask for a card with the names of the peaks at the information centre (by the ferry dock). At the summit of each mountain is a different hole puncher. When you've summited all seven peaks, hand in your fully punched card and receive a certificate stating that you've completed the challenge. Henceforth you can call yourself: 'Fjallagarpur Seyðisfjarðar'. Every Fjallagarpur's name is documented in a registry and there's a special registry for those who complete the challenge in 24 hours. Always submit your travel plan and pay attention to the weather: safetravel.is.

GETTING AROUND

Once you've driven the 30 minutes from Seyðisfjörður to Egilsstaðir, most other destinations in the vicinity can be reached in about 1½ hours. To the north lie Borgarfjörður Eystri and Vopnafjörður, via Stuðlagil, and to the south, Reyðarfjörður, Fáskrúðsfjörður, Eskifjörður and Neskaupstaður.

Beyond Seyðisfjörður

Deep fjords, tall mountains and peaceful seaside villages, each with their own attractions. Discover their history and natural wonders.

The Eastfjords await. By definition, they include every fjord along the rugged eastern coastline, from Djúpivogur to Borgarfjörður Eystri. Pre-tunnels, you had to drive in and out of every fjord to travel between villages. Pre-roads, people used to travel by sea or hike across mountain passes. While scenic drives and treks are enjoyable when you have time and the weather plays along, the tunnels are a welcome improvement – and more are in the pipeline. The larger towns are connected by paved roads but there are still places that are quite isolated (including Mjóifjörður with its 15 inhabitants) and fjords like Loðmundarfjörður, which was abandoned in the 1970s. Many treasures can be discovered while journeying between the fjords.

TOP TIP

Want to party with the locals and listen to some of the hottest Icelandic acts? Bræðslan Music Festival is held in Borgarfjörður Eystri in July.

IMAGEBROKER/OLAF KRUEGER/GETTY IMAGES ©

Stórurð (p284)   283

GESTUR GISLASON/SHUTTERSTOCK ©

Former French hospital, Fáskrúðsfjörður

PUFFIN WATCHING

Approximately 5km out of town, down at the marina, is islet **Hafnarhólmi**, where puffins and other seabirds nest in summer. It has a birdwatching house where you can sit comfortably and watch puffins peek out from their burrows, fly out to sea to catch fish for their chicks and return with full beaks. The harbour also has a cafe, which doubles as a storage and shower facilities for fishers, with a wonderful view out to sea.

Admire the Colours of Borgarfjörður Eystri
THE PAINTER'S MUSE

Drive from Seyðisfjörður towards Egilsstaðir on Rte 93, then take Rte 94 to Borgarfjörður Eystri. On the way, look out for an unassuming little hut. It plays an important part in Iceland's art history as it was the summerhouse of painter Jóhannes S Kjarval (1885–1972). He grew up in Borgarfjörður Eystri and, as an adult, returned here every summer to seek inspiration from the colourful landscapes and work on his art in the quiet countryside. He painted the altarpiece for Bakkagerðiskirkja, the local church, in 1914, showing Jesus standing on Álfaborg – an elf-inhabited mound in Bakkagerði village – delivering his Sermon on the Mount with Dyrfjöll mountains in the background.

For hikers and bikers, there are plenty of trails and opportunities for enjoying the spectacular nature at your own pace, from brief outings to multiday tours. The hike to **Stórurð** below Dyrfjöll peaks is among the more popular. It's a spe-

WHERE TO EAT IN THE FJORDS

Beituskúrinn – The Bait Shack
Simple, tasty, traditional food with international flair in a renovated bait shack. €€

Randulff's Sea House
Inside an old Norwegian herring processing station, sublime seafood is served with other regional treats. €€€

L'Abri
French cuisine meets Icelandic ingredients. Delicious food, stunning ocean view from the old French hospital. €€€

cial natural phenomenon where turquoise ponds have formed between massive boulders. From the parking area off Vatnsskarð Eystra there's a 16km marked round trip. Fjord Bikes offers mountain-bike rentals and varied tours around Borgarfjörður Eystri of varied lengths, as well as snowshoeing and cross-country skiing tours in winter. For more action still, try RIB (Rigid Inflatable Boat) safari tours by Puffin Adventures, which include birdwatching – puffins and other seabirds – and sometimes seals and whales can be sighted, too.

Frystiklefinn Restaurant serves local food and beer brewed in the KHB Brewery next door. Blábjörg Resort has accommodation and also a spa, offering beer baths and kelp wraps, among other treatments.

Step Onboard Fáskrúðsfjörður's History

THE FRENCH VILLAGE

Thousands of names, appearing briefly, then disappearing into the waves. *Ocean of Memories* is a video artwork dedicated to the estimated 5000 French schooner sailors whose lives were lost in Icelandic waters. Hypnotisingly powerful, it turns Fáskrúðsfjörður's French history into a palpable experience mixed with a tinge of seasickness. It takes approximately one hour to drive from Seyðisfjörður to Fáskrúðsfjörður on Rte 1. The town is renowned known for its French Museum, where visitors are invited to step into history. Housed in the former French hospital, built in 1903 and now operated as a hotel, it includes a detailed encounter of the massive operations of French fishers off Iceland in the late 1800s and early 1900s. Fáskrúðsfjörður was one of the main fishing stations.

As you enter the museum, it seems that you've entered the hospital's waiting room, where injured sailors have lined up for treatment. Learn about the hardships the sailors faced and their relationship with the locals on multimedia screens. Then enter a replica of the tight living quarters inside the schooners and feel sorry for the lifelike wax figurines, squeezing into narrow bunks and sitting hunched at a table, cold and exhausted after hours of fishing.

Judging by the bilingual street signs, the locals treasure their French history. They look after the graveyard where the sailors, who didn't end up in a watery grave, were buried. They also celebrate an annual French Days festival – nurturing their relationship with Gravelines, the town from which most of the sailors came – at the end of July.

FILMING FORTITUDE

Fans of British television series *Fortitude* may recognise the black corrugated iron building and neon fox sign by the harbour in Reyðarfjörður. Tærgesen guesthouse and adjacent Kaffi Kósý cafe and bar played a big role in the thriller, the town standing in for Svalbard in Norway. The mural on the building next door shows an Inuit hunter and, upon closer look – a crazed polar bear.

 WHERE TO SLEEP IN THE FJORDS

Mjóeyri
Charming huts by the quiet Eskifjörður seaside. Also has bedrooms with a shared bathroom. €€€

Hildibrand Apartment Hotel
Stylish family-run hotel offering self-catering apartments in Neskaupstaður inside the town's old co-op. €€€

Fosshotel Eastfjords
Design hotel inside the beautifully renovated 1903 French hospital by the Fáskrúðsfjörður harbour. €€€

SUDDEN SNOWSTORM & ACT OF BRAVERY

During the Allied occupation of Iceland in WWII, troops set up camp around the country, including in Reyðarfjörður, or Búðareyri, as the town was known. On 20 January 1942, a large group of British soldiers hiked up Eskifjarðarheiði mountain pass with full equipment for training purposes. They were planning to cross over to Eskifjörður but took a longer route due to slippery conditions. Suddenly a snowstorm hit and the situation looked dire. One of the men noticed a light – it was a candle in the window of farm Veturhús. He collapsed outside the door but was luckily found by Páll, the farmer's son, who went to fasten the sheep house door. Páll and his brother Magnús braved the storm and carried 48 men into their house, saving their lives. Sadly, eight men perished.

Explore the Fair Fjords
OUTDOOR RECREATION AND NATURE EXPLORATION

Reyðarfjörður nestles at the foot of majestic mountains in East Iceland's longest fjord. It takes one hour to drive there from Seyðisfjörður on Rte 1. A historical centre for fishing and trade, it also became the centre for Allied operations from Iceland at the height of WWII. On 1 July 1940, British troops set up camp here, outnumbering the local residents 10 times over. Some of the barracks they built still stand. Reyðarfjörður is also a centre for employment in East Iceland, as the Alcoa-Fjarðaál aluminium smelter is located here.

A mere 15km drive will take you to **Eskifjörður**, another picturesque fjord and seaside town. It's a great base for hiking; Mjóeyri, a local travel service, is one of the organisers of Gönguvikan, a weeklong hiking festival held annually in Fjarðabyggð municipality. Outside Eskifjörður is **Helgustaðanáma**, a former Iceland spar mine now under protection. The clear, transparent calcite mineral was used to create navigational instruments and for various inventions.

A tunnel takes you onwards to **Neskaupstaður** in Norðfjörður, the easternmost town in Iceland, enclosed by tall mountains. While the main industry is fishing, volleyball has an unusually strong foothold. Heavy metal is another local passion, culminating in the annual music festival Eistnaflug. **Oddsskarð** ski resort is a beloved playground for skiers and snowboarders in winter. The swimming pools in Eskifjörður and Neskaupstaður have fun water slides, along with areas for swimming and relaxing.

The High Road to Vopnafjörður
ENTERING EAST ICELAND'S LAST OUTPOST

The northernmost town in East Iceland is **Vopnafjörður**, connected to Egilsstaðir by one of the most scenic – and highest – mountain roads in Iceland. When travelling from Seyðisfjörður, take Rte 93 to Egilsstaðir, then Rte 1 northwards, and make a turn off the main road onto Rte 917. Open in summer only, this gravel road takes you across Hellisheiði Eystri on which you climb 655m up the mountain. While not recommended for inexperienced drivers or those afraid of heights, the view from the top over the sandy beach of Héraðsflói is magnificent. If you'd rather stay on the beaten path, continue on Rte 1 until you can make a turn on Rte 85, which also leads to Vopnafjörður.

Outside the town, on Rte 920, is **Hofsárdalur** valley, through which salmon river Hofsá flows. It's popular among the En-

 BEAUTIFUL BEACHES

Héraðssandur
At 25km, Héraðssandur by Hérðasflói Bay is one of Iceland's longest black-sand beaches.

Sandvík
This long black beach in the innermost part of Vopnafjörður is popular with local families – and birds!

Urðarhólavatn Beach
Extraordinary white beach by lake Urðarhólavatn at a comfortable walking distance from Borgarfjörður Eystri.

Bustarfell, Hofsárdalur

THE RISKY NATURE OF THE MOUNTAINS

In December 2020, following heavy rainfall, Seyðisfjörður was hit by several landslides, damaging or destroying 10 buildings. Thankfully, no one was harmed.

In March 2023, two avalanches hit Neskaupstaður, smashing windows and damaging houses. No lives were lost and no one was seriously injured, partly thanks to avalanche barriers that blocked some of the snow.

Before the barriers were built, in December 1974, 12 people died when two avalanches ravaged the town. These disasters are a reminder of the risk the mountains pose under certain conditions and that further protection is necessary.

glish aristocracy and members of the royal family, including King Charles himself. This is also where one of the oldest and best-preserved traditional turf farms is located. Charming **Bustarfell**, with red wooden panels and grass on the roof, dates back to 1532 and is still owned by the same family. It is now preserved as a museum, taking visitors through the developments of Icelandic farm life of the past centuries.

While technically not in North Iceland, Vopnafjörður is included in the Birding Trail of Northeast Iceland. On birding trail.is you can find vast information on the bird species you can expect to see, and where and when you're likely to find them.

Experience the Exotic Attraction of Stuðlagil

NATURE'S CATHEDRAL

One of East Iceland's most popular attractions lies just off the Ring Road and used to be hidden in plain sight. It takes about 1½ hours to drive there from Seyðisfjörður. Take Rte 93 to Egilsstaðir, then Rte 1 northwards until you take a turn

 FUN FESTIVALS

Vopnaskak
Art, culture, activities and family fun. Held in Vopnafjörður in late June/ early July.

Eistnaflug
This friendly heavy metal festival takes place in Neskaupstaður in early July.

Franskir Dagar
French Days are celebrated in Fáskrúðsfjörður in late July in honour of its history.

SALMON & SWIMMING

Two of Iceland's best salmon fishing rivers, Hofsá and Selá, are located in Vopnafjörður. In addition to Atlantic salmon, Arctic char and sea trout can be caught there. The lodges offer first-class accommodation, breakfast, lunch and dinner by the resident chef and view of the rivers from the bedroom windows. See thesixriversfoun dation.com for more information.

While not everyone can afford a fly-fishing adventure, everyone can enjoy a swim along the banks of a salmon river. The public swimming pool in Vopnafjörður, the small country pool Selárdalslaug, was built on the banks of the Selá in 1949 and is still in operation.

on Rte 923. Of course, locals in Jökuldalur were aware of Stuðlagil, the ravine through which Jökulsá á Dal flows and its spectacular columnar basalt formations. However, the glacial river used to be more voluminous and the water murkier. In 2007, the Kárahnjúkar power plant was built and, to create the Hálslón dam, the water flow to Jökulsá was drastically reduced. As a result, the full 30m extent of the columns was exposed, including a layer of red rock, and the water gained an exotic turquoise colour.

The adventure begins by crossing the bridge across Jökulsá á Dal by the farm Klaustursel, followed by a 10km walk along a dirt road. Enjoy the sight of sheep and goats grazing peacefully, the sound of clucking geese, and 5km on, you reach a second car park (accessible by 4WD vehicle). Make a point of bringing a small amount of money for the donation box. It's for the hospitable farmers of Klaustursel who are working on improving the facilities. Take in the beauty of Stuðlafoss waterfall before continuing to Stuðlagil. If you'd rather skip the long walk, you can drive past Klaustrsel to the viewing platform at Grund.

But up close is more impressive. When the conditions are safe, you can even climb down into the ravine and take in its full beauty. It feels a bit like standing inside a cathedral, except these columns aren't made by humans; it's nature's artwork, the columnar basalt formed in an ancient eruption when the lava contracted while cooling. Straight, slanting and irregular – some rusty red – they form a magnificent frame to the blue-green river.

Stop at a Ring Road Curiosity

SCENIC PIT STOP

After driving from Seyðisfjörður on Rte 93 through Egilsstaðir and onwards to North Iceland on Rte 1 northwards, you'll pass the road sign to Stuðlagil in 1½ hours. Soon, you'll notice a change in scenery. No trees, no grass, no sign of life, just barren landscapes and a black-sand desert. This is **Möðrudalsöræfi**, a part of the Ring Road leading through the highland plateau. It can get very windy here, and in winter snowstorms are not uncommon.

At the intersection of Rte 1 and Rte 901, approximately two hours from Seyðisfjörður, is **Beitarhúsið**, perhaps the most curious pit stop on the Ring Road. The restaurant and cafe are an outpost from Möðrudalur á Fjöllum (p305) – Iceland's highest-located farm – built in the style of a stately turf house, with a wooden panel front and grass on the roof. Here you can try traditional Icelandic fare. Warm up on lamb soup and

 MEMORABLE MUSEUMS

East Iceland Maritime Museum
Learn about the history of seafaring in the Eastfjords in an old store in Eskifjörður.

Neskaupstaður's Museum House
Learn about natural history, a local painter's art and seafaring, and visit an old smithy.

Auroras Iceland
A collection of spectacular Northern Lights pictures by local photographers in Fáskrúðsfjörður.

Stuðlagil (p287)

RJÚKANDI WATERFALL

Slow down before reaching Stuðlagil, because if you don't, you'll miss Rjúkandi (also known as Ysti-Rjúkandi). The 139m-high waterfall can be seen from the Ring Road. Park the car and walk for a few minutes to take in the view of the tiered fall and Jökuldalur valley. It's also possible to follow the marked trail to the edge of the waterfall and sign the guestbook kept there. Further to the west is another waterfall called Rjúkandi, or Fremsti-Rjúkandi, which can also be seen from the road. It's popular to walk between the two sister falls.

have delicious *ástarpungar* (love balls) doughnuts with your coffee while enjoying the view of Herðubreið mountain. You can fuel up your car too!

If you continue on Rte 901, you'll reach Möðrudalur. At a height of 469m, the farm is the last hint of human habitation before the vast northeastern highlands take over. The weather can get pretty rough here; in fact, the coldest temperature ever recorded in Iceland (-38°C) was in Möðrudalur in January 1918. Today, tourism company Fjalladýrð offers visitors authentic Icelandic experiences at Möðrudalur, accommodation in a traditional turf farm and hearty homemade food, along with tours of the wilderness.

GETTING AROUND

The gravel mountain road (Rte 953) to Mjóifjörður, which has only 15 inhabitants, is often closed, especially in winter. From October through May a ferry goes from Neskaupstaður to Mjóifjörður twice a week.

XIU YU PHOTOGRAPHY/SHUTTERSTOCK ©

THE HIGHLANDS

RUGGED, RAW, WILD ICELANDIC INTERIOR

Challenging routes cross Iceland's hinterlands, accessible only in the height of summer, when roads open and soaring volcanic landscapes beckon.

The interior highlands' undulating multi-coloured lava flows, creeping glaciers, seething volcanoes, and vast, unbroken horizons of sand, rock and mountain feel like another world. Gazing across the unspoilt, remote expanses, you could imagine yourself, as many have noted, on the moon or Mars. Those aren't overactive imaginations – Apollo astronauts trained here before their lunar landing and NASA trains here for Mars missions.

The highlands are home to Iceland's King and Queen of the Mountains, and the only sign of life you'll see (besides other homo sapiens) is an occasional delicate moss or flower, or the vibrant ripple of bright green where vegetation grows along a hot river. The isolation and the humbling scale of the natural world in its rawest form are the reason people visit.

The solitude is exhilarating, the views unending. But there are practically no services, accommodation or bridges over rivers – or guarantees if something goes wrong, so travel to the highlands is not something to be undertaken lightly. It's vital to research road access, weather conditions and refuelling spots, and to choose the right vehicle and travel supplies for your trip (a 4WD is a necessity; you will need to self-cater). You can simplify things by opting for a bus or super-Jeep tour. Be prepared with logistics and your spirit of adventure.

ANNASOFFIA / 500PX/GETTY IMAGES ©

THE MAIN AREAS

KJÖLUR ROUTE
North–south with all rivers bridged.
p294

SPRENGISANDUR ROUTE
North–south with large rivers to ford.
p298

ASKJA ROUTE
Access from Iceland's north to Askja caldera, Herðubreið and Holuhraun. **p301**

KVERKFJÖLL ROUTE
From the north or east to Kverkfjöll ice caves and glacier.
p306

Above: Herðubreið (p303). Left: Moss growing on lava   291

Find Your Way

Access to the highlands depends on mountain roads being open – which is determined by weather conditions. Check road.is for practical information, or phone 1777 for updates.

Askja Route (Öskjuleið), p301

Rte F88 or F905/910. Hike across the lava field, drinking in the caldera views, then gazing at the waters of Víti crater.

Kverkfjöll Route, p306

Rte F905, F910, then F902. Marvel at the openings of geothermal caves in a vast glacier.

Kjölur Route, p294

Rte 35. Spice up endless vistas of rock and ice with stops at hot springs and climbable crags.

Sprengisandur Route, p298

Rte F26. Pity the melancholy ghosts and outlaws on Iceland's longest, loneliest north–south track.

4WD VEHICLES

Highlands routes are strictly for robust, high-clearance 4WD vehicles (not 4WD passenger cars or little Dacia Dusters), as jagged terrain and treacherous river crossings are common. Know how to cross a river before setting out – this is not the place to learn – and ask rangers/visitor centres/experienced locals about current river conditions before going. The easiest route to drive is the Kjölur Route. Always make sure your rental vehicle is insured for F-road travel. River crossings are not insured (ie you'll be stuck with the bill).

GUIDES

Licenced tour operators sometimes gain access to roads before and after regular people are allowed in. They are, by definition, safer bets for highland travel, plus knowledgable guides offer fascinating information on this unusual terrain.

Note: Roads in this area are subject to flooding.

Móðrudalur

Drekagil

Askja (Öskju) Caldera

Askja Route (Öskjuleið)

Kverkfjöll Route

Virkisfell

Kverkfjöll

Holuhraun

Vatnajökull

Íshólsvatn

Sprengisandur Route

Jökulfall

Dyngjujökull

Bárðarbunga

Old Gæsavatnaleið (Rjúpnab)

Grímsvötn (1719m)

Tungnafellsjökull

Nýidalur (1083m)

Skaftafell (Vatnajökull National Park South)

Torfufell (1241m)

Laugafell

Laugafell (879m)

Skagafjörður Approach

Hofsjökull

Berghnúkstest

Hágnupur

Blöndulón Reservoir

Áfangi Hut

4WD Only

Hveravellir Nature Reserve

Geirsalda

Beinahóll

Kerlingarfjöll

Highland Base Kerlingarfjöll

Héraðsdalir

Versalir

Kjalvötn

Gíslaskáli Hut

Langjökull

Hvítárvatn

Blágil (1204m)

4WD Only

Fremstaver Hut

Gullfoss

50 km
30 miles

0
0

Askja caldera (p304)

Plan Your Time

The interior highlands have few sleeping options: basic campsites, few huts (reserve ahead) and a couple of mountain lodges. Most people stay on the edge of the highlands then make forays to the interior.

Preparation & Safety

● **Safety** Read up on alerts and advice on safetravel.is; enquire about conditions and river crossings along your way with rangers (national park maps have their phone numbers), visitor centres and local experts.

● **Weather Conditions** Fickle and it can snow, even in midsummer. Check vedur.is (and its app) for forecasts.

● **Log Your Plan** Leave a travel plan at safetravel.is. When you stop into huts write your plan in the guestbook and tell rangers where you are going.

● **Mapping** Have good paper maps and GPS gear – don't just rely on your mobile phone, which will lose signal.

● **Supplies** Depending on your itinerary you may need additional fuel. You will certainly need food – only three or four places sell any.

SEASONAL ACCESS

PLAN AHEAD
It's vital to research road access, weather conditions and refuelling spots, and to choose the right vehicle.

SUMMER ROADS OPEN
Openings occur any time from June to early July.

AUTUMN ROADS CLOSE
Roads become impassable and are closed again in September or October.

WINTER ACCESS
Possible to some areas, but only on guided tours by snowmobile or super-Jeep, driven by local professionals.

KJÖLUR ROUTE

Kjölur Route

☉ REYKJAVÍK

If you want to sample Iceland's central deserts but don't like the idea of ford crossings, the 200km Kjölur (pronounced *kyu*-loor) route has had all of its rivers bridged. In summer there have even been high-suspension buses, but at the time of writing there were none in operation. The route got jazzed up in 2023 by the first luxe highlands establishment: Highland Base Kerlingarfjöll.

From the south, Rte 35 starts just past Gullfoss, passing between two large glaciers before emerging near Blönduós on the north-west coast. It reaches its highest point (around 700m) between the Langjökull and Hofsjökull ice caps, near the mountain Kjalfell (1000m). Its northern section cruises scenically past Blöndulón, a large reservoir used by the Blanda hydroelectric power station. Road conditions in the north are better than those in the south.

The Kjölur route usually opens in June, and closes sometime in September, depending on weather conditions.

TOP TIP

Kerlingarfjöll, Árbúðir (Kaffi Kjölur) and Hveravellir offer food, but you need to bring self-catering supplies for all other overnighting options. Huts generally have kitchen access, but utensils are not guaranteed and campers are not allowed in some huts. Campers need to bring cooking equipment and stoves (campfires are not permitted).

ALBERTO LOYO/SHUTTERSTOCK ©

Hveradalir (p296)

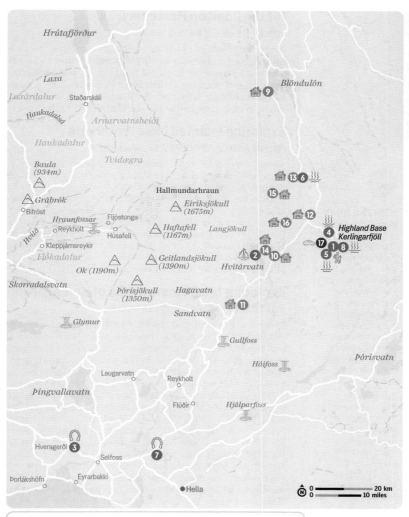

HIGHLIGHTS
1 Highland Base Kerlingarfjöll

SIGHTS
2 Hvítárvatn

ACTIVITIES, COURSES & TOURS
3 Eldhestar
4 Highland Base Baths

5 Hveradalir
6 Hveravellir Nature Reserve
7 Íslandshestar
8 Snækollur

SLEEPING
9 Áfangi Hut
10 Árbúðir Hut
11 Fremstaver Hut

12 Gíslaskáli Hut
13 Hveravellir New Hut/ Old Hut
14 Hvítárnes Hut
15 Þjófadalir Hut
16 Þverbrekknamúli Hut

TRANSPORT
17 Parking Area/Mt Keis

Hit the Road on Horseback

RIDING THE OPEN RANGE

What better way to catch old-world vibes than to cover the Kjölur route on horseback. Multiday tours follow the track, a slow-mo way to feel the wind in your hair. **Íslandshestar** has rides overnighting in their three huts on the route, while **Eldhestar** horse farm's offerings also take in the Sprengisandur region. Look online and search the term 'Kjalvegur' too.

Exploring Isolated Lake Hvítárvatn

HIKING AND CAMPING AT A GLACIAL LAKE

The pale-blue lake Hvítárvatn, 35km northeast of Gullfoss, is the source of the glacial river Hvítá – popular for white-water rafting. A glacier tongue of Iceland's second-largest ice cap, Langjökull, calves into the lake and creates icebergs occasionally, adding to the beauty of this rarified spot.

In the marshy grasslands northeast of Hvítárvatn is Ferðafélag Íslands' (Iceland Touring Association; fi.is) oldest hut, **Hvítárnes Hut** (N 64°37.007', W 19°45.394'), built in 1930. It has a warden for most of July and some of August and sleeps 30. The kitchen has a stove, but no utensils. Beds must be reserved.

Exploring the Coloured Hills of Kerlingarfjöll

HOT SPRING VALLEYS AND STRIPED HILLS

Icelanders believed that the Kerlingarfjöll mountain range (10km off Rte 35 on Rte F347) harboured the worst outlaws. It was thought they lived in the heart of the 150-sq-km series of peaks in an isolated Shangri-la-type valley. It was only in the mid-19th century that anyone ventured into Kerlingarfjöll. In 1941 the range was properly explored by Ferðafélag Íslands.

The colourfully dramatic landscape is broken up into jagged peaks and ridges, the highest of which is **Snækollur** (1477m), and it's scattered with hot springs. The striated steaming geothermal valley **Hveradalir** is a highlight. A stunningly colourful but difficult 5km hike ascends from Highland Base Kerlingarfjöll to this roiling pot of geothermal mist and colourful scree hills. Check on conditions before undertaking it, though – it's usually too muddy to be safe until well into July. Most people opt to drive the 15 minutes to a **parking area at Mt Keis**, from where Hveradalir is a short, steep walk downhill.

Prebook to join one of the several different guided hikes offered by Highland Base Kerlingarfjöll twice daily July to mid-September (except one on Monday).

BEST MULTIDAY HIKES

Old Kjalvegur route
An easy and scenic three-day hike (39km) from Hvítárvatn to Hveravellir (or vice versa) follows the original horseback Kjölur route (west of the present road), via the Hvítárnes, Þverbrekknamúli and Þjófadalir mountain huts (fi.is).

Hringbrautin
The challenging three-day circuit (47km) around Kerlingarfjöll starts and ends at Highland Base Kerlingarfjöll with huts at Kisubotnar and Grákollur opening in autumn 2024.

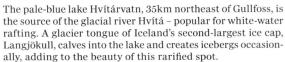

HUTS ON THE KJÖLUR ROUTE

Beds in huts run by Ferðafélag Ísland (fi.is; 568 2533) and Íslandshestar (islandshestar.is; 699 2004) must be booked in advance. Some huts have bathrooms and cooking facilities, and space to pitch a tent.

There are three well-appointed Íslandshestar huts on or just off the Kjölur route, for drivers, hikers and horse riders.

Ferðafélag Ísland day-use fee is 500kr to use toilets or the outdoor grill.

Living It Up at Highland Base Kerlingarfjöll
HOT POOLS, SNOWMOBILING, TREKKING AND MORE

For many years, Kerlingarfjöll was the site of a highland centre used by Icelanders for hiking and skiing. In 2023 the Blue Lagoon company completed a massive renovation to transform it into Highland Base Kerlingarfjöll. Designed as a year-round venue, it has a rich offering in hikes as well as the chance to rent electric mountain bikes in summer.

Launched in October 2023, the **Highland Base Baths** have a trio of hot-pots, cold plunge and sauna, and there's also a natural hot springs a half-hour walk from the base.

In winter, Amazing Tours leads adventures from Hveradalir snow-shoe treks to snowmobiling on Hofsjökull glacier and back-country skiing. They offer super-Jeep transfers to Highland Base in winter as the roads are closed (18,000kr one way).

The complex offers a broad range of accommodation, from a hotel to shared and private huts, and camping. Plus there's a restaurant, with sweeping views, which serves lunch à la carte and a dinner buffet (8900kr). They operate two mountain huts, allowing a three-day loop walk in the area.

Unwinding at the Hveravellir Oasis
HOT SPRINGS AND SUSTENANCE

The popular geothermal area of fumaroles and hot springs called **Hveravellir Nature Reserve** (hveravellir.is; summer 452 4200, year-round 894 1293) is located between Gullfoss and the Ring Road. Among its warm pools are the brilliant-blue Bláhver; Öskurhólshver, which emits a constant stream of hissing steam; and a luscious human-made bathing pool. Another hot spring, Eyvindurhver, is named after the outlaw Fjalla-Eyvindur. Hveravellir is reputedly one of the many highland hideouts of this renegade. Lovely trails crisscross the area and you can pick up information from helpful staff at the **New Hut**, which has private rooms with shared bathrooms (no cooking facilities). The **Old Hut** sleeps about 30 in dorm beds (linen available for 2200kr) with cooking facilities. There's also a campsite, simple cafe and teeny store, as well as device charging and wi-fi hot spot for a fee. It also operates the **Áfangi Hut**, about 38km north, near Blöndulón reservoir.

A service fee (500kr) applies for all day guests using parking, the hot-pot, toilets or showers.

THE BADLANDS

Historically in Iceland, once a person had been convicted of outlawry they were beyond society's protection and aggrieved enemies could kill them at will. Many outlaws (*útilegumenn*), such as the renowned Eiríkur Rauðe (Erik the Red), voluntarily took exile abroad. Others escaped revenge killing by fleeing into the mountains, valleys and broad expanses of the harsh Icelandic interior, where few dared pursue them.

Undoubtedly, anyone who could live year-round in these bitter, barren deserts must have been extraordinary. Icelandic outlaws were naturally credited with all sorts of fearsome feats, and the general populace came to fear the vast badlands, which they considered to be the haunt of superhuman evil. The *útilegumenn* thereby joined the ranks of giants and trolls, and provided the themes for popular tales such as the fantastic *Grettir's Saga*.

GETTING AROUND

The Kjölur route is labelled Rte 35 (not F35), but it is still a mountain road, and while it is technically possible to drive a 2WD along the route, it is absolutely not sanctioned (posted signs are clear on this!). Car-hire companies expressly forbid the use of 2WD rentals on the route and you will be liable for any damage (there are potholes and puddles that could almost swallow a small car, you'll damage the car's underside, and your journey will be slow and very bumpy).

Drivers with 4WD vehicles should be able to manage the Kjölur route. If you're in a 2WD and curious for a taste of the highlands, you can drive the first 14km of the route (north of Gullfoss), which is sealed.

SPRENGISANDUR ROUTE

Sprengisandur

⟳ REYKJAVÍK

To Icelanders, the name Sprengisandur conjures up images of outlaws, ghosts and long sheep drives across the barren wastes. The Sprengisandur route (F26) is the longest north–south trail, and crosses bleak desert moors that can induce a shudder even today in a 4WD. An older route, now abandoned, lies a few kilometres west of the current one.

This route requires large river fords so is best kept to a tour or those with highland river-crossing experience and a hardy high-suspension 4WD vehicle. In addition to the in-demand accommodation at the Highland Center Hrauneyjar, there are huts along the route (BYO sleeping bag) and camping areas. It's necessary to prebook hut beds and pack all of your food (and remove all your rubbish). This route usually opens late, from late June to mid-July, and closes sometime in September, depending on weather conditions.

TOP TIP

There's no fuel along the route. Goðafoss to Hrauneyjar is 240km. The nearest petrol stations are: Akureyri (from the Eyjafjörður approach); Varmahlíð (from the Skagafjörður approach) or Fosshóll, near Goðafoss (if you're coming from the north along the main route through Bárðardalur). In the south there is petrol at Hrauneyjar.

ANDY SUTTON/ALAMY STOCK PHOTO ©

Nýidalur range

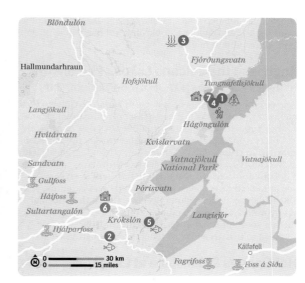

SIGHTS
1 Tungnafellsjökull

ACTIVITIES, COURSES & TOURS
2 Landmannahellir
3 Laugafell
4 Nýidalur
5 Veiðivötn

SLEEPING
6 Highland Center Hrauneyja
7 Nýidalur Hut

Hiking Around the Nýidalur Range

TRAMPING IN THE MIDDLE OF ICELAND

Nýidalur (also known as Jökuldalur), the range just south of the **Tungnajökull** ice cap, was discovered by a lost traveller in 1845. With facilities including a campsite and huts, plus appealing hiking trails, it's the most popular rest spot for travellers along the Sprengisandur route. It's about 100km from Hrauneyjar. The Vatnajökull National Park ranger (vjp. is; July and August, 842 4377) stationed here in summer can advise on trail conditions and routes like the one up to Tungnafell or along Mjóháls ridge into Vonarskarð. It's smart to let them know you are going before you head out.

There are two rivers en route to Nýidalur – the one 500m from the hut is usually difficult to cross (even for a 4WD). Ask locally for advice on conditions and always check weather forecasts as it can snow up there (830m).

The **Nýidalur Hut** (fi.is; N 64°44.130', W 18°04.350'; July and August, 860 3334) is actually two huts (sleeping up to 79

ÞÓRISVATN

Before water was diverted from Kaldakvísl into Þórisvatn from the Tungnaá hydroelectric scheme in southwest Iceland, it was 70 sq km. Now it's one of the country's largest lakes at 85 sq km. The glacial-blue-green lake is 11km northeast of the junction between Rte F26 and the Fjallabak route (F208) and about 19km northeast from Hrauneyjar.

HIGHLAND CENTER HRAUNEYJAR

At the crossroads of the Sprengisandur route (F26) and the F208 to Landmannalaugar, the Highland Center Hrauneyjar is handy for highland attractions. A Vatnajökull National Park ranger (vjp.is, 842 4376) in summer advises on local conditions and walking trails. You can buy basic supplies, petrol and diesel, but bring most necessities from further afield.

The centre has a year-round guesthouse and hotel in the middle of lava and scree fields west of Þórisvatn. The simpler guesthouse has smaller rooms, sleeping-bag accommodation and a restaurant. The hotel, about 1.4km away, offers larger, more luxurious rooms, a smart restaurant, hot-pot and sauna.

MULTIDAY HIGHLAND TOURS

In addition to day tours to Askja, Kverkfjöll and Laugafell, multiday tours explore the central highlands. Operators such as **Fjalladýrð** (fjalladyrd. is) at Möðrudalur and **Geo Travel** (geotravel. is) at Mývatn offer overnight excursions.

Ferðafélag Akureyrar (ffa.is) organises five-day hut-to-hut hiking tours along the Askja Trail.

Eldhestar (eldhestar.is) leads six-day wilderness horse-riding treks along the Kjölur and Sprengisandur routes, for very experienced riders, as does **Íslandshestar**.

Icelandic Mountain Guides (mountainguides. is) offers 10-day winter ski trips on the Sprengisandur route.

people) with kitchen facilities, showers (500kr) and a summer warden (July and August). Book your bed in advance. Campers cannot use hut facilities.

Angling at the Volcano Lakes of Veiðivötn
FISH FOR TROUT AND SLEEP UNDER THE MIDNIGHT SUN

You will always remember the beautiful area of Veiðivötn (pronounced *veeth*-i-vutn), just northeast of Landmannalaugar – a shimmering entanglement of small desert lakes in a volcanic basin. It's a continuation of the same fissure that produced Laugahraun in the Fjallabak Nature Reserve and besides gazing in wonder, it's a popular place for trout fishing.

It's about 30km from the Highland Center Hrauneyjar's accommodation, or there are basic huts and camping available in summer, plus fishing licences. Check the informative veidivotn.is site or email ampi@simnet.is. Licences for lakes further south are sold at **Landmannahellir**.

Access to this area is via Rte F228, east of Hrauneyjar.

Hot Springs & Sunshine at Laugafell
GEOTHERMAL SOAKING AND HIGHLAND HUTS

Wonderful Laugafell is an 879m-high mountain with hot springs bubbling on its northwestern slopes. You can stay nearby at the hiker huts (ffa.is; N 65°01.630', W 18°19.950'; July and August, 833 5697) operated by Ferðafélag Akureyrar, whose best feature is the geothermally heated, natural swimming pool. The two huts have 32 beds and a kitchen, plus are heated using the local geothermal water. Cushy! There's a warden on-site in July, August and early September.

Laugafell is on both the Skagafjörður approach (93km via Rte 752 and F752) and the Eyjafjörður approach (87km south of Akureyri via Rte 821 and F821) to the Sprengisandur route. A few tour companies out of Akureryi/Mývatn offer 4WD day tours to this area, including Geo Travel.

APPROACHING SPRENGISANDUR FROM THE NORTH

In the north, the Sprengisandur route offers several variations. The route proper begins at Rte 842 near Goðafoss in northwest Iceland. After 41km, you'll pass through a metal gate as the road turns into F26. A billboard explains the sights and finer points of the route, and 1km later you'll come upon one of Iceland's most photogenic waterfalls, Aldeyjarfoss. Water bursts over the cliff's edge as it splashes through a narrow canyon lined with honeycomb columns of basalt. Just a bit further lie the multiple chutes of Hrafnabjargafoss, 1km down a signposted turnoff.

After the waterfalls, the route continues through 240km of inhospitable territory all the way to Þjórsárdalur. There are two other ways to approach Sprengisandur, both of which link up to the main road about halfway through:

Eyjafjörður Approach From the north, the F821 from southern Eyjafjörður (south of Akureyri) connects to the Skagafjörður approach at Laugafell.

Skagafjörður Approach From the northwest, the 81km-long F752 connects southern Skagafjörður (the nearest town is Varmahlíð on the Ring Road) to the Sprengisandur route. The roads join near the lake Fjórðungsvatn (pronounced fyorth-ungs-vatn), 20km east of Hofsjökull.

The main route opens around the start of July.

ASKJA ROUTE

Askja Route ●

⊘ REYKJAVÍK

The brilliant Askja route (Öskjuleið) runs across the multihued highlands to Herðubreið (1682m), the Icelanders' beloved 'Queen of the Mountains'; the idyllic, green oasis Herðubreiðarlindir; and onward to the region's most popular marvel, the immense Askja (Öskju) caldera with its lake. Not to be forgotten is the little crater lake, Víti, alongside with its cerulean waters shining brighter than Askja's grander one.

Rock formations are another star of the show, with everything from one of Iceland's newest lava fields, Holuhraun, to dragon-shaped pinnacles at Drekagil, plus volcanic soils and rocks in myriad hues.

The usual access road is Rte F88, which leaves the Ring Road 32km east of Mývatn and has deep rivers that are not safe for smaller 4WDs. The route slightly east via Rtes F905 and F910 (close to Möðrudalur) has more reliable river crossings. The route tends to open sometime in mid- to late June.

TOP TIP

Askja is part of the vast Vatnajökull National Park – see vjp.is for excellent information and hiking maps. A visitor centre is due to open near Mývatn at Skútustaðir. National park rangers are stationed at Drekagil (842 4357), Herðubreiðarlindir and Askja in summer, and give daily walking tours, from mid-July to mid-August at Askja, Herðubreiðarlindir and Holuhraun.

NIKPAL/GETTY IMAGES ©

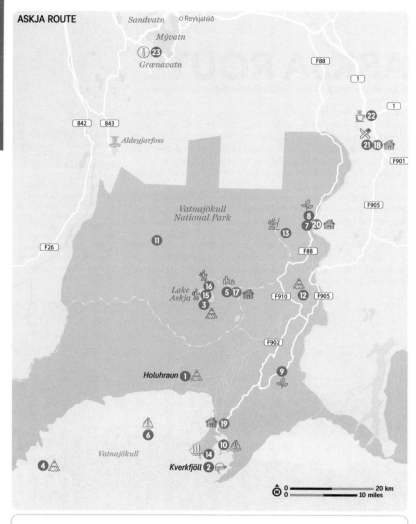

ASKJA ROUTE

Sandvatn ○ Reykjahlíð

Mývatn

Grænavatn

Aldeyjarfoss

Vatnajökull National Park

Lake Askja

Holuhraun

Vatnajökull

Kverkfjöll

N 0 ——————— 20 km
   0 ——————— 10 miles

HIGHLIGHTS
1 Holuhraun
2 Kverkfjöll

SIGHTS
3 Askja (Öskju) Caldera
4 Bárðarbunga
5 Drekagil
6 Dyngjujökull
7 Fjalla-Eyvindur

8 Herðubreiðarlindir
9 Hvannalindir
10 Kverkjökull
11 Ódáðahraun
12 Upptyppingar Hills

ACTIVITIES, COURSES & TOURS
13 Herðubreið
14 Hveradalur

15 Öskjuvatn
16 Víti

SLEEPING
17 Dreki Huts
18 Möðrudalur
19 Sigurðarskáli Hut
20 Þorsteinsskáli Hut

EATING
21 Fjallakaffi

DRINKING & NIGHTLIFE
22 Beitarhúsið

INFORMATION
23 Skútustaðir Visitor Center

Hiking in Verdant Herðubreiðarlindir

OUTLAW HIDEOUT IN LUSH LANDS

The oasis Herðubreiðarlindir, a nature reserve thick with green moss, angelica and the pinky-purple flower of the Arctic river beauty *Epilobium latifolium*, was created by springs flowing from beneath the Óðáðahraun lava. You get a superb close-up view of Herðubreið from here (unless, of course, you're greeted by dense fog and/or a wall of blowing sand).

Stay at the appealing hut and campsite here, with a summertime ranger station. Behind the hut is a **Fjalla-Eyvindur** 'convict hole'. Outlaw Eyvindur (p306) is believed to have occupied it during the winter of 1774–75, when he subsisted on angelica root, raw horsemeat stored on top of the hideout to retain heat inside, and water from the stream running through the hole.

The popular 25-bed **Þorsteinsskáli Hut** (ffa.is; N 65°11.544', W 16°13.360'; 822 5191) offers a greener, more welcoming landscape than that encountered at Drekagil. The cosy lodge has showers (500kr) and a kitchen. Book hut beds in advance. It's operated by the Touring Club of Akureyri and is the start of the Askja Trail, an ambitious five-day trek best tackled on one of their guided hikes.

Herðubreiðarlindir is about 60km from Hrossaborg, at the northern point of Rte F88, and another 35km on to Drekagil.

Herðubreið, the Queen of the Mountains

THAT'S ONE DISTINCTIVE PEAK

Icelanders call Herðubreið (pronounced *hair*-the-breth), its most distinctive mountain (1682m), the 'Queen of the Mountains'. Majestic Herðubreið (meaning 'Broad Shoulders') is visible for miles around, and it crops up time and again in the work of local poets and painters, entranced by its beauty.

It's a *móberg* mountain, formed by subglacial volcanic eruptions. In fact, if Vatnajökull was to suddenly be stripped of ice, Grímsvötn and Kverkfjöll would probably emerge looking more or less like Herðubreið. From the Þorsteinsskáli hut in Herðubreiðarlindir, a marked trail runs to Herðubreið.

If you wish to climb the mountain, beware: as serenely beautiful as the queen may be, the hike is unrelenting and dangerous if you're not properly prepared. In the spring, falling rocks alter paths and topography. Clouds often shroud

NORTHERN HIGHLANDS

Elísabet and Villi, the farm owners and hotel, restaurant and tour operators at Möðrudalur, come from a long line of Möðrudalur folk. They share what they love about their home region. @fjalladyrd, fjalladyrd.is

The highlands north of Vatnajökull are a hidden gem. If you are looking for peaceful and powerful nature with little traffic we recommend visiting Hvannalindir, Kverkfjöll and Hafrahvammagljúfur. We enjoy them on a perfect day trip from Möðrudalur farm...where you can experience the wilderness spirit, untouched expanses, black sand, lava fields, silver-sparkling rivers, the presence of the glacier, rugged highland vegetation and wildlife.

TOURS IN THE ASKJA AREA

If you're short on time, grab an exhilarating scenic helicopter flight from Möðrudalur with Glacier Heli (glacierheli.is).

Several operators run super-Jeep tours to Askja, from mid- to late June until September or October as weather permits.

From Akureyri, it's a long day (up to 15 hours); a better base is Reykjahlíð at Mývatn (even then, the tour time is around 11 to 12 hours),

or better yet Möðrudalur (nine or 10 hours). For a more relaxed pace (and a chance to experience the highlands' evening stillness), consider a two-day tour.

Bring a packed lunch and water. Some operators stop for late-afternoon coffee at Möðrudalur en route home. Don't forget your swimsuit and towel in case you fancy a chilly dip in Víti crater.

BIRTH OF A LAVA FIELD

On 16 August 2014, sensors picked up increased seismic activity around **Bárðarbunga**, one of many volcanoes underneath Vatnajökull. The magma in Bárðarbunga formed an 'intrusive dike' (tunnel of magma) through the ground under an outlet glacier named Dyngjujökull. On 29 August, the magma surfaced – a fissure eruption, complete with spectacular lava fountains, began in Holuhraun, a 200-year-old lava field about 5km away from the Dyngjujökull glacial edge.

The eruption continued for almost six months; Iceland's largest for 230 years. Impressive stats: 85 sq km in area (larger than the island of Manhattan), averaging about 10m to 14m thick, and weighing about the same as a herd of 600 million elephants.

the mountain. A GPS is a must, as is a helmet, crampons and ice axe (and experience using them). Don't go alone, prepare for foul weather, and it is required that you discuss your intentions with the wardens at Herðubreiðarlindir. Consider joining a tour – Fjalladýrð at Möðrudalur can arrange this.

Chasing Waterfalls in Drekagil

WALK UP 'DRAGON CANYON'

The name of the gorge Drekagil, 35km southwest of Herðubreið, means 'Dragon Canyon', after the shapes of dragons in the craggy rock formations that tower over it. A hike up the twisting gorge (behind the Dreki huts) leads to an impressive waterfall that is only accessible when the river is low enough to pass.

The **Dreki huts** (ffa.is) are an ideal base for exploring the area. Day-use of the facilities (toilet etc) costs 500kr per person. You can also walk (or drive) 8km up the marked trail to Askja, and take a 20km trail to the Bræðrafell (pronounced bri-thra-fetl) hut. Book with Dreki summertime rangers (842 4357; 8am to 7pm) first, as the hut is locked.

Walking Fresh Lava in Holuhraun

SEE SOME OF ICELAND'S NEWEST LAVA

The huge lava field Holuhraun is young as can be, created in 2014–15 during the Bárðarbunga eruption. Sightseeing flights (p303) grant you a sense of its vastness, or reach it by road (F910) following signs from Drekagil for 24km to reach a car park. The marked trail clearly reveals the difference between the old lava field and the new, and the interplay of lava and river.

Park rangers at Drekagil provide information and safety precautions about Holuhraun and offer free one-hour walking tours starting at the car park (once daily, mid-July to mid-August). The area is still volcanically active: stay on the tracks and signed trails at all times. Some Askja day tours also visit Holuhraun.

Investigating Askja & its Two Crater Lakes

CERULEAN WATERS AND SENSORY DELIGHT

The utterly remote and inspiring Askja caldera is the main destination for all tours in this northeastern part of the highlands. This immense 50-sq-km caldera shouldn't be missed – as you walk into the multicoloured snow-rimmed site you'll find it difficult to imagine the sorts of forces that created it.

Wait for your first glimpse of the sapphire-blue lake **Öskjuvatn**, at the heart of the crater, as you crunch through sienna

ASKJA ROUTE PRACTICAL PLANNING

There's no public transport, but there are plenty of tours. Or, hire a large 4WD jeep and prepare for a rocky ride (seek local/ranger advice on fording rivers). There are no fuel stops anywhere on the route. The nearest ones are at Möðrudalur (90km from Askja) and Mývatn (120km from Askja). Plan accordingly.

FOR MOUNTAIN CLIMBERS

If you love a good mountain ascent, other thrilling climbs include littler **Laki** (p159) or Iceland's tallest, **Hvannadalshnúkur** (p156).

Holuhraun lava field

and magenta stones. The lake stands in contrast to the milky cerulean waters inside the small, steep crater **Víti**, adjacent to the caldera.

Although a bit on the chilly side (temperatures are currently about 22°C), a dip in Víti's milky blue pool was once a highlight of an Askja adventure (sometimes done sans swimsuit). But low PH and high uncertainty level on volcanic activity means park officials have had to prohibit swimming in it for safety reasons since 2021.

Free, ranger-led, one-hour hikes leave from the Askja car park daily mid-July to mid-August. The closest huts and camping are at Drekagil and in the more inviting, fertile area at Herðubreiðarlindir. Bring your own food (none for sale here) and picnic by the Dreki huts or on Öskjuvatn's shores on a fine-weather day.

From Drekagil an 8km road leads to the Askja car park (which has toilets), and then it's a gorgeous 2.5km walk into and through the caldera (easy to moderate, depending on snow melt and weather conditions) across lava fields to reach Víti and the lake.

ICELAND'S HIGHEST FARM

Möðrudalur is the closest farm to the northern highlands, and Iceland's highest farm altogether (469m). You'll see its petrol pump and yummy cafe Beitarhúsið (p288) on the Ring Road between Egilsstaðir and Mývatn, and if you continue south on Rte 901 you'll be welcomed at the main farm with a full range of accommodation from stylish private rooms to rustic guesthouse and view-blessed camping. Their restaurant **Fjallakaffi** serves delicious local fare and they are the leading regional tour operator (called Fjalladýrð) for Askja and Kverkfjöll.

 ASKJA ROUTE OPTIONS

If you take F88 in (the deep rivers here are not safe for smaller 4WDs), it's a good idea to leave along F910/F905 (with more manageable rivers) for variety's sake. Other options from Askja include heading east towards Egilsstaðir, or west on the extremely difficult Gæsavatnaleið route (F910 west) to Sprengisandur (ask locally for advice on conditions – it's only for super-Jeeps). To reach Kverkfjöll, head east on F910, then south on F902.

FROM HIGHLAND LORE TO LUNAR LANDERS

The highlands are the setting of countless tales about **Fjalla-Eyvindur** ('Eyvindur of the Mountains'), a charming but incurable 18th-century kleptomaniac. He fled into the highlands with his wife and today you'll see hideouts attributed to him and hear lore of his ability to survive in impossible conditions while always staying one jump ahead of his pursuers.

If sci-fi is more your scene, visit the otherworldly grey-sand desert and jagged lava formations of **Ódáðahraun** where 1960s NASA astronauts of the *Apollo* mission twice made astro-geologic field-training trips in the area south of the F910 east of Askja and near Drekagil. Nowadays NASA uses the area to test Mars Exploration Rovers.

The cataclysm that formed the lakes happened relatively recently (in 1875) when 2 cu km of tephra was ejected from the volcano. The force was so strong that debris landed in Continental Europe. Ash poisoned cattle in northern Iceland, sparking a wave of emigration to America.

After the initial eruption, a magma chamber collapsed and created a humongous, craterous 11-sq-km hole, 300m below the rim of the original crater. Part of this new depression filled with water and became the lake Öskjuvatn, the second-deepest in Iceland at 220m.

In the eruption a vent near the northeastern corner of the lake exploded and formed the tephra crater Víti, which contains geothermal water. This is one of two well-known craters called Víti, the other being at Krafla near Mývatn. (FYI: Víti means 'hell' in Icelandic.)

Expanding into the Kverkfjöll Route

GET EVEN MORE REMOTE

Not far from Askja, but a veritable world away, the Kverkfjöll (pronounced *kverk*-fyutl) route creeps across the highlands to the **Kverkfjöll** area at the northern margins of the Vatnajökull ice cap. Kverkfjöll is actually a cluster of peaks, the third highest in Iceland, formed by a large central volcano and it's partially capped by the ice of **Kverkjökull** (a northern tongue of Vatnajökull). Over time, the name Kverkfjöll has also come to refer to the hot-spring-filled ice caves that often form beneath the eastern margin of the **Dyngjujökull** ice due to the heavy geothermal activity in this area.

Along the rugged access road F902 (off Rte F910) thrilling sites include the twin pyramid-shaped **Upptyppingar hills** near the Jökulsá á Fjöllum bridge, and the **Hvannalindir** oasis, about 20km north of **Sigurðarskáli Hut** (Kverkfjöll's accommodation, campsite and information base). Check vjp. is for information and hiking ideas.

A 2km-return marked hike from behind the hut takes you up Virkisfell (1108m) for a spectacular view over Kverkfjöll and the headwaters of the Jökulsá á Fjöllum (pronounced yuk-ul-sow ow fyu-tloom).

Besides being the source of the roiling Jökulsá á Fjöllum, central Iceland's greatest river, Kverkfjöll is also one of Iceland's largest geothermal areas. The lower Kverkfjöll ice caves lie 3km from the Sigurðarskáli hut; they're about a 15-minute

---

ROUTE F88 FROM THE RING ROAD THROUGH ÓDÁÐAHRAUN

Route F88 leaves the Ring Road at Hrossaborg, a 10,000-year-old crater shaped like an amphitheatre, used as a film set for the Tom Cruise sci-fi flick *Oblivion* (2013). For much of the way it's a flat journey, following the western bank of the Jökulsá á Fjöllum glacier river, meandering across tephra expanses and winding circuitously through rough, tyre-abusing sections of the 4400-sq-km Ódáðahraun (pronounced *o*-dow-tha-roin; Evil Deeds Lava Field).

Then there are two river crossings, one of which routinely swamps smaller Jeeps. Check on conditions before setting out.

Kverkfjöll

KVERKFJÖLL GUIDED TOURS

Without a robust 4WD vehicle, the only way to visit Kverkfjöll is on a tour. If you do have your own vehicle, you can park and walk up to the viewing area for the mouths of the ice caves (entrance strictly prohibited) – anywhere further is highly ill-advised without a guide.

Some summers, the park rangers stationed at Sigurðarskáli hut offer guided hikes onto the Kverkjökull outlet glacier or to the geothermal area at 1700m, known as Hveradalur. Email ferdaf@ferdaf.is or call 863 9236 (in summer) to see what tours are being offered.

There are tour packages involving transport and guiding. Fjalladýrð has a two-day tour from Möðrudalur. From Mývatn, Geo Travel has a two-day Askja–Kverkfjöll tour. Glacier Journey guides snowmobile rides for experienced snowmobilers.

walk from the 4WD track's end. Here the hot river flows beneath the cold glacier ice, and clouds of steam swirl over the river. It is not possible to enter the caves (they have claimed the life of one person), but depending on the year you can see different openings in the glacier ice.

Ranger-led tours continue up onto the glacier itself. The longer guided tours head over the glacier to the remarkable **Hveradalur** geothermal area. Always log any independent hike plans with the rangers.

The road to Kverkfjöll (F902; in Icelandic known as Kverkfjalaleið) usually opens mid- to late June. The Kverkfjöll route connects Möðrudalur (70km east of Mývatn, off the Ring Road) with the Sigurðarskáli hut via the F905, F910 and F902. Or, after visiting Askja, follow up with a 70km trip to Kverkfjöll by driving south along the F902. Drivers note: the petrol stop at Möðrudalur is the last place to fill up.

ROUTE F88 FROM HERÐUBREIÐARLINDIR TO ASKJA

After the long journey through hypnotic lava- and flood-washed plains, you reach the lovely oasis of Herðubreiðarlindir, at the foot of Herðubreið. The route then scoops westwards through ever-more-remote dunes and lava flows, past the Drekagil gorge and up the hill towards Askja, where you leave your car to walk the remaining 2.5km into the caldera.

TOOLKIT

The chapters in this section cover the most important topics you'll need to know about in Iceland. They're full of nuts-and-bolts information and valuable insights to help you understand and navigate Iceland and get the most out of your trip.

Arriving
p310

Getting Around
p311

Money
p312

Accommodation
p313

Family Travel
p314

Health & Safe Travel
p315

Food, Drink & Nightlife
p316

Responsible Travel
p318

LGBTIQ+ Travellers
p320

Accessible Travel
p321

Take Care of Iceland
p322

Nuts & Bolts
p323

Language
p324

✈ Arriving

International travellers flying to Iceland arrive at Keflavík International Airport, about 49km southwest of Reykjavík. A weekly ferry service runs from northern Denmark to Seyðisfjörður and back, stopping at the Faroe Islands each way. Several cruise lines sail to Iceland from Canada, Europe and the UK.

Visas

Citizens or residents of the US, Australia, Canada, the UK, Japan, New Zealand, and EU and Schengen countries do not need a visa for visits under 60 days.

Wi-Fi

Fast, free wi-fi is available at Keflavík International Airport and on local and airport buses. Most accommodation and many bars, restaurants and tourist sites also provide free wi-fi.

Border Crossing

You will need to go through passport control if you're coming from outside the Schengen Area. This includes visitors from North America, the UK and Australia.

Airport Buses

Airport bus schedules are coordinated with flight schedules and fares are less than a third of what a taxi from Keflavík International Airport to Reykjavík would cost.

Public Transport from Airport to City Centre

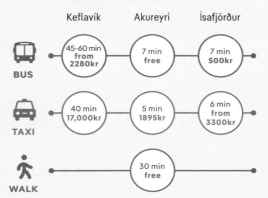

	Keflavík	Akureyri	Ísafjörður
BUS	45-60 min from 2280kr	7 min free	7 min 500kr
TAXI	40 min 17,000kr	5 min 1895kr	6 min from 3300kr
WALK		30 min free	

AIRPORT SERVICES

Keflavík is the best-equipped of Iceland's airports. Several companies offer pick-up services that can include everything from assistance with baggage to personal escorts through security. Travellers can request VAT refunds at the airport by submitting original purchase receipts and Tax Free forms signed by retailers. You'll quickly notice that everything is more expensive in Iceland, including alcohol and cigarettes. To save money, stock up at the duty-free shop before leaving Keflavík International Airport. Services are limited at Iceland's smaller airports. Airports in Akureyri and Egilsstaðir have cafes. There's also a postbox for VAT forms in Akureyri.

Getting Around

Best ways to get around Iceland

Nothing beats the freedom of renting a car, especially if you plan to explore small towns and off-the-beaten-path natural wonders.

TRAVEL COSTS

Rental
10,800kr/day

Petrol
Approx
362kr/litre

Bus in Reykjavík
570kr per ride

EV charging
1900–3750kr

Road Conditions

Major roads in Iceland, like the Ring Road (Rte 1), are paved and well-maintained throughout. Secondary roads may be gravel roads but are accessible to all types of vehicles. F roads are challenging mountain roads that should only be attempted by experienced 4WD drivers.

Cycling

Iceland's Ring Road is a major draw for cyclists, but there are no bike lanes along this route. Cold, rain and wind can make for uncomfortable conditions and contingency planning is key. Bike rentals are available in Reykjavík and a handful of other towns.

RIDESHARING & HITCHHIKING

Iceland has about as many cars as it has people. And while it doesn't allow ridesharing services like Lyft and Uber, it does have a vibrant carpool scene. People submit routes they're driving on samferda.net, and passengers can request rides and offer to split costs. Because public transport is limited outside of Reykjavík, carpooling is a popular option for getting between cities. It's also not uncommon to see hitchhikers, particularly along Rte 1.

TIP

Download the Strætó app to purchase individual bus tickets. Activate your ticket before you ride.

DRIVING ESSENTIALS

Drive on the right

Seat belts are required for all occupants.

.05
Blood alcohol limit is 0.05%

Trains & Buses

Unlike most of Europe, there's no public train system in Iceland. Reykjavík has an extensive bus system, but it's harder to get around by bus beyond Selfoss on the southern coast and Borgarnes to the north. Akureyri, Ísafjörður, Reykjanesbær and the Eastfjords also have local bus systems.

Ships & Ferries

Iceland is becoming an increasingly popular cruise destination with several lines sailing to Iceland from North America and Europe. It's also getting easier to circumnavigate the island on a cruise ship. There's a weekly ferry service from Denmark via the Faroe Islands.

Planes

International flights arrive at Keflavík International Airport. A domestic airport in Reykjavík connects the capital to three other Icelandic cities: Akureyri, Egilsstaðir and Ísafjörður. Domestic connecting flights through Keflavík may require a change of airports.

 # Money

CURRENCY: **ICELANDIC KRÓNA (KR OR ISK)**

Cash or Card?

Don't feel pressured to visit an ATM. Most places in Iceland accept credit cards and digital payments, even for small purchases. Some public restrooms require payment, so may want to keep some coins on hand if you're taking a long-distance road trip.

Chips & PINs

If you don't have a chip-based credit card, you'll need a PIN to use your plastic in Iceland. PINs aren't required with chip-based cards.

Taxes & Refunds

Iceland's standard VAT is 24%. Books, food and accommodation are taxed at a lower 11%. Visitors who live outside of Iceland can claim a tax refund on transactions of 6000kr or more – ask for a form to fill in and a receipt from the shop, and drop these off at the airport.

Tipping

Taxes and service charges are always included in Iceland. However, rounding up restaurant bills or leaving an additional tip for exceptional service is always appreciated.

HOW MUCH FOR...

An espresso
600kr

A museum ticket
2500kr

Golden Circle tour
10,000kr

Northern Lights tour
7600kr

HOW TO... **Save Some Króna**

The best way to save money is to limit restaurant visits and alcohol. Book accommodation with kitchen access and cook for yourself as much as possible. When you do go out to eat, opt for lunches at casual cafes, hot-dog stands or food halls. Alcohol is heavily taxed in Iceland, which is one of the most expensive places to drink in Europe, and $20 glasses of wine aren't unusual.

Find more money-saving tips

LOCAL TIP

Don't waste your money on bottled water. Iceland has some of the cleanest tap water in the world, and you can drink as much as you want for free.

ICELAND FOR FREE

If you're looking for a cheap holiday, Iceland isn't it. After flights, allocate the largest portion of your budget towards accommodation. Stretch the rest of your budget by filling your itinerary with free activities. Visit waterfalls, national parks and geothermal areas across the country. Go hiking. Take in epic views. Walk across the red lava fields at the Heiðmörk Nature Reserve. Check out the Harpa concert hall and the Reykjavík Botanic Garden. Set out in search of the Northern Lights. Believe it or not, the best things in Iceland are free.

Accommodation

Hotels

Many of Iceland's most luxurious hotels are located in and around Reykjavík, but you'll find a few scattered across the countryside as well. Don't be surprised if the nicest properties set you back 100,000kr a night during the busiest seasons. Iceland is one of the more expensive countries in the world for travellers, and even budget hotels here will likely cost more than you're used to, even for a basic room.

Hostels & Guesthouses

Hostels and guesthouses tend to be more affordable than hotels, but you may need to share bathrooms and other facilities. Expect to pay at least 5000kr for a hostel dorm. Some places offer private rooms, sometimes with ensuite bathrooms, or family rooms with plenty of space for everyone.

Sleeping Bag Accommodation

Bring your own sleeping bag or sheets and you'll save money at some guesthouses, rural hotels, hostels and farm stays. Sleeping bag accommodation is often dorms with bunk beds but no sheets, but that isn't always the case – you could find yourself sleeping in an attic or with a room to yourself. Expect to pay up to 50% less by choosing sleeping bag accommodation.

Camping

Camping is an affordable way to see Iceland, but it isn't free, and you can't set up your tent just anywhere. Camping is only allowed at designated campsites or in camper vans on private property with the owner's permission. Iceland has a vast network of campsites with toilets and electricity. Some offer cooking facilities and playgrounds. Expect to pay between 1500kr and 2500kr per night per person.

HOW MUCH FOR A NIGHT IN...

A hostel dorm
4000kr

A 3-star hotel
22,000kr

A 4-star hotel
36,500kr

Explore Icelandic accommodations

Bubbles, Domes & Cabins

There are a growing number of bubbles and cabins with expansive glass walls for travellers who want to experience the Northern Lights without the cold. Expect to pay around 30,000kr each night to stay in one.

HIGH SEASON & TOURIST TAXES

Summer is peak tourist season in Iceland. Prices tend to spike for accommodation and car hire, and you'll want to book tours and activities in advance. Accommodation taxes were suspended from April 2020 to December 2023, but the 11% tax is typically included in displayed room prices. This tax applies to hotel rooms, guest rooms, hostel beds and campsites. An 11% tax rate is also charged by tour operators and travel agencies – these taxes are included in quoted prices.

Family Travel

Iceland doesn't need amusement parks or exciting rides to entertain children. The entire country is a natural wonderland that feels a little like a film set coming to life. Go horse riding across red lava fields or whale watching off the coast. Explore ice caves and check out geysers. Learn about volcanoes. Chase Northern Lights. Your kids won't get bored here.

Sights

With its ample natural wonders and wide variety of outdoor activities, Iceland may be the world's best playground. You'll find lots of kid-friendly hikes. Activities including snowmobiling, ATVs and ice-cave experiences welcome children with some age restrictions. The Blue Lagoon allows children two and older. The Sky Lagoon doesn't admit children under 12.

Facilities

Some hostels and guesthouses offer family rooms, which may help you save money. Some hotels offer connecting rooms. Campsites offer discounted rates for children, and some have playgrounds. You'll find lots of kid-friendly fare like hot dogs, hamburgers and chicken nuggets across the country, and many restaurants have children's menus. Most restaurants have a toilet with a changing table.

KID-FRIENDLY PICKS

Perlan (p65)
Wander through an artificial glacier indoors.

Lava Centre (p126)
Learn about volcanoes and experience an earthquake.

Raufarhólshellir Lava Tunnel (p124)
Walk across a lava field and into a long lava tunnel.

Húsavík Whale Watching (p250)
Take a boat tour from the harbour to look for blue whales.

Reykjavík Puffin Tour (p61)
Take a boat tour from Reykjavík's Old Harbour to look for puffins.

Laugardalslaug (p64)
This Reykjavík swimming pool is practically a waterpark.

Breastfeeding

Breastfeeding is such a non-issue here that an Icelandic government official once addressed parliament during a live television broadcast while breastfeeding her six-week-old, and it was no big deal.

Car Seats

Car hire companies also rent car seats. Blue Car Rental, for example, offers booster seats for a one-time charge of 500kr. Baby seats for children up to three incur a one-time fee of 4000kr. Child seats for children between four and eight are also 4000kr.

GLACIERS & ICE CAVES

Take kids six and older on a journey through a natural ice cave. Strap on crampons and head into the Katla Ice Cave to traverse icy paths and check out the various shades of blue and black. These markers tell stories of volcanic eruptions, glaciers and the formation of Iceland. Or head to Jökulsárlón glacier lagoon, which might feel a bit like seeing the home of *Frozen*'s Elsa of Arendelle. Most glacier snowmobiling tours are open to children eight and older though drivers must be 18 and hold a valid driving licence.

Health & Safe Travel

INSURANCE

Iceland is generally considered a safe place to travel, but theft, illness and accidents can happen anywhere. Travel insurance policies offer coverage for each of these situations, but you'll need to check the fine print to see if potentially dangerous activities like paragliding, ATVs or ice climbing are covered.

Scan to find out more

Personal Safety

Iceland is one of the safest countries in the world for visitors. It reports few violent crimes and murders compared with other countries. Mass shootings and sectarian violence are non-existent, and burglary rates are low. Theft, sexual assaults and car accidents do occur. Use common sense and never leave your drink alone.

Nature

Animals may not try to kill you in Iceland, but nature might. Never walk on glacial ice or swim in a glacial lagoon – hypothermia can set in within minutes. Never turn your back on the black-sand beaches near Vík as people have been known to get washed away. And always be prepared for the weather to change, sometimes drastically, in minutes.

TAP WATER

It's not only safe to drink from the tap in Iceland, it's delicious. Iceland has some of the cleanest, purest tap water in the world.

ROAD SIGNS

Speed limit
Speed limits in kilometres

Gravel road
Bumpy gravel road ahead

4x4 only
Off-limits to anyone without a 4WD

Extremely difficult
Challenging terrain, even for experienced drivers

Road Safety

Iceland's roads present unique hazards that include wildlife, rivers and unpredictable weather. Follow speed limits, check weather conditions frequently, and don't attempt an F road without a 4WD. If you're skidding on a gravel road, turn into the skid as you would on ice to regain control of your vehicle.

VOLCANIC ERUPTIONS

Follow safetravel.is for updates on conditions and closures. Stay on designated trails and out of hazard zones. Be prepared to hike for several hours. Pack food, water and a power bank. Bring an N95 mask for smoke pollution and consider a gas mask. You can notify Icelandic officials of your hiking plans online and find local officials to answer questions on-site.

Food, Drink & Nightlife

When to Eat

Breakfast (9–11am) Most coffee shops don't open until 8am. Many cafes open at 10am or later.

Lunch (11am–2pm) Many restaurants close in the late afternoon. Expect limited dining options between 3pm and 5pm.

Dinner (7–9pm) Restaurant kitchens start closing at 10pm, and it's hard to find anything to eat after midnight.

Land of Greenhouses

It won't take long for you to notice the Icelandic countryside is dotted with greenhouses. These greenhouses allow Icelandic farmers to grow cucumbers, strawberries, lettuces, peppers, mushrooms, herbs and flowers year-round. At Friðheimar (p100) in Southwest Iceland, guests can dine inside a greenhouse on farm-fresh tomatoes grown on-site at the family-owned farm. Or head to Farmers Bistro (p100) where you can sample the bounty from Flúðasveppir, Iceland's only mushroom farm. It doesn't get any more farm-to-table than this.

MENU DECODER

Matseðill Menu
Barnamatseðill Children's menu
Morgunmatur Breakfast
Smjör Butter
Drykki Drinks
Vatn Water
Byor Beer
Eftirréttur Dessert
Bragðarefur Ice cream swirled with three toppings
Reikningur Bill
Servíetta Napkin
Ávextir Fruits
Fiskur dagsins Fish of the day
Grænmetisæta Vegetarian

Sólagrænmetisætur Vegan
Kjöt Meat
Hangikjöt Smoked lamb
Kjúklingur Chicken
Hákarl Fermented shark
Harðfiskur Stockfish
Plokkfiskur Fish stew
Pylsur Hot dog
Humar A small Icelandic lobster, also known as langoustine
Rúgbrauð Icelandic rye bread
Skyr A thick creamy yoghurt that's technically a cheese
Kleinur Doughnut twist

HOW TO... Pick the Right Milk

Iceland has a vibrant dairy industry and one of the highest milk-consumption rates in the world. And while Iceland is a small country, there's a surprising amount of variety in the Icelandic milk scene. This can be incredibly confusing, especially if your Icelandic is non-existent. Most coffee shops offer dairy milk and non-dairy alternatives like almond milk, soy milk, coconut milk and oat milk. Here's what you need to know:

Nýmjólk Full-fat milk
Léttmjólk Low-fat milk
Undanrenna Skimmed milk
Fjörmjólk Fortified and enriched skimmed milk
AB Mjolk Basically runny *skyr*. This will feel like adding a dollop of yoghurt to your coffee.
G-Mjolk Milk processed at ultra-high temperatures that's typically added to coffee.
Kókómjólk Chocolate milk; popular among adults as well as kids.

HOW MUCH FOR...

A coffee
400–600kr

A beer
1050–1700kr

A wine
1500–1750kr

Pýlsur
300–600kr

Hamburger
2500–3000kr

Main course
4500–7000kr

A soft drink
400–600kr

A dozen eggs
800kr

HOW TO...

Eat Skyr

Skyr is a rich, creamy dairy product that's packaged like a yoghurt but technically defined as a cheese, like ricotta or mascarpone. Icelanders have been eating *skyr*, which is made from cow's milk, for centuries. It's high in protein, low in fat and packed with calcium and B vitamins.

Skyr can be eaten for breakfast or as a snack, and is used to make desserts like cheesecake or an Icelandic twist on tiramisu. It can form the base for drinks and smoothies, and there's a runny *skyr* that's essentially a milk.

Skyr is often eaten on the go with individual servings packaged with disposable spoons. Pick up a carton at a shop or visit a *skyr* bar for a bowl topped with fruit, nuts, peanut butter and more. Try a *skyr* and oatmeal breakfast like many Icelanders do.

You'll encounter *skyr* on lots of restaurant menus. Have a *skyr* bowl for breakfast at Cafe Laundromat (p52) in Reykjavík. At Cafe Loki (p52), you can try a *skyr* cake or *skyr* as a pancake topping. Tapas barinn on Vesturgata in Reykjavík uses *skyr* as a base for sauces.

Try *skyr* from the source at Efstidalur II (p89), a farm that makes *skyr*, feta and ice cream. In Höfn, don't miss the *skyr* volcano at Pakkhús (p166).

Did You Know?

It takes four cups of milk to make a single cup of *skyr*, and it's that milk that makes *skyr* so much thicker and creamier than traditional yoghurts.

ICELAND & BEER: IT'S COMPLICATED

Icelanders were beer drinkers from the time this island was settled until prohibition came into effect in 1915. Wine was legalised in 1922 and spirits followed in 1935, but beer remained illegal until 1989. Icelandic lawmakers took the stance that beer would lead to more depravity because of its cheaper price. They declared that beer could contain a maximum of 2.25% alcohol by volume, half that of average beer.

As Iceland fought for its independence, beer became closely associated with its Danish rulers. Drinking beer was considered unpatriotic. For years, home brewing and smuggling were the only ways to get full-strength beer. Some people took to spiking their 2.25% beer with Brennivín, a cumin-and-caraway-flavoured local spirit. In 1979, an Icelandic businessman argued he should have the same right to buy beer at Iceland's duty-free shop as foreign visitors and flight crews. Davíð Scheving Thorsteinsson lost his case, but his action helped to change attitudes in the country.

Beer became legal again in Iceland on 1 March 1989. Nowadays you can find quality craft breweries across the country. Beer is also sold at government liquor stores. Icelandic beer is made with Icelandic water, giving these lagers, pilsners, pale ales and stouts an exceptional taste that can't be matched. The two largest brewers in Iceland are Egill Skallagrímsson Brewery and Víking, but there are more than two dozen smaller beer brands in Iceland. Look out for the words *brugghús* and *ölgerð* – both are markers of a brewery.

Responsible Travel

Climate Change & Travel

It's impossible to ignore the impact we have when travelling, and the importance of making changes where we can. Lonely Planet urges all travellers to engage with their travel carbon footprint. There are many carbon calculators online that allow travellers to estimate the carbon emissions generated by their journey; try resurgence.org/resources/carbon-calculator.html. Many airlines and booking sites offer travellers the option of offsetting the impact of greenhouse gas emissions by contributing to climate-friendly initiatives around the world. We continue to offset the carbon footprint of all Lonely Planet staff travel, while recognising this is a mitigation more than a solution.

Order Fish Not Beef

Beef production is one of the largest drivers of climate change. Minimise the environmental impact of your holiday by opting for the fish of the day in this seafood capital of the world.

Shop Local

One of the things that makes Iceland so charming are its independent restaurants, bars and shops. Help keep these open by eating, drinking and shopping at locally owned businesses. Opt for locally grown produce labelled *íslenskt*.

Time Your Visit Just Right

The peak summer months can put a lot of pressure on Icelandic businesses and the environment. Visit at other times of year to remove some of that pressure and save some money.

Iceland is known for its pure, clean water. Bring a reusable water bottle, or pick up a new one in Iceland, and refill it at the tap.

You'll find lots of electric and hybrid car hire options, and charging stations across the country. Some rental companies include free charging.

EMBRACE SLOW TRAVEL

Make the most of your journey by settling into places and embracing slow travel. Become part of a community instead of just crossing it off a list to minimise the carbon footprint of your trip.

STAY OFF THE MOSS

There's nothing Icelanders hate more than tourists damaging precious moss that can take hundreds of years to grow back. As tempting as it may be, stay off the moss, especially if there are signs telling visitors to keep off.

Don't Eat Whale

About 2% of Icelanders report regularly eating whale meat; tourists are its most frequent consumer. Conservation groups are urging visitors to meet the whales not eat them, and more than 60 restaurants have pledged to stop serving whale.

Look For This Label

The orange Vakinn label shows that a tourism business meets the Icelandic Tourist Board's standards for ethical, professional and environmentally sustainable operations. There's a list of certified companies at vakinn.is/en/certified-companies.

Iceland is a geothermal energy pioneer that uses renewable sources to generate all of its electricity.

Purchase carbon offsets to fund wetland restoration through the Icelandic Wetland Fund at votlendi.is/carbon-offset.

2030

More than half of the new cars registered in Iceland each year are electric or hybrid. Iceland plans to stop issuing new registrations for fossil-fuel-powered vehicles in 2030.

A Leader in Carbon Capture

Iceland is home to the world's largest carbon-capture facility. The plant in Hellisheiði can remove up to 4000 metric tonnes of carbon dioxide from the air each year and runs on renewable geothermal power.

Stay on the Road

Icelandic roads can be narrow and rarely have hard shoulders. Avoid pulling over in places without a hard shoulder unless it's an emergency – the perfect photo opportunity does not qualify as an emergency.

RESOURCES

visiticeland.com/carbon-offset
Calculate the carbon footprint of your trip.

globalclimatepledge.com/global/iceland
Promise to be a responsible tourist in Iceland by signing the Icelandic Pledge.

LGBTIQ+ Travellers

Icelanders are open and accepting of LGBTIQ+ travellers, and Iceland is one of the world's most friendly countries for people who identify as gay, lesbian, bisexual or transgender. It was among the first to give same-sex couples equal access to adoption and IVF. Both Icelandic Parliament and the Church of Iceland support same-sex marriage.

Reykjavík Pride

This epic pride party takes over Reykjavík for a week each August. Thousands of people flood the Icelandic capital for what's become one of the country's largest annual events. The parade is the biggest party of Reykjavík Pride, but the event also includes lectures, concerts, a family festival and a post-parade dance party. Reykjavík held its first pride parade in 2000 after several years of local protests. In 2015, an estimated 100,000 people celebrated pride in Reykjavík, a number equal to almost one-third of the Icelandic population.

GAY REYKJAVÍK

Reykjavík is where you'll find the beating heart of the Icelandic gay scene. The city is so small there's no clearly defined gay neighbourhood. There's a gay bar in Reykjavík called Kiki Queer Bar (p55), and you'll see rainbow flags and stickers in the windows of lots of other businesses.

Reykjavík Bear

If you're a bear or bear admirer, this is an Icelandic event not to miss: Iceland's premier bear party. This festival started by a group of volunteers more than 15 years ago has since grown into an international event attracting visitors from around the world. Reykjavík Bear includes a Golden Circle tour, a shirtless party, a visit to the Blue Lagoon and a night of clubbing.

TOUR COMPANIES

Pink Iceland is a gay-owned tour operator. This company won't just arrange your tours, they also arrange weddings and are happy to answer any questions about local LGBTIQ+ culture.

Out Adventures is a Canadian company that specialises in small-group tours for LGBTIQ+ travellers. They host a few trips to Iceland each year.

THE NATIONAL QUEER ORGANIZATION

This organisation was founded in 1978 and has been a driving force in promoting acceptance across Iceland. As well as counselling and support groups, it has an extensive offering of youth programmes and is developing a queer certification programme for workplaces in Iceland.

Dating Apps

Tinder and Grindr are popular in Iceland, but remember this is a country so small that there's an app to help people avoid dating potential relatives. Whichever app you choose, expect to see the same small pool of people, especially outside of Reykjavík.

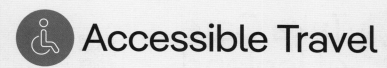

Accessible Travel

Accessibility is still a work in progress in Iceland, but the country has made major strides in recent years. Lifts and accessible bathrooms are the norm in modern buildings, and wheelchair ramps are increasingly common.

Ramping Up

Many businesses along Laugavegur, Reykjavík's main shopping street, have wheelchair ramps, thanks to Ramp Up Reykjavík. The grassroots effort has driven the construction of 450 ramps, with plans for 1600 more.

Airport

Keflavík International Airport offers travellers with reduced mobility assistance with checking-in, security screening, boarding and stowing hand luggage on board. Assistance must be requested through a passenger's airline at least 48 hours ahead of their departure.

Accommodation

Look for newer hotels and holiday rentals. Buildings constructed after 2012 are required to have lifts and accessible bathrooms. Many campsites and some hostels are accessible.

RESOURCES

wheelmap.org
An online map for searching and marking wheelchair-accessible places.

sjalfsbjorg.is
The National Confederation of Physically Disabled People provides short-term mobility equipment rental and curated lists of accessible hotels, restaurants and transportation services.

wheelchairtraveling.com
Destination-specific travel content for travellers in wheelchairs.

PUBLIC TRANSPORT

Public buses are wheelchair-accessible, but users must enter and exit the bus on their own. Wheelchair accessibility is limited on buses outside of Reykjavík.

Taxis

Hreyfill and City Taxi provide accessible taxi services in Reykjavík. City Taxi offers fixed-rate rides between Reykjavík and Keflavík International Airport. Call ahead to arrange.

Attractions

Key tourist sites including Gullfoss, the Geysir geothermal area and Þingvellir National Park are wheelchair-accessible. In Reykjavík, the Harpa concert hall, Hallgrímskirkja, National Museum, Perlan and most shops along Laugavegur are accessible.

LAGOONS

Several of Iceland's top lagoons including the Blue Lagoon, Sky Lagoon and Laugarvatn Fontana geothermal pools are wheelchair-accessible, as are many of the country's swimming pools.

Iceland Unlimited offers accessible day tours of the Golden Circle, Reykjanes Peninsula and the southern coast. GJ Travel and BusTravel Iceland can accommodate travellers with foldable wheelchairs, however, travellers must be able to enter and exit tour buses on their own.

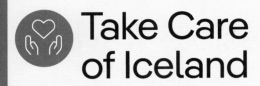

Take Care of Iceland

Start planning a Northern Lights trip

Iceland is a small country that sometimes struggles under the weight of its popularity. Nature is its biggest resource, and visitors haven't always respected the land. The country launched the Icelandic Pledge in 2017 to encourage respectful tourism. Sign it online and join the effort by following these guidelines.

Don't Venture off the Road

Tyres can do a lot of damage to delicate ecosystems, so stay on roads and off the moss. Off-road driving is illegal in Iceland, and pulling over just anywhere can be dangerous for you, other drivers sharing these roads, and the nature you came to see.

Camp in Designated Areas

Just because you have a tent doesn't mean you can set it up anywhere. Wild camping isn't allowed in Iceland. Only camp at designated areas, and park motorhomes and camper vans in designated spaces at campsites.

Park in Designated Areas

Get the owner's permission before parking on private property or set up camp at one of the country's many campsites. Parking self-sufficient camper vans or motorhomes just anywhere isn't allowed.

Use Designated Toilets

Icelanders are so annoyed with tourists using nature as their toilet that they've taken to shooting videos to shame them. Don't be that person. Public toilets are available at campsites and other locations across the country.

LEAVE PLACES AS YOU FOUND THEM

There's no need to carve anything anywhere to let the world know you've been to Iceland. Leave places as you've found them, and take everything you bring with you when you leave.

DON'T BE LIKE JUSTIN BIEBER

Justin Bieber's 'I'll Show You' music video, filmed in Iceland in 2015, is a good lesson on what not to do in Iceland. In the music video, Bieber goes swimming in a glacier and frolicking through a pristine canyon with jagged rocky edges and postcard-perfect views.

In reality, swimming in a glacial lagoon is incredibly dangerous. The water is also icy cold, so it would be far less pleasant than soaking in one of the many geothermal lagoons that are scattered across the country.

And that canyon Bieber frolicked through? Officials had to close it in 2019 because so many fans were damaging the moss by rolling around on it. Look closely at the Bieber video, and you'll notice the moss starting to tear in places. While it looks like a lush carpet, Icelandic moss is delicate and can take years to regrow after being trampled.

There are few things Icelanders hate more than tourists that go destroying their delicate moss for silly reasons. Don't be that tourist.

Nuts & Bolts

OPENING HOURS

Supermarkets 7am–midnight. Some open as late as 10am and close as early as 8pm.

Government-owned liquor stores (Vínbúðin) 11am–6pm Monday through Saturday. Closed on Sundays.

Shops 9am–6pm. Weekend hours may vary.

Bars To 1am Sunday to Thursday, and as late as 5.30am on Fridays and Saturdays.

Internet

Free wi-fi is widely available at hotels, restaurants, attractions and public libraries, but network availability can be limited in remote areas. Portable wi-fi devices are available to rent.

Weights & Measures

Iceland uses the metric system. Distances and speeds are measured in kilometres.

Smoking

It's illegal to smoke inside restaurants, bars and clubs, but smoking is allowed outdoors.

GOOD TO KNOW

Time zone
Western European Time
(equal to GMT)

Country code
354

Emergency number
112

Population
394,000

Electricity 220V/50Hz

Type C
220V/50Hz

Type F
230V/50Hz

PUBLIC HOLIDAYS

There are 13 public holidays in Iceland. Banks and government offices are closed on these days. Businesses and non-essential services may be closed, and demand can be high for accommodation and restaurant tables.

New Year's Day 1 January

Easter March or April; Maundy Thursday and Good Friday to Easter Monday (changes annually)

Labour Day 1 May

Ascension Day 18 May

Whit Sunday and Whit Monday May or June (changes annually)

Independence Day 17 June

Commerce Day First Monday in August

Christmas Eve 24 December

Christmas Day 25 December

Boxing Day 26 December

# Language

Most Icelanders speak English, so you'll have no problems if you don't know any Icelandic. However, any attempts to speak the local language will be much appreciated.

Basics

Hello. Halló. *ha·loh*
Goodbye. Bless. *bles*
Yes. Já. *yow*
No. Nei. *nay*
How are you? Hvað segir þú gott? *kvadh say·yir thoo got*
Fine. And you? Allt fínt. En þú? *alt feent en thoo*
Thank you. Takk./Takk fyrir. *tak/tak fi·rir*
Excuse me. Afsakið. *af·sa·kidh*
Sorry. Fyrirgefðu. *fi·rir·gev·dhu*
My name is ... Ég heiti ... *yekh hay·ti ...*
Do you speak English? Talarðu ensku?. *a·lar dhoo ens·ku*
I don't understand. Ég skil ekki. *yekh skil e·ki*

Directions

Where's the (hotel)? Hvar er (hótelið)? *kvar er (hoh·te·lidh)*
What's your address? Hvert er heimilisfangið þitt? *kvert er hay·mi·lis·fown·gidh thit*
Can you show me (on the map)? Geturðu sýnt mér (á kortinu)? *ge·tur·dhu seent myer (ow kor·ti·nu)*

Signs

Inngangur Entrance
Útgangur Exit
Opið Open
Lokað Closed
Bannað Prohibited
Snyrting/Salerni Toilets

Emergencies

Help! Hjálp! *hyowlp*
Go away! Farðu! *far·dhu*
I'm lost. Ég er villtur/villt. (m/f) *yekh er vil·tur/vilt*
Call ...! Hringdu á ...! *hring·du ow ...*
  a doctor lækni *laik·ni*
  the police lögregluna *leukh·rekh·lu·na*
Where are the toilets? Hvar er snyrtingin? *kvar er snir·tin·gin*

Eating & Drinking

What would you recommend? Hverju mælir þú með? *kver·yu mai·lir thoo medh*
Cheers! Skál! *skowl*
Do you have vegetarian food? Eruð þið með grænmetisrétti? *er·udh thidh medh grain·me·tis·rye·ti*
  breakfast morgunmat *mor·gun·mat*
  lunch hádegismat *how·day·yis·mat*
  dinner kvöldmat *kveuld·mat*

Shopping & Services

I'm looking for ... Ég er að leita að ... *yekh er adh lay·ta adh ...*
How much is it? Hvað kostar þetta? *kvadh kos·tar the·ta*
It's faulty. Það er gallað. *thadh er gat·ladh*
Where's the ...? Hvar er ...? *kvar er ...*
  bank bankinn *bown·kin*
  market markaðurinn *mar·ka·dhu·rin*

NUMBERS

1 **einn** *aydn*
2 **tveir** *tvayr*
3 **þrír** *threer*
4 **fjórir** *fyoh·rir*
5 **fimm** *fim*
6 **sex** *seks*
7 **sjö** *syeu*
8 **átta** *ow·ta*
9 **níu** *nee·u*
10 **tíu** *tee·u*

Phrases to Sound Like a Local

Cool! Kúl! *kool*

No worries. Engar áhyggjur. *ayng-ahrr ow-higyrrö*

Sure. Vissulega. *viss-ö-lehkh-ah*

No way! Ekki séns! *ehky-i syens*

Just joking! Bara grín! *ba-rrah grreen*

Too bad. En leitt. *ehn layt*

What a shame. En leiðinlegt. *ehn layth-in-lehcht*

What's up? Hvað segirðu (gott)? *kvahth sagy-irr-th (gott)*

Well done! Vel gert! *vehl gyehrt*

Not bad. Ekki slæmt. *ehky-i slaimt*

GIMLI, MANITOBA, CANADA

The town of Gimli has a large Icelandic community, having been established for Icelandic immigrants fleeing poverty.

Icelandic Origins

Icelandic is a North Germanic language. Iceland was settled primarily by Norwegians in the 9th and 10th centuries. By the 14th century Icelandic (Old Norse) and Norwegian had grown apart considerably, due to changes in Norwegian.

Reading the Sagas

Icelandic has changed so little through the centuries that the sagas and the *Poetic Edda*, written about 700 years ago, can be enjoyed by modern-day speakers of Icelandic.

Icelandic names

Icelanders use the ancient patronymic system, where *son* (son) or *dóttir* (daughter) is added to the father's or, less commonly, mother's first name. For example, Jónsdóttir or Gunnarsson.

Telephone book entries are listed by first names.

WHO SPEAKS ICELANDIC?

Icelandic *(íslensku)* is spoken by about 350,000 people, mainly in Iceland.

Iceland

Ð/ð is pronounced as the 'th' in 'lather'.

Þ/þ is pronounced as the 'th' in 'thin'.

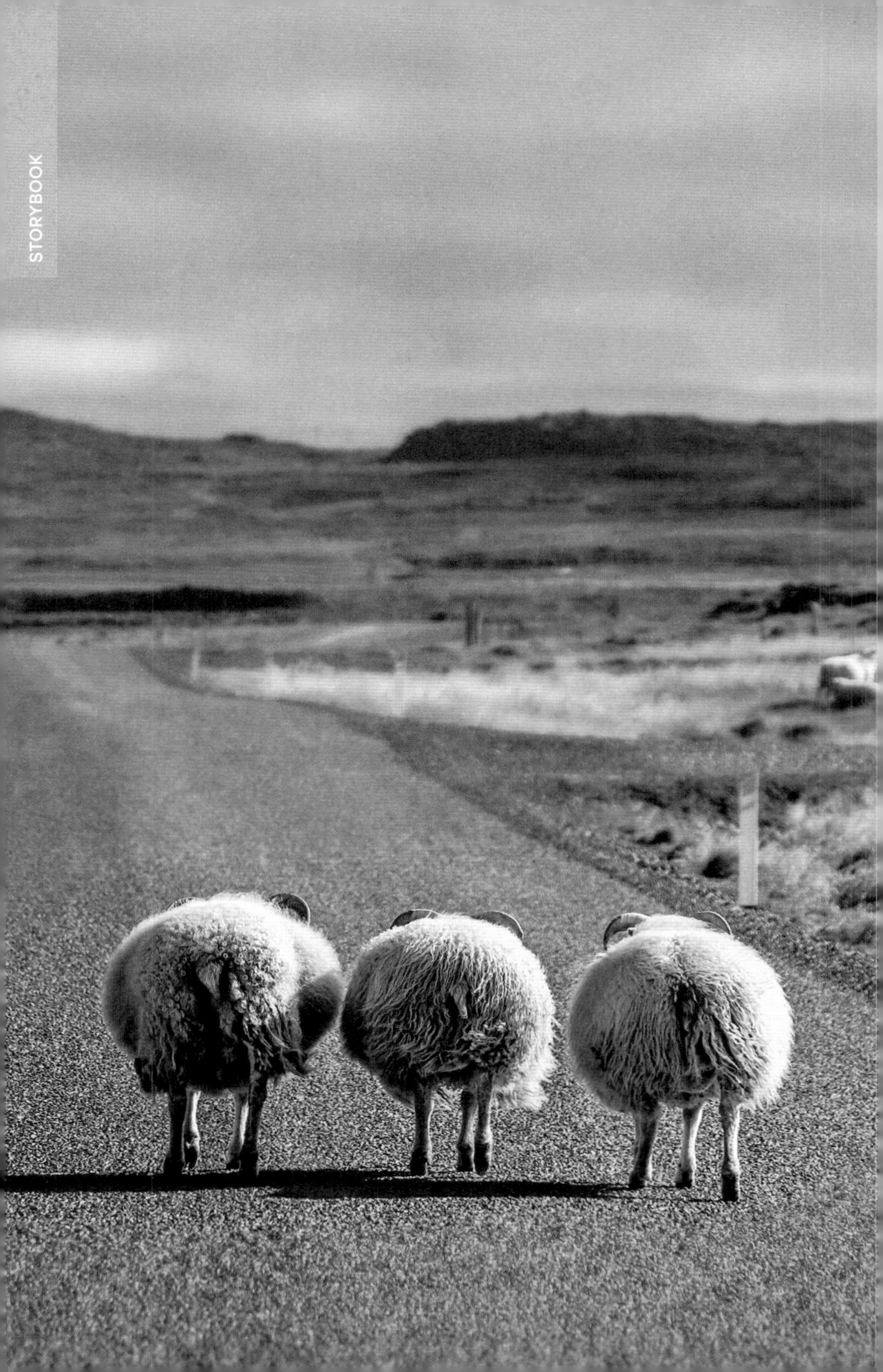

THE ICELAND

STORYBOOK

Our writers delve deep into different aspects of Icelandic life

A History of Iceland in 15 Places

Trace Iceland's past from its earliest Viking settlements to the present

Meena Thiruvengadam

p328

Meet the Icelanders

Debunking the myths – or confirming them?

Eygló Svala Arnarsdóttir

p332

Iceland Minus the Ice

The devastating effects of climate change on Iceland's glaciers

Egill Bjarnason

p334

Fire in the Blood

Volcanoes: givers and takers of life

Eygló Svala Arnarsdóttir

p337

Iceland's Pop-Rock Juggernaut

Iceland has a rich and wildly varied music scene

Alexis Averbuck

p340

A HISTORY OF ICELAND IN
15 PLACES

Iceland packs 1200 years of history into a small island in the North Atlantic Ocean. Iceland itself is a result of shifting tectonic plates, a remote island created by the volcanic activity that mesmerises so many visitors. Its story is one of Viking exploration, Danish colonisation, religious conflict and modern development.
By Meena Thiruvengadam

ONE OF THE northernmost inhabited places on the planet, Iceland is like a geology book come to life. Several chapters of Icelandic history are missing, but it's believed Norse and Celtic settlers came to this rugged island about the size of Switzerland over 1200 years ago. In 930 CE, Iceland became the first country to establish a democratic parliament.

In 1980, Iceland was the first in the world to democratically elect a female president. It had the world's first openly gay head of government in 2009, was the first country in the world to legalise abortion in 1935, and the first in the world to jail bankers after the 2008 financial crisis.

Icelanders have a history of resilience, a requirement for living in this environment. Plagues gutted the Icelandic population in the 15th century, and a volcanic eruption almost forced out the population in the 18th century. Denmark colonised Iceland in 1602, maintaining a grip on the country until 1944.

WWII ushered a fishing-based agricultural economy into the industrial age. An airport left behind by Allied forces gave way to the rise of tourism, and the rest of the story is best told through these 15 places.

1. Húsavík
VIKINGS AND EUROVISION

This tiny North Icelandic town was home to one of Iceland's earliest Viking settlements. Archaeologists have found 9th-century Viking ruins nearby, suggesting this area predates Reykjavík by several decades and could be the earliest settlement in Iceland. Today, Húsavík is a hub for whale watchers and Eurovision fans. Nearly two dozen species of whale – including the gigantic blue whale – make appearances here. A Eurovision Museum opened in 2021. The 2020 Netflix film *Eurovision Song Contest: The Story of Fire Saga* was set and filmed in Húsavík, which is also the title of a song performed by Will Ferrell and Molly Sandén in the film.

For more on Húsavík, see page 249

2. Þingvellir National Park
WHERE DEMOCRACY BEGAN

Few places are more historically significant to Iceland than Þingvellir National Park. In 930 CE, this became the site of the Alþingi, the world's first democratic parliament. This is also where Iceland formally adopted Christianity in 1000 CE and where it declared independence from Denmark in 1944. Iceland's parliament met at a site along the Öxará river until the 18th century, and in 1930 this became the country's first national park. Follow the hiking path for a walk through early Icelandic history, and snorkel the Silfra Fissure to see where the North American and Eurasian tectonic plates converge.

For more on Þingvellir National Park, see page 88

3. Árbær Open Air Museum
JOURNEY INTO THE PAST

Wander through history at this open-air museum in a Reykjavík suburb where costumed guides explain what Icelandic life was like a century ago. Walking around this area and exploring its turf houses feels like walking into another time. Costumed guides usher guests through a collection of 20 historic buildings put together to form a town square, a village and a farm. While this was the site of a working farm in the 20th century, the structures here were relocated from Reykjavík.

For more on Árbær Open Air Museum, see page 68

4. Gásir
WHERE FORTUNES WERE MADE

This plot of land along the Eyjafjörður fjord, about 14km north of Akureyri, springs to

Medieval festival, Gásir

ICELAND/ALAMY STOCK PHOTO ©

life every summer during a medieval festival commemorating its history. Gásir was a key trading post in North Iceland and regularly made appearances in 13th- and 14th-century Icelandic sagas. This area is believed to have housed a trading post until the 16th century as Akureyri was developing into a commercial centre. The Gásir medieval festival takes travellers back in time every July with costumed actors and craftsmen who bring history to life.

For more on Akureyri, see page 235

5. Skálholt Cathedral
MORE THAN MEETS THE EYE

This cathedral may look relatively new, but it's a key piece of Iceland's Viking history. Built in 1963, the cathedral now standing at the site is the 10th to occupy the property. The history of this site can be traced to the 11th century, when sharp religious disputes defined the nation. Iceland's first church was built here around 1000 CE, when this was a large town and Christianity was rapidly spreading in Iceland. Iceland's last Catholic bishop was executed in Skálholt in 1550 alongside his two sons for opposing the Reformation imposed by the Danish king.

For more on Skálholt Cathedral, see page 96

6. Reykholt
A READER'S DELIGHT

Head to this small town in West Iceland to walk in the footsteps of Snorri Sturluson, the country's best-known writer of sagas, the legendary family stories that defined the literary landscape of medieval Iceland. Sturluson lived here, writing his books on calfskin and taking breaks to soak in an idyllic pool that's one of Iceland's earliest archaeological remains. Sturluson was a legendary literary figure in Iceland – a feat in a country with some of the most voracious readers on the planet – and there's no better place to get acquainted with his work.

For more on Reykholt, see page 177

7. Eiríksstaðir
HOME OF LEGENDARY EXPLORERS

Take a detour to the 10th century at this West Iceland historic site that was the home of Erik the Red, father of legendary explorer Leifur Eiríksson. This is where the younger Eiríksson is believed to have been born. Archaeologists have found the remains of two buildings here: a Viking longhouse and a separate pit house. The site is still visible to visitors, and a reconstructed longhouse shows what a typical Viking farmhouse would have looked like at the time. Each summer, costumed performers take visitors back in time to tell the story of this adventurous family.

For more on Eiríksstaðir, see page 184

8. Kirkjubæjarklaustur

A TINY VILLAGE WITH HUGE TALES

On the southern coast, Kirkjubæjarklaustur offers a peek into Iceland's Celtic history. Irish monks once lived in this little village, best known for a convent of Benedictine nuns that have inspired numerous folk tales. Kirkjubæjarklaustur was the site of a monastery in the 9th century, according to the Book of Settlement, Iceland's leading history text. A paved area of basalt stones resembles the Giant's Causeway in Northern Ireland, but its origin is just one of many Icelandic mysteries. The convent here closed in 1550 when Iceland moved away from Catholicism and toward Lutheranism.

For more on Kirkjubæjarklaustur, see page 157

9. Vestmannaeyjar

AFTER THE ERUPTION

These volcanic islands are largely uninhabited. Heimaey, the main island in this archipelago, offers a look at a key event in Icelandic history: the 1973 eruption of the Eldfell volcano, which decimated a thriving town, leaving it buried in a blanket of lava and ash. A swift evacuation left one casualty from the natural disaster. A museum on the island tells the stories of people forced to quickly leave home and shows how destructive volcanic activity can be to daily life. Another island that's visible from Heimaey, Surtsey, is the result of an underground volcanic eruption that lasted from 1963 until 1967.

For more on Vestmannaeyjar, see page 134

10. Raufarhólshellir Lava Tunnel

A TUNNEL TO THE PAST

Journey thousands of years into the past just a half-hour's drive from Reykjavík. This is one of the largest lava tunnels in Iceland and one of the easiest to visit from Reykjavík. Walk through a tunnel carved by the boiling lava that ferociously flowed through here thousands of years ago. See the iron-oxide formations that have developed over the centuries, and learn what the interior of the tunnel can teach us

Basalt stones, Kirkjugólf (p158)

FELIX LIPOV/SHUTTERSTOCK ©

about the history of this area. Two tour options are available, and safety gear is provided.

For more on Raufarhólshellir lava tunnel, see page 124

11. Keflavík International Airport

AN AIRSTRIP THAT CHANGED ICELAND

The airport that welcomes most visitors to Iceland is a remnant of WWII, a time when British and US forces occupied the country leaving behind a key piece of infrastructure. Keflavík International Airport opened in March 1943 and has been a key driver of commercial aviation growth in Iceland. This airport made it easier for Icelanders to travel the world and has helped Iceland become a layover tourism pioneer. Until 1987, civilian and military passengers shared a terminal. A separate civilian terminal, the Leifur Eriksson Terminal, named after the first European to reach the Americas, has served all civilian travellers since.

For more on Keflavík International Airport, see page 310

12. Settlement Exhibition

HOW ICELAND CAME TO BE

Dive deep into Viking history with a short trip underground at this museum in downtown Reykjavík. The Settlement Exhibition surrounds a collection of excavated Viking ruins and tells the story of the settlement of Iceland. The remains of a Viking settlement here were unearthed in 2001 and are the oldest human-made structures that have been discovered in Iceland. The Settlement Exhibition is connected to the Reykjavík City Museum – where you'll find the oldest house in central Reykjavík, dating to 1762 – by an underground tunnel.

For more on the Settlement Exhibition, see page 51

13. Hallgrímskirkja

REYKJAVÍK'S DEFINING FEATURE

This Lutheran church is the tallest in Iceland and one of the tallest buildings in the country. A distinctive curved spire and side wings have helped it become an international symbol of Iceland since it was completed in 1986. Construction on the church began in 1945 and the tower, which has come to define the Reykjavík skyline, was among the first portions of the church to be completed. The statue of Leifur Eiríksson in front of the church predates its construction. It was a gift from the US to Iceland in honour of the 1000th anniversary of Iceland's parliament convening at Þingvellir.

For more on Hallgrímskirkja, see page 49

14. Höfði House

A COLD WAR ICON

The gleaming white house overlooking the water became a Cold War icon in 1986 when US president Ronald Reagan and Soviet president Mikhail Gorbachev met here towards the end of the Cold War. The wooden house was built to serve as a French consulate in 1909 when French fishermen frequented the island. The structure was imported from Norway. It is the best-known of several 'catalog-style' homes in Iceland. Nowadays, this space is occasionally used for official events. Visitors can walk around the outside of the building and check out a chunk of the Berlin Wall.

For more on Höfði House, see page 63

15. Eyjafjallajökull

ICELAND'S BEST-KNOWN VOLCANO

In April 2010, this stratovolcano in South Iceland became a household name few people could pronounce when its eruption forced hundreds of people from their homes and wreaked havoc with European air traffic for six days. Several heads of state, including US president Barack Obama, German chancellor Angela Merkel and French president Nicolas Sarkozy were among those affected. As a result of the eruption, Eyjafjallajökull became Iceland's most famous volcano. A glacier sits on top of the caldera, and Eyjafjallajökull is part of a volcano chain that stretches across Iceland. Before 2010, its last recorded eruptions were in 920 and 1612.

For more on Eyjafjallajökull, see page 143

MEET THE ICELANDERS

Sword-swinging, hard-headed Vikings or peace-loving, elf-whispering farmers? Who are the Icelanders really? EYGLÓ SVALA ARNARSDÓTTIR debunks some myths and reaffirms others while introducing her people.

ICELAND WAS SETTLED by independent Norse chieftains who would not bow to the rule of a dictator…or so the legend goes. Evidence suggests that the origin of the Icelanders is more complex. Celtic influence on the Icelandic language and culture is more extensive than commonly perceived, and DNA research shows that more than 50% of female settlers were Celts. Today roughly 18% of Iceland's inhabitants are immigrants.

Icelanders are fiercely protective of their legacy, independence and language, a nation of storytellers. But now, the Icelandic language is under siege by English influences. In the 19th century during Danish colonisation, Danish influence on the Icelandic language was widespread, and Icelanders fought to save their native tongue. A new awakening is necessary, columnists write, to make young Icelanders proud of their language again. But, as we say whenever the outlook is bleak, *þetta reddast,* 'everything will work out in the end'.

Icelandic humour is distinctively dark, from the ancient Eddic poem 'Þrymskviða' – where Thor wears a wedding gown, pretending to be Freyja to reclaim his precious hammer, killing the groom – to Hugleikur Dagsson's death-themed cartoons and Ragnar Kjartansson's neon sign *Scandinavian Pain,* based on the Hotel Holt sign in Reykjavík. While Icelanders may seem cold – not wasting too many words, smiles, hugs or kisses – they usually warm up to you once the ice is broken, which might take a few drinks. At their core, Icelanders are hospitable and helpful.

Icelanders don't plan things a long time ahead, because the weather is so unreliable. If it happens to be sunny, you start haymaking. If it looks stormy, cancel the fishing trip. In summer, campers 'follow the weather' – go wherever the forecast is best. Even though most people live in urban areas, they're rural by nature, exercising outside and staying in countryside cabins.

This connection to nature can materialise as superstition. People often ask if Icelanders believe in elves. The short answer is 'no'. Yet, once in a while, for example during road construction, 'elf boulders' are moved out of respect for the hidden people. Because even though people don't believe in elves, they don't feel comfortable denying their existence either. Why risk a curse?

The Book of Icelanders

Íslendingabók (islendingabok.is) is an online database containing genealogical information about the inhabitants of Iceland more than 1200 years back in time. People can look up their relatives and ancestors and discover that they are indeed all related – if generations back.

Pictured clockwise from top left: Fisherman; Priest in traditional Viking clothing, Hvalfjörður; Young woman, Reykjavík; Farmer, Hornafjörður

332

WHAT I LOVE ABOUT ICELAND

There was a time when I couldn't get away from here fast enough. My fellow Icelanders were narrow-minded, I thought, and nothing exciting ever happened. I lived abroad for many years – and, granted, I still miss the European summers. But once I returned, I experienced Iceland from an outside perspective and started appreciating the clean tap water, the abundant hot water, *skyr* and the close proximity to nature. And I appreciated my people more. With all their faults, they also have their charms, and there's a certain informality about them that often makes life easier. You don't lose hours every day commuting to work, and children grow up free and independent, playing outside on their own and cycling to soccer practice. Life, for the most part, is uncomplicated. And when I need to blow off steam, nature is right there: I run along the shore, bike through green areas or drive 15 minutes to hike up the next mountain.

ICELAND
MINUS THE ICE

In the future, Iceland will have less ice and more trees. Native flowers and fauna will lose ground to invasive species. The real surprise is how fast predictions, along with the landscape itself, are changing. By Egill Bjarnason

A FEW YEARS ago, a completely new crop of news stories appeared in Icelandic media: celebrities, particularly musicians, who had fallen prey to biting midges on calm summer nights. 'Damn this newcomer', drummer Karl Tomasson – his arms swollen – said of the *Culicoides* midges spreading across the southern lowlands at an alarming rate. Rappers posted pictures of their tattooed chests after being 'sniped at' during sleep.

The red bumps disappeared and the topic faded. The midges returned the next summer but, by then, as part of the landscape and everyday life.

When a glacier recedes it leaves behind piles of soil and rock, known as moraine. On every glacial floor, these hills of sediments show plainly and simply – stone-black versus snow-white – how far the glacier once reached. Look over the rest of Iceland, however, and the effects of climate change are less visible to an outsider.

Passengers on whale-watching boats today expect to see species of whales that were considered a novelty in Icelandic waters some 10 or 20 years ago, including the humpback whale, linked to changes in the ocean food web. Locals may not notice either, until a black-backed gull steals a steak from the barbecues. Aggressive

seagulls are the side-effect of a collapse in the sand-eel stock – their preferred steak – believed to be caused by warmer winter ocean temperatures. Nearly every seabird population is in decline. Puffins, a bird that symbolises Iceland in the age of tourism, is listed as 'vulnerable' by the International Union for Conservation of Nature, suffering a 70% fall in its population since 1975.

But who wants to read about starving puffins! As a reporter based in Iceland, the climate stories getting the widest reach have a positive spin to them – for example, a technical solution turning carbon dioxide into rocks or a public policy promoting electric cars, forestry and new agriculture. In reality, nature controls Iceland, not the other way around.

Drive the Ring Road in early summer and it's like barrelling down a road paved straight through purple-blue fields of lupine, as if the flowers came before the road. Far from it. The invasive Nootka lupine is an experiment that blew up in Iceland's face and left a permanent purple mark, brought to the country in an effort to fight soil erosion. Buoyed by climate change, it is spiralling towards places previously protected from the plant by cold temperatures and low rainfall.

If extreme rainfall continues, the effects will cause soil erosion by setting off landslides, previously a rare hazard. In 2020, parts of Seyðisfjörður were abandoned after a massive landslide, with plans to relocate the buildings.

Within a few years, drivers may also pass the first wind parks. Roughly 70% of electricity in Iceland is produced by hydroelectric power plants in rivers streaming from the glaciers. As the glacial melt increases – almost half of the total melt witnessed in the last 150 years has occurred within the last 30 years – the rivers grow more powerful, producing ever more electricity. But only for the time being. The state-run energy company Landsvirkjun is installing more wind turbines to prepare for a looming energy shift.

In 2019, Vatnajökull National Park, the area surrounding Europe's largest glacier, became a UNESCO World Heritage Site precisely for its ephemeral landscape, a sort of lab, UNESCO notes, to 'explore the impacts of climate change on world glaciers and the landforms left behind when they retreat'. Under the Paris Climate Agreement, a policy framework meant to keep temperatures from rising 2°C above pre-industrial levels, the mighty Vatnajökull, up to 1km in thickness, will still shrink to between 30% and 60% of its current size. The other 14 ice caps could go the same way, and the smaller will most definitely disappear. Breiðamerkurjökull, the glacial tongue calving icebergs into the famous Jökulsárlón glacier lagoon, is receding faster than any other glacial outpost due to rising ocean temperatures mixing with the lagoon. Ice caves, another popular sight at the base of Vatnajökull, are currently unsafe to visit outside the solidly frozen months from October to March; a time period that's bound to shrink if autumn and spring temperatures continue to rise.

Researching this book, I took the Arctic Coast Way from Hvammstangi to Langanes. The winding road passes pristine beaches with a wide ocean view: beyond the horizon are just a few tiny islands of dry land and definitely no trees. Yet the beaches are littered with driftwood – originating, largely, from trees felled by logging in the Yenisei catchment in central Siberia. The multiyear journey, thousands of kilometres long, is made possible by sea ice, according to a 2022 study Global and Planetary Change. With less ice, the driftwood is more likely to sink before it can make it to shore. By 2060, the study predicts that, based on sea-ice simulators, Iceland's driftwood supply will cease.

Midway along the 900km Arctic Coast Way, I stop at the turf farm Glaumbær constructed almost entirely from earthy material: turf, rocks, more turf. Windows were made with the afterbirth of a cow. The wealthy Glaumbær farm was inhabited until 1946 when the last two families moved out. Had it not been bought for protection, the structure would have rotted into the ground like any other turf farm. The first thing typically unearthed by archaeologists is driftwood – the lumber holding up roofs for most of Iceland's history – a pillar now sinking out of sight.

WHEN A GLACIER RECEDES IT LEAVES BEHIND PILES OF SOIL AND ROCK... LOOK OVER THE REST OF ICELAND, HOWEVER, AND THE EFFECTS OF CLIMATE CHANGE ARE LESS VISIBLE.

FIRE
IN THE BLOOD

Volcanoes shape the land, fertilise the soil, heat the water but also threaten to destroy life. By Eygló Svala Arnarsdóttir

THERE ARE 32 active volcanoes in Iceland and eruptions occur frequently. At the time of writing, volcanologists believe the series of eruptions on Reykjanes Peninsula may continue for several years, similar to Kröflueldar in North Iceland (1975–84). So far, the three Reykjanes eruptions since 2021 have been small and accessible – so-called 'tourist eruptions' – and not caused any damage to infrastructure or posed severe risk to human lives.

Each of the three eruptions were preceded by powerful earthquakes, the largest of which measured magnitude 5.8. They could easily be felt in Reykjavík but have affected the inhabitants of Grindavík, the town closest to the eruption site, the most. Objects fell from shelves and smashed against the floor, cracks formed in walls and people woke with a start in the middle of the night.

Bogi Adolfsson, head of local search and rescue team Þorbjörn, explains that they had prepared for every scenario, eruptions near the town and instant evacuation, but not the hordes of people wanting to view live eruptions. The volunteers of Þorbjörn – along with search and rescue teams from around the country – took shifts guiding people to makeshift car parks, making hiking routes through rough terrain, monitor-ing gas levels and hurrying people away from danger zones. When accidents occurred and people got lost, they came to fetch them.

While these latest eruptions may seem rather harmless, national hazard specialist Salóme Jórunn Bernharðsdóttir stresses that they are not. Molten lava should obviously not be played with and the gas that accumulates can prove life threatening.

Historical Eruptions

Subglacial eruptions are usually more dangerous. In 2010, a phreatic eruption in Eyjafjallajökull in South Iceland grounded aircraft around the world. Ashfall and massive flooding caused problems for farmers in the region, and part of the Ring Road was damaged. The most dangerous eruptions in living memory include Vestmannaeyjar in 1973. Thousands of people had to be evacuated in the middle of the night. Houses were buried in lava and ash and a new mountain, Eldfell, was formed. One person died.

Through history, eruptions have caused devastation and destruction, including the eruption in Askja in 1875. Ashfall in East Iceland propelled mass emigration to North America. The poisonous gas from the Skaftáreldar (River Skaftá Fires) eruption in

1783–85 is believed to have caused the death of 75% of livestock and of every fifth inhabitant in Iceland. The eruption in Öræfajökull, Iceland's largest volcano, in 1362 caused severe ashfall and flooding, turning the lush region at its foot into wasteland. The Hekla eruption in 1104 had a devastating effect on life in the blooming Þjórsárdalur valley and marked the beginning of the end of farming in the area.

Not much is known about the effect of earlier eruptions, as they were rarely mentioned in sources. In the Book of Settlement, documenting the settlement of Iceland in the 9th century CE, eruptions are mentioned twice, briefly, in the context of people relocating as a consequence. Archaeologist Bjarni F Einarsson says that in spite of lack of written sources, it is clear that eruptions had immense consequences on habitation. He theorises that the 934 Eldgjá eruption, one of the largest to have occurred in the world in the past 2000 years, made a large region in South Iceland uninhabitable. Bjarni reasons that people fled to the mountains – closer to the eruption – because there, trees protruded from the ash and could be used for feeding livestock. The population eventually collapsed, and the remaining people moved back to the lowlands when the vegetation recovered. The Eldgjá eruption is believed to have slowed down the settlement of Iceland.

Ash Analysis

Now, thanks to volcanoes, the story of Iceland's settlements may have to be rewritten. Archaeologists use ash layers from eruptions to determine the age of relics found during excavations, among other methods. Bjarni is currently leading an excavation project in Stöðvarfjörður, East Iceland, where a layer from an eruption in Grímsvötn that occurred in 875 was found in a turf wall of a longhouse. Underneath is an older house, which dates back to 800–850, prior to the official settlement. Bjarni believes that these were seasonal dwellings that were used as a base for workers hunting and processing whales – oil made from whale blubber was a sought-after product at that time.

Geothermal Benefits

With volcanic activity comes geothermal activity, used for energy production, heating and bathing – naturally hot water is used for swimming pools and bathing lagoons around the country. Icelandic bathing culture has developed over centuries, at least going as far back as the Middle Ages when the sagas were written, describing people bathing in natural pools. Snorralaug, in which saga author Snorri Sturluson used to soak at his home in Reykholt, still exists. Bjarni says there is no evidence of Iceland's first settlers having used the natural hot water for bathing – they may have, even though the practice probably seemed alien to them at first. For hundreds of years, the hot ground and water have been used for baking and cooking, and the hot springs were convenient for doing laundry. In Laugardalur in Reykjavík there are pools that were used for doing laundry in the 19th and early 20th century, before houses had running water.

For better or for worse, volcanoes have shaped the country, culture and the Icelandic mentality. While the threat of a serious eruption is looming, Icelanders take solace in the fact that a team of scientists monitors all of the country's volcanoes and that action plans are in place were one to erupt near inhabited areas. In recent times, people generally seem keener to run towards eruptions than away from them. 'I'd say that Icelanders are excited about living in a country with volcanic activity,' says Salóme. 'We have fire in our blood.'

THE MOST DANGEROUS ERUPTIONS IN LIVING MEMORY INCLUDE VESTMANNAEYJAR IN 1973. THOUSANDS OF PEOPLE HAD TO BE EVACUATED.

Eyjafjallajökull eruption (p331)

ICELAND'S POP-ROCK
JUGGERNAUT

Icelandic musicians draw on deep roots for rich modern-day creativity. By Alexis Averbuck

ICELAND BLOWS AWAY concerns such as isolation, continuous winter darkness and its small population with a glowing passion for music and all things cultural. From its earliest high-action medieval sagas, which were recited aloud, to the present day where many Icelanders play in a band, the country produces a disproportionate number of world-class musicians in all manner of styles. Their creativity and influences – like the grand landscape, Rekyjavík life and capricious weather – blend with the literature and sounds of yore.

Roots

Until rock and roll arrived in the 20th century, Iceland was a land practically devoid of musical instruments and singing was the sole form of music.

The most famous song styles were *rímur* – poetry or stories from the sagas performed in a low, eerie chant (Sigur Rós have dabbled with the form) – and *fimmundasöngur,* which were sung by two people in harmony. Cut off from other influences, the Icelandic singing style barely changed from the 14th century to the 20th century. It also managed to retain harmonies that were banned by the church across the rest of Europe for being the work of the devil. You'll find choirs around Iceland performing traditional music, and various compilation albums, such as *Inspired by Harpa – The Traditional Songs of Iceland* (2013), give a sample of Icelandic folk songs or *rímur.*

Eddic & Skaldic Poetry

Lyric writing goes back to the earliest days of Icelandic life. The first settlers brought their oral poetic tradition with them from other parts of Scandinavia, and the words of the poems were later committed to parchment in the 12th century.

Eddic poems were composed in free, variable meters with a structure very similar to that of early Germanic poetry. Probably the most well known is the gnomic *Hávamál,* which extols the virtues of the common life – its wise proverbs on how to be a good guest are still quoted today.

Skaldic poems were composed by skalds (Norwegian court poets) and are mainly praise-poems of Scandinavian kings, with lots of description packed into tightly structured lines. As well as having fiercely rigid alliteration, syllable counts and stresses, Skaldic poetry is made more complex by kennings, a kind of compact word riddle. Blood, for instance, is 'wound dew', while an arm might be described as a 'hawk's perch'.

The most renowned skald was saga anti-hero Egil Skallagrímsson. In 948, after being captured and sentenced to death, Egil composed the ode *Höfuðlausn* (Head Ransom) for his captor Eirík Blood-Axe. Flattered, the monarch released Egil unharmed.

Early Instruments

The Vikings brought the *fiðla* and the *langspil* – both a kind of zither where a two-stringed box rests on the player's knee and is played with a bow. Never solo instruments, they served to accompany singers. In the 19th century, harmonicas and accordions arrived, but mostly, instruments were an unheard-of luxury until the 20th century. You can see some of the push-and-pull of international influence in the film *Djöflaeyjan* (Devil's Island; 1996), which depicts the lives of Icelandic families inhabiting the US military barracks left in Keflavík after WWII.

Björk & the Sugarcubes

By most measures, the first modern-era internationally famous Icelandic musicians were the Sugarcubes. They received worldwide acclaim with their album *Life's Too Good* (1988), which included the hit single, 'Birthday'. They were also part of the influential Reykjavík indie label, Bad Taste (Smekkleysa), which still champions Icelandic musicians, artists, poets and writers, and was an early ground for fostering Icelandic creative artists. You can visit their shop at Hjartatorg and Hverfisgata 32 in Reykjavík.

When the Sugarcubes disbanded in 1992, lead vocalist, Björk, spun off into a smashing solo career spanning a fecund range of styles from her platinum album *Debut* (1993) to her most recent, *Fossora* (2022). You'll hear historic roots in her song from *Fossora* called 'Sorrowful Soil', which is influenced by a 17th-century elegiac Icelandic hymn. Check out her bestselling *Gling Gló*, a collection of jazz standards and traditional Icelandic songs.

Björk is a force, not only as a singer, songwriter and record producer, but also as an actor and for her daring fashion collaborations and eclectic style and persona. She is an early example of how many Icelandic musicians and visual artists are seri-ous creative artists in multiple disciplines. Others who are making a splash overseas include Ragnar Kjartansson – part painter, actor, director and musician. Reykjavík Art Museum's Hafnarhús and the Reykjavík art galleries and collectives do a superb job showcasing these kinds of creatives, as does the Reykjavík Arts Festival (late May/early June).

Sigur Rós

The wildly creative band Sigur Rós have followed Björk to international stardom. Their album *Ágætis Byrjun* (A Good Beginning; 1999) brought them worldwide attention for lead singer Jónsi's unique vocals (usually sung in Icelandic or an improvised vocalisation they dub Volenska) and the band's bowed guitar techniques. Their biggest-selling album *Takk…* (Thanks… ; 2005) garnered rave reviews around the world and firmly cemented them on the international stage.

Seek out their concert film *Heima* (Home; 2007), a must-see for its blend of brilliant music and Icelandic settings captured during a series of free concerts they gave around the country upon returning from their 2006 concert tour.

One of their albums, *Route One* (2017), was assembled from music created while the band drove the entire Ring Road in midsummer 2016. And, in 2023 they toured internationally with a full orchestra behind their latest album *Átta* (Eight; 2023), featuring a singing style reminiscent of early Icelandic devotional music.

Lead singer Jónsi also had success with his joyful solo album *Go* (2010), and the music of Sigur Rós is used widely in film and television. It's emblematic of the international reach of Icelandic composers in general, like Hildur Guðnadóttir, who won an Academy Award for her score to *Joker* (2019) and has collaborated with all manner of rock, metal and classical musicians. For example, she used to record with Icelandic band múm, making experimental electronica mixed with traditional instruments (try their album *Smilewound* from 2013).

Indie-Folk Stars

Understandably, with its rich folk music history, indie-folk bands hit well in Iceland. Of Monsters and Men stormed the

US charts as well in 2011 with their debut album, *My Head Is an Animal*. The track 'Little Talks' from that album reached number one on the Billboard US Alternative Songs chart. B*eneath the Skin* (2015) debuted at number three on the US Billboard 200 and their latest albums are *Fever Dream* (2019) and *EP Tíu* (2022).

KALEO, a popular blues-folk-rock band from Mosfellsbær, hit the international stage with a splash – the song 'No Good' from their 2016 studio album *A/B* garnered a Grammy Award nomination and the album peaked at 16 on the US Billboard 200. Their latest release is *Surface Sounds* (2021).

Singer-songwriter Ásgeir Trausti, who records simply as Ásgeir, had a breakout hit with *In the Silence* (2014), sung mostly in moody English, and sells out concerts internationally. His latest albums are *Afterglow* (2017), *Bury the Moon / Sátt* (2020) and *Time on My Hands* (2022).

Seabear, an indie-folk band, has spawned several top music-makers like Sin Fang (try *Flowers* from 2013) and Sóley (*We Sink* from 2012). Árstíðir records minimalist indie-folk and had a 2013 YouTube viral hit when they sang a 13th-century Icelandic hymn a cappella in a train station in Germany.

The Scene

Reykjavík's flourishing music scene rocks with a constantly changing lineup of new bands and sounds – see icelandmusic.is for a sampling and check website/paper *Grapevine* for music news and performances. If your trip coincides with one of the country's many music festivals, go! Fabulous Iceland Airwaves (held in Reykjavík in November) showcases local and international acts. Aldrei fór ég Suður shakes up

Ísafjörður every Easter, while the Þjóðhátíð (National Festival) in Vestmannaeyjar, attracts over 16,000 people for four days of music and debauchery in late July or early August.

Iceland and electronica go hand in hand, as demonstrated by Mosfellsbær-born and Grammy-nominated Ólafur Arnalds. GusGus, a top pop-electronica act has 11 studio albums while Kiasmos is an Icelandic-Faroese duo which mixes moody, minimalist electronica – check out *Kiasmos* (2014) or EPs like the excellent *Blurred* (2017).

In September 2016, Sturla Atlas, the Icelandic hip-hop/R&B phenomenon, opened for Justin Bieber (whose video 'I'll Show You' was shot in Iceland). Other well-known Icelandic rappers include pioneering Quarashi, Gisli Pálmi, rap collective Reykjavíkurdætur (Daughters of Reykjavík), Cyber and Emmsjé Gauti.

Vestmannaeyjar-born Júníus Meyvant's 2016 debut, *Floating Harmonies,* is a creative blend of beautifully orchestrated folk, funk and soul.

Other local acts include FM Belfast (an electronica band who set up their own recording label to release their first album, *How to Make Friends;* their latest is *Island Broadcast*); Hafdís Huld (spiky female popstress); pop-rockers BSÍ; and theremin-playing Hekla (check out *Xiuxiuejar*), among many others.

And you can't forget idiosyncratic pop-meister and Eurovision star Daði Freyr who rocketed to stardom with his 2020 'Think about Things' and whose videos are a Dadaesque study in humour.

REYKJAVÍK'S FLOURISHING MUSIC SCENE ROCKS WITH A CONSTANTLY CHANGING LINEUP OF NEW BANDS AND SOUNDS.

Sigur Rós

XAVI TORRENT/REDFERNS/GETTY IMAGES ©

Listen to Iceland's music online

INDEX

Map Pages **000**

Map Pages **000**

Map Pages **000**

Valahnúkamöl (p118) is one of the most scenic parts of the southern Icelandic coast. This is where towering cliffs meet crashing waves, a place that can look wildly different depending on the season and time of day.

Eskifjörður (p286), a picturesque fjord and seaside town, is a great base for hiking.

Mapping data sources:
© Lonely Planet
© OpenStreetMap http://openstreetmap.org/copyright

THIS BOOK

Destination Editor
Amy Lynch

Production Editor
Barbara Delissen

Book Designer
Fabrice Robin

Cartographer
Chris Lee-Ack

Assisting Editors
Karyn Noble, Mani Ramaswamy

Cover Researcher
Marc Backwell

Thanks Kate James, Gabrielle Stefanos

MIX
Paper from responsible sources
FSC™ C021741
www.fsc.org

Paper in this book is certified against the Forest Stewardship Council™ standards. FSC™ promotes environmentally responsible, socially beneficial and economically viable management of the world's forests.

Published by Lonely Planet Global Limited
CRN 554153
13th edition – Mar 2024
ISBN 978 1 83869 361 9
© Lonely Planet 2024 Photographs © as indicated 2024
10 9 8 7 6 5 4 3 2 1
Printed in China